Lu Hsün's Vision of Reality

Lu Hsün on September 24, 1930, age fifty. Photographed in Shanghai.

Lu Hsün's Vision of Reality

WILLIAM A. LYELL, JR.

UNIVERSITY OF CALIFORNIA PRESS

BERKELEY • LOS ANGELES • LONDON

The woodcut illustrations are from Feng Tzu-k'ai's
Hui-hua Lu Hsün hsiao-shuo (illustrating Lu Hsün's stories)
(Hong Kong: Wang-yeh shu-tien, 1954).

University of California Press
Berkeley and Los Angeles, California
University of California Press, Ltd.
London, England
ISBN 0-520-02940-2
Library of Congress Catalog Card Number: 74-30527
Printed in the United States of America

CONTENTS

The chief commander of
China's cultural revolution,
he was not only a great man of letters
but a great thinker and revolutionary.
Lu Hsün was a man of unyielding integrity,
free from all sycophancy or obsequiousness;
this quality is invaluable among colonial
and semi-colonial peoples.
Representing the great majority of the nation,
Lu Hsün breached and stormed the enemy citadel;
on the cultural front he was
the bravest and most correct, the firmest,
the most loyal and the most ardent national hero,
a hero without parallel in our history.
The road he took was the very road of
China's new national culture.

Mao Tse-tung,
"The Culture of New Democracy" (1940)

PREFACE

As with almost everything else in China during the first half of this century, so too in fiction there was a revolution. Since this "fictional" revolution demanded changes in both form and content, the modern Chinese writer faced formidable challenges. What is surprising is not that there were so many failures, but that there was a fair number of successes. In the realm of the short story, Lu Hsün led the pack. It is likely that a hundred years from now his two slim volumes of stories, *Call to Arms* (1923) and *Wandering* (1926), will be read as twentieth century classics.

The purpose of this book is not to have the last say on Lu Hsün, but rather to introduce the man and his stories to the general reader as a means of "sharing the wealth." I have cast the discussion of his stories in such a way as to allow those who have not yet read them to follow along. In the Appendix I have included my own translations of Lu Hsün's very first short story, "Remembrances of the Past" (1911) and "Some Rabbits and a Cat" (1922). A selected list of English translations of the other stories may be found in Section A of the Appendix.

To those readers who are already familiar with the works of Lu Hsün, either in Chinese or in translation, I express my hope that this book will enhance their understanding and appreciation of Lu Hsün and his stories.

I should like to express my appreciation to Professor H. C. Creel, of the University of Chicago, for his books and teaching, which first interested me in Chinese civilization; and to Professor David Tod Roy, of the University of Chicago, who served as my adviser for the dissertation upon which this book is based. To my colleagues at The Ohio State University, I tender thanks for their intellectual stimulation and moral support. I am indebted to both The Ohio State University and the Center for East Asian Studies at Stanford University for the financial support that made my research possible. My colleagues in the Department of Asian Languages at Stanford University have been generous with their time in answering questions related to the final revision of the manuscript, and the provocative questions of my students have given me many new insights on the meaning of the stories. My friend and colleague, Professor William R. Schultz of the University of Arizona, obligingly checked the final draft for errors.

I have often heard unpleasant anecdotes about the problems authors have with editors. I had none. Jesse M. Phillips was constantly critical, as a good editor should be, but he was also ever gracious and gave me a new sense of respect for the English language.

Finally I should like to thank my wife Ruth for the suggestions she has contributed to this book, and my children, Miriam, Sean, Deirdre, and David, for putting up with me during the course of my work. Needless to say, any mistakes that remain are also my children.

William A. Lyell, Jr.

Stanford, California
July 1975

1

SHAOHSING AND ITS "SHIH-YEH"

Any Chinese familiar with the works of Lu Hsün (pen name of Chou Shu-jen, 1881-1936) will certainly be aware that he was from Shaohsing, a southeastern city in Chekiang Province famed equally for producing fiery drinks and clever men. In a Western reference early in the nineteenth century we find: "The inhabitants of this city are considered to be the most formidable shysters in all of China. At least, they enjoy the reputation of being so well-versed in knowledge of the law that the provincial governors and high-ranking mandarins select all their secretaries from among them."[1] Secretaries (*shih-yeh*) from Shaohsing were to be found in government service all over the country. There was a popular saying to the effect that there were three things which could be found anywhere in the empire: beancurd, sparrows, and Shaohsing men.[2] If you killed your own father on Main Street at high noon and were lucky enough to get hold of a Shaohsing *shih-yeh*, you might very well get off scot-free—such was the reputation of those clever Shaohsing fellows. It was a reputation that simultaneously acknowledged their sprightliness of mind and deplored their amorality. Enemies of the adult Lu Hsün would sometimes dismiss him contemptuously as a Shaohsing *shih-yeh*, clearly

1. J. B. G. A. Grosier, *De la Chine, ou Description Générale de cet Empire* (3d ed.; Paris, 1818), I, 109. For a recent discussion of *shih-yeh*, and a study of the whole informal political structure of which they were a part, see Kenneth E. Folsom, *Friends, Guests, and Colleagues: The Mu-Fu System in the Late Ch'ing* (Berkeley and Los Angeles 1968).
2. W. Gilbert Walshe, "The Ancient City of Shaohsing," *Journal of the China Branch of the Royal Asiatic Society*, XXXIII (1900-1901), page 48 of the last fascicule in the volume.

intending the pejorative connotation of a clever charlatan. This was both inaccurate and unfair, but if we substitute "intelligent" for "clever," and "cultural critic" for "charlatan," we can grasp something of the positive influence that the Shaohsing *shih-yeh* tradition had on Lu Hsün, who was, indeed, a highly intelligent critic of Chinese culture.

From Hangchow, the provincial capital of Lu Hsün's native Chekiang, one usually went down to Shaohsing by canal. A member of the British consular service who took a journey through Chekiang in 1883, when Lu Hsün was just two years old, has left a description of the northern approaches to Shaohsing from about forty miles out:

This is without exception the fattest stretch of land I have ever seen in China or elsewhere . . . Shan-yin and K'uai-chi are the prefectural districts, and seem to reek with richness. Substantial villages and market towns, many as large as the more Western district-cities, succeed one another at distances of half-a-mile, and are to be seen thickly dotted over the country. . . . With the exception of the substantial stone pathways between cities, there seems to be little means of inter-communication except by boat, and these boats are externally adorned with such consummate art that they have the appearance of being made of fine porcelain. Large and small, they are all fitted up with rainproof telescope mats, and can be used as dwellings, cargo boats, or passenger and pleasure barges; they fully merit the name of gondola; many of the small ones are worked with the feet, and thousands are passed during a day's travel. [The] highroad canal runs both around and through Shaohsing, and the passage of 10 *li* through the busiest part of the town affords an excellent opportunity of inspecting it at ease.[3]

Crisscrossed by canals and small waterways, Shaohsing lay in "water country (*shui-hsiang*)" and a trip of any distance—whether it was a case of Lu Hsün's going into the countryside to see a village opera or his father's going to Hangchow to sit for the civil service examinations—would be made by boat.[4]

3. E. H. Parker, "A Journey in Chekiang," *Journal of the China Branch of the Royal Asiatic Society*, n.s., XIX, pt. I (1884), 44.
4. For boat travel in and around Shaohsing see Chou Tso-jen, "Wu-p'eng ch'uan" [Black-canopied boats], in *Hsien-tai Chung-kuo hsiao-p'in san-wen hsüan* [A selection of contemporary Chinese informal essays and prose] (Shanghai, 1926); hereafter cited as *WPC*. (An alphabetical list of abbreviations for Chinese sources is to be found in the Bibliography.)

In Shaohsing itself the British visitor in 1883 saw from his boat a Protestant mission and a memorial arch, the latter with a dedication in French to Lieutenant Le Brethon de Caligny, who had died fighting the Taiping rebels.[5] A Protestant missionary who was stationed in Shaohsing at the turn of the century reported that many traces of the rebellion were still to be seen:

A great disaster happened to the ancient city in the 11th year of Hsien-feng [1862] when on the 29th of the 9th moon, the "Long-haired" advanced from Ko-ch'iao and took possession. . . . Many of the women and children had been sent to the hills before the occupation of the city whilst their husbands "remained by the stuff," but alas in many cases they never met again. . . . Meanwhile, the rebels dressed themselves in the finest silks and satins, in the manufacture of which the Shaohsing people excel, and every morning hundreds of boats laden with produce arrived at the gates of the city, brought by the country people, who to save themselves from extinction had taken the oath, and accepted the small flags which the rebels distributed as a mark of loyalty and protection against attack. The whole country was ravaged, and many evidences of the "fury of the oppressor" remain to this day both in city and country.[6]

The missionary's description of the occupation of Shaohsing by the long-haired Taiping rebels so closely matches the one given by an old servant in Lu Hsün's first short story, "Remembrances of the Past (Huai-chiu)," that there can be but little doubt that this was the orthodox history of the period as engraved on the tongues of the city's natives.

The t'aimen, or family compound, where Lu Hsün was born in 1881 was called the New T'aimen to distinguish it from the two compounds in which collateral branches of the Chou family lived nearby. It too was redolent with old reminders of the great rebellion that had ravaged the country and almost toppled the dynasty in the 1850s and 1860s. There was a mound of broken tile in the main yard that had probably been piled there when repairs

---

Now connected with Hangchow by rail, Shaohsing is a favorite tourist attraction in the People's Republic, both because of its association with famous revolutionaries and writers, and because of its beautiful scenery. See Jen Wei-yin, *Shaohsing san-chi* [Random impressions of Shaohsing] (Shanghai, 1956), pp. 1-5; hereafter cited as *SHSC*.

5. Parker, "A Journey in Chekiang," pp. 44-45.
6. Walshe, "The Ancient City of Shaohsing," p. 48.

on the buildings of the compound were made after the final defeat
of the rebels. An adjoining yard was known as the "ghost yard,"
because so many corpses of people who had died during the
rebellion were buried there.[7] People as well as things reminded one
of the rebellion. Lu Hsün's governess, Ah Ch'ang, used to enterain
the boy with spine-tingling tales of how it was back in the terrible
days of the Long Hairs.[8] His great-great-uncle, known in the
family as Twelfth Old Gentleman, had been killed during the
rebellion and was posthumously awarded lowest grade of Manchu
nobility in recognition of his loyalty to the dynasty.[9] Twelfth Old
Gentleman's son, and thus Lu Hsün's great-uncle, Tzu-ching,
taught his grandnephew to read the *Book of Mencius*[10] and would
later provide the model for the protagonist of one of Lu Hsün's
finest short stories.[11]

A vivid reconstruction of Shaohsing as it appeared at the time of
Lu Hsün's birth is given by one of the ablest of his biographers:

The city itself was under the joint jurisdiction of the Shan-yin and
K'uai-chi districts. The Shan-yin District yamen was in the western half
of the city; that of the K'uai-chi District, in the eastern half; while the
prefectural yamen was situated at the foot of a hill at the southwest
corner of the city—the Hill of the Reclining Dragon. The largest yamen,
however, was that of the Manchu Garrison Commander, which was
situated in the very heart of the city and commonly referred to as "the big
yamen." The resident of this yamen then was a military officer and in
front of the gate one could see a flagpole, reviewing stand, buglers, and
drummers. In short, it was the most awesome of all the yamens. Here it
was that a cannon was fired to announce the dawn and here it was that in
the evening the firing of a cannon set the first watch of the night. Then
the beating of the watchman's bamboo sticks would begin and by the
time that the hollow, rhythmic striking of the first watch had ended,

---

7. Chou Hsia-shou (Chou Tso-jen), *Lu Hsün te ku-chia* [Lu Hsün's old home]
(Hong Kong, 1962), pp. 8-10; hereafter cited as *LHKC*. For Tso-jen's later book
of reminiscences see chap. 2, n. 14.
8. *Selected Works of Lu Hsün*, trans. Yang Hsien-i and Gladys Yang (4 vols.;
Peking, 1956-60), II, 366-67; *Lu Hsün ch'üan-chi* [Complete works of Lu Hsün]
(10 vols.; Peking, 1957-58), II, 228-29. The *Selected Works* are hereafter cited as
SWLH and the complete works in Chinese as *LHCC*. Unless stated otherwise, I
have quoted from *SWLH*, though often I have silently altered the Yang's
translation when a different rendering seemed closer to the original.
9. *LHKC*, p. 25.
10. Ibid., p. 124.
11. "The White Light (Pai-kuang)."

pedestrians would have disappeared from the main streets and back lanes, and a silence would have settled in over the ancient city.

Within the city there were several parallel and intersecting flagstone streets, and on almost every one of them t'aimen of various sizes were to be seen. On the gates of the larger ones one could see plaques proclaiming the civil service degrees its residents had won or the titles that they held. Huddled close by these t'aimen, one would see clusters of small, dark, damp rooms. Facing the door at an angle there would be wine-making vats and other odds and ends. These were the homes of the artisans. The commercial center of town, such as it was, consisted of a few large streets within the city on which were clustered the larger variety stores, bookstores, and stationery shops. And all over the city one could find tearooms, wineshops, and the stores that sold the tinfoil money burned at funerals.

In the evening, too, there came the sound of church bells from the spires of mission churches that shot up at various points in the city.[12]

Thanks to the reminiscences of Lu Hsün's brother, Chou Tso-jen, written during the 1950s, it is possible to focus on the neighborhood in which Lu Hsün grew up.[13] The New T'aimen was on the north side of a quiet east-west street called Tung-ch'ang Lane, a term that referred to both the street and the neighborhood. The boundary of the neighborhood was drawn on the west by a north-south street and marked on the east by the Fu-p'en Bridge. If you stood in the middle of the intersection that marked the western limit of the neighborhood, you would find a small business on each of the four corners. On the northwest corner was a stand that sold *ma-hua*, long twists of fried dough resembling pretzels; on the southwest corner, across the street from the pretzel stand, there was an herb shop whose proprietor was commonly known by the unattractive epithet of Mangy-Beard Runt. On the southeast corner stood a wineshop.

If you left your precarious station in the middle of the intersection and walked eastward along the north side of the street, you would pass a fruit store on the northeast corner and then, a few doors beyond, a store that sold cured meats, another herb shop, the Liang family's t'aimen, and, just past that, the Chou family's New T'aimen. Since the western corner of the family compound had been leased to a coffin store, the approach to the Chou

12. Wang Shih-ching, *Lu Hsün chuan* [A biography of Lu Hsün] (Peking, 1962), pp. 4-5; hereafter cited as *LHC*.

13. *LHKC*, pp. 112-48.

residence from this direction was less than auspicious. On the eastern side lived a family whose fortunes had declined. It was from them that the Chous had bought the New T'aimen.

If you went much further to the east, you would get into a different neighborhood. Let us turn around then, and walk back, along the south side of Tung-ch'ang Lane. You would first pass one of the tinfoil-money stores for which Shaohsing was famous, then a firewood shop, a godown, and, next to that, the Hsien-heng Wineshop that Lu Hsün was later to immortalize. To this wineshop often came a pathetic failed scholar whom people nicknamed "Master Mencius"—he would become the model for the protagonist of one of Lu Hsün's stories, "K'ung Yi-chi." Past the wineshop was a rice store, and next to that, if you turned left, you could go down to a wharf that accommodated small boats on one of Shaohsing's many waterways. A few doors beyond the wharf was the residence of Mangy-Beard Runt, owner of the corner herb shop. He provided one of the few bits of mystery in the neighborhood when, one day as he sat in his home after lunch, his life was brought to an unceremonious end by a brick hurled from outside. The assassin was never found.

For the most part, people stuck pretty close to the neighborhood, for Tung-ch'ang Lane was some distance from the main shopping area. For the convenience of marketing close to home, however, the residents had to pay prices that were slightly exorbitant. As a studious little boy, Lu Hsün regretted the distance of Tung-ch'ang Lane from the business center, for it was there that the bookstores were located.[14]

Shaohsing winters were rather mild, though they brought some snow. Due to a lack of central heating and adequate insulation, one would often be awakened in the middle of the night by the cold. The cold was such that one had to contend with chilblains. Lu Hsün's younger brother, Tso-jen,[15] had chilblains so often that even as an old man he would still be able to see the scars they had left on his feet. The mosquitoes that the summer brought in swarms must have been of truly heroic proportions, for Tso-jen (writing from the vantage point of the 1950s) declared with some

14. *LHC*, p. 9.
15. Lu Hsün was the eldest of three brothers. Chou Tso-jen was second; Chou Chien-jen, third.

degree of civic pride that even the post-World War II wonder bug-killer, DDT, would have been helpless against them. Reminiscing about waking up from the cold in the winter and pushing through the thick smoke used as a mosquito repellent in the summers, Tso-jen concluded that the climate was the very last thing that would make one miss Shaohsing.

Within the New T'aimen lived a veritable community consisting of several branches and generations of the Chou family, a large number of servants, and persons with no blood ties who rented rooms. According to Tso-jen, in and around Shaohsing the word *t'aimen* was used to denote the residence of a scholar-gentry family. Anyone who lived within the walls of a t'aimen was referred to (regardless of age or economic status) as "t'aimen goods" and considered qualitatively different from ordinary people. There were certain activities that members of t'aimen families could properly engage in without losing status, but the number was limited. They could sit for the civil service examinations and thus become officials, or failing that, they could become yamen secretaries (and yamen secretaries from Shaohsing, or Shaohsing *shih-yeh*, were, as we have seen, both famous and infamous throughout the empire). Failing to become either officials or secretaries, they might go into business, preferably managing a savings and loan shop or a pawnshop. The operation of a yard-goods store, such as abounded in Shaohsing, was considered beneath them. If the fortunes of a t'aimen family sank into continuous decline, its members would eventually settle back down into the mass from which they had originally sprung. Such a fate would most often be brought on by the besetting weakness of the gentry: too much easy living, an opulent comfort that made them so lazy and incompetent that even imminent disaster could not rouse them from their hapless torpor. According to the reminiscences of Chou Tso-jen, it was this kind of gradual devitalization of moral fiber that usually brought down the great t'aimen families.

In a set of admonitions to posterity, Lu Hsün's grandfather once pondered the problem of familial decline. He posited a family of three brothers in which the eldest was an official, the second owned a silk store, and the youngest ran a shop which made and sold beancurd. He then imagined that the official lost his post and the silk store failed, so that the children of the brothers were all reduced to working in the lowly beancurd shop. Then and only then, he opined, would the younger generation be able to make something of themselves. According to Tso-jen, against the cliché-ridden background of Grandfather's admonitions, this passage stood out like a gem. Evidences of the degeneration of the Chou t'aimen must have been painfully apparent during Lu Hsün's youth, for Tso-jen remembers that as soon as he and Lu Hsün were old enough to apprehend what was going on, they became aware that the t'aimen had already settled into a state of gradual decline, a decline concurrent with that of the fortunes of the Manchu dynasty.

2

THE FAMILY

As the adult Lu Hsün moved through the worlds of his everyday realities, he was silent on the subject of his family.[1] Although in daily contacts with friends and acquaintances he kept the doors of the New T'aimen tightly closed, in the world of his stories he threw wide the gates and invited in one and all for the grand tour. Even in that let's-pretend world of fiction, however, there were still a few rooms that he was reluctant to show.[2]

The fictional use of relatives and neighbors was by no means something that Lu Hsün first learned as an adult. Right up into their teens, he and his younger brother, Chou Tso-jen, had created and acted out plays for their own amusement whose characters were based on relatives and neighbors in Shaohsing. A big-headed man in Tung-ch'ang Lane who was raising a goat became an evil giant who had taken possession of a cave from which he and his animal worked violence on innocent people. Twenty-eighth Gramps, a relative belonging to their grandfather's generation, had become freakishly thin through opium addiction and, as a consequence, had a unique and unforgettable way of shrugging his meatless shoulders; as one of the heroes of the play, it was he who captured the evil giant by clamping him between his own chopstick-like shoulder blades.[3]

1. Sun Fu-yuan, *Lu Hsün hsien-sheng erh-san-shih* [A few things concerning Lu Hsün] (Shanghai, 1949), p. 65; hereafter cited as *ESS*.
2. Especially the rooms of his grandfather and the young woman, Chu An, to whom his mother married him. Takeuchi Yoshimi has pointed out that the names of these two figures are taboo throughout Lu Hsün's works, and takes this as an indication of the intensity of the pain that they caused him. *Rojin* [Lu Hsün] (Tokyo, 1948), pp. 39-43; hereafter cited as *RJ*.
3. *LHKC*, pp. 60-62.

When as an adult writer Lu Hsün would occasionally use a few deft strokes of the writing brush to pay back a real or imagined wrong suffered in the realm of everyday reality,[4] this too was something that he had already learned to do as a child in the New T'aimen. Eight-Pounder Shen,[5] a rough boy a few years older than Lu Hsün, used to bound about the New T'aimen, bamboo spear in hand, intimidating everyone with shouts of "Kill! Kill!" Although this bothered Lu Hsün, traditional Chinese family mores prohibited him from doing anything so crass as fighting Eight-Pounder (even if we assume for the moment that he had either the strength or the nerve to do so), but there was one way in which he could get even. And so it was that Lu Hsün's father one day discovered a stitched booklet of sketches done by his son; leafing through them, he came across one with a title. It showed a boy lying on his back with an arrow protruding from his chest and bore the inscription, "Eight-Pounder Killed by an Arrow."[6]

If the memories of the New T'aimen that Chou Tso-jen recorded a half century later are at all accurate, it is no wonder that Grandfather Chou was moved to ponder the causes of the decline of gentry families. One would have to search long and hard to find a really strong male in Tso-jen's reminiscences of the family. The family compound was populated with kindly old pedants like Great-Uncle Chao-lan (in whose study the bookish Lu Hsün liked to browse),[7] skeletal opium addicts like Twenty-eighth Gramps, and highly unstable failed scholars like Great-Uncle Tzu-ching,[8] or even Lu Hsün's own father, a man for whom alcohol and opium had become serious problems.[9]

4. For instance, Chou Tso-jen has suggested that the shabby treatment given Mrs. Yen in "So-chi (Trifling Notes)"—*LHCC*, II, 263-70—reflects the fact the character is based upon the great-aunt who, along with her husband, introduced their father to the use of opium. See *LHKC*, pp. 39-40.

5. Children were sometimes given these tags on the basis of their weight at birth. Here, "pounds" is a rough translation of *chin*, and "eight pounds" is not to be taken as equivalent to eight of our pounds.

6. *LHKC*, p. 38.

7. Ibid., p. 70; *LHCC*, II, 230.

8. *LHKC*, pp. 26-30. Tzu-ching was the model for Ch'en Shih-ch'eng, protagonist of "The White Light (*Pai-kuang*)." See Chou Hsia-shou (Tso-jen), *Lu Hsün hsiao-shuo li te jen-wu* [The characters in Lu Hsün's stories] (Shanghai, 1954), pp. 122-27; hereafter cited as *HSJW*.

9. *LHKC*, pp. 39-41.

The only really strong, active, enterprising adult male in the New T'aimen seems to have been the patriarch of the family, Grandfather Chou, who had climbed the civil-service-examination ladder of success from *hsiu-ts'ai* (the lowest degree awarded), through the *chü-jen*, on up to the third and highest degree, the *chin-shih*. Those who stood highest on the *chin-shih* list of successful candidates were usually appointed to the Han-lin Yuan—the Imperial Academy—in Peking and known thenceforth as Han Lin,[10] the highest academic-official honor to which one could aspire in Ch'ing-dynasty China. Grandfather Chou had even achieved that. Unfortunately, he was also capable of dishonesty. It was this fault in him that led the family into the steep economic decline that the adult Lu Hsün was to remember with a touch of bitterness as one of the formative experiences of his youth:

I think that anyone who falls from comfortable affluence into poverty will, on the way, probably be able to discern what the people of this world are really like.[11]

Grandfather Chou was brought to trial in 1893 for attempting to suborn a civil service examiner; he was sentenced, by imperial edict, to decapitation and was imprisoned at Hangchow, the provincial capital, to await execution in the autumn, the time for carrying out capital sentences. The family back in Shaohsing, however, managed to have his execution postponed from autumn to autumn until the old man was eventually allowed to return home in early 1901 under the general amnesty that was issued in the wake of the Boxer Rebellion.[12] The postponements of execution had, no doubt, been obtained with costly bribes, thus hastening the impoverishment of the family. After his release, Grandfather Chou remained in Shaohsing until his death in 1904.[13]

Chou Tso-jen traces the beginning of this chain of events back to the death of Grandfather Chou's mother, at the age of

---

10. For a succinct description of the Imperial Academy and the examination system see Kenneth Scott Latourette, *The Chinese: Their History and Culture* (New York, 1954), pp. 522-33.

11. *LHCC*, I, 3; *SWLH*, I, 1-2.

12. *LHKC*, pp. 46-48.

13. *ESS*, p. 66; *LHC*, p. 26.

seventy-nine, on New Year's Eve (of the lunar year, February 16) in 1893. When Lu Hsün and Tso-jen were young, the boys' great-grandmother was a rather senile, albeit still somewhat stern, old lady. Having learned by telegram of his mother's death, Grandfather took leave from his official duties in Peking and returned to Shaohsing with his concubine, surnamed P'an, and his twelve-year-old son, Po-sheng. Po-sheng's own mother, Concubine Chang, had died when he was very young, and hence Concubine P'an was bringing him up.[14]

For the young people in the New T'aimen, Concubine P'an (in her twenties) was a welcome contrast to a grandfather who, having been away for so long, was almost a stranger and (worse yet from the children's point of view) was easily irritated. In his old age Tso-jen would still remember the intensity of Grandfather Chou's outrage when he rose early one morning after his return from the capital and discovered that no one else was yet up—a sure sign of familial decline. He was probably particularly irked that Lu Hsün's father (whose opium addiction precluded an early rising) was still abed.[15]

While Grandfather Chou was there, the prefectural examination for the *chü-jen* degree was held.[16] Knowing that he was acquainted with the head examiner, some relatives made the disastrous suggestion that he get together a group of well-to-do candidates and have them put up 10,000 ounces of silver with which to bribe the head examiner and thus ensure their success. As middleman in this transaction, Grandfather Chou, of course, would not go unrewarded. The suggestion was acted upon, a promissory note for the stated amount was drafted, and Grandfather Chou went off to Soochow in order to intercept the head examiner on his way to Chekiang and make the illegal arrangements. Soon after a preliminary meeting with the head examiner,

14. Chou Tso-jen, *Chih T'ang hui-hsiang-lu* [Reminiscences of Chih T'ang (Chou Tso-jen)] (2 vols.; Hong Kong, 1971), I, 7-12; hereafter cited as *HHL*. This work duplicates much of the material to be found in Tso-jen's other works on Lu Hsün. It differs, of course, in that the focus is on Tso-jen's own life.
15. Ibid.
16. Although the degree and the education they represent are quite different, some readers may like to remember them as *hsiu-ts'ai* (B.A.), *chü-jen* (M.A.), and *chin-shih* (Ph.D.). If our degrees automatically entitled one to the possibility of appointment as councilman, mayor, or governor, the similarity would be closer.

Grandfather Chou sent a letter with the promissory note enclosed. As ill luck would have it, the assistant examiner happened to be visiting with the head examiner when the runner bearing the letter from Grandfather arrived. No doubt aware of the contents, the head examiner put it aside unopened. The runner, something of a bumpkin to begin with, began to complain loudly that he ought to have a receipt for a letter with money in it, and clamored on until the cat was out of the bag. The Soochow prefect to whom the case was reported was prepared to slough off the whole thing on the grounds that Grandfather Chou had a history of mental upsets and accordingly ought to be pardoned. The whole thing might well have ended then and there. Grandfather, however, would have none of it. Loudly insisting that he was no lunatic, he proceeded to call out the names of many persons who had bought the *chü-jen* degree—a clear indication, as far as he was concerned, that there wasn't anything all that untoward about his own behavior. At this impasse, there was nothing for it but to turn the whole case over to the provincial government, which, in turn, requested instructions from the Board of Punishments in Peking. The final disposition of the case, as we have seen, resulted in the imprisonment of the old man under sentence of decapitation.

Within the family there was another explanation as to why the affair had been blown up to such serious proportions. Years back, one Ch'en Ch'iu-fang had married into the clan and during a low period in his career had spent some time living with his in-laws, prompting Grandfather Chou to opine: "Anyone who huddles under the petticoats of his wife's family is a hopeless lout. He'll never become an official!" Upon hearing of this, Ch'en left the house, vowing never to return until he had become an official. Later he did in fact pass the *chin-shih* examination and was serving as a secretary to the Soochow prefect at just the time when Grandfather Chou's case came up. According to the family, it was Secretary Ch'en who insisted that the case be handled according to the letter of the law.[17]

This was a hectic and frightening period for the people in the New T'aimen. When the order was issued for his arrest, Grandfather went into hiding, making things still more difficult for the family; for the law of the empire stipulated that in the event that a

17. *HHL*, pp. 12-14.

culprit could not be apprehended, the other males in his family
would be taken into custody.[18] Thus, by way of precaution, Lu
Hsün and Chou Tso-jen were whisked off to the countryside to
hole up with relatives. At first they stayed at Huang-fu village
with their mother's family, whose surname, Lu, would later form
part of Lu Hsün's pen name. The Lu family seat was originally at
An Ch'iao T'ou; Lu Hsün's maternal grandfather, Lu Ch'ing-
hsüan, after obtaining the *chü-jen* degree, had moved the family
to Huang-fu village. By the time the boys hid out there, this
grandfather had already passed away, leaving their maternal
grandmother and two maternal uncles (both holders of the
hsiu-ts'ai degree) in the village. Since the younger of the two
uncles had a quartet of daughters, it was decided that it would be
better for the boys to stay with the elder uncle, who had a son as
well as a daughter. This uncle wasn't very much fun, however,
being an opium addict and seldom up and about. Toward the end
of 1893 it was decided that the younger uncle should return to the
family seat of An Ch'iao T'ou, while the elder went to live with
in-laws at Hsiao Kao Fu, whither the Chou boys accompanied
him. Because of the chaos that he was causing in the family,
Grandfather Chou finally turned himself in, thus allowing the
boys to return to their own home in Shaohsing in the early part of
1894.[19]

Grandfather's imprisonment must have been a severe shock to
Lu Hsün, who was just coming into his teens at this time. The
successful old patriarch off in Peking had, no doubt, been held up
to him as an example of what a man might make of himself; this
must have been doubly impressive, given the relative unsuccess of
the other adult males living within the walls of the New T'aimen.
Furthermore, Grandfather Chou was the first and only *chin-shih*
that the family had produced. Then, suddenly, Lu Hsün was
deprived of the reflected prestige of this great and honored
forebear, was transformed into the grandson of a convicted
corrupt official, and was even forced to flee to the countryside to
avoid possible involvement. Some three decades later he would
write: "I was deposited at a relative's house where I was sometimes

---

18. Chu Cheng, *Lu Hsün chuan-lüeh* [Outline biography of Lu Hsün] (Peking,
1956), p. 7; hereafter cited as LHCL.
19. LHKC, pp. 49–53; HHL, pp. 14–19; LHCL, pp. 7–8.

even called a beggar."[20] Tso-jen, on the other hand, remembers their period of exile as rather pleasant. It was a leisurely time during which he and Lu Hsün had the opportunity to meet interesting people, copy illustrations from books, and read novels which were not as readily available at the New T'aimen.[21]

In 1896 tragedy struck the family a second blow. Lu Hsün's father died after a protracted illness against which doctors had proved helpless.[22] The father's illness cost the family dearly in doctors' fees and medicines. On the basis of a definition of the curing arts that equated "curing" with "associating ideas" (the two ideographs were similar in pronunciation), a drink of ink was prescribed when Lu Hsün's father started coughing blood: "black can cover up red."[23] Lu Hsün would never forgive this sort of thing. Throughout his life he was to remain an implacable enemy and critic of traditional Chinese medicine.

The year after the father's death, it was decided that Tso-jen should go to Hangchow and stay with Concubine P'an so that he might periodically visit Grandfather Chou in prison. Concubine P'an had rented quarters next to the prison and Po-sheng (Grandfather's son by Concubine Chang) had joined her there in 1896 to help keep his father company.[24] In 1897, Po-sheng left to attend the Naval Academy in Nanking, and thus it was that Tso-jen was sent up to fill in. He stayed at Hangchow for nearly two years.[25]

Even while imprisoned, the old patriarch was apparently in firm control of the affairs of the New T'aimen. In jail or out, he was still the eldest male and therefore entitled to respect. Furthermore, whatever else he may have been, he was, at least, strong. In Hangchow the teen-aged Tso-jen at first missed the relative spaciousness of the New T'aimen and found the tenor of life rather boring; however, he gradually became accustomed to his new

20. Meng Chin, comp., *Lu Hsün tzu-chuan chi ch'i tso-p'in* [Autobiography of Lu Hsün, together with some of his works] (bilingual edition, English translation by Meng Chin; Hong Kong, 1959), pp. 2-3; hereafter cited as *LHTC*.

21. *LHKC*, pp. 49-53.

22. Ibid., pp. 91-92.

23. Ibid., p. 92.

24. Tso-jen's memory of this date differs in his *LHKC* and *HHL*. For a number of reasons, the *LHKC* date seems more likely.

25. Chou Tso-jen, "Wu-shih-nien-ch'ien te Hang-chou fu-yü (The Hangchow prefectural prison fifty years ago)" in *Chih T'ang (Chou Tso-jen) yi-yu wen-pien* (Hong Kong, 1962), p. 89; hereafter cited as *YYWP*. See also *HHL*, p. 36.

situation and settled down to doing his stint. He thought Concubine P'an a rather good sort and wrote off any shortcomings in her personality as being due to her awkward social position as a concubine.[26] Other than studying on his own and presenting Grandfather periodically with practice examination essays for criticism and correction, his main duty was to spend one day out of every three or four at the prison keeping his grandfather company.[27] Tso-jen would later remember him as a very talkative, outgoing man who liked to chat with his jailers and fellow prisoners. Fond as Grandfather was of lashing out against people (from the Emperor and the Empress Dowager down to the younger members of his own family), Tso-jen never heard him castigate either the criminals or the jailers at the Hangchow prison.[28]

Lu Hsün made occasional trips to see Grandfather, visit with Tso-jen, and buy things for the people in the New T'aimen. These trips must have been welcome breaks in the routine of life. Since he was almost constitutionally disinclined to sightseeing, it is unlikely that he appreciated the famous scenery of Hangchow, but, studious lad that he was, Lu Hsün probably was excited by the opportunity for browsing through bookstores.[29]

Imprisonment seems not to have tamed Grandfather Chou one whit. Upon returning to the New T'aimen after his release in 1901, he continued to give scope to his explosive temper.[30] He would scold this one and gossip about that one with little regard for the feelings of the persons involved.[31] Solely exempted from this were Concubine P'an and Po-sheng. Though nominally Lu Hsün's uncle, Po-sheng was actually one year younger than his nephew. Grandfather's treatment of the two was quite different. Later on, when both boys were attending school in Nanking, if Po-sheng came in second from the bottom on an examination list, Grandfather would praise him for having done enough work to avoid coming in at the tail end; on the other hand, if Lu Hsün came in second from the top, the old bear would castigate him for not having put forth enough effort to come in first.[32]

26. *HHL*, pp. 38-39.
27. *YYWP*, p. 90.
28. Ibid., p. 91.
29. *HSJW*, pp. 242-43.
30. *HHL*, p. 36.
31. *LHKC*, pp. 48, 87.
32. Ibid., p. 48.

And what of Grandfather's influence on Lu Hsün? The apparently systematic avoidance of reference to him throughout Lu Hsün's writings suggests some intensity. We know that the old man created a climate in the New T'aimen which encouraged the reading of novels, something slightly unusual among bookish families of the time. He held, for instance, that children ought to be allowed to read Wu Ch'eng-en's novel *Journey to the West* (*Hsi-yu chi*) at an early age because the pleasant experience of reading this delightful and adventurous tale would give them a feel for language which would carry over to the reading of the classics.[33] The normal practice was to start youngsters out on such dull-to-children Confucian fare as *The Great Learning* and *The Doctrine of the Mean*. How they felt about their teachers' forcing them to read and memorize such works may be gauged from a children's ditty of the time:

> The *Great Learning*, the *Great Learning*—
> They whack your butt until it's burning!
> The *Doctrine of the Mean*, the *Doctrine of the Mean*—
> They beat your ass to a jelly bean![34]

Lu Hsün's youngest brother, Chou Chien-jen, has pointed out that, in addition to holding unusual views on education, Grandfather Chou was intellectually independent in other ways, and has suggested that the grandfather's failure to have a distinguished career in the civil service followed from his refusal to curry favor with superiors and his fondness for telling people off. On his first assignment away from Peking, Grandfather Chou was given the rather lowly position of district magistrate. In that capacity he carefully attended to all litigation under his jurisdiction and even sent a young nephew spying into the jail to make sure that no torture was being employed. He dealt severely with any jailer caught maltreating prisoners. Although Lu Hsün may not have approved everything his grandfather did, says Chien-jen, he could not help being influenced for the better by such relatively enlightened attitudes.[35]

33. Ibid., p. 87. The abridged translation by Arthur Waley, entitled *Monkey*, has long been a favorite with Western readers of Chinese fiction.
34. *HHL*, p. 25. My very free translation seeks to convey the spirit.
35. Ch'iao Feng (Chou Chien-jen), *Lüeh chiang kuan-yü Lu Hsün te shih-ch'ing* [A general discussion of the affairs of Lu Hsün] (Peking, 1955), p. 12; hereafter cited as *LHSC*.

Regardless of whether Lu Hsün ever sought to be the man that Grandfather had been before his detour from the path of official integrity, we can be fairly sure that he did not identify with his father. Grandfather, at least, had once enjoyed the power and the glory that inspired admiration in traditional Chinese society. Lu Hsün's father never had any part of either. A rather withdrawn soul, the father was not very close to those around him. His use of opium would not in itself explain his introversion (as we shall see, some of the users in the New T'aimen were garrulous and outgoing); more likely it was a matter of temperament. Under the influence of alcohol he occasionally told stories to the children, and then as he kept on drinking he would become dejected and the children would scatter.[36] He seems to have been neither attractive nor lively. The children seldom approached him.[37] In turn, it is scarcely surprising that he took little interest in their education. When they came home from school, he simply allowed them to play without supervision.[38]

There is a well-known instance in Lu Hsün's works where his father appears briefly in the stereotypic paternal role of teacher and disciplinarian. This occurs in "The Fair of the Five Fierce Gods (*Wu-ch'ang hui*)," a reminiscence of childhood written in 1926. Here, the stern father will not allow Lu Hsün to go on an outing to watch the religious festival named in the title until he has memorized and recited between twenty and thirty lines of the *Rhymed History (Chien-lüeh)*, a work which gave a rhymed account of the essentials of Chinese history, from

> In the beginning was P'an Ku,
> Born of primeval void;
> He was the first to rule the world,
> The chaos to divide . . .

on up to the end of the Ming dynasty (1368-1644). Chou Tso-jen (who again and again warns that there is a strong element of fictionalization in Lu Hsün's reminiscences) points out that this incident, if it did in fact take place, was the exception and not the rule.[39] Moreover, the youngest of the brothers, Chien-jen, notes

36. *LHKC*, p. 40.
37. Ibid., p. 45.
38. Ibid., p. 78.
39. *HSJW*, p. 212. For the incident itself see *LHCC*, II, 241, and *SWLH*, I, 374. I have used the *SWLH* translation of the *Rhymed History* lines.

that in that time and context their father would have been considered rather "democratic" for agreeing to let Lu Hsün go to a religious festival of the common people in the first place. Chien-jen reminds us that Lu Hsün often exaggerated facts to make a point.[40] Because of his opium habit, drinking, and retiring disposition, the father rarely spent time with his sons, eating at the same table with them only on New Year's, and otherwise taking his meals alone. He seems to have been kind and understanding, but very remote.[41]

It is difficult to assess the effect of this kind of father on Lu Hsün. Surely it can hardly have been as serious as the case would be in a nuclear family, for there were other males in the New T'aimen who could serve as surrogates. With emotions widely diffused in so large a family, there would not be the need for intense relationships with a very few people that arises in nuclear families. Yet, both the stories and essays that Lu Hsün wrote as an adult would lead one to believe that as a boy growing up in the New T'aimen he felt emotionally undernourished and experienced a need for intimate and intense relationships, perhaps even a need for love.

In a real sense, judged by the traditional Chinese ideals of what family life should be, the opium- and failure-ridden atmosphere of the New T'aimen was hardly capable of offering Lu Hsün the more satisfying kind of familial relationships that might otherwise have existed. Later on, he would become aware of the possibility of other forms of relatedness, a knowledge derived from exposure to another culture during his student days in Japan and through wide reading of the literatures of other countries. After he ventured beyond the walls of both the New T'aimen and of China, he had bases for comparison (the outsider's point of view) and may well have perceived that the relationships he had known in the t'aimen were seriously lacking. Thus one can posit both a real need experienced in childhood and an elaborated and partly imagined one that was projected back from adulthood.

His boyhood relationship with his mother does not seem to have been close. In 1881, when Lu Hsün was born, his mother was twenty-four. A mere female, she had, of course, been given no formal instruction, though she had learned enough characters to

---

40. *LHSC*, p. 8.
41. *LHKC*, pp. 39-41.

read rhymed romances and some fiction. She once scandalized the
New T'aimen by unbinding her feet in response to the Natural
Foot movement. When a reactionary relative started the rumor
that she had unbound her feet in order to marry one of the
"foreign devils," she responded to it by saying, "You never can
tell—I just might do that!" She was to live a long and full life,
during which most of her needs would be filially attended to by an
apparently devoted Lu Hsün. Dying in 1943, she survived her
famous son by seven years.[42] Despite this faithful attention to her
welfare, there is some ground for doubting that Lu Hsün received
any great influence from his mother during his formative years.
Both in Chou Tso-jen's recollections and in Lu Hsün's fictionalized
reminiscences of boyhood in the New T'aimen, the mother
impinges on the life of her sons only in a peripheral fashion.[43]

In contrast, the servants and Grandmother Chiang seem to have
been Lu Hsün's intimates. It was this grandmother—the wife of the
old bear—who told him the folk tales that he would reuse and
reinterpret as an adult.[44] It was she who gave him riddles to guess
as he lay on a table under a cassia tree, seeking coolness on a hot
summer's night.[45] She would later appear as a leading character in
a story, "The Isolate *(Ku-tu che)*."[46] It is probable that she also
had much to do with the formation of a strong feminist element in
Lu Hsün's adult thought, for he was very close to her and she was
treated badly. As a young boy, he was once told rather coldly that
she was not his real grandmother. He was shown a painting of his
"real" grandmother almost as though he were expected to love the
artist's representation more than the flesh-and-blood old lady
whom he knew as Granny.[47]

His real grandmother had been a Sun. She had given birth to a

---

42. Ibid., pp. 156-57.

43. Lu Hsün's biographers in the People's Republic of China tend to make much
of the influence of his mother because of her supposed roots in the common
people. Lu Hsün's reminiscences of his early years lend themselves easily to such
an interpretation. William Schultz, in "Lu Hsün: The Creative Years" (Ph.D.
dissertation, University of Washington, 1955), makes it clear that she was of the
gentry (p. 10).

44. For example, *SWLH*, II, 82-84, and *LHCC*, I, 279-280.

45. *LHCC*, II, 221.

46. *HSJW*, pp. 187-89.

47. *SWLH*, I, 224; *LHCC*, II, 94-95. For confirmation of the factual elements in
these reminiscences see *HSJW*, pp. 188-89.

daughter in 1858, and a son in 1860 (Lu Hsün's father), and had
died not long after that. The woman whom Lu Hsün knew as
Granny was a second wife (née Chiang), whom Grandfather had
married after the death of Grandmother Sun. Grandmother
Chiang, born in 1842, lived into her late sixties, dying in 1910. She
had presented Grandfather with only one child, a daughter, born
in 1868.[48] This girl, thirteen years Lu Hsün's senior, was very kind
to her young nephews, and they repaid her with great affection.
The day that she was married out of the New T'aimen, the
children were so heartbroken that some of them tried to get into
the bridal sedan chair with her. When in 1894 the news came that
she had died in childbirth, it was a great blow to her nephews, and
a far greater one to Grandmother Chiang: having given birth to no
son of her own, she was never to be anything more in the New
T'aimen than a stepmother to Lu Hsün's father. Her daughter, at
least, had been of her own body and had given her some sense of
fulfillment and purpose. Now even that was gone.[49]

Grandmother Chiang's later years were also clouded over by the
suspicion that she had directly contributed to the death of her
predecessor's daughter. Born in 1858 to Grandmother Sun, this
girl, whose baby name was Te, was a full sister to Lu Hsün's
father, and thus a paternal aunt to his sons. When she reached the
age to marry, Grandfather Chou was so choosy about finding her
a mate that he procrastinated until Aunt Te fell victim to a rather
unadmirable Shaohsing custom: any girl who had passed the age
of twenty without a husband was called an old maid and assumed
to be defective in some way or other, the proof being that she was
still unmarried. Once a girl had been placed in this category there
was little chance of marrying her off as a proper bride. Her family
could consider themselves lucky if they were able to get her into a
good home as a replacement for a wife who had died. This is
exactly what happened to Aunt Te. She was married, as a
replacement, to a Mr. Ma from Wu-jung village.

One year, during the hottest part of summer, Aunt Te came
back to Shaohsing to pay her respects on the anniversary of her
mother's death. Because the weather was so foul that day, it was
suggested that she stay overnight instead of going back the same
day, as she would normally have done. When she informed her

48. *LHKC,* p. 63.   49. Ibid., pp. 63-64.

stepmother, Grandmother Chiang, of this suggestion, the latter assented to it in such a way as to offend Aunt Te, who then insisted on going back at once to Wu-jung village. Soon after she left, there was a terrible storm. Toward evening, word came that the boat she was on had tossed about so violently that Aunt Te had been thrown overboard and was drowned. Quite a few in the family commented that if her mother had been still alive such a thing would never have happened. Such talk must have weighed heavily on Grandmother Chiang, whose position in the family was insecure to begin with.[50] Nominally Grandmother Chiang was the wife of a Han Lin, and that was quite an honor, but in reality Grandfather had gone off to Peking, abandoning her in the countryside, while he pursued an official career and picked up a succession of concubines in the process. And then when he finally returned to Shaohsing, he brought with him one of the concubines that he had acquired while away, along with a son that he had begotten by still another. To add insult to injury, whenever the mood was upon him, he amused himself by cursing Grandmother Chiang.[51]

Grandfather Chou died in 1904; Grandmother Chiang would survive him by six years. After Grandfather's death, understandably, Concubine P'an's position in the New T'aimen was not so strong as it had been previously. She became increasingly unhappy and it was finally agreed that she be allowed to quit the Chou household. Grandmother Chiang drew up an agreement certifying that Concubine P'an, objecting to the present straitened circumstances of the Chou household, was leaving with permission. On her part, Concubine P'an presented Grandmother Chiang with a document certifying that she was leaving of her own free will and absolving the Chous of all future responsibility for her welfare. If Grandmother Chiang had her sorrows, so had Concubine P'an. Chou Tso-jen later wrote some poetry containing the following lines in memory of Concubine P'an:

> Born in Peking, Mistress P'an
> Began serving Grandfather while her hair was still in girlish tufts.
> Though she had wed a poor capital official,
> Still it seemed that she had found a proper haven.
> It must have been an unkind fate

50. *HHL*, pp. 651-52.
51. *HSJW*, pp. 188-89.

That involved her in [Grandfather's] troubles.
Still worse, in middle years she was cut adrift
To float—who knows where?[52]

In the course of his reminiscences, Tso-jen repeatedly points out that few, if any, of the people at the t'aimen were really bad. The family system, which concentrated so much power in the hands of the eldest male and permitted such practices as concubinage, made people what they were and caused inestimable suffering.[53]

The general impression one derives from reading either Chou Tso-jen's factual reminiscences of the New T'aimen or Lu Hsün's fictionalized ones is that of gloom. Tso-jen's recollections, especially, abound in unhappy and unfulfilled people; the few minor victories in the everyday battle of life that one finds scattered here and there through the pages of his reminiscences are scarcely enough to modify an overall impression of defeat. The bleak lives of many of the residents of the New T'aimen would later be reflected also in the stories that Lu Hsün would write, and in his essays as well. For example, in "Random Thoughts" (no. 25) written in 1918, Lu Hsün discusses the role of "father" in traditional Chinese society:

The Austrian misogynist, Otto Weininger, divided women into two categories: mothers and prostitutes. Similarly, men can be classed as fathers and profligates. The fathers again can be graded into two groups: the fathers of children and the fathers of "men." Since all the former can do is beget children, not bring them up, they still have something in common with profligates. The latter not only beget children but also try to educate them, in order that they may be genuine men in the future.

At the end of the Ch'ing dynasty, when a normal college was first set up in a certain province, an old gentleman was horrified. "Why should one have to learn to be a teacher?" he demanded indignantly. "At this rate, there will soon be schools teaching men to be fathers!"

This old gentleman thought that the only thing required of a father was to beget children, and since everyone knows instinctively how to do this, there is no need to learn it. But the fact is that China today needs schools for fathers, and this old gentleman should be enrolled in the lowest class.

For in China we have many fathers of children, but in the future we want only fathers of "men."[54]

52. *HHL*, p. 651.
53. Ibid., pp. 649-51.
54. *SWLH*, II, 26-27; *LHCC*, I, 375-76.

Tso-jen suggests that in this passage Lu Hsün had in mind one of his uncles, Chou Feng-t'ung, who was born in 1877 and was thus only four years older than himself. The mother of Feng-t'ung had died soon after his birth. When he was still very young, he was left with his maternal grandmother while his father (cousin to Grandfather Chou and great-uncle to Lu Hsün) wandered off in search of a relative in Honan Province who was an official and hence might be able to advance his career in some way. Over the course of the years, Fent-t'ung's father returned to the New T'aimen only once.[55] After that visit he wandered off again and nothing was heard of him until news of his death came from Honan.[56]

Uncle Feng-t'ung was probably a bit slow-witted to begin with. Be that as it may, the maternal grandmother's family did not bother to give him any kind of education. (He was, after all, of a different surname and not really kith and kin.) When the grandmother died, her sons refused to be responsible for him any longer and sent him back to the Chous.[57] Some members of the New T'aimen managed to wangle him a job at Mangy-Beard's herb shop, a kindness that Uncle Feng-t'ung returned by throwing in a little extra whenever anyone from the New T'aimen bought anything there. Just as things seemed to be going very well for him, there occurred the incident when Mangy-Beard Runt was struck and killed by an assassin's stone, and Feng-t'ung was out of a job. At this point a collection was taken up in the t'aimen to set him up in a business as a roving hawker of pretzels and fried cakes. This time, unfortunately, he repaid their kindness by periodically taking whatever money he had taken in and going off on an alcoholic binge. The family would then have to repay the stand from which he had gotten his consignment for that day.[58] Once, bemoaning his fate, he said that his father had sired him in exactly the same way that a mosquito begets its offspring— dropping the larvae and then simply forgetting the whole thing.[59] It does indeed seem likely that Lu Hsün had the unfortunate Feng-t'ung's father in mind when he distinguished between real fathers, who not only beget but also nourish their sons, and the

55. *LHKC*, p. 100.
56. Ibid., p. 36.
57. Ibid., p. 101.
58. Ibid., pp. 102-3.
59. Ibid., pp. 144-45.

profligates, who are capable of nothing more than sexual congress.[60]

There was no shortage of people like Feng-t'ung within the walls of the family compound. Three brothers of a collateral branch of the Chou family living in the New T'aimen were so undistinguished that they were referred to merely by their weights at birth: Four-seven (four pounds [*chin*] and seven ounces [*liang*]), Five-ten, and Six-four. Since they were older than Lu Hsün's father, the boys called them *po-po*, or "uncle senior to my father."[61] The most successful of the three was Six-four; he had married (the other two had not), and had fathered two children, and he was gainfully employed.[62] Four-seven, a repulsive kind of man, was a hopeless opium addict and if you had met him on the street, Chou Tso-jen avers, you would have taken him for a downright bum.[63]

Five-ten, on the other hand, was rather personable and had about him something that attracted one. Thin as the opium pipe he smoked, he was forever smiling at people and agreeing with everything that was said to him. However, he was inordinately fond of gossip, and hence he often stirred up trouble. Grandfather Chou thought him no damned good, yet loved to listen to his gossip. Five-ten's gossip apparently exerted a malign influence on the old patriarch, for when Five-ten died, Grandmother Chiang unconsciously let a "Thanks be to Buddha!" escape her lips.[64] It is unlikely that Four-seven and Five-ten exerted any great influence on the young Lu Hsün (madness would seem the only conceivable result), though they must have done much to add to the number of gloomy shadows that squatted in the corners of the New T'aimen. As we shall see when we come to discuss the stories, they also provided models for characters that would come to life in his fictionalized world.

And what of the influence of Lu Hsün's siblings? In all, his mother gave birth to five children. There were four sons: Shu-jen (Lu Hsün), born in 1881; Tso-jen, 1885; Chien-jen, 1889; and Ch'un-shou, 1893 (he died of pneumonia in 1898).[65]. The only

60. Ibid., p. 145.
61. Ibid., p. 73.
62. Ibid., p. 94.
63. Ibid., p. 96.
64. Ibid., pp. 99-100.
65. Dates from *LHKC*.

daughter, Tuan, did not survive the year of her birth, 1888.[66] Of the three surviving children, Lu Hsün and his next younger brother, Tso-jen, were very close as youngsters and remained so until a quarrel in the 1920s permanently estranged them. The eight years that separated him from Chien-jen probably inhibited the development of a close relationship there.[67]

The familial atmosphere was at once interesting (as a madhouse is interesting) and gloomy (as a madhouse is gloomy). It was an ambience characterized by failure and lack of human fulfillment. Everywhere one looked there were shattered lives: women married to effete or profligate men; children of uninterested or absent parents; men who had come to prefer the sweet visions of opium to the reality of the human debris around them. It was an atmosphere that did much to determine the way that Lu Hsün saw China. He would always prefer describing the stark realities of the present to rhapsodizing over the imagined glories of the past; he would ever choose to depict human relationships as he knew them rather than attempt to present them in such a way as to accord with the hollow ideals of long-lost classical traditions. Throughout his life he would, in effect, be concerned with one of the oldest problems in the history of Chinese thought, that of *ming* and *shih* (name and reality). He had been introduced to the ideals of Chinese culture (the *ming*) through the classics; he knew the reality (the *shih*) only too well through his experience in the New T'aimen. He would emerge from all his varied familial experiences with a lifelong sensitivity to sham.

66. Tso-jen caught smallpox and infected Tuan with the disease. Lu Hsün had been inoculated in a sporadic government campaign that had fallen into disuse when Tso-jen reached the proper age for inoculation. Tso-jen attributed his coming through without scars to the fact that his grandmother bound his hands so that he couldn't scratch. *HHL*, pp. 4-5.

67. For instance, Chien-jen excuses himself for not knowing many details about Lu Hsün's youth on the grounds that there were simply too many years between them. *LHSC*, p. 1.

3

STUDY AND PLAY

Though the high-speed methods of modern printing were coming into vogue in the treaty ports while Lu Hsün was a youngster, most of the books to be found around the New T'aimen were wood-block editions. Two pages of Chinese characters, carved on wooden blocks, were printed on one side of a single sheet of paper which was then folded down the middle to form two pages with the fold on the outer edge; such sheets were stitched together into *ts'e* (complete booklets, or parts of a longer book), and a book might consist of a small or large number of *ts'e*. It was, of course, also possible to carve sketches onto the blocks and thus produce illustrations. Of the various interests Lu Hsün had as a boy, his enthusiasm for books in general, and illustrated ones in particular, was probably most decisive for his later development as a writer: his adult prose would be distinguished by a rough-hewn quality reminiscent of the stark line-sketches presented in the woodblock prints he so loved in his early youth.

Of all the various relatives who lived at the New T'aimen, it was Great-Uncle Chao-lan who most influenced him in the direction of books. With this man he began his studies at the age of five,[1] and some four decades later he wrote of him with loving nostalgia:

A fat and kindly old man, he liked to grow plants such as chloranthus or jasmine, or the rare silk tree. . . . This old man was a lonely soul with no one to talk to, so he liked children's company and often even called us his "young friends." In the compound where several branches of our clan

1. Wang Yeh-ch'iu, *Hsin-hai ke-ming ch'ien te Lu Hsün hsien-sheng* [Lu Hsün before the Republican Revolution] (Shanghai, 1957), p. 79; hereafter cited as *KMCLH*.

27

lived, he was the only one with many books, and unusual items at that. He had volumes of the essays and poems written for the examinations, of course; but his was the only study where I could find Lu Chi's *Commentaries on the Flora and Fauna in the Book of Songs*, and many other strange titles. My favorite in those days was *The Mirror of Flowers* with all its illustrations. He told me that there was an illustrated edition of the *Classic of Hills and Seas* with pictures of man-faced beasts, nine-headed snakes, three-footed birds, men with wings, and headless monsters who used their teats as eyes. . . . Unfortunately, he happened to have mislaid it.[2]

Much to young Lu Hsün's surprise and delight, Ah-ch'ang, his amah, eventually secured an illustrated copy of the *Classic of Hills and Seas (Shan-hai ching)* for him. It was the first book that he ever owned, and it launched him almost immediately on a career of collecting illustrated volumes.[3] Up to the time when Lu Hsün started building his own modest library, there were only two collections of books at the New T'aimen (not very impressive for a family with at least some pretentions to scholarship). The other one belonged to his father. Largely confined to the narrow purpose of preparing a candidate for the examinations, it was not nearly so interesting as that belonging to Great-Uncle Chao-lan.[4] The enthusiasm that the old man kindled in his grandnephew gradually expanded to include all books.[5] It was a love-affair that was to last a lifetime and was to continue to grow until it included such varied activities as collecting rubbings from stone monuments and promoting the craft of woodblock printing.[6]

The boy Lu Hsün approached his play with a seriousness that might be reserved for work. Characteristically, he was fastidious about his own books. He housed them in a red leather suitcase (insects might penetrate an ordinary wooden box) that was kept in his mother's room and provided with an arsenal of camphor balls against the possible forays of bookworms. Occasionally, after carefully wiping down a table, he would favor his brothers with the showing of an illustrated volume. They were free to lean on

2. *SWLH*, I, 367-68; *LHCC*, II, 227-30.
3. *SWLH*, I, 359-60; *LHCC*, II, 230-31. For corroboration see *HSJW*, p. 207.
4. *LHKC*, pp. 76-77.
5. *HSJW*, p. 209.
6. As a boy he often watched the cutting of woodblocks at Hsü Kuang-chi's establishment in Shaohsing. *LHCC*, II, 296.

the table and enjoy his treasure as he carefully leafed through it, but they were not allowed to touch it.[7]

In the days before he was able to buy anything with which to stock the red suitcase library, he contented himself by making hand copies of favorite books. Getting his hands on an illustrated edition of a novel, he would trace out the woodblock portraits of the leading characters on separate sheets and then stitch them all together to make a little book of his own. Or gaining temporary access to a particularly interesting text, he would make a personal copy. The first such copy consisted of separate sheets on which he copied the old forms of characters given in the *K'ang Hsi Dictionary*, afterward stitching the sheets together to form a small volume. From this he went on to copying poems and then to copying entire books that he borrowed from Great-Uncle Chao-lan's library.[8]

At the age of eleven, in early 1892, Lu Hsün began attending a private school (*ssu-shu*) known as the Three Flavor Study.[9] According to his own testimony, even here he found time during class to trace illustrations from novels:

[Before long] I had a big volume each of illustrations from *Suppressing the Bandits* (*Tang-k'ou chih*) and *Journey to the West* (*Hsi-yu chi*). Later, because I needed money, I sold them to a rich classmate.[10]

Occasionally too, while their teacher was absorbed in a book, the boys would surreptitiously stage battles with puppet warriors. These were modeled after illustrations in novels and made of colored paper which was cut and pasted into helmets (worn perched on the thumb) and suits of armor (worn draped over the hand). Weapons were wielded pinched between the fingers. Competition for quality was so intense that if a boy fashioned a warrior elaborate enough to arouse the envy of his peers, a jealous schoolmate might well slip a cockroach into the drawer where the doughty hero was stored, in the hope that it would take a few bites

7. *LHSC*, pp. 1-5.
8. *LHKC*, pp. 77-78.
9. *KMCLH*, p. 79.
10. *LHCC*, II, 256; *SWLH*, I, 393. Tso-jen states that while the illustrations from *Journey to the West* may have been traced out in the Three Flavor Study, those from *Suppressing the Bandits* were done while the boys were in exile at Huang Fu village. *LHKC*, p. 51.

out of him. The models for these warriors were the same black-on-white line prints that Lu Hsün had traced from novels.[11]

In 1926, in an essay titled "Illustrations of the Twenty-four Celebrated Examples of Filial Piety *(Erh-shih-ssu hsiao-t'u),*" Lu Hsün—then in his forties—noted with approval that illustrated children's books were beginning to appear in China. When he was in school, teachers did not like children to have anything that was illustrated and would punish them if they were caught with such materials. Feeling strongly that in the traditional China of his youth the natural esthetic appetite of the young had been starved virtually out of existence, he saw the appearance of illustrated books as a great improvement. Fortunately in his own case it appears that, once away from supervision at the school and safely behind the walls of the New T'aimen, he was perfectly free to read illustrated works.[12]

Even though the New T'aimen may have appeared permissive in comparison, it is not likely that the Three Flavor Study was very strict. As we have seen, Lu Hsün was not sufficiently intimidated to be prevented from copying illustrations from novels when the teacher's back was turned.[13] The master of the school, Shou Huai-chien, was an affable and kindly old gentleman who only occasionally resorted to physical punishment, and that of the lightest sort.[14] When Lu Hsün wrote a "reminiscence" of the Three Flavor Study in 1926, however, he chose to emphasize the negative aspects of the school. (We are reminded again of Tso-jen's admonition against treating his brother's recollections of childhood as pure biographical data.)[15] Something may be divined of the comparatively liberal atmosphere of the Three Flavor Study by comparing it with another private school nearby, the Hall of Comprehensive Thought. Before going to the latrine, pupils in this neighboring institution were required to come forward and request one of the bamboo permission slips kept in a holder on the teacher's desk. In the Three Flavor Study, when bladders became uncomfortably distended the children were free to leave the

---

11. *LHSC,* p. 1.
12. *LHCC,* II, 233-34.
13. *KMCLH,* p. 79.
14. *LHKC,* p. 56; *HHL,* pp. 21-24.
15. See "From Hundred Plant Flower Garden to Three Flavor Study" in *SWLH,* I, 387-93, and *LHCC,* II, 252-56. The Three Flavor Study, the Chou family

classroom and go to the latrine without any intervening ritual. Granted that the neighboring school was a bit formal, by modern standards the business of the bamboo slips does not appear extreme. Even so, it made Lu Hsün, Tso-jen, and their peers so righteously indignant that during their lunch hour one day they went to the school where this "cruel" and "oppressive" custom prevailed and, under the flags-flying leadership of Lu Hsün, broke all the bamboo slips and threw the teacher's inkstone on the floor. They completed the punishment of what they considered to be a dictatorial schoolmaster by scattering his writing brushes and ink sticks in all directions.[16] All of this would lead one to suspect that discipline in the Three Flavor Study cannot have been very strict.

Shou Huai-chien was, at least, a considerable improvement over the great-uncle in the New T'aimen who tutored Lu Hsün in reading the *Book of Mencius* at about this time. This great-uncle, Tzu-ching, was so incompetent and unstable that it would seem unlikely that Lu Hsün could have learned very much from him.[17] However, as we have noted earlier, he provided a model for the protagonist for one of Lu Hsün's best short stories, "The White Light (*Pai-kuang*)."[18] Tzu-ching lived alone in a single room at the t'aimen called the "orange-tree room" by the children since the window faced a tiny courtyard in which an orange tree grew. Was he a bit crazy because he was alone or was he alone because he was a bit crazy? Tzu-ching's father was the "Twelfth Old Gentleman" who disappeared in 1861 during the Taiping Rebellion. When captured by the rebels, he was disguised as a coolie; hence the rebels put him to work as a carrier. Later on he was killed and the government considered him a martyr (he had not gone over to the rebel side), granting him a posthumous rank of Manchu nobility in

---

compound, and the Hundred Plant Flower Garden—a backyard at the compound—are now parts of the Lu Hsün museum in Shaohsing. *LHCC*, II, 448, n. 5.

16. *LHKC*, p. 58; *HHL*, p. 23.

17. *LHKC*, pp. 24, 26.

18. For remarks on how Lu Hsün transformed the stuff of Tzu-ching's life into fiction, and a comparison of his techniques with those employed by writers of traditional Chinese fiction, see the discussion by the Soviet scholar V. I. Semanov quoted in Zbigniew Slupski's informative *The Evolution of a Modern Chinese Writer: An Analysis of Lao She's Fiction with Biographical and Bibliographical Appendices* (Prague, 1966), p. 20.

recognition of his loyalty.[19] Twelfth Old Gentleman's wife survived until 1901; she preferred staying with a married daughter in Hangchow to living with her eccentric son at the t'aimen in Shaohsing. Tzu-ching married, but his wife died early, leaving him with two sons, Eight-Pounder and Ah-kuei (the name connoted August, the month in which he was born). For one reason or another (some said that Tzu-ching used to beat them), both sons left home, whereupon their father became a recluse in the orange-tree room.[20] His eventual insanity and incredibly inept suicide figure heavily in "The White Light" and we shall come back to Tzu-ching when that story is discussed.

As has been pointed out, of all the teachers Lu Hsün had as a youth, Great-Uncle Chao-lan probably exerted the greatest, most lasting, and most wholesome influence; his large library and personal example kindled Lu Hsün with a lifelong enthusiasm for books and prints. Yet even this good man's life impinged upon that of his grandnephew in ways that were sometimes painful. The first bit of unpleasantness was primarily the work of Chao-lan's well-meaning daughter-in-law, Mistress Ch'ien. A very capable young woman, she had long been a favorite of Lu Hsün's mother. Later on, when Lu Hsün was a student in Japan, Mistress Ch'ien requited his mother's affection by putting herself forward as a go-between for Lu Hsün and one of Chao-lan's grandnieces on his wife's side of the family. Even as an old man, Tso-jen would continue to blame her for this particular match. An extremely pretty woman herself, Mistress Ch'ien arranged a match with a girl of the Chu family who was almost freakishly small, as if her growth had been abnormally stunted. Since Mistress Ch'ien must have known what the girl was like, Tso-jen could only conclude that she had intentionally tried to put something over on the Chous by foisting off this relative of Chao-lan's wife on Lu Hsün.[21] Their marriage having been duly arranged, Lu Hsün did in fact, upon his mother's command, marry this girl, but he never really regarded her as his wife. According to one biographer, in conversation with an old friend, Hsü Shou-shang, Lu Hsün once com-

---

19. *HSJW*, pp. 122-23, *LHKC*, pp. 24-25. There are some discrepancies between the two accounts.
20. *LHKC*, p. 27.
21. *HHL*, p. 172; *LHKC*, p. 69.

mented with a melancholy sigh: "She's a gift to me from Mother, and the only thing I can do is to take care of her."[22]

The second bit of unpleasantness relating to Great-Uncle Chao-lan occurred in 1897, the year Lu Hsün's father died. A clan meeting was held in which the primary order of business was the disposition of the deceased's property. The elders of the clan had reached an agreement and wanted Lu Hsün to assent to it as his father's eldest son. Chao-lan pressured him to sign in such an overbearing manner that the sixteen-year-old grandnephew was left with a residue of resentment and indignation; characteristically, Lu Hsün was only able to purge himself of it by pouring it out on paper—this time in his diaries.[23] Chao-lan died in the following year (1898). Perhaps his death took the edge off Lu Hsün's resentment and caused his memory of the old man to retain only the good things; or perhaps, in retrospect, he blamed the family system more than he did his great-uncle. At any rate, according to Tso-jen, the affection and respect that Lu Hsün had for Chao-lan prevailed over any lingering rancor. For although Chao-lan never amounted to much in the everyday sense, he was, after all, a literary man graced with an air of learning and art that must have made him very attractive to the young, serious, and bookish Lu Hsün.

Childhood was not entirely a matter of books and study. Lu Hsün had his lighter moments, and there were even occasions when he was more Tom Sawyer than model student. One of the best documented of these occurs in Chou Tso-jen's extended reminiscence of the unfortunate Aunt Te. It seems that not far from Wu-jung village, to which Aunt Te had gone when she married, were two places along the ocean that were famous for the magnificent waves that came each year on the eighteenth of the eighth lunar month. One summer, Aunt Te was about to go back

---

22. Lin Ch'en, *Lu Hsün te shih-chi k'ao* [Tracing down some of the facts of Lu Hsün's life] (Shanghai, 1957), p. 84; hereafter cited as *SCK*.

23. Tso-jen says (*HSJW*, p. 209) that the following remark by Wei Lien-shu in "Ku-tu-che (The Isolate)" refers to this business: "When I was a child and my father died, I cried bitterly because they wanted to take the house from me and make me put my mark on the document." *SWLH*, I, 220; *LHCC*, II, 91-92.

In both *HSJW* (p. 209) and *LHKC* (pp. 71, 231) Tso-jen is somewhat reticent about this event. The exact nature of the dispute is not clear; nor is it clear to what extent Lu Hsün gave in to the pressure.

to Wu-jung village after a visit to Shaohsing when she happened to notice that it was the seventeenth of the eighth lunar month and asked if anyone would like to go back with her and her young daughter, Pearl, to see the famous tide the next day. The only takers were Lu Hsün, his brothers Tso-jen and Chien-jen, and an uncle, Ming-shan (a mere four years older than Lu Hsün). Aunt Te could hardly have foreseen what she was in for. It was a trip which one made, of course, by boat, for in the "water country" around Shaohsing almost all travel was done that way. The boat was hardly out of town when the four boys grew restless and began to act up. They stood two on each side of the boat and managed to rock it enough to annoy the boatman and scare little Pearl into a fit of tears. Despite Aunt Te's and the boatman's remonstrances, the boys kept on until the boat reached its destination. During the few days that they stayed with Aunt Te, there seemed no limit to the pranks they were prepared to play. She unthinkingly acceded to their request that they be allowed to take their meals alone. At mealtimes they would be sent a generous selection of dishes and a wooden tub of rice. Sometimes they would eat everything on one group of dishes and leave everything on another. Sometimes they would eat every last grain of rice while leaving their meat and vegetables untouched. Sometimes they would reverse the process.

When Aunt Te thoughtfully provided them with snacks to take to their room at night they would wait until she was in bed and then pretend to be having a bloody battle over the snacks to see who got what. When she got up and came to their room to arbitrate the quarrel, they would pretend to be fast asleep. She provided their room with a covered commode to use at night. They used it both night and day, and refused to let the servant empty it until it was so full that the cover was floating. In sum, they disported themselves as a foursome of utter little nuisances, prompting Aunt Te to complain at one point: "I should never have invited rotten guests like you in the first place." Despite everything, however, she continued to treat them well and was even polite enough to ask them to linger longer when their short visit was over.[24] Perhaps the temporary freedom from the restraints of life in the New T'aimen had been more than the boys could resist.

24. *HHL*, pp. 653-55.

During his youth in the New T'aimen, Lu Hsün displayed a lively interest in religious processions and festivals. They had an aura of drama and mystery that intrigued him; it was an aura made all the more romantic by the feeling that here was something forbidden, a realm of freedom far removed from the restrictions of gentry life in a t'aimen. Reminiscing, he wrote in 1926:

Though these processions were not prohibited by the authorities . . . still, women and children were not allowed to watch them, and educated people or the so-called literati seldom went to look on either. . . . I do, however, remember once witnessing a rather fine show myself. First came a boy on horseback called the Announcer. Then, after a considerable interval, the High Pole arrived. This was a great bamboo pole to which a long banner was attached, and it was carried in both hands by a huge fat man dripping with perspiration. When in the mood he would balance the pole on his head or teeth, or even on the tip of his nose. He was followed by stilt-walkers, children on platforms carried by men, and other children on horseback, all masquerading as characters from operas. There were people dressed in red like felons, too, loaded with cangues and chains, some of whom were also children. To me each part was glorious and each participant extremely lucky—I no doubt envied them the chance to show off. I used to wish that I could have some serious illness, so that my mother would go to the temple to promise the god that I would masquerade as a felon. . . . So far, though, I have failed to have any association with these processions.[25]

He was fascinated, as a boy, by the color, excitement, and drama of folk religion, and later on, as an adult, by the stark—almost crude—symbolism of the dusk-to-dawn religious operas danced and sung on stage on festival days in honor of the deities. Two characters in particular caught his fancy: Nü-tiao (the Hanging Woman) and Wu-ch'ang (Nothing Is Constant). The Hanging Woman was a mythical personification of the oppressed spirits of all women who had been wronged throughout the ages; she had been a child bride, so mistreated that she was finally driven to suicide by hanging.[26] Most religious operas had a villain, and, as sunrise drew near, the King of Hell would issue a warrant for the villain's arrest. Wu-ch'ang, a frightening-yet-humorous personification of death who sported on his hat the phrase "As soon as you see me, you'll be in for a great piece of luck (*yi-chien*

25. *SWLH*, I, 373; *LHCC*, II, 240. See also *HSJW*, p. 214.
26. *SWLH*, I, 438; *LHCC* VI, 502-3.

Fig. 1. Wu-ch'ang as drawn by Lu Hsün in 1927.

ta-chi)," was the arresting officer. He would mount the stage, sneeze 108 times, and fart 108 times before even bothering to introduce himself, a lively lad by anyone's standards.[27]

While writing his reminiscences in the 1920s, Lu Hsün got so caught up in the spell of Wu-ch'ang that he became something of an expert on the various kinds of woodblock prints that portrayed him. He devotes much of the Afterword of *Dawn Blossoms Plucked at Dusk* (*Chao-hua hsi-shih*) to the subject and includes various representations of Wu-ch'ang, discussing the merits of each and even adding a drawing of his own.[28]

From all of his varied interests as a boy growing up in the New T'aimen a recognizable pattern begins to emerge, a pattern that individualizes Lu Hsün, that sets him apart from countless other lads who received essentially the same kind of education toward the end of the Ch'ing dynasty. Generally speaking, his education was what one would expect it be for a boy of his class. He was led down the usual path of the Four Books and Five Classics,[29] toward the gates of the examination halls and a career as an official of the Manchu empire.[30] Certain peculiar characteristics in the somewhat permissive (if only by default) environment of the New T'aimen, however, lent a tinge of individuality to this pattern of training. For instance, he was not only allowed, but positively encouraged to read novels. He was even allowed to read illustrated books and, more importantly, allowed to copy them. When his father came across the sketch showing Eight-Pounder vicariously murdered, he questioned the boy in a bemused manner about the sketch and ripped that page from the volume, but did not object to any of the other sketches or berate his son for indulging in such a frivolous pastime.[31]

Lu Hsün was undoubtedly taught the history of his country and introduced to its gods and heroes through the written word of the classical sources and even novels, but gods and heroes whose bodies were made of words seem never to have been so real or

27. *LHCC*, II, 248; *SWLH*, I, 383.
28. *LHCC*, II, 294-300.
29. *LHSC*, p. 7. The Four Books were *The Great Learning*, *The Doctrine of the Mean*, the *Analects* (of Confucius), and the *Book of Mencius*; the Five Classics were the *Book of Changes*, the *Book of Odes*, the *Book of History*, the *Book of Rites*, and the *Spring and Autumn Annals*.
30. *HSJW*, p. 244.
31. *LHKC*, p. 38.

attractive to him as the characters (real or mythical) that he saw presented in religious processions or pictured in the pages of an illustrated book. Heroes became more "real" when he could copy them out of an illustrated edition of a novel and feel them under the very tip of his writing brush, and became even more exciting when colored paper and paste turned them into miniature puppet-warriors that could be matched in honorable combat. The development of this plastic sense, this ability to make things while seeing them in the mind's eye, was to have its effect on the stories he would write as an adult; it would become one of the distinguishing characteristics of his style.

In these interests we may also see a foreshadowing of the content of Lu Hsün's stories, which was derived in large part from the experiences of the relatives and acquaintances who lived within the walls of the New T'aimen. Since many of these lives were wrecked or thwarted, the content reflects an attitude that we could characterize as anti-establishment. If we pose the tradition of the scholar bureaucracy against that of the ordinary people, then it is fair to say that most of Lu Hsün's interests belonged more to the latter. For instance, despite his love for books and illustrations, he never had the scholar's typical interest in calligraphy[32] and preferred woodblock prints to the high art of China that one finds in museums and the homes of wealthy connoisseurs.[33] In theatricals, too, he was throughout his life more interested in the folk drama of religious festivals than in the sophisticated operas of the cities. Writing in 1936 (the year of his death), he remembered fondly:

The Shaohsing I knew was the Shaohsing of forty years ago. Since there were no high officials there at that time, there were no private performances in the houses of the great. All performances were a kind of religious drama.[34]

Writing in 1922, he noted that in twenty years he had been to the opera only twice and had seen nothing in it.[35]

32. LHSC, p. 3.
33. Chih T'ang (Chou Tso-jen), "Kuan-yü Lu Hsün hsien-sheng" [On Lu Hsün], Yü Chou Feng, XXIX (November 16, 1936), 262; hereafter cited as KYLH.
34. SWLH, I, 433; LHCC VI, 499.
35. SWLH, I, 136; LHCC, I, 139.

It would be very difficult to dismiss this sympathy with the tradition of the ordinary people as a mere pose; Lu Hsün's identification with it is too thoroughgoing and the tone of his language too sincere for that. Here we see the shadows of a bittersweet contradiction, a contradiction that would be reflected in many of the stories he was to write as an adult: though the little tradition of the ordinary people may have differed in the degree to which it observed the Confucian mores of the big tradition of the scholar-bureaucrats, it did not differ qualitatively and hence could not provide an alternate tradition that could be used to replace or revitalize the old culture of the governing class.

There were good reasons, of course, for his sympathy with the culture and traditions of the ordinary people. The gentry people with whom he lived and from whom he came were far too effete, and even ugly, to invite the emulation of a sensitive and intelligent boy. Then there was the humiliation brought upon the family by Grandfather Chou's disgrace, and the chicanery (or so he felt) of the traditional doctors who had slowly killed his father at great expense. Such a childhood was likely to produce a young man in revolt against his own background. Indeed his was a childhood that formed a young man who had both feet planted firmly in the world of traditional China but was so disenchanted with that world that the muscles in the legs above those feet were taut and had been long cocked for a leap to something new and different.

4

NANKING AND
MILITARY SCHOOL

Reminiscing in 1926 about his departure from home in his eighteenth year (1898), Lu Hsün recalled that he had left at a time when his spirits were doubly dampened by the narrow parochialism of the Shaohsing natives in general and the perfidy of some members of the t'aimen in particular:

I simply had to go seek out a different kind of people, to seek out those very people whom the natives of S[haohsing] City found most despicable, be they beasts or devils. At that time the cynosure of ridicule and vituperation in S City was a school that had not been open very long, called the Sino-Occidental Academy. In addition to Chinese [subjects] they taught some foreign languages and mathematics, a circumstance that had already made the school a common target for attack. In fact, the local *hsiu-ts'ai*, steeped as they were in the works of the sages, culled sentences from the Four Books and put them together to make an eight-legged essay ridiculing the school. . . . But to tell the truth I was not quite satisfied with the Sino-Occidental Academy, myself: Chinese, mathematics, English, and French were the only course offerings they had. Of course, if you wanted a school where you could find fairly new and interesting courses, there was always the Ch'iu Shih College at Hangchow, but the tuition was high. Since there were tuition-free schools at Nanking, there was nothing for it but to go there.[1]

1. *LHCC*, II, 265. Chiang Monlin, who attended the Sino-Occidental Academy at the turn of the century, states that the major part of the curriculum consisted of Chinese studies that would prepare one for the civil service examinations; but students were also introduced to the basic concepts of Western science, and Japanese was taught, as well as English and French. According to Chiang, the Ch'iu Shih College at Hangchow was, in its early phase, similar to the Sino-Occidental Academy—which he characterizes as "an old-style Chinese school whose curriculum included some foreign languages and science teaching." *Tides from the West* (New Haven, 1947), pp. 40-41, 49-50.

Probably what most influenced him to decide in favor of Nanking was the fact that he had a great-uncle there who was dean of the Engineering Section of the Kiangnan Naval Academy. Because of the convenience afforded by this relative's position, no fewer than four of the boys from the Chou t'aimen attended this school: Lu Hsün was the third, and Tso-jen the fourth.[2]

This great-uncle, Chou Ch'ing-fan, was a holder of the *chü-jen* degree who had originally gone to Nanking as an expectant district magistrate (one who would be appointed to a district magistracy when a vacancy occurred). While waiting, Ch'ing-fan got on good terms with a member of his wife's family, a man who was serving as a secretary in the yamen of the governor-general of Kiangsu and Chekiang. This relative was a wily fellow (wiliness was an occupational necessity for yamen secretaries) who had managed to remain secure in his post through a succession of changes in administrative superiors, apparently because he was valued for his knowledge of things foreign. Through the good offices of this relative, Great-Uncle Ch'ing-fan had managed to secure a post there in Nanking at the Kiangnan Naval Academy, one of the schools established during the latter part of the nineteenth century when Chinese officials decided that it was vital for China's self-preservation to learn the superior military techniques of the Western powers. He taught classical Chinese while serving as dean of the Engineering Section and held onto this post for about a decade until a change of school directors in 1903 forced him into retirement. He then returned to Shaohsing and set up shop in the New T'aimen as a private teacher. Priding himself on being a strict moralist, he nevertheless rapidly gained a reputation as something of a "dirty old man." Once he made advances to an old maid who struck him for taking such liberties. His second daughter-in-law saw the whole thing out the window and shouted: "A splendid blow! Why don't you beat the stupid old lout to death?" According to Chou Tso-jen, many such incidents occurred during Ch'ing-fan's declining years.[3]

Tso-jen has pointed out that Lu Hsün would not really have needed the familial connection to gain admission to the school, for the entrance examination was not at all difficult. He has added, however, that there is little doubt that Lu Hsün chose a school so

2. *LHKC*, pp. 79–82.
3. Ibid., p. 83.

far from home because he had learned of it through Ch'ing-fan, whose presence there, at the very least, facilitated things.[4] As late as March and April of 1898,[5] Lu Hsün was still practicing away at the kind of eight-legged essay and poetry that one had to write for the civil service examinations.[6] It was not time wasted, for the entrance examinations for the Naval Academy involved writing essays very similar to those required in the imperial examinations. Lu Hsün's successful performance on the entrance examinations for the academy was, at best, a mixed blessing: attendance at such half-Chinese, half-foreign institutions was so little prestigious that Great-Uncle Ch'ing-fan had the Chou boys change their names as soon as they arrived on campus.[7] The civil service examinations were not abolished until 1905; hence at this time any other road to social advancement was still considered irregular. Following a non-Chinese curriculum was considered especially reprehensible. In the famous Preface to his *Call to Arms (Na-han)* Lu Hsün recalled:

... society in general considered the so-called "study of foreign things" a course of action embarked upon only by people who had met dead ends at every other turn and had nothing left but to sell their souls to the foreign devils; hence such people were severely ridiculed and even ostracized.[8]

Because the cadets wore uniforms, the contempt of society was in this case exacerbated by traditional Chinese disdain for men in the military.[9]

From the academy's point of view, Po-sheng, Grandfather Chou's son by Concubine Chang, was probably the most successful of the four Chou boys from Shaohsing, in that he spent the rest of his life in the service, and had risen to the rank of chief engineer on the warship *Lien Ching* by the time of his death, in 1918, when he was in his thirty-seventh year.[10] He had entered the academy in

4. Ibid., p. 81.
5. I have converted the lunar dates of my Chinese sources into the more familiar solar approximations.
6. *HSJW*, p. 247, 296-97.
7. *LHKC*, p. 80. The change, of course, was in their given, not their family, names.
8. *LHCC*, I, 4; *SWLH*, I, 2.
9. *HSJW*, pp. 222, 293.
10. *LHKC*, p. 80.

1897, in his fifteenth year, and graduated in 1904. Basically a rather intelligent lad, he had an unfortunate aversion to study and made it through the school by the skin of his teeth. Having spent his earliest years in the imperial capital, Po-sheng had a Peking fondness for the opera which Great-Uncle Ch'ing-fan saw as an improper frivolity and tried to curb. There was a time during his school years in Nanking when Po-sheng would go to the opera every Sunday. Unfortunately, to get out he had to sneak past Ch'ing-fan's window. Although Ch'ing-fan was terribly near-sighted, there was nothing amiss with his hearing, and he often detected the sound of Po-sheng's squeaking leather shoes as the lad tried to tiptoe past his window. Recognizing the telltale sound, he would call out to Po-sheng, who would be foiled again. Great-Uncle Ch'ing-fan did his damndest to keep Po-sheng away from the opera; sometimes on Saturday he would invite Po-sheng over for a snack on Sunday (his opera day). Once, when Sunday arrived and Po-sheng didn't, Ch'ing-fan went to his dormitory to get him. In front of the bed his boots were still in place and the mosquito net was pulled down all around as though he were still sleeping; however, when Ch'ing-fan got close enough to see inside the net, he realized that Po-sheng was probably well on his way to the theater.[11] It will be recalled that Po-sheng's mother, Concubine Chang, died when he was still just a little tyke and that he was brought up by Concubine P'an—who happened to be an opera lover. No wonder that when Po-sheng and Lu Hsün were at the Naval Academy together, Grandfather Chou was pleased if this son of his managed to keep from coming in last on an examination, and was displeased if Lu Hsün came in anywhere but at the top of the list.

Lu Hsün left Shaohsing for the Naval Academy on the eleventh of the intercalary third month (May 1, 1898) and arrived in Nanking six days later.[12] Reminiscing in 1926, he remembered that as soon as you entered Nanking through the I-feng Gate in the West Wall, you would immediately spot the lofty mast and smokestack that marked the location of the school.[13] The cadets had to learn to climb the mast as part of their training,[14] and

11. Ibid., pp. 88-89.
12. *HSJW*, p. 246.
13. *LHCC*, II, 265.
14. *HSJW*, pp. 311-12.

though it was quite high, the danger was greatly reduced by a net spread out beneath to save inept fledgling seamen. Lu Hsün did not remember anyone ever having fallen.[15] Formerly there had been a pool in which the cadets were taught to swim, but after two drownings it was filled in and a small shrine to the God of War was erected over it to keep the watery ghosts of the departed from harming anyone else. Apparently as a further precaution against the possible malevolence of the ghosts, the school authorities invited Buddhist monks in to conduct masses for the dead on every feast of All Ghosts' Day.[16]

Almost four full days of the week were devoted to English; another full day was taken up with composing essays in Chinese. The upperclassmen in this three-year school had the best rooms and lorded it over the lowerclassmen in many ways.[17] Both Lu Hsün and Tso-jen (who entered the same academy in 1901)[18] were unimpressed with the quality of the education they received there. Tso-jen remarks that the cadets objected to the slipshod manner in which the courses were taught and to the bureaucratic airs of the instructors.[19] The level of English teaching was very low, as was even the instruction in Chinese.[20] Lu Hsün characterized the school as a "total mess."[21]

Toward the end of 1898, Lu Hsün returned to Shaohsing—he had, it would seem, quit the academy in disgust.[22] A few weeks later, he, Tso-jen, and two of their uncles—Po-wen and Chung-hsiang—all took the K'uaichi District examination for the *hsiu-ts'ai*, lowest of the traditional civil service examination degrees. The two uncles, both sons of Great-Uncle Ch'ing-fan, were about Lu Hsün's age albeit one step higher in the generational hierarchy.

15. *LHCC*, II, 266.
16. Ibid., pp. 266-67 and p. 451, n. 11. This was the "Yü-lan-p'en-hui," a Buddhist festival celebrated on the 15th of the 7th month, during which sutras were recited and food was offered to hungry ghosts.
17. Ibid., p. 266.
18. D. E. Pollard, "Chou Tso-jen and Cultivating One's Garden," *Asia Major*, n.s., XI, pt. 2 (1965), 184.
19. *HSJW*, p. 316.
20. Ibid., pp. 320-22.
21. *LHCC*, II, 267.
22. *HSJW*, p. 247. I have not seen a clear statement as to why he returned to Shaohsing at this time. In *LHKC* (p. 85), Tso-jen says that he "took leave and returned home"—to prepare for the examinations, perhaps?

The results were published in January 1899; they had all passed. On a list of approximately 550 successful candidates, Uncle Chung-hsiang (the younger of Ch'ing-fan's sons) placed 24th; Lu Hsün, 137th; Uncle Po-wen, (Ch'ing-fan's eldest), 169th; and Tso-jen, 484th.[23]

The district examination was the first of three hurdles that one had to clear in order to obtain the *hsiu-ts'ai* degree, the next two being the prefectural and provincial examinations.[24] But the day after the young men took the examination, Lu Hsün and Tso-jen's youngest brother (fourth in order of birth), Ch'un-shou, became seriously ill and died quite suddenly, in only his sixth year.[25] According to Tso-jen, Lu Hsün was so shaken by his little brother's death that he had no heart to sit for the prefectural examination and therefore returned to Nanking that same month. Dissatisfied with the Naval Academy, he made arrangements for transferring to the School of Mines and Railroads attached to the Kiangnan Army Academy, where he began a course of study in the spring.[26]

His return to Nanking early in 1899 meant that he would miss the prefectural examination and thus disqualify himself for the third and final round of the *hsiu-ts'ai* examinations. For this reason Lu Hsün's mother was prevailed upon to employ a "spearman (*ch'iang-shou*)" to take the second examination for him and thus preserve his place on the list of candidates. At first she objected on the grounds that it would cost too much money and that Lu Hsün had already committed himself to a modern-style school in Nanking, but in the end she was won over and a brother-in-law of Uncle Chung-hsiang was employed as spearman. He earned a rather low pass for Lu Hsün on a list of successful candidates that was published in February.[27] While Grandfather Chou was still in prison at Hangchow it seems incredible that the family would employ a spearman and thus flout

23. Ibid., pp. 247-49.
24. Etienne Zi (Siu), *Pratique des examens littéraires en Chine* (Shanghai, 1894), p. 14.
25. *HSJW*, p. 248; *LHKC*, p. 85.
26. *HSJW*, p. 248. In *LHKC*, the eleventh is given as the date of his return to Nanking, but it seems probable that this is in error. The date in *HSJW* occurs in the course of a more detailed entry and seems preferable.
27. *HSJW*, pp. 249-50; *HHL* p. 51.

proprieties again, yet that is exactly what they did. One can only conclude that they were not very awed by imperial law, for this practice was specifically forbidden, the spearman and those who employed him all being liable to severe punishment.[28] Perhaps the practice was so widespread that the family felt there were few chances of being caught.

As it turned out, this was a waste of time and money, for Lu Hsün never took the final examination for the *hsiu-ts'ai*. The other three Chou boys sat for it, but only Uncle Chung-hsiang won the degree. K'uaichi District was only alloted forty degrees that year, and Chung-hsiang was in last place on the list. Chou Tso-jen and Uncle Po-wen did less well and failed to appear on the list of new *hsiu-ts'ai*.[29] Po-wen, the elder of the two uncles, was furious. He was, to all appearances, a rather harmless type who was rather good at calligraphy and had eyes that bubbled out far enough to earn him the nickname "Goldfish." The younger brother's success, however, was enough to set him off. Back at the t'aimen he threw himself on the ground, grabbed a cassia tree at the base, and, straining for all he was worth, pulled it out by the roots. He loudly proclaimed that his leviathan ire had nothing to do with the success of Chung-hsiang. No, he was infuriated, he said, because the person who occupied the numbered examination cubicle next to him had passed. It was as though he looked upon the examinations as one might view a lottery: he had missed by just one digit![30]

During all of this, Lu Hsün was studying at the School of Mines and Railroads in Nanking, from which he graduated near the end of 1901.[31] The curriculum here differed somewhat from that at the Naval Academy. Although the readings in Chinese were approximately the same, the subjects assigned for composition were farther-ranging; at one point the students were even asked to write an essay on George Washington. There were also classes in the natural sciences, geology, and mineralogy. Lu Hsün found these fresh and stimulating, and in general appears to have been somewhat more satisfied than he was at the Naval Academy.[32]

In 1901 Lu Hsün and Great-Uncle Ch'ing-fan decided that it would be well for Tso-jen to fill an opening in a supplementary

28. Zi, *Pratique*, p. 37, n. 1.
29. *HSJW* pp. 249-50.
30. *LHKC*, pp. 83-84.
31. *HSJW*, p. 248.
32. *LHCC*, II, 266-67.

quota of students and come to Nanking to enroll in the Naval Academy.[33] Thus Tso-jen arrived in September. Since Lu Hsün did not leave for Japan until March of the following year, the brothers had about six months together. Their schools were not far apart, and they had occasion to visit back and forth, and to wander around Nanking, visiting famous sites, browsing through bookstores, and sampling the various teas and snacks to be had in the area.[34]

Thus, though in different schools, they shared a common environment. Nanking—a bustling center of activity far closer to the heart's blood of a changing China than was their remote, provincial Shaohsing—exposed them to the exciting and somewhat terrifying new world into which old China was being reluctantly thrust. Here on every side was talk of K'ang Yu-wei (1858-1927) and Liang Ch'i-ch'ao (1873-1929), the constitutional reformers who had tried abortively to have a young Manchu emperor goad the great frog of traditional China into leaping into the pond of the modern world, and who had found it necessary to flee for their lives to Japan. Here one could easily obtain foreign novels translated into the elegant classical diction of Lin Shu (1852-1924), or the works of Western intellectuals rendered into the equally refined prose of Yen Fu (1853-1921). The separate reminiscences of the brothers give the impression that the metropolitan ambience exerted more influence on them than the content of the formal courses they pursued at school. The course work was probably not very demanding. According to a lifelong friend, Hsü Shou-shang, Lu Hsün found time to devour novel after novel and still do well on the examinations.[35]

A new director of studies, quite a liberal and progressive one, was appointed to the School of Mines and Railroads during the second year that Lu Hsün was there. Lu Hsün later described the effects of his arrival:

Thereupon the reading of new books became prevalent and I came to know that there was a book in China called *Evolution and Ethics*. On Sunday I went down to the south suburbs and bought a copy. It was a thick, lithographed edition on white paper and sold for five hundred cash even. I opened it and looked in; it was printed in very good characters. It

33. *HSJW*, p. 263.
34. Ibid., pp. 224-27.
35. Hsiao Hung (ed.), *Hui-yi Lu Hsün hsien-sheng* [Reminiscences of Lu Hsün] (Shanghai, 1948), p. 61; hereafter cited as *HYLHHS*.

began: "Huxley, back to the mountains, facing the plains, sat alone in his room in southern England. Beyond his threshold the various views were all in order like the threads on a loom. He then began to imagine what the scenery had been like before the Roman general, Caesar, arrived in England. He reckoned that there had been nothing but primordial darkness."

Wow! To think that there was actually a Huxley in this world who had sat in his study and thought in that way, in such a unique way! I read the book straight through. I came across the concepts of "the struggle for existence" and "natural selection" and the names of Socrates and Plato. Here too I encountered the Stoics. And then a periodical room was set up in the school where one could read the *Journal of Collected Translations*, not to speak of the *Chinese Progress*.[36]

Among those who made translations from foreign languages into Chinese at this time the two giants were Lin Shu and Yen Fu. Yen Fu's version of T. H. Huxley's *Evolution and Ethics* (*T'ien-yen lun*), published in 1898, was not, strictly speaking, a translation, but rather an abridged summary that Yen Fu used as a platform for preaching the gospel of social Darwinism by means of his own commentaries on the original.[37] In 1898 Yen Fu began the serial publication of his *Ten-Thousand Word Memorial*, a document that was never actually submitted to the throne. In the memorial he set forth priorities for China's attempts at reform and modernization, and argued that spiritual concerns (the nurture of men of ability, changes in customs and in men's minds) should take precedence over more material ones (military modernization, financial reform, and proper diplomacy).[38] Yen Fu's predilection for the spiritual over the material was to be reflected in Lu Hsün's own writings as a student in Japan a few years later. One might also read into Yen's priorities a preference for the intellectual over the political leader, the thinker over the activist, that appears also throughout the adult life of Lu Hsün, who was much more comfortable alone in his study with books, writing brushes, and ideas than he could ever be in the political hurly-burly of a changing China. The Republican Revolution (1911) would not belong to him in the way that the May Fourth movement (1919) would.

36. *LHCC*, II 268.
37. Benjamin Schwartz, *In Search of Wealth and Power* (Cambridge, Mass., 1964), pp. 95, 99.
38. Ibid., pp. 84-85. The characterization of these concerns as spiritual (or intellectual) and material is my own.

Lu Hsün's attitude toward the relative merits of Chinese and Western cultures was undoubtedly partly influenced by the thought of Yen Fu, who was much impressed by the sheer vigor of the West. Benjamin Schwartz has summarized Yen's view at this time in these words:

. . . the Western values of dynamism, self-assertion, realization of capacities—of freedom, democracy, and science—starkly confront the Chinese exaltation of inertia, sterile social harmony, and the negative authoritarianism which had dammed up the physical and intellectual energies of the race.[39]

It would probably be difficult to overestimate the influence of Yen Fu on the young Lu Hsün, who was so taken with the *Evolution and Ethics* that he committed large chunks of it to memory.[40]

Lu Hsün was an almost equally avid fan of the second giant of late-nineteenth-century translators, Lin Shu. While Yen Fu was introducing his compatriots to the thought of the West, Lin Shu was, through scores of translations into classical Chinese prose, exposing them to its literature. While in Nanking, Lu Hsün obtained at least three of Lin's translations: a retelling of various adventures of Sherlock Holmes, a translation of one of Rider Haggard's novels, and (perhaps the most popular of all Lin's translations) a Chinese rendering of *La Dame aux camélias*. Working with collaborators (he knew no language other than his own), Lin worked rapidly and turned out a prodigious number of books. Lu Hsün bought them as fast as they came out. Later, as a student in Japan, he expressed dissatisfaction with Lin's fondness for the works of Rider Haggard and Conan Doyle and once greeted a friend with the disgruntled observation: "Lin Shu's gone and done still another Haggard novel!"[41] This is understandable when one considers that Lin Shu did eleven of them in 1905 alone.[42]

During this time some of Lin Shu's judgments of traditional China seem to have corresponded rather closely to those of Yen Fu. For instance, Lin regarded Robinson Crusoe (he had translated the novel) as an embodiment of the true meaning of the Confucian

39. Ibid., p. 81.
40. Hsü Shou-shang, *Wang-yu Lu Hsün yin-hsiang-chi* (Impressions of my departed friend Lu Hsün) (Peking, 1953), p. 10; hereafter cited as *YHC*.
41. Ibid.
42. Ou-fan Lee, *Lin Shu and His Translations: Western Fiction in Chinese Perspective* (Cambridge, Mass., 1965), p. 176.

golden mean. Crusoe's attitude "gave the lie to that trouble-dodging, fence-sitting, play-it-safe attitude in Chinese social practice, which Lin called the 'golden mean of the mediocre.' "[43] This view of a passive, play-it-safe China that valued continuity (often seen as mere survival) over progress, and quantity over quality, was one that Lu Hsün shared with both Yen Fu and Lin Shu. It was a view that would be fundamental for the essays written during his student days in Japan, and would later provide the world-view from which his first short story was written, on the eve of the Republican Revolution. By the time of the May Fourth movement, however, Yen Fu and Lin Shu would have abandoned many of their earlier stands and become conservatives in the eyes of a new generation, while Lu Hsün, during the same period would, if anything, have grown more radical.

If the second year of Lu Hsün's attendance at the School of Mines and Railroads brought a blessing (in the person of the progressive director who created a liberal atmosphere), it also brought a threat; a rumor was bruited about that the school was to be closed. The reason for locating such a school in Nanking in the first place had been the city's proximity to the coal deposits at Ch'ing Lung Mountain, where a mine was already in operation. It was hoped that the new institution would be able to help in the exploitation of the deposit, but a series of administrative blunders seriously impaired the productivity of the mine. By the time of the rumor about closing the school, barely enough coal was being produced to supply power for two pumps which were used to keep the mine floor dry. "The pumps cleared the water out so that the coal could be mined, and the coal that was mined was, in turn, used to run the water pumps."[44]

Despite all this, both school and mine remained in operation, and the rumor died, though in the end it did not prove totally groundless. Lu Hsün's was the first and only class that the institution graduated, in 1901, before closing down.[45] It was not without cause that Lu Hsün had some misgivings about his future.

Of course, everyone looked forward to graduation, and yet, once it came, I somehow felt as though I had made a mistake. Having done no

43. Ibid., p. 181.
44. *LHCC*, II, 269.
45. *HSJW*, p. 224.

more than climb a mast a few times, I was certainly not qualified to be even half a sailor; having attended a few years of lectures and gone down into a mine a few times, could I [really be expected] to be able to run right out and start mining the five metals? . . . I had climbed two hundred feet into the sky and burrowed two hundred feet into the earth, and as a result of all that I was still without a single, solitary ability. . . . There was only one road left: to go abroad.[46]

46. *LHCC*, II, 269.

5

TOKYO AND THE
KŌBUN INSTITUTE

China's defeat by Japan in 1895, the debacle of the Hundred Days
reform of 1898, the Boxer fiasco of 1900—this series of political
disasters created a climate of intense interest in (and a demand for)
foreign education.

In the decade of the 1900's the Manchu government undertook a selective
adoption of Western institutions in a desperate attempt to bolster itself
against the crushing Western impact. As a part of this effort, students
were encouraged to study abroad in order to acquire Western knowledge. This resulted in a movement—volcanic in its suddenness—of
thousands of Chinese students across the Yellow Sea in search of the
"new learning."[1]

Sent to Japan on a government scholarship soon after his graduation, Lu Hsün was one of these students.[2] A substantial farewell
dinner was given for him by Great-Uncle Ch'ing-fan, and he was
off.[3]

He arrived in Tokyo in early 1902 and entered the Kōbun
Institute, a school that had been established to teach Chinese
students enough Japanese to enable them to enter the institutions
of higher learning in Japan. He spent two years there, graduating

1. Roger F. Hackett, *Chinese Students in Japan, 1900-1910*, (Cambridge, Mass.,
1949), p. 63.
2. Nakagawa Shun, *Rojin nempu* [A chronology of Lu Hsün] (Tokyo, 1966), p.
8; hereafter cited as *RJNP*.
3. *HSJW*, p. 270.

Lu Hsün as a youth. Photographed in Tokyo.

in 1904.[4] Lu Hsün has not dealt extensively with this period in any
of his reminiscences, and since Chou Tso-jen was still attending
the Naval Academy in Nanking, we would have scant information
about this part of his life were it not for the friendship that Lu
Hsün formed with a fellow native of Shaohsing, Hsü Shou-shang
(1882-1948). It was a lasting friendship, and we have two books of
reminiscences by Hsü that include some account of this period.[5]
Hsü says that he does not remember exactly how they first met; his
earliest clear impression of Lu Hsün dates from the latter's sudden
change of hair style. Many Chinese students in Tokyo, especially
those who were pursuing accelerated courses and who would not
be there long anyway, simply coiled their queues up on top of
their heads during their Japanese sojourns. They would pull their
student caps down over the resulting piles, creating a number of
near-to-hand miniatures of distant Mount Fuji, visible from
Tokyo on a clear day. Others had the barber cut the long braid,
and this was the solution chosen by both Lu Hsün and Hsü.[6] In
reminiscing over their student years in Japan, Hsü has left one of
the most detailed physical descriptions of his friend to be found in
all the voluminous writings about Lu Hsün.

In physique he was not at all tall. His forehead was broad; his
cheekbones, slightly raised. From his crystal-clear eyes came a warm
gaze that was slightly tinged with melancholy. You could tell at a glance
that he was a compassionate and sensitive person. He had strong arms
and would from time to time take a deep breath and hold it for a second
while he flexed and rubbed them. His step, brisk and strong, immediately
bespoke a high-strung kind of person. When barefooted, he would often
gaze at the tops of his feet and say: "They're awfully high. I wonder if it
could be the inherited influence of mother's bound feet?" In sum, there
was hardly a single movement, word, or expression about him that didn't

4. Ts'ao Chü-jen, *Lu Hsün nien-p'u* [A chronology of Lu Hsün] (Hong Kong,
1967), pp. 18-21; hereafter cited as *LHNP*.
Basic science courses were also taught at the Kōbun Institute, but what Lu Hsün
gained there was essentially a working knowledge of Japanese. Chou Ch'i-ming
(Chou Tso-jen), *Lu Hsün te ch'ing-nien shih-tai* [The period of Lu Hsün's youth]
(Peking, 1957), p. 40; hereafter cited as *CNST*.
5. *Wang-yu Lu Hsün yin-hsiang-chi* [Impressions of my departed friend Lu
Hsün] (Peking, 1953), written in 1947, and *Wo so jen-shih te Lu Hsün* [The Lu
Hsün I knew] (Peking, 1952), a posthumous collection of essays written between
1936 and 1947; hereafter cited, respectively as *YHC* and *WTLH*. In *WTLH*, the
complier of the volume, Wang Shih-ching, states that Hsü was assassinated in
Taiwan by Nationalist agents.
6. *YHC*, pp. 2-3.

reveal a combination of compassion and toughness—the two characteristic qualities that filled his life, pervaded his works, and made him a
great writer and brave fighter, the very soul of the Chinese people.[7]

In his personal life, Hsü recalls, the young Lu Hsün was rather
Spartan, caring little for fine clothing or good food. He did display
one gastronomic preference: he was abandonedly fond of hot
pepper, a liking that later caused, or at least aggravated, the
stomach disorders that afflicted him toward the end of his life.
He smoked a lot and quaffed prodigious quantities of tea. He
liked hard liquor, but thoughts of how little it had done to
improve his father's disposition kept him from going too far.
Generally, his conversation created an atmosphere of warmth and
intimacy, though it is true, Hsü admits, Lu Hsün did enjoy cursing
people out (as did Grandfather Chou). Finally, Hsü remembers
that Lu Hsün—and we have already seen something of this in
Shaohsing—loved books to the point of fastidiousness. He knew
papers, stitchings, and the like, and was later to take a great interest in the physical production of his own works.[8]

As schoolmates in an institution that was a collection point for
new student arrivals from China, Lu Hsün and Hsü Shou-shang
shared an intellectual environment that would greatly influence
them both.

[The] Japan of that day was a remarkable contrast with [the Chinese
student's] native land. The city of Tokyo had made great strides toward
modernization which were nothing short of startling. . . . This was his
real introduction to the possible accomplishments of Western learning.
Modern transportation, modern communications, efficient postal service
—these were before him, not only as constant reminders of Japan's
progress, but as rude awakeners of the backwardness of his homeland.[9]

Living conditions in the Kanda section of Tokyo, where the
Chinese students were concentrated, were less than ideal, but there
were compensations. Being in a foreign land, they were largely
free from the pressures of their own social milieu in China and
could think about it with a degree of objectivity that would have
scarcely been possible at home. Furthermore, this time of relative
freedom from the ordinary constraints of family and culture
roughly coincided with the period during which the individual
would carve out his adult identity. Here Lu Hsün would wear a

7. Ibid., p. 16.
8. Ibid., pp. 99-104.
9. Hackett, *Chinese Students*, p. 146.

Japanese school uniform, grow a moustache, and cut off his pigtail; here he would be forced into taking his own stand on such problems as his marriage and the political future of China.[10] In short, during his long sojourn in Japan, from 1902 to 1909, he would come to know better what it meant to be "Lu Hsün" as well as what it meant to be Chinese. When, the year after his arrival in Japan, Lu Hsün brought his self-image more clearly into focus by cutting off his queue, he commemorated the event by having a photograph taken; on the back of the copy he presented to Hsü Shou-shang, he inscribed the following poem:

My heart knows not how to dodge
   the arrows loosed by love of country;
Storms weigh down like boulders and twilight
   the gardens of my native land.
Though I have begged the lonely stars to hasten my warnings home,
   my people take no heed and will not wake.
There is nothing I can do—save consecrate this
   life's blood to the land of the Yellow Emperor.[11]

His outward change of appearance expressed an inward change of attitude. The reference to the early Chinese culture hero, the Yellow Emperor, in the last line is clearly directed against the alien Manchu race that had ruled China since 1644. Like other young Chinese of similar background and education, Lu Hsün was expected to know how to write poetry and had written other poems before this one. The earlier ones, however, had "expressed

10. For a provocative discussion of this period in Lu Hsün's life see Li Ou-fan, "Lu Hsün te ch'eng-nien" [Lu Hsün's years of maturation], *Ming Pao*, LXI (January 1971), 53-60.
11. Chiang T'ien, *Lu Hsün shih hsin-chieh* [New interpretations of Lu Hsün's poetry] (Hong Kong, 1967), pp. 15-18; hereafter cited as *SHC*. The original is a short four-liner of 28 characters; my translation, though very loose, conveys the spirit of the poem. The Chinese expression which Lu Hsün uses for "arrows" is *shen-shih*. In an unpublished paper, "Lu Hsün's Poetry," written at Stanford University in 1974, Cynthia L. Chennault points out: "Lu Hsün read Greek and Roman mythology in translation during his years of study in Japan. Although the *shen-shih* originally mean the arrows of Cupid which are blindly shot to instill a sexual kind of love, Lu Hsün means these arrows to instill love of country. The modification in meaning was inspired by Byron's poem *Lara* in which a young nobleman returns to his native country from abroad, leads an uprising of serfs and is fatally wounded in battle by an arrow shot by the opposing army of feudal chieftains." (p. 19.) She notes also that the expression I have translated as "my people take no heed" was taken verbatim by Lu Hsün from Ch'ü Yuan's poem "Encountering Sorrow *(Li-sao)*," written in the fourth century B.C. (pp. 22-23.)

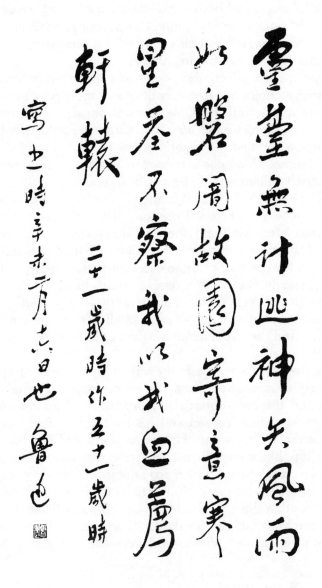

Fig. 2. The subscript (in smaller characters) following the poem reads:
"Composed in my twenty-first year; written in my hand on February 16,
1931, during my fifty-first year—Lu Hsün."

his love of flowers and books, his nostalgia at being away from home, or his concern for his family; this poem expresses an ardent commitment to the future of his country."[12] It represents a turning point in his view of his role in society.

Essentially, the student who pondered China's future was confronted with a choice between constitutional monarchy or revolution. From 1902 until 1907 the constitutionalist position was represented by Liang Ch'i-ch'ao's *New Citizen's Fortnightly* (*Hsin-min ts'ung-pao*),[13] and the revolutionary one (after 1906) by the *People's Journal* (*Min pao*), propaganda arm of Sun Yat-sen's Revolutionary Alliance (T'ung-meng hui), under the editorship of Chang T'ai-yen (1868-1922).[14] Liang Ch'i-ch'ao had become an influence to be reckoned with among the Chinese students in Tokyo soon after his flight there in the wake of the abortive Hundred Days reform movement of 1898. He made his opinions felt through his creation of three excellent periodicals, printed in Japan but widely read in progressive circles back in China: the above-mentioned *New Citizen's Fortnightly*, the *Journal of Disinterested Criticism* (*Ch'ing-yi pao*; published every ten days, 1899-1901), and the *New Fiction Magazine* (*Hsin-hsiao-shuo pao*; 1902-5).[15]

During the years when Lu Hsün was in Japan, student opinion increasingly moved away from the more moderate suggestions of Liang and the constitutional monarchists toward the revolutionary stand of Sun Yat-sen and his followers.[16] Early in their student careers in Japan both Hsü Shou-shang and Lu Hsün took this direction, like many of their student-compatriots, and at one point broke off relations with an acquaintance who had gone over to the constitutionalist camp.[17] The students often saw themselves as members of an elite that would be responsible both for the overthrow of the Manchus and for the establishment of a new government that would guide China toward a democratic regime. Most of

---

12. Chennault, "Lu Hsün's Poetry," p. 23.

13. Hackett, *Chinese Students*, p. 149.

14. Marius B. Jansen, *The Japanese and Sun Yat-sen* (Cambridge, Mass., 1954), pp. 117-21.

15. Liang Jung-jo, *Wen-hsüeh shih-chia chuan* [Biographies of ten authors] (Taipei, 1966), pp. 363-64; hereafter cited as *SCC*.

16. Robert A. Scalapino, "Prelude to Marxism: The Chinese Student Movement in Japan, 1900-1910," in Albert Feuerwerker et at., ed., *Approaches to Modern Chinese History* (Berkeley and Los Angeles, 1967), p. 194.

17. *YHC*, pp. 10-12.

them held that the masses were not ready for such a government; hence the same student elite would have to educate the people for it through a sustained period of tutelage.[18]

Faced at every turn with the amazing political and material progress that Japan had made since the Meiji Restoration of 1868, the Chinese students were doubly disheartened—by the all too apparent backwardness of their own country in comparison, and by the debilitating attitudes that went with it:

Possessed in the past of a great civilization, the Chinese people had become morally bankrupt. Now they were characterized by lethargy, a profound ignorance of the world in which they lived, and a totally self-centered attitude devoid of any sense of patriotism or public spiritedness.[19]

The stark contrast between the lethargy of the Chinese people and the serious-minded diligence of the Japanese must have made a strong impression on Lu Hsün. Years later, when Sino-Japanese relations were straining toward the breaking point in the period just before the Eight-Year War of Resistance (1937-45), he saw this lethargy as all-pervasive, telling a Japanese friend:

Four hundred million Chinese have, to a man, caught the disease of being mindlessly slipshod. If we don't cure this, we can't save China. It's really in Japan that one can find a potent medicine to cure it—the serious-minded attitude of the Japanese people. Even if we reject everything else Japanese, we will still have to buy that medicine.[20]

Many who expressed themselves in student publications of the early 1900s saw China's problem as a moral one, nothing less than "how to reshape the basic character of Chinese man." When Lu Hsün and Hsü Shou-shang discussed China's predicament, they too framed it in ethical terms, often pondering three interrelated questions:

What is the nature of the ideal human being?
[With respect to this ideal,] what is most lacking in the character of the Chinese people?
What is the reason for this lack?[21]

18. Scalapino, "Prelude," p. 211.
19. Ibid., p. 195.
20. Shen Yin-mo et al., *Hui-yi wei-ta te Lu Hsün* [Reminiscences of the great Lu Hsün] (Shanghai, 1958), p. 207; hereafter cited as *HYLH*.
21. *WTLH*, p. 19.

They eventually answered the second question with "love" (*ai*) and "sincerity" (*ch'eng*)—a most significant reply in view of the short stories that Lu Hsün would later write, whose characters so often display a singular lack of human sympathy and an alarming capacity for self-deception.

The rather leisurely pace of student life at the Kōbun Institute gave Lu Hsün time to read works of philosophy and literature.[22] He had already begun to buy books in Japanese: the poetry of Byron in translation, a biography of Nietzsche, works on Greek and Roman myths, and a Japanese edition of *Encountering Sorrow* (*Li-sao*), the long poetic lament attributed to Ch'ü Yuan, the patriot-poet of the fourth century B.C.[23] Lu Hsün did not have many books on specifically Japanese subjects; he would use this new language primarily as a key to the learning and literature of the world at large. Periodical literature, especially that issued by Chinese political and student organizations in Japan, was also a staple in his reading diet. The first issue of the *New Fiction Magazine*, on November 29, 1902, contained an essay on literature that exerted a strong influence on him.[24] This essay, by Liang Ch'i-ch'ao, explained the reasons for initiating such a journal, and the title, "On the Relationship between Fiction and Public Order (*Lun hsiao-shuo yü ch'ün-chih chih kuan-hsi*)," reflected the rather narrow, utilitarian attitude toward fiction that Liang held at the time. Because of its importance in the development of modern Chinese literature in general and its influence on Lu Hsün in particular, it will be well to recapitulate the essentials of this essay.[25]

One of Liang's points is that intellectuals in China had traditionally disdained the production of popular fiction (though they have always read it, he notes), with the result that they abandoned their responsibility for its content to mere storytellers and commercial publishers. This was so, despite the fact that fiction provided a ready means whereby the intellectuals (rulers, scholar-officials, the establishment) could establish contact with the Chinese masses and educate at least the semiliterate element

---

22. Ibid., p. 8.
23. *YHC*, p. 5.
24. *SCC*, p. 364.
25. In the following discussion I use the text in *Yin-ping-shih ch'üan chi* [Complete works from the ice-drinker's studio (Liang's study)] (Shanghai, 1917), *ts'e* 5, 19a–19b; hereafter cited as *YPSCC*.

which, though inaccessible through the more profound, classical Chinese forms of learning, could be reached through the popular novel.

Noting that intellectuals, who could presumably read much better stuff, still displayed a veritable passion for fiction, Liang opines that the reason for its popularity cannot reside solely in the simplicity of the vernacular style in which it is presented. He suggests, rather, that the almost universal appeal of popular fiction may properly be attributed to its providing an escape from the humdrum (or even painful) round of daily life and to its being occasionally able to make a man realize things about his own life that he had never adequately been able to verbalize before.

On a short-term, conscious level, fiction makes its impact felt by stimulating the emotions, and even by shocking; on a long-term, unconscious level, it exerts its influence by seeping into the very pores of the reader and, in effect, marinating him in new ideas and attitudes. But fiction's greatest power to influence lies perhaps in its presentation of models with whom a reader can vicariously identify. Significantly, the list of proper models that Liang cites contains a mix of East and West: Washington, Napoleon, Confucius, and Buddha.

Traditional fiction is faulted for encouraging people to lust after money and high position in the open society, or to become bandits in one of the secret ones; above all, old fiction is scored for encouraging beliefs in such varied superstitious claptrap as geomancy, physiognomy, divination, and penitential sacrifices for rain. The building of railroads and the opening of mines had been impeded precisely because of the existence of such beliefs. Widespread superstition is also blamed as a factor that contributed to the Boxer fiasco of 1900. In view of the tremendous power of fiction, it is high time, says Liang, that the leaders of society begin to pay attention to it.

While the unflagging instructions of the sages and wise men, embodied in tens of thousands of words, are still not enough [to mold society], one or two [such] works . . . are more than sufficient to destroy it. The more that cultured gentlemen are loath to concern themselves with this kind of thing, the more it will be left in the hands of frivolous authors and booksellers.

The social consequences of this, of course, are truly frightening: it means that social mores are formed by a tiny part of the population that is not, either by training or position, fit for the task:

. . . the frivolous authors and [unscrupulous] booksellers thereupon seize and control the sovereignty of an entire nation. . . . Therefore, if we are to improve today the social order, we must begin with a revolution in the realm of fiction. If we are to renovate the people, we must begin by renovating fiction.

It is clear that Liang expects this revolution in fiction to come about when intellectuals infiltrate the ranks of the writers from the top down. He is not suggesting that novelists become serious gentlemen, but rather that serious gentlemen become, in part at least, novelists. Given the elitist tendencies of Chinese students in Japan that we have already observed, it is not difficult to see the appeal of such a suggestion. In view of Lu Hsün's own early interest in popular literature, an interest that was nurtured by the somewhat permissive atmosphere of the Shaohsing t'aimen, we can well imagine that he read the essay in a receptive frame of mind: Liang's essay at once affirmed the intellectual's responsibility for leadership in society and legitimized popular fiction as an area of serious concern. Although Lu Hsün would quickly reject Liang's narrowly utilitarian conception of literature, he would retain the idea of its importance as a formative influence on a changing society. It was, after all, an idea in accord with the traditional Confucian notion that "writing is to be used to carry forward the way of morality (*wen-yi tsai-tao*)." Liang expands the meaning of "writing" to include even popular fiction and broadens "the way" until it is wide enough to accommodate Western learning.

Liang's implied suggestion for a positive type of censorship to be imposed on literature by the nation's elite assumes that the leaders of society know where they are going, know what kind of models should be set up for the masses to emulate. Lu Hsün, however, during most of his creative life, would never be sure where society should go, would never be sure that he was in possession of models proper for emulation: he would always remain somewhat suspicious of those who sanguinely assumed that they knew what was good for China. He was to remain essentially a critic of the old society, not a builder of the new one. To be sure, in his latter years (especially after the Kuomintang brutally purged itself of leftist elements during the White Terror of 1927), Lu Hsün began to see an answer to China's problems in the rising communist movement, but that was after the bulk of his creative work had been completed.

By temperament and the circumstances of his social station and experiences, he was drawn to realism (describing things as they are) in literature, for it was through realism that he could give full scope to his analytic talents. The kind of fiction that Liang's essay envisaged, on the other hand, was more positive, more properly suited to that kind of romanticism which, with some degree of hope and confidence, depicts society as it should or could be. The kind of thing that he had in mind is perhaps best exemplified by a translation that Liang made and published serially under the pen name "A Young Man of China" for the opening issues of the *New Citizen's Fortnightly*.[26] His source was a Japanese rendering, by Morita Shiken, of an English translation of Jules Verne's *Deux ans de vacances*. Liang gave his Chinese version a title meaning *Fifteen Young Heroes*, and he was clearly pleased with having the opportunity to present, as the title indicates, a gallery of foreign models worthy of emulation by the youth of China. He tells us that in translating the Japanese text he nearly doubled the fourteen chapters of that version in order to come out with segments of the right length for serial publication in his journal, and also that he has reshaped the work into the form in which Chinese novels usually appear. He introduces the novel with a lyric poem (*tz'u*), translates into a Chinese novelese diction, and maintains suspense with the time-honored "and if you'd like to know what happened next, please turn to the explanation at the beginning of the following chapter."

Before long, the young Lu Hsün would reject the idea of presenting morally illustrative material for the general improvement of the population; he would also reject the notion that foreign works had to be stripped of their foreign clothing and freshly raimented in the Chinese fashion before being presented to the public. However, there is evidence that for a time he was strongly influenced by Liang's translation style. For instance, in 1903, while still at the Kōbun Institute, he translated Jules Verne's *De la terre à la lune* into Chinese (*Yüeh-chieh lü-hsing*). This

26. I have used the 1956 Taiwan reprint of the magazine done by the Wen-yi yin-shu-kuan.

translation, based on Inoue Tsutomu's Japanese rendering,[27] appeared serially in one of the student magazines the same year. In the translator's introduction,[28] written in classical Chinese, Lu Hsün approvingly notes Verne's achievement in popularizing science through the medium of fiction. He reminds his readers that there is a Chinese precedent for popularization. The *Romance of the Three Kingdoms* (*San-kuo-chih yen-yi*), for example, retells as fiction incidents contained in the officially sanctioned *History of the Three Kingdoms* (*San-kuo-chih*), so that even men who have never glimpsed the official history can still speak with familiarity of the period; similarly, readers of *Flowers in the Mirror* (*Ching-hua yuan*) are made aware of the myths and fantasies contained in the *Classic of Mountains and Seas* (*Shan-hai ching*) even though they may never have seen the original. It follows from all this that it is possible to increase a man's general knowledge almost without his being conscious of it, as long as you present it to him in a pleasant package. Furthermore, one can, in this way, break down inherited superstitions, improve thought, and aid the cause of civilization. On the other hand, Lu Hsün complains, there has been a proliferation of love stories, tales of the supernatural, and the like (Liang's frivolous authors have been hard at work), and there is a dearth of such potentially wholesome fare as science fiction. "Therefore," the young Lu Hsün would have us know, "if one wants to make up for this lack in the present-day world of translation, and [thus] lead the Chinese masses to progress, then he must certainly begin with science fiction." This idea—and even the way it is expressed—shows a young man who is under the influence of Liang's thought. Yet in essays that he wrote just a few years later, we will find Lu Hsün scoring all those who, out of hand, condemn the common people's superstitions instead of trying to understand them. According to Chou Tso-jen, he was quite taken with Liang's essay on fiction when he first read it, but later moved beyond Liang's narrow concern with political and scientific novels.[29]

27. Inoue's translation, made in 1880, was based on an American one. M. Nakamura, *Modern Japanese Fiction* (Tokyo, 1968), p. 23. Lu Hsün's is in Vol. I of *Lu Hsün yi-wen-chi* [The collected translations of Lu Hsün] (10 vols.; Peking, 1959); hereafter cited as *LHYW*. The publisher's foreword notes that Lu Hsün's translations appeared in thirty separate books during his lifetime.
28. *LHYW*, I, 3-5.
29. "Kuan-yü Lu Hsün chih erh" [On Lu Hsün, pt. 2], *Yü Chou Feng*, XXX (December 1, 1936), 303; hereafter cited as *KYLH*, pt. 2.

The Japanese translation of Verne's novel was in 28 chapters. Lu Hsün rearranged them into 14 and provided each with a double title referring to two main incidents within the chapter, thus putting his translation into essentially the form of a traditional "serially chaptered" (*chang-hui*) piece of fiction. Further, he ended every chapter but the last with some version of the storyteller's traditional formula. Chapter 13, for instance, ends with: "If you want to know whether the projectile made it to the moon or fell back to the earth, wait until the next chapter." This device, of course, was not employed in the original.[30] With regard to diction he explained:

At first I intended to translate it [entirely] into the vernacular (*su-yü*) in order to make it a bit easier for readers, but [I found] that if I used the vernacular exclusively, it would be too wordy; therefore, I also mixed in [some] classical Chinese to save space. Where the wording was dull or not suited to [the experience] of my fellow countrymen, I have made a few changes and deletions.[31]

We can see in this first major translation venture an endorsement of Liang's concern for popularization, together with his own feeling, which he would never quite abandon, that colloquial Chinese was too wordy.

It was probably about this time that Lu Hsün made a translation of a second Verne novel, *Voyage au centre de la terre* (*Ti-ti lü-hsing*), although it was not published until 1906.[32] In general arrangement and style, it seems to have been informed by the same rather carefree principles that he applied to *De la terre à la lune.* Both of his Verne translations appeared in serialized form in the *Chekiang Tide* (*Che-chiang ch'ao*), a magazine published in Japan by students from Lu Hsün's native province.[33] In the same magazine he published an essay on China's mineral wealth, in

---

30. I do not know whether Inoue employed it in his translation.

31. *LHYW*, I, 4-5.

32. *RJ*, p. 281. At about this time, Lu Hsün made another translation, "Pei-chi t'an-hsien chi" (Verne's *Les Anglais au Nord Pole* perhaps?). No publisher was ever found for this one and it was subsequently lost. *KMCLH*, p. 44.

33. *LHC*, pp. 44-45. Apparently only parts of the second work appeared in the *Chekiang Tide*. See Shen P'eng-nien, *Lu Hsün yen-chiu tzu-liao pien-mu* [A bibliography of materials for the study of Lu Hsün] (Shanghai, 1958), p. 37; hereafter cited as *YCTL*. Like Liang's publications, the *Chekiang Tide* was circulated in China as well as Japan. For more on this see Harold Z. Schiffrin, *Sun Yat-sen and the Origins of the Chinese Revolution* (Berkeley and Los Angeles, 1968), pp. 277-78.

large part the fruit of knowledge he had gained in the School of Mines and Railroads. In this piece, "A Brief Sketch of the Geology of China (Chung-kuo ti-chih lüeh-lun)," he condemns as "bandits preying on the people" those of his countrymen who lead foreigners on mineral-hunting expeditions into the interior of China, hoping to get rich through performing this service. In an impassioned statement of nationalism, he affirms:

What is meant by "China" is the China of the Chinese people. Non-Chinese may study [the country], but they may not explore [with a view of determining what of the national wealth is worth taking]. Non-Chinese may gasp [at the country] in admiration, but they are not to be permitted to stand around licking their chops in anticipation.[34]

Chou Tso-jen is, no doubt, right when he says that Lu Hsün's thought during these years in Japan could be summed up in one word—nationalism.[35]

Lu Hsün's connection with the *Chekiang Tide* seems to have been due to his friendship with Hsü Shou-shang. After taking over the editorship, Hsü felt isolated and lonely, and knew that Lu Hsün was in the same mood; therefore, to dispel somewhat the forlorn atmosphere, he asked Lu Hsün to contribute something to the magazine. Lu Hsün said that he would. Much to Hsü's pleasant surprise, the manuscript of "The Soul of Sparta (Ssu-pa-ta chih hun)" was handed to him the next day. The alacrity with which Lu Hsün fulfilled promises was, says Hsü, a notable characteristic of his friend.[36]

Written in a rather difficult style of classical Chinese, "The Soul of Sparta" recounts the tale of the heroic stand of the Greeks against the Persians at Thermopylae. Singled out for particular praise is a young Greek woman who disowns her man because he has returned home ignominiously alive from the battle. In the introduction to the piece, Lu Hsün challenges young Chinese men to emulate the martial valor of this antique foreign maid—clearly the kind of fiction Liang Ch'i-ch'ao would have approved, although Liang might have been miffed that it was addressed to

34. *LHC*, p. 45; *LHCC*, VII, 218. Lu Hsün also made use of what he had learned of mining in collaborating on a book on China's mineral resources, *Chung-kuo k'uang-ch'an chih*, in 1906. *LHC*, p. 45; *YCTL*, p. 21.
35. *KYLH*, pt. 2, p. 307.
36. *YHC*, p. 14.

restricted readership with literary teeth sharp enough to gnaw through the lumpy classical Chinese sentences in which it was presented.[37]

During 1903 also, Lu Hsün also published in the *Chekiang Tide* an article recounting the discovery of radium by the Curies in 1898. "On Radium (*Shuo jih*)," was written with the intention of stimulating Chinese students to the study of science.[38] Thus it was a productive time for the young Lu Hsün; in his twenty-third year he had translated three novels and worked up a historical short story and two articles. Probably the most accurate assessment of these works is his own, in a preface to a collection that included some of them, published in 1935. Here he admits that he is not proud of all of them—some would make him blush—but, he notes, unless he had undergone some such apprenticeship in his early years, he probably would not have been able to produce the works of his more mature period. With reference to "The Soul of Sparta" and "On Radium" in particular, he says:

As I remember it, my attainments in chemistry and history at that time were certainly not of a level [that would have permitted me to compose such essays]. Thus I must have lifted the materials from some place or other, but later when I tried to recall from just where I had made the theft, try as I would, I just could not remember. Moreover, at that time I had just begun my study of Japanese and I was anxious to read [anything I could get my hands on], even though I hadn't really gotten the grammar yet. And then I was equally eager to translate, even though I hadn't understood what I'd read very well. Hence I think that the content of these two essays is rather suspect. Moreover, the diction is downright peculiar, especially in "The Soul of Sparta." Looking at it now is enough to make me blush. At the time, however, it was thought that that was the way to write. You had to be dramatic and a bit bombastic before people would praise your style. . . . My diction was also influenced by Yen Fu. For instance, I would use the Chinese transliteration of the Latin word for

---

37. *LHCC*, VII, 9-17. V. I. Semanov, because of certain structural devices in the story and because it was included in a 1934 collection of Lu Hsün's works—*Chi-wai-chi* [Collection of uncollected works]—in which no other translations appeared, treats it as a creative work. See Charles J. Alber, "Soviet Criticism of Lu Hsün (1881-1936)" (Ph.D. dissertation, Indiana University, 1971), pp. 307-10. *Keikoku bidan* [Laudable anecdotes of able statesmanship] (1883), by Yano Ryūkei, seems a likely source for "The Soul of Sparta," but I have not been able to examine it. See Nakamura, *Modern Japanese Fiction*, p. 29.

38. *LHCC*, VII, 18-26. See also *LHCL*, p. 20.

nerve and write *nieh-fu*. I'm afraid that I'm the only one around who would understand that word today. Later, I was influenced by Chang T'ai-yen and began going antique in style, but none [of the essays written under his influence] is included in the present collection.[39]

In general, the essays and translations of this early period are truly works of apprenticeship. They are run-of-the-mill and could well have been written by any number of other Chinese students living in Tokyo at that time, for there is little about them that exhibits the style that we later come to associate with Lu Hsün. His mature style is associated with understatement, not the bluster of something like "The Soul of Sparta." The prose of his later years is distinguished also by dispassionate analysis, not the near-demagogic tribal calls of "A Brief Sketch of the Geology of China." These early translations, done while he was at the Kōbun Institute, are cut, snipped, and rearranged in order to make them look more Chinese. This method is totally at odds with the painfully literal translation technique that he was to employ five or six years later on the eve of his return to China in 1909, a technique which would faithfully preserve the foreign strangeness of the material he translated. As we shall see in due course, the change that would occur in Lu Hsün's translation style in the interim between these early days at the Kōbun Institute and his return to China in 1909 would reflect an equally radical change in his thought.

39. *LHCC*, VII, 4.

6

SENDAI AND
MEDICAL SCHOOL

Upon graduation from the Kōbun Institute in 1904, Lu Hsün decided to study medicine. In retrospect, both he and his friends have offered a variety of reasons for this choice: his father's death at the hands of traditional Chinese doctors; his vague feeling that medicine was somehow associated with the rapid and successful modernization of Japan; a desire to learn how to help Chinese women who had let out their bound feet (as his mother had done); and, finally, an excruciating toothache that he had once suffered.[1] While his choice of medicine as a field is not surprising, his choice of a school was.

According to Japanese educational regulations of the time, as a graduate of the Kōbun Institute, he was on a par with Japanese high school graduates and therefore eligible to apply to a specialized school of medical studies, although his level of preparation was not considered high enough to enable him to apply to one of the medical colleges attached to a university. Upon graduating from a specialized school of medical studies, he could set himself up in practice just as a graduate of one of the medical colleges could. There was some difference in the degree awarded,[2] and a degree from a medical college was more prestigious than one from a specialized school, but the nicety of that distinction would probably have been lost back home in the China of that day.

Tokyo was burgeoning with Chinese students and there were several specialized schools of medical studies among which they

1. *WTLH*, pp. 19-20.
2. *HSJW*, p. 230.

might choose in the event that they opted for a medical career. The most logical choice was the school just across Tokyo Bay at Chiba. Lu Hsün did not make that choice; instead, he decided in favor of the specialized school at Sendai, hundreds of miles to the north. It was an odd choice: Sendai was far removed from the cosmopolitan centers of contemporary Japanese culture. On the surface, it was a choice for the boondocks.

Both he and Chou Tso-jen have indicated that it was disgust with the narrow pragmatism and unseemly frivolity of Chinese students in Tokyo that prompted him to go trundling off to the chilly North, to a city in which he would be the only Chinese student. His distaste for the majority of Chinese students in Japan at that time was virtually boundless. Many of them were studying practical subjects (likely to lead to a government career) such as law or police administration while at the same time pursuing, by way of extracurricular activities, the newest and most frivolous trappings of Western civilization. Writing in 1926, Lu Hsün remembered his decision to leave Tokyo in much the same way that he had remembered his decision to leave Shaohsing for Nanking: in both cases he was getting away from people with whom he was, for one reason or another, fed up.

In the gatehouse of the Chinese Students' Union there were always some books on sale, and it was worth going there sometimes. In the mornings you could sit and rest in the foreign-style rooms inside. But toward the evening the floor of one room would often be shaken by a deafening tramp of feet, and dust would fill the whole place. If you questioned those in the know, the answer would be: "They are learning ballroom dancing."

Then why not go somewhere else?

So I went to medical school in Sendai.[3]

Lu Hsün seems by temperament to have been almost equally attracted and repelled by the hurly-burly of life. He is occasionally to be found in the ballroom of society; he will stay for one or two numbers and then slip away in search of solitude and silence. Chou Tso-jen, writing of Lu Hsün's daily habits in Tokyo, says that he often browsed through bookstores, but seldom went to visit friends, tending rather to wait for them to come to him.[4]

3. *LHCC*, II, 271; *SWLH*, I, 402.
4. *LHKC*, p. 190.

During his stay at Sendai he went to theatricals with school-mates,[5] and even journeyed up the coast a bit to see the beautiful tree-covered islands famed all over Japan as the Pine Islands (Matsushima).[6] But on the whole, here in Sendai too he seems to have been a rather bookish loner. Since he was not charged tuition and had a regular remittance from the Manchu government, he had more pocket money than did many of his Japanese fellow students, at least one of whom remembered him as having a sweet tooth. He was often seen at a small shop close to campus consuming large amounts of coffee and fruit. Apart from this modestly hedonistic lapse, however, the same classmate remembers him as a fairly studious fellow who kept pretty much to his room and books—in sum, a rather diffident type whose subsequent fame no one would have suspected.[7] One feels that he was not too different in personality at this point from what he was years later when he observed to a former student in a letter: "I don't get around too much, and for the most part, it is black characters on white pages . . . that put me in contact with society."[8]

In 1926, already a famous author, Lu Hsün wrote a warm reminiscence of an instructor at Sendai, a certain Fujino Genroku, who introduced him to anatomy and a number of other subjects. Professor Fujino had him turn in his class notes every week and then checked them over, put in supplements, and even corrected grammatical mistakes. Lu Hsün was forever grateful.

I had the lecture notes he corrected bound into three thick volumes and kept them as a permanent souvenir. Unfortunately seven years ago when

5. Ibid., p. 200.

6. *YHC*, p. 29. The modern Japanese writer Dazai Osamu (1909-1948) wrote a novel *Sekibetsu* [Regrets at parting], describing Lu Hsün's life in Sendai. He visited Sendai in 1944 to gather material for his book, which was completed the following year. In general, Dazai's novelistic account accords with what we know of Lu Hsün's life in Sendai from other sources. Dazai presents the novel as the reminiscences of a doctor who had been a fellow student of Lu Hsün's at the medical school. I am indebted to Miss Yuri Kondo for an interpretation of this novel. *Sekibetsu* is in Vol. 7 of the definitive edition, *Dazai Osamu Zenshū* [Complete works of Dazai Osamu], published in Tokyo by the Chikuma Bookstore in 1962, pp. 133-232; this book is cited in the Bibliography as *SB*.

7. Yamada Norio, *Rojin den* [A biography of Lu Hsün] (Tokyo, 1968), p. 69; hereafter cited as *RJD*. He was known also among his compatriots as having a sweet tooth; *LHKC*, p. 199.

8. *Lu Hsün shu-chien* [Lu Hsün's letters] (Hong Kong, 1960), I, 29; hereafter cited as *SC*.

I was moving house, a case of books broke open on the road and half the contents were lost, including these notes. I asked the transport company to make a search, but to no effect. So all I have left is his photograph which hangs on the east wall of my Peking lodging, opposite my desk. At night if I am tired and want to take it easy, when I look up and see his thin, dark face in the lamplight, as if about to speak in rhythmic tones, my better nature asserts itself and my courage returns. Then I light a cigarette, and write some more of those articles so hated and detested by "upright gentlemen."[9]

Fujino himself, reminiscing in 1938 (two years after Lu Hsün's death), considered the intensity of his former student's gratitude a bit odd and intimated that it may have been due to the relatively poor treatment accorded him by other Japanese. For in spite of the fact that the Sino-Japanese War had been over for a decade, there was still a great deal of residual resentment in Sendai against Chinese, who were contemptuously referred to as "Chinks" (*chanchan bozu*). According to Fujino, even some of Lu Hsün's classmates shared this disdainful attitude.[10] Also, the stay at Sendai coincided in large part with the period of the Russo-Japanese War (1904-5). Lu Hsün was occasionally accosted on the street by Japanese who ridiculed him.[11] The wartime atmosphere seems to have inflated Japanese nationalism and latent hostility against Chinese out of all proportion.

Nevertheless, Lu Hsün made it through his first year with the following grades:

Dissection	59.3	German	60.0
Anatomy	72.7	Physics	60.0
Physiology	63.3	Chemistry	60.0
Ethics	83.0		

His cumulative average was 65.5 (60 was passing) and in a class of 142 he placed sixty-sixth.[12] Whatever his first year had been, it had not been spectacularly easy. He spent the summer vacation of 1905 in Tokyo, taking advantage of the trip down from Sendai to

9. *SWLH*, I, 409; *LHCC*, II, 277.

10. *RJD*, p. 68. Chou Chien-jen, Lu Hsün's second brother, has speculated that Fujino's reminiscences may have been doubly distorted by temporal distance and the anti-Chinese atmosphere in Japan during the late 1930s. *LHSC*, p. 44.

11. *LHSC*, p. 43.

12. *RJD*, p. 55.

stop off and visit the tomb of Chu Shun-shui, a Ming dynasty loyalist who had died in exile rather than return to a China under the control of the alien Manchus.[13]

During his second year at Sendai, some of his Japanese classmates accused him of receiving unfair assistance from Professor Fujino. In correcting and supplementing his notes, they said, Fujino had given out advance information as to what would be emphasized on the examination. Lu Hsün reported this allegation to the teacher and was supported in his indignation by some of his more sympathetic classmates. Finally, the whole affair died a natural death. However, it had left a deep mark on Lu Hsün. In 1926 he described how he had felt in the following words:

China is a weak country, therefore the Chinese must be an inferior people, and for a Chinese to get more than sixty marks [passing] could not be due simply to his own efforts. No wonder they suspected me.[14]

Sendai is in Miyagi Prefecture. In order to recover some of the wartime atmosphere there, a Japanese scholar, Yamada Norio, has gone through the chronological tables of the prefectural history for the period and copied out various entries that bear on the Russo-Japanese War. Yamada reminds us that Sendai was an army as well as a university town; the Second Division of the reserves had its headquarters there. An order for mobilization was received in Prefecture on February 5, 1904, and by February 14 the Second Division was activated as a line combat unit. By May, the division had already seen action, and the residents of Sendai followed its fortunes with an enthusiasm that was apparently not dissimilar to that engendered in the United States by local athletic teams. Army capes taken from Russian prisoners soon became the rage, and Sendai shops did a brisk business in them. Then finally in the fall of 1905 the Second Division embarked on its triumphant return; all Sendai was drunk with the success of its fighting men.[15] It was against this background that the incident occurred which Lu Hsün refers to in the following quotation:

In our second year we had a new course, bacteriology. All the bacterial forms were shown in slides, and if we completed one section before it was

13. *WTLH*, pp. 77-79.
14. *SWLH*, I, 407; *LHCC*, II, 275.
15. *RJD*, pp. 56-58, 62.

time for the class to be dismissed, some news pictures would be shown. Naturally at that time they were all about the Japanese victories over the Russians. But in these lantern slides there were also some Chinese who had acted as spies for the Russians and were captured by the Japanese and shot, while other Chinese looked on. And there was I, too, in the classroom.

"Banzai!" the students clapped their hands and cheered.

They cheered everything we saw; but to me their cheering that day was unusually discordant.[16]

He recalls the same incident (or one like it) in the preface of his first collection of short stories, *Call to Arms:*

I do not know what advanced methods are now used to teach microbiology, but at that time lantern slides were used to show the microbes; and if the lecture ended early, the instructor might show slides of natural scenery or news to fill up the time. This was during the Russo-Japanese War, so there were many war films, and I had to join in the clapping and cheering in the lecture hall along with the other students. It was a long time since I had seen any compatriots, but one day I saw a film showing some Chinese, one of whom was bound, while many others stood around him. They were all strong fellows but appeared completely apathetic. According to the commentary, the one with his hands bound was a spy working for the Russians, who was to have his head cut off by the Japanese military as a warning to others, while the Chinese beside him had come to enjoy the spectacle.

Before the term was over, I had left for Tokyo, because after this film I felt that medical science was not so important after all. The people of a weak and backward country, however strong and healthy they may be, can only serve to be made examples of, or to witness such futile spectacles; and it is not necessarily deplorable no matter how many of them die of illness. The most important thing, therefore, was to change their spirit, and since at that time I felt that literature was the best means to this end, I determined to promote a literary movement.[17]

16. *SWLH*, I, 407-8; *LHCC*, I, 275-6.
17. *SWLH*, I, 3; *LHCC*, I, 4-5. The Yangs have translated *tien-ying*, which ordinarily means "motion picture," as "lantern slides." Jay Leyda thinks that "motion picture," is what Lu Hsün meant and that he saw a newsreel. In the photograph that he offers as evidence, however, the executioner is Chinese, not Japanese. See Leyda, *Electric Shadows: An Account of Films and the Film Audience in China* (Cambridge, Mass., and London, 1972), pp. 13-14 and plate 3. Lu Hsün says that the "forms" of microbes were shown (which implies slides), and since his wording makes it clear that the news scenes and microbes were shown by the same method, one can only conclude that he must have seen a

Perhaps we ought to discount to a certain extent (just how much I am not sure) Lu Hsün's public-spirited explanation as to why he changed from medical studies to literature. We know, for instance, that despite his high intellectual capacities he was not doing correspondingly well in his studies. And in background and temperament he was perhaps better suited to the humanities than to the sciences.

Hsü Shou-shang began to have doubts about his friend's stability when he saw him again in Tokyo. Years later Hsü remembered the encounter in detail:

"I've quit school," he said.

"Why?" I asked in surprise, fearing privately that he had become infirm of purpose. "Weren't you just at the point where you were beginning to find your studies interesting? Why do you want to quit in the middle of things?"

"There's truth in what you say." He hesitated for a bit and finally said: "I've decided to study literature. How can China's idiots, her rotten idiots, ever be cured by medical science?"

We looked at each other and exchanged a grim smile, for the twin categories of "idiots" and "rotten idiots" had long been stock phrases in our everyday conversation.[18]

"still" news slide. It seems unlikely that at that time motion pictures could have been perfected to the point of microphotography. Further, in both passages he says that the execution was "about to" take place, wording that one would not expect had he seen the whole thing in a newsreel. It will be noted that there is a discrepancy between the two accounts: in one there is about to be an execution by gunfire of some Chinese captives (or a single captive—it is not clear in the original); in the other, the prisoner is going to be decapitated. The former version is from *Dawn Blossoms Plucked at Dusk* [Chao-hua hsi-shih]. Since there is a strong element of fictionalization in this book of reminiscences, I am inclined to accept the decapitation version in the preface to *Call to Arms* [Na-han].
18. *WTLH*, pp. 8-9.

7

TOKYO AGAIN AND A
LITERARY CAREER

Lu Hsün left Sendai and returned to Tokyo in the spring of 1906. Whether his reason for doing so was entirely as he states, or whether he understood it completely, we shall never know. Then in the summer an odd thing occurred. His mother called him back to China. It seems that a rumor had reached Shaohsing that he had married in Japan and was now the father of a child. His mother, who with Mistress Ch'ien's assistance had already betrothed him to a girl of the Chu clan, was panic-stricken. She managed to get him to Shaohsing on the pretext that she was ill. Once he was at home, the marriage—an old-fashioned one with all the trimmings —quickly followed. Apparently Lu Hsün put up virtually no resistance, unless his return to Japan a few days after the wedding can be interpreted as such. For the rest of his life he was not often to live in the same house with Miss Chu, and during one extended period in Peking when he did (1919-26), they occupied separate rooms. Thus, though he was financially responsible for his wife, it would seem that he was never really a husband to her.[1]

Su Hsüeh-lin, one of his most hostile critics, probably is not totally unjustified in her opinion, expressed in 1966, that "Lu Hsün had no feeling for his wife," and even one of his earliest and most sympathetic biographers, Professor Takeuchi Yoshimi, is troubled by this matter, finding his compliance in the marriage

1. Ts'ao Chü-jen, *Lu Hsün p'ing-chuan* [A critical biography of Lu Hsün] (Hong Kong, 1957), pp. 298-99; hereafter cited as *LHPC*.

incredible.[2] After all, Takeuchi points out, Lu Hsün was a mature young man of twenty-six who had been baptized in the "new learning" and who was, moreover, wise in the ways of the world. Yet he did comply. Can the pressure from home have been so great? As Takeuchi notes, Chou Tso-jen apparently felt free to marry a Japanese in Tokyo a few years later. But aquiescence to arranged marriages was fairly common among revolutionary young Chinese during the early decades of this century. They comforted themselves with the thought that theirs was a sacrificial generation and promised themselves that they, at least, would liberate the next one.

Grandfather Chou's son Po-sheng was also to become a victim of well-intentioned matchmaking. Lu Hsün's mother took her responsibility very seriously; she was fond of saying that a mistress of a household who failed to make early provision for the marriage of her children was no longer fit for her position. Genuinely fond of Po-sheng, who looked upon her almost as a mother, she arranged a marriage for him that he did not want. This was during the first year of the republic (1912). Po-sheng became so dissatisfied with this match that he briefly considered a divorce. He eventually solved the problem by taking a second wife, a circumstance which presented a complication with regard to the disposition of his naval death-benefits when he passed away in 1918. After his debts had been paid, there was only 250 dollars left. This amount was divided, rather equitably one would think, by giving the first wife 100 dollars and the second 150 dollars in recognition of the fact that she already had one small child and another on the way. Thus, both Lu Hsün and Po-sheng sacrificed women to the good intentions of Lu Hsün's mother and old family morality.[3]

About the time of his elder brother's wedding, Chou Tso-jen was also awarded a government scholarship for study in Japan. And so it was that Lu Hsün returned to Japan, not with his wife,

---

2. Su Hsüeh-lin, *Wo lun Lu Hsün* [I have my say on Lu Hsün] (Taipei, 1967), p. 5; hereafter cited as *WLLH*. *RJ*, pp. 39-43.
Su adds: "Since an old-style woman could not hope to remarry, Miss Chu had no choice but to spend her life waiting on her mother-in-law as a grass widow in the Chou household."
3. *HHL*, pp. 298-99.

but with the beloved brother of his childhood. They went to Tokyo in the fall of 1906 and took up quarters in the Fushimi Boarding House in the Hongō ward of the city. Since, upon leaving Sendai, Lu Hsün had decided that he would no longer pursue a formal course of study, he now began to devote his energies to the study of language and literature. He started learning German, while his younger brother worked on Japanese. Tso-jen formally enrolled in a language class organized by the Chinese Overseas Students' Association; it met from nine o'clock in the morning until noon at the association's headquarters, a foreign-style building conveniently located at the juncture of the Kanda and Hongō sections, not far from the boarding house. Despite his sporadic attendance and the odd teaching method employed (the teacher wrote colloquial Chinese on the board while saying the same thing in Japanese), Tso-jen began to pick up the rudiments of the language. He had little chance to speak it, however, for as long as the brothers remained together in Japan it was usually Lu Hsün who negotiated with the Japanese around them.[4]

For Tso-jen, Japan was a case of love at first sight; Tokyo so delighted him that he would, ever after, refer to it as his second home (*ku-hsiang*) and constantly look back upon his six-year sojourn as one of the happiest periods in his life.[5] He was never to meet with the kind of unpleasantness that Lu Hsün went through in Sendai and, hence, would remain very open to his experience. He would delight in the Japanese architecture, food, courtesy, and esthetic sense, and would eventually take a Japanese wife. Like many of his compatriots, he loved Japan in part because he thought that it preserved much of what had been beautiful in Chinese culture of an earlier period—the China that existed during the T'ang dynasty, before the Mongol and Manchu invasions wrenched it off course.[6] It is interesting that Lu Hsün (as we have noted above) attributed what he saw as the defects of Chinese personality to just such periods of foreign domination.

The brothers' stay at the Fushimi Boarding House was not to last long. A few years earlier, repugnance for the frivolous lives of the Chinese student population in Tokyo had caused Lu Hsün to bypass medical school in nearby Chiba in favor of remote Sendai;

4. LHNP, p. 25; HHL, p. 193.
5. HHL, pp. 179-82, 188.
6. YYWP, pp. 143-44.

now a similar antipathy made the brothers decide to seek new quarters. A number of the student boarders were unruly and uncouth, and Lu Hsün suspected that under the guise of helping China they were really pursuing courses of study in such practical things as law, politics, and railroading in hopes of eventually enriching themselves. Furthermore, the rascals had a veritable passion for the bath (so did Lu Hsün) and when the water was hot, like children in a toy department, they would toss all rules of propriety and precedence into the nearest waste-can and scurry devil-take-the-hindmost into the bath. This was more than the brothers could take and they moved out.[7]

Lu Hsün arranged for them to live in a place nearby, the Nakakoshi Boarding House. Originally this was nothing more than a family dwelling in which rooms were rented out, but, because three boarders were staying there, police regulations required that the family hang out a little sign proclaiming its status as a commercial boarding house. It was in a clean, quiet neighborhood, and for that reason the rates were rather high. In general it seems to have been a pleasant place, though there were one or two things about the landlady that repelled the slightly finicky Lu Hsün: he found her obsequious old-style courtesy rather annoying, and her habit of waking her daughter to tell her to hurry up and get to sleep because tomorrow was a school day, downright ridiculous.[8] At this time he was nominally enrolled in the language school of the Germanic Alliance, but was never fully a student there. He did, however, continue to receive thirty-three dollars a month from the Manchu government in financial support.[9] The government was apparently very lax in its supervision of students in Japan and would support any one who went through the motions of officially reporting his whereabouts even if no formal enrollment was involved.[10]

Lu Hsün would usually awaken in the morning sometime after ten o'clock, lie back again for a while, and smoke one or two cigarettes before getting up to take his bath and have breakfast. After eating, he would read the papers until it was time for lunch.

7. *LHKC*, pp. 177-78.
8. Ibid., pp. 178-80.
9. Ibid., p. 182, 191. Tso-jen remembers that Lu Hsün attended classes there only rarely, when the mood took him. *CNST*, p. 51.
10. *HHL*, p. 192.

Well aware of his habits, his friends would usually come to see him only after lunch. If no one came, then he would set out for a browse through the bookstores, and though he did not always have enough money to pick up even a secondhand book, he usually had a coin or two with which he might buy one of the German magazines which he and Tso-jen mined for the precious ore of German translations of Eastern European authors.[11]

During part of the time that they were at the Nakakoshi Boarding House, the brothers would, after supper, go over to the Kanda section, where they and some friends (including Hsü Shou-shang) studied Russian with a Jewish refugee named Maria Konde. Returning from these study sessions, Lu Hsün would stay up very late and read by the light of a kerosene lamp long after everyone else had gone to bed. How late he had stayed up on any particular night could be gauged by the size of the pile of cigarette butts in his ashtray the next morning. The class did not hold together very long, however, and the group learned but little Russian. Distressed by rumors concerning herself and some Russian youths who visited her quarters, Maria clumsily attempted suicide with a pistol. Although the class continued after her wound had healed, the friends began to lose interest. The man who had organized it decided to drop out and go to Nagasaki to study bomb making with the Russians there. This was a skill which would prove useful in the revolution against the Manchus. The class faded away.[12]

Life at the Nakakoshi Boarding House seems to have been quite agreeable and it is likely that the Chou brothers would have stayed longer had not Hsü Shou-shang suggested that they and two other friends join him in renting a house together.[13] The house that they took was in the Nishikata district, long a center of Tokyo cultural life, and it was said that the well-known novelist Natsume Sōseki (1867-1916) had once lived there. The five young men moved in during the spring of 1908 and renamed their house the "Hall of the Five."[14]

In the beginning, life at the Hall of the Five was pleasant: the house was spacious, the garden flourishing, and the view beautiful. Perhaps it was the esthetic influence of this fresh environment

11. *LHKC*, p. 191.
12. Ibid., pp. 184, 191.
13. Ibid., p. 181.
14. *YHC*, p. 28; *HHL*, p. 215.

that enabled Hsü to persuade Lu Hsün to venture out to Ueno Park one day to view the cherry blossoms; in Hsü's opinion, Lu Hsün was willing to go mainly because he could browse through the Nankō Bookstore on the way. The two friends enjoyed the cherry blossoms and the teashops, and Hsü in particular was impressed with the respect that the Japanese showed as they passed the statue of that embodiment of the samurai spirit, Saigō Takamori (1827-1877).[15]

In later years, Hsü recalled fondly that he and Lu Hsün did everything together in those days. They would spend their last dime on a book, smile at each other, and say: "Broke again!"[16] It was a pleasant period, but it did not last long, for after living in the Hall of the Five for ten months, they moved out early the next year. It seems that while Hsü and the Chou brothers got on famously, the other two members of the group felt left out and decided that it would be better to split up. The Chou brothers and Hsü continued to remain together, taking up more modest quarters in the same district.[17] But Lu Hsün was not to stay at this new place for very long either; he ended his sojourn in Japan and returned to China in the summer. It was 1909. He had been in Japan for most of seven years.[18]

Because of the high rent charged for a nice place in a prestigious neighborhood, it had been necessary for Lu Hsün to pinch pennies. The monthly thirty-three dollars from the Manchu government proved insufficient. At this point, Hsü helped out by giving him a job reading the proofs of a Chinese translation of a Japanese work on China's economy.[19] The fate of this translation was to be indirectly related to that of Chang T'ai-yen, the bold revolutionary leader who had come to Japan in 1906, just after serving a three-year prison term in China,[20] and was now editor of

15. *YHC*, p. 29. Saigō Takamori was instrumental in bringing about the return of power from the feudal lords to the emperor (the Meiji Restoration of 1868) with a minimum of disruption. After the restoration, he became dissatisfied with the treatment accorded the military class and with Japan's foreign policy. When some of his more radical followers revolted, his sense of personal loyalty moved him to join them, and he died in the Satsuma Rebellion of 1877.

16. *YHC*, p. 30.

17. *LHKC*, p. 181.

18. *LHNP*, p. 29.

19. *LHKC*, p. 182.

20. Arthur W. Hummel, ed., *Eminent Chinese of the Ch'ing Period (1644-1912)* (2 vols.; Washington, D.C., 1944), II, 769.

the *Peopole's Journal* (*Min pao*), propaganda organ of the newly organized Revolutionary Alliance, which took into its fold a number of anti-Manchu groups.[21] While living at the Hall of the Five, Lu Hsün was one of a group that met regularly on Sundays at the office of the *People's Tribune* to hear lectures that Chang T'ai-yen gave at their request. Chang's subject was the ancient etymological dictionary, *Shuo-wen chieh-tzu*, but Lu Hsün has said that he was far more interested in the lecturer as a revolutionary than as a scholar.[22] Yet he was, by his own testimony, influenced by Chang's style of classical Chinese,[23] of which there was an abundant sampling in the *People's Tribune*, for Chang was its most prolific contributor as well as its editor.[24]

When the newspaper was eventually prohibited by the Japanese authorities in 1908,[25] a fine of 150 dollars was levied against it, and Chang, as editor, had either to pay the fine or to work it off at the rate of a dollar a day in jail. He did not have the money. Hsü Shou-shang solved the problem by paying the fine with part of the money earmarked for printing the translation that Lu Hsün was proofreading. Lu Hsün was quite displeased that the Revolutionary Alliance had not borne its responsibility for the fine. When the *People's Tribune* later resumed publication, in Paris, the issue that Chang had already prepared for the press was scrapped in favor of a new one. This further incensed Lu Hsün To be sure, Chang's diction was a bit archaic and might not be readily understood by overseas Chinese in Southeast Asia (whose financial support was important to the revolution), but Lu Hsün knew that Chang was influential among Chinese students in Japan, and felt that it was shortsighted of Sun Yat-sen and the Alliance not to realize that.[26]

Curiously, despite the fact that he was often in the offices of the

21. Marius B. Jansen, *The Japanese and Sun Yat-sen* (Cambridge, Mass., 1954), p. 119. Under the charismatic leadership of Sun Yat-sen (1866-1925), the Revolutionary Alliance, a federation of dissident groups, was formed in the summer of 1905. Sun was exceedingly effective in leading Chinese students in Japan away from the constitutional reform position toward determined commitment to revolution. For a summary of events of this period see Michael Gasster, *China's Struggle to Modernize* (New York, 1972), pp. 19-31.

22. *LHCC*, VI, 442.

23. *LHCC*, VII, 4.

24. Michael Gasster, *Chinese Intellectuals and the Revolution of 1911* (Seattle and London, 1969), p. 57.

25. Ibid.

26. *LHKC*, pp. 186-87.

People's Tribune and had several friends who belonged to the Revolutionary Alliance, Lu Hsün himself was never very active in the group. Moreover, he was at this time on rather intimate terms with T'ao Ch'eng-chang (d. 1911), who had been one of the founders (by virture of his connections with Chekiang secret societies) of a slightly older revolutionary group, the Restoration Society (*Kuang-fu hui*).[27] Yet, according to Chou Tso-jen, his brother never showed any interest in joining this group, either; Tso-jen has said that this struck him as odd at the time. Some biographers have argued that Lu Hsün did, in fact, join the Restoration Society.[28]

There is little doubt that during his years in Japan Lu Hsün was no political activist. As we have seen, he tended to attribute ulterior motives to those students who said they were pursuing this or that course of action in Japan in order to help China. It would seem likely that this kind of suspicion would have precluded his joining any of the revolutionary organizations in Tokyo at the time. Besides, as we have seen, he tended to be a loner. The wife of his later years, Hsü Kuang-p'ing, has said that during all the time that he was in Japan he was never willing to participate in any positive action.[29] Reminiscing in 1949, she stated that he was not a seeker of danger and did not want people close to him to court it. She recalled that he once said, "When a revolutionary tells you to do something, you simply have to do it, no questions asked. But I ask questions and gauge the value of this or that course of action. Hence, I cannot be a revolutionary." As she remembered him, he was a thinker, not an activist.[30]

While Lu Hsün was in Tokyo, also present was another native of Shaohsing, the famous Ch'iu Chin (1879?-1907). She participated in a number of revolutionary groups and attended many meetings, her arrival often generating mixed feelings because of her sharp tongue. On one occasion Lu Hsün and Hsü Shou-shang were among those upon whom she vented wrath for disagreeing with her.[31] Because females were a rarity in the Chinese student population, Ch'iu Chin would be asked to stand and give a speech whenever she went to a gathering of her countrymen. Her

27. *KYLH*, pt. 2, p. 307.
28. *SCK*, pp. 1-13.
29. *ESS*, p. 49.
30. Ibid., p. 50.
31. *LHKC*, pp. 161-62.

speeches were invariably punctuated by chain explosions of enthusiastic applause. Later, while she was serving as principal of the Ta-t'ung Academy in Shaohsing and simultaneously organizing a secret army, her plot for the seizure of Shaohsing was exposed. She was taken into custody, tried before a Manchu judge, and beheaded.[32] Lu Hsün apparently felt that the thunderous applause she received in meetings had made her overconfident and rash, for when the news of her death arrived in Japan, he remarked, "Ch'iu Chin was clapped to death. And yet when you come right down to it, she didn't accomplish a thing."[33]

In Lu Hsün's aloofness from the various forms of political activity that were popular among the Chinese students in Tokyo and in his comment on the death of Ch'iu Chin we discern two aspects of his personality that also characterize his mature style as a writer: dispassion, and realistic irreverence. Much of his depth as a writer is attributable to his distaste for enthusiasms and his ready suspicion of righteous advocacies of any kind. His tendency to see some of the most sacred people and events of the hagiography of modern Chinese history as "full of sound and fury, signifying nothing" undoubtedly did much to earn him his reputation for being caustic.

In general, the even tenor of Lu Hsün's life after his return to Tokyo in 1906 indicates a period of intellectual ferment. In the preface to his first collection of stories, *Call to Arms* (1922), he gives the impression that when he left Sendai he was newly committed to a cause. In all likelihood, this impression is accurate. However, one would suppose that it was as yet a general commitment: it is doubtful that he knew just how he would use literature to reform his countrymen, or that he had any definite idea as to what the content of that literature should be.

Speaking of this period, Chou Tso-jen has said that it was in Tokyo in 1906 that Lu Hsün first made a really serious study of literature. Previously he had loved and appreciated it, but had not rid himself of traditional concepts as to what it was.[34] There is evidence of this ferment in an incident that occurred while he was attending Chang T'ai-yen's lectures at the *People's Tribune* office. Chang asked for a definition of literature and Lu Hsün answered:

32. Hummel, *Eminent Chinese*, pp. 169-70.
33. *ESS*, p. 51. A tall stone monument stands in Shaohsing today at the place where she was executed.
34. *KYLH*, pt. 2, p. 307.

"Literature is something different from philosophy. Philosophy is that whereby men's thoughts are stimulated, but literature is that whereby men's feelings are enriched." Chang commented that although this definition was better than the old ones, it was still unsound. After all, he observed, referring to two famous prose-poems, neither "The River," by Kuo P'u (276-324), nor "The Sea," by Mu Hua (*fl.* 290), was capable of moving anyone, and yet both were commonly considered to be literature. Lu Hsün did not openly disagree with him, but after class he observed to Hsü Shou-shang that Chang defined literature too broadly; there should be some distinction made between literature and mere writing. "Although 'The River' and 'The Sea' are rich and exotic in vocabulary, it is difficult to say just what their literary value is," he confided to Hsü. At this point, for Lu Hsün, "literature" was no longer a simple descriptive term; it was a normative one, and hence one that was to be applied carefully.[35]

As a first step toward seeing what could be done with literature as an instrument for reforming the people, in 1907 Lu Hsün, Chou Tso-jen, and Hsü Shou-shang decided to launch a periodical.[36] In the preface to *Call to Arms* we are told of the plans for this venture and why, not surprisingly, it came to naught:

There were quite a few Chinese students in Tokyo studying everything from law, politics, physics, and chemistry on down to police work and industrial [planning], but there was no one in literature or art. Even in this uncongenial atmosphere, however, I was fortunate enough to find some kindred spirits. We gathered the few others that we needed and, after discussion, our first step of course was to publish a magazine, the title of which denoted that this was a new birth. Since we were rather classically inclined at that point, we called it *New Life* [*Hsin-sheng*].

As the time for publication drew near, some of our contributors dropped out, and then our funds were withdrawn, until finally there were only three of us left, and we were penniless. Since we had started our magazine against the trend of the times in the first place, there was naturally no one we could very well complain to when it failed.[37]

With regard to his reading during this time, it is to be noted that Lu Hsün sought out in Japanese translation the literatures of the

---

35. *YHC*, p. 27.
36. *RJNP*, p. 9.
37. *SWLH*, I, 3-4; *LHCC*, I, 5. Reminiscing as an old man, Tso-jen saw the new literature movement of the May Fourth period as a continuation of the effort that had gone into the *New Life* "movement." *HHL*, p. 232.

oppressed, the literatures of those who had cried out and resisted. For this reason he tended to focus on Russia, Eastern Europe, and the Balkans.[38] Chou Tso-jen, in the course of a lecture given in 1932, made a similar connection between his own intense feelings of nationalism at this same time and his interest in the literatures of weak, oppressed nations; Tso-jen traced this interest to the lectures by Chang T'ai-yen that he and Lu Hsün attended in the *People's Tribune* office. Since Chang T'ai-yen was an elder and much admired *landsmann (t'ung-hsiang)* of the Chou brothers, there can be but little doubt that it was Chang's influence that also moved Lu Hsün to a concentration on these literatures.[39] Despite a good command of the Japanese language (gained in part as the only Chinese student in the medical school at Sendai), Lu Hsün did not during these years display any marked interest in the literature of Japan as such, but rather used the language to acquire the literatures of those countries that especially interested him because of their political similarity to China. Chang T'ai-yen saw the Manchus as enslavers of the Han people, and when Lu Hsün and Hsü Shou-shang decided that the Chinese as a people were most lacking in "love" and "sincerity," they further concluded that these defects were largely due to the experience of having been twice enslaved by non-Chinese races.[40] Against this background it was only logical that the Chou brothers should seek out the literatures of other oppressed peoples.

Although indifferent to Japanese works in general, Lu Hsün did display an interest in the novels of Sōseki, and it was from Sōseki, or so Tso-jen would opine in later years, that he derived a certain

38. *LHCC*, I, 392.

39. Chou Tso-jen, *Chung-kuo hsin-wen-hsueh te yuan-liu* [The course of new Chinese Literature] (Peking, 1932), p. 21; hereafter cited as *WHYL*.

The term *t'ung-hsiang* refers to people from the same province or division thereof. Though *landsmann* refers to fellow natives of Germany (Chinese use *t'ung-pao* for fellow Chinese) or fellow natives of some geographic or political divisions of the country, it still seems a useful Western approximation of *t'ung-hsiang*, a most significant term in the pattern of Lu Hsün's adult relationships, most of which were formed with people from his native province, especially those from his home town area, Shaohsing. They so often got each other jobs and published each other's works that one is tempted to reach down to the ball off the toe of the boot below Germany and speak of a Chekiang or Shaohsing "Mafia." *Shaohsing shih-yeh* carries something of this pejorative connotation. Since provincial affiliations were important throughout China, however, it may not be fair to single out Chekiang.

40. *WTLH*, p. 19.

smack of lightness and grace in his satire.[41] Further, while he tended to use Japanese primarily as a passkey to the literatures of other countries, it can hardly be overemphasized that it was precisely the vigorous state of Japanese letters at that time which made this possible. Ever since the 1870s, the Japanese had been eager translators of Western fiction. By 1885 a critical study, *The Essence of the Novel* (*Shōsetsu shinzui*), was published by Tsu-bouchi Shōyō; and little more than a decade later, Futabatei Shimei published an important novel written completely in collo-quial diction.[42] By the early 1900s, when the Chou brothers were in Tokyo, the literary scene in Japan was flourishing. The times were distinguished also by the high tide of naturalism that followed in the wake of the Russo-Japanese War, though in addition to the naturalistic school there existed literary groups that reflected almost all of the current European modes.[43]

Neither China nor the majority of Chinese students in Tokyo was ripe for such cultural ferment. China had not even begun to make a good beginning toward solving its political problems, whereas Japan had taken its first giant step several decades earlier, in 1868, with the Meiji Restoration. In 1918, speaking at Peking University before a group organized for the study of the novel, Chou Tso-jen said that contemporary Chinese literature was in a state similar to that of Japan in 1884 or 1885. In this same speech (in which he seemed to view the nascent Chinese literary revolu-tion of 1918 as a recapitulation of the Japanese experience) Tso-jen called for more translation and for more imitation of foreign

41. In analyzing the characteristics of his brother's style, Tso-jen has similarly noted that it was from a Russian and a Pole, from translations of Gogol and Sienkiewicz, that Lu Hsün learned how to describe cruel events with a humorous pen. *KYLH*, pt. 2, p. 306.

42. Donald Keene, *Modern Japanese Literature* (New York, 1960), pp. 13-28. For more on these two men and on the difficulties they faced in creating a colloquial diction for use by novelists see Masao Miyoshi, *Accomplices of Silence: The Modern Japanese Novel* (Berkeley and Los Angeles, 1974), pp. 3-37.

43. Chou Tso-jen, "Jih-pen chin san-shih-nien hsiao-shuo chih fa-ta (The development of Japanese fiction during the last thirty years)," in *Chung-kuo hsin-wen-hsueh ta-hsi—ti yi chi* [A corpus of China's new literature—first collection] (10 vols.; Hong Kong, n. d.), pp. 315-16; Tso-jen's article is hereafter cited as *JP*. The original edition of the ten-volume corpus was published in Shanghai, 1935-36. For a discussion of its contents see Fairbank and Liu, *Modern China: A Bibliographic Guide to Chinese Works, 1898-1937* (Cambridge, Mass., 1961), pp. 478-81.

models. He saw what the Japanese had done as "creative imitation" and exhorted his audience to try the same kind of thing. He also called for the creation of a theoretical work on the novel that would serve for China the function that Tsubouchi Shōyō's critical study had earlier for Japan.[44]

There can be little doubt that during their sojourn in Tokyo both Lu Hsün and Chou Tso-jen were already well prepared for the literary revolution that would begin in China a decade later. They were prepared; China was not: "Since we had started our magazine against the trend of the times . . . there was naturally no one we could very well complain to when it failed." Although *New Life* had never really gotten off the ground, the intellectual and emotional stake that Lu Hsün put into the venture was the first expenditure in a subsequent lifetime of energy devoted to the moral regeneration of China through literature. This initial commitment led logically down a road to his mature works during the May Fourth period.

Little daunted by the failure of *New Life*, the brothers continued to read, write, and translate. Much of the writing that Lu Hsün had done for the first issue of *New Life* appeared later in the magazine *Honan* (published in Japan by the association of students from that province).[45] This writing consisted of essays, in classical Chinese, three of which are especially interesting for the light they throw on Lu Hsün's thought with regard to literature: "The Erratic Development of Culture (*Wen-hua p'ien-chih lun*)," "The Power of Mara Poetry (*Mo-lo shih-li shuo*)," and "On Breaking through the Voices of Evil (*P'o e-sheng lun*)." He wrote the first two in 1907, the third in 1908.

"The Erratic Development of Culture"[46] clearly reveals one of the characteristics of Lu Hsün's thought that was to dominate both the stories and the essays of his mature period: his questioning of the motivation of people who espouse various kinds of programs. In this essay Lu Hsün tells his readers that in modern times it seems that whenever China faces a problem, a number of intellectuals immediately stand up and begin hawking the merit of various

44. *JP*, pp. 308-19. For a capsule presentation of the contents of this work see Miyoshi, *Accomplices of Silence*, pp. 20-21.
45. *LHYW*, p. 51; *HHL*, p. 217.
46. This discussion is based on "Wen-hua p'ien-chih lun" as that essay appears in *LHCC*, I, 179-93.

remedies for the problem at hand. Each of them, like a quack doctor, loudly proclaims the superior efficacy of the particular medicine that he happens to be hawking at the time. Lu Hsün reminds his readers that they ought never to forget that these medicine men are being paid for their services and are often more interested in their fees than in the fate of China: "A" says that China needs railroads. It may, but how much is "A" going to pocket in the process of building them? "B" says that China needs a strong military. It does, but how much of "B's" effort is actually going to be expended for the sake of making China strong and how much of it will go into advancing "B's" own power and prestige? Throughout this essay Lu Hsün is as interested in *why* a man says this or that as he is in *what* the man actually says. As we have seen, in conversations with Hsü Shou-shang he arrived at the conclusion that honesty was one of the things most lacking in Chinese character. It is hardly surprising, then that he sees hypocrisy at every turn and treats the *argumentum ad hominem* as a device for establishing truth rather than a logical fallacy. A present-day Japanese scholar, Imamura Yoshio, says that in "The Erratic Development of Culture" Lu Hsün in effect made a "scathing and cynical critique of the basic programs of that enlightment movement which constituted the mainstream of con-temporary thought—a movement that sloganized in favor of such things as enriching the country and strengthening the military, increasing productivity while fostering industry, and even estab-lishing a constitutional monarchy."[47]

Lu Hsün felt that the dominant trends of thought in nineteenth-century Europe, materialism and social democracy, were the consequences of an overreaction to the spiritualism of the Catholic church and the despotism of the state. In its intensity, this overreaction led to a crude materialism that caused people to lose faith in the life of the intellect; it led to a false kind of democracy that bullied the individual in the sacred name of the majority. Lu Hsün invokes the names of Nietzsche, Schopenhauer, Kierke-gaard, and Ibsen, all of whom, he assures us, were reacting against

---

47. *Rojin to dentō* [Lu Hsün and tradition] (Tokyo, 1967), p. 199; hereafter cited as *RJ&DT*. Lu Hsün's critique as summarized here was not, of course, original; much of it can, for instance, be found in Li Po-yuan's novel, *Wen-ming hsiao-shih* [A short history of civilization], which was published in book form in 1906.

the nineteenth-century leveling process that stifled all individuality. The civilization of nineteenth-century Europe had arisen out of the Reformation and was based primarily on the concept of resistance to old, pre-Reformation ways: thus that civilization had gone to an extreme in its almost uncritical preference for materialism and social democracy. It was to correct this extremism, Lu Hsün feels, that the neo-idealists (for so he labels Nietzsche and the others) first began to speak out. He goes on to observe, however, that culture moves as a river from its own particular source, with tributary streams coming in here and there along its course, and one is free to change it only within limits. Hence the culture of China can be influenced from the outside only within definite limits. Those who would totally Westernize China are wrong. It is right and proper that Chinese culture should be selectively influenced by the new culture of the West, but it is beyond all reason to think that the one can suddenly be replaced by the other.

It is important, he says, that China not be misled by the present "erratic" development of European culture. China ought rather to move in the direction of Europe's future, and it is likely that the trend of that future will be away from the narrow materialism and social democracy of the nineteenth century and toward the individualism and spirituality mapped out by the neo-idealists. Hence China ought now to honor the individual and expand the realm of the intellect, or spirit. Once the Chinese people, as individuals, are established and made strong, everything else will follow; any other course would be self-defeating. Here we have the concrete expression of the intellectual framework that would inform most of Lu Hsün's mature literature; the spiritual (psychological) liberation of the individual is a precondition for the liberation of the collective energy of the Chinese people and the eventual establishment of a new, strong and vigorous society. In the short stories that Lu Hsün was to write in later years, he would describe the fetters that bound the Chinese spirit, hoping that abler men would find some way to liberate it. Toward the end of the essay he affirms that the real strength of China and Europe lies in their people, a spiritual factor that is not so readily observable as are the fruits of labor (heavy machinery, trains, ships, and the like). Therefore, if China is to achieve domestic tranquility and become powerful enough to drive its enemies away from its shores, it must first establish its people, for once the people are established everything else will follow.

In the second of the essays, "The Power of Mara Poetry,"[48] Lu Hsün is primarily interested in the satanic spirit of nonconformity and revolt that he saw exemplified in Byron (he admired translations by Su Man-shu [1884-1918]) and Shelley. The word "Mara," which he glosses as equivalent to the devil, was first applied, he notes, to Byron; however, he proposes to apply it to all those poets who cried out in rebellion against heaven and man in order to stir their contemporaries to a more meaningful, free, and robust mode of being.[49]

The emergence of the individual genius of men like Byron and Shelley influenced such poets as Aleksander Pushkin (1799-1837) in Russia, Adam Mickiewicz (1798-1855) in Poland, and Sándor Petöfi (1823-1849) in Hungary. All of these "Mara poets" were, in one way or another, associated with arms and bloodshed, for they were warriors—not ordinary fighters, but warriors of the spirit. China, says Lu Hsün, stands in need of just such warriors. These "warriors of the spirit" give a culture its voice. When a culture is silent it is nearing death. The works of these warriors constitute the "voices of the mind (hsin-sheng)." These voices articulate the feelings, hopes, and fears of an entire people, and they are voices that are often prophetic, either exhorting the culture to reform or stirring its people to resistance against oppression.

One of the voices that Lu Hsün singles out for special attention in the course of this essay is that of Nikolai Gogol, (1809-1852), for his was a voice that broke a Russian silence of centuries. He made Russia, and the world at large, aware of the hitherto invisible traces of tears on the tragic faces of a suffering people. He brought nineteenth-century Russia to an awareness of the dark side of life. Lu Hsün would remain a lifelong admirer of Gogol and would perform in twentieth-century China a function not entirely dissimilar to that of Gogol in nineteenth-century Russia. Singled out as examples of German voices of the mind are Ernst Moritz Arndt (1769-1860) and Karl Theodor Körner (1791-1813). The voices of these men stirred the German people to heroic resistance

48. The discussion in this section is based on "Mo-lo shih-li shuo" as that essay appears in LHCC, I, 194-234.

49. "The Power of Mara Poetry" rambles over far more topics than my discussion indicates. "The main purpose of the article," however, is to "celebrate the writer as a rebel who hurled challenges at society." V. I. Semanov, "Lu Hsün and His Predecessors" (Lu Sin' i ego predšestvenniki [Moscow, 1967], unpublished trans. by Charles J. Alber), chap. 1, p. 20.

when the fatherland faced possible extinction at the hands of Napoleon. Lu Hsün emphasizes their example to show his Chinese readers that countries are not preserved by weapons and technology alone.

The voices of the mind give a nation its literature, and literature is as necessary to a people as food, clothing, or shelter. This is especially true in the modern world, a world so concerned with scientific utilitarianism that it has virtually neglected to provide sustenance for man's intellect. Perhaps the most important function of literature, however, is its ability to bring to light the hidden springs of human existence, to show human life to the reader in a way that is denied to science and the academic disciplines. One might well employ the disciplines of physics and physiology to describe ice to a man who has grown up in the tropics, but the same man would have a much clearer conception of ice, of course, if one were to give him a piece of it to handle. Similarly, the academic disciplines, though able to describe human life in great detail, are not able to place it in their readers' hands; literature, on the other hand, gives the reader the cake of ice.

In "On Breaking through the Voices of Evil"[50] Lu Hsün continues his search for spiritual warriors who will sound a clarion blare to awaken their sleeping compatriots to a new and more meaningful mode of existence. In this third essay, too, he seriously questions the motivation of his various contemporaries with their sundry programs for curing China's ills. His suspicion remains the same: under the guise of various high-sounding slogans, they are out to further their own selfish interests. He restates his fear that all groups interested in modernization would further supress individuality in the name of the majority or the national good. The central theme of "On Breaking through the Voices of Evil," however, lies in another direction, a direction that is in itself a gauge of the distance that now separates him from Liang Ch'i-ch'ao's position on the place of fiction in society. Imamura Yoshio well sums up the content of this new theme:

The anti-superstition movement, part of the reform movement led by Liang Ch'i-ch'ao and his group, was then thriving. Political novels,

---

50. The discussion in this section is based on "P'o e-sheng lun" as that essay appears in *LHCC*, VII, 235-47. I am indebted to Dr. Vladislav Sorokin, (Lu Hsün expert from the U.S.S.R. Academy of Sciences) for helping me to improve my translation of the title; I met Dr. Sorokin when he visited the Stanford campus in February of 1975.

taking anti-superstition as their theme, were being written in great numbers. These dedicated scholars of the anti-superstition cause (1) saw religion as an illusion, (2) would prohibit religious fairs, and (3) disdained mythology. In opposition to this, Lu Hsün . . . made the refutation [contained in this essay].[51]

Lu Hsün's refutation of these "dedicated scholars of the anti-superstition cause" is intimately related in his view of the gentry and the peasantry. For, though not explicitly set forth in those terms, the anti-superstition movement does lend itself to class analysis. In effect, Lu Hsün in "On Breaking through the Voices of Evil" says that the gentry, instead of accepting any responsibility for the contemporary plight of China, find it more convenient to lay the country's ills at the doorstep of the peasantry. Blinded by their own overwhelming concern with personal success, the gentry have lost that reverence for nature and sensitivity to its beauties that the peasant possesses. Having lost such sensitivity themselves, they are unable to comprehend its true significance among the peasants. They label it superstition and blame the peasant for China's backwardness. They do not seem to realize, notes Lu Hsün, that if one examines Chinese history, he will find that those who have caused the altars of the land and grain to be destroyed and family temples to be razed have not been peasants, but rather members of the scholar-gentry. He concludes that "the most urgent thing today is to get rid of hypocritical members of the scholar gentry; we can well afford to retain superstition!"[52] In this regard, he notes that some of his more empty-headed contemporaries have used biology to disprove the existence of the Chinese dragon! But, he comments, people have not been as disposed to employ modern science to disprove the existence of the equally imaginative symbols of more powerful states. In his view, instead of being ashamed of the Chinese dragon, people ought to be proud of the imaginative power of the people who produced it. But since China is weak, he concludes, people assume that everything Chinese must necessarily be inferior. As we have seen, similar considerations led him to leave Sendai and devote himself to literature in the first place.

The greatness of Lu Hsün lies, in part, in his fiercely independent and rather consistent point of view vis-à-vis Chinese culture and the West. It was a point of view that he developed through

51. *RJ&DT*, p. 214.
52. *LHCC*, VII, 240.

decades of coming-and-going fads in thought and politics. Here, in 1908, long before the writings of Karl Marx were much known in china (and, so far as I know, long before Lu Hsün knew much about Marxism), we find him undertaking something very close to a class analysis of society. Little wonder, then, that he was not to be an ardent enthusiast for "science" or "democracy" during the May Fourth period. During the years in Japan, Lu Hsün's interest shifted to finding out where the Chinese people actually were rather than dreaming about where he would like them to be. He became capable of looking at his own people for what they were and not being ashamed, not wishing immediately to make them all into pragmatists, or Christians, or Marxists, or disciples of democracy. It was an attitude that made it possible for him (at a deep level) to be comfortable in being Chinese, and this sense of belonging in turn made it possible for him to look things in the face without being embarrassed or threatened in his estimate of his own worth, or China's. In "On Breaking through the Voices of Evil," students, too, get a bit of the lash of his writing brush. He says that there is a rather simple-minded movement afoot in China that cavalierly takes over the holy places of the Buddhists and converts them into schools. Schools for temples—it seems a poor exchange, for Buddhism is one of the world's great religions, a religion of proven worth; the students turned out by the schools, on the other hand, are at best of a rather low level. And yet those very students smugly consider themselves precious gifts to modern China.

In this essay, for the first time, Lu Hsün takes a critical look at the uses to which the doctrine of social Darwinism had been put. In the West its high-sounding phrases are, he points out, used to justify the subjugation of weaker peoples. (If China has its hypocrisies, the West has its own, too.) He also notes with a trace of alarm that there are those Chinese who in resisting their Western oppressors are fully prepared to copy them in this respect. There are some, for instance, who ridicule countries like India and Poland for having lost their sovereignty. (A Chinese army ditty of the day proudly contrasted China's fate with that suffered by others: "Poland is crushed and India is lost / The last of the Jews to the four winds are tossed.")[53] China should not become powerful in order to lord it over others or seek revenge,

---

53. Ibid., I, 516, n. 18.

but should rather seek after strength to become able to help the oppressed and downtrodden by going to their succor much as Byron (the Mara poet par excellence) did when he went to the aid of the Greeks. In all three of these essays one is struck by the author's critical perceptiveness. Lu Hsün's view of China and the West was a reasoned one, achieved only after mature reflection and was the result of much study and love; it was reached through hard work and was uniquely his own.

In "The Erratic Development of Culture," Lu Hsün saw China's weaknesses and strengths as proceeding from the same cause— isolation. Because China had come to maturity apart from the other centers of civilization, it had developed its own style of life, a style that would stand comparison with that of any of the other great cultures. Because of the distance from other centers, how- ever, China was never exposed to genuine stimuli from the outside and the result had been slow atrophy. For this reason, one might say, the function of translator is as important in Lu Hsün's thought as that of the creative writer. Just as the Mara poet breaks the silence that shrouds the land, so the translator tears down the barriers that isolate one culture from another. The translator provides the stimulus which prevents paralysis from setting in. Throughout his career Lu Hsün translated, selflessly checked over the proofs of the works of younger translators, and cried out for more and better translations. The twin enemies of his personal life—silence and loneliness—were also China's enemies. Mara poets would slay the first monster, and translators the second.

His first efforts at tearing down the barriers that sequestered China resulted in the two-volume collection of short stories that he and his brother translated and published in 1909. The cost of printing was defrayed by a banker friend of Hsü Shou-shang's from Hangchow who had come to Tokyo in 1908 for an ear operation. When he was told of plans for the production of such a collection, to be called *Tales from Abroad (Yü-wai hsiao-shuo chi)*, the banker was quite enthusiastic and offered to help in financing it. This man, a certain Chiang Yi-chih, subsidized the first volume with 100 dollars and the second with 50. This was enough money to print 1,000 copies the first volume and 500 of the second.[54] The venture, thus, went much further than the ill-fated

54. *LHKC*, p. 163. Tso-jen and Lu Hsün translated a total of sixteen stories for *Tales from Abroad*. By country of origin, there were one each from England,

New Life. It had almost everything required for success except—alas!—readers.

It was sold at two locations, one in Tokyo, the other in Shanghai. Of the Tokyo stock, 21 copies of the first volume and 20 of the second were sold. Nothing is known of how well the Shanghai stock sold; furthermore, the unsold copies were lost in a fire five or six years later.[55] Once again the brothers were ahead of the times. Ready and itching for a literary renaissance (if not a revolution), they had rushed into print; they were ready, but their compatriots were not. The political revolution that would establish, in name at least, the Republic of China was only two years off, but the literary revolution for which they were anxiously prepared was still more than a decade away. In the preface to *Tales from Abroad*, the brothers state that they have tried to remain faithful to both the form and the content of the originals, and that they hope to give impetus to the making of Chinese translations and to put their readers in contact with the great spiritual voices of other lands.[56] They are, in effect, helping their readers see beyond the wall.

Instead of bestowing Chinese names, the brothers painfully transliterate all the original names of the characters, syllable by syllable.[57] All of the material added to the original text for the benefit of Chinese readers not familiar with the customs of other lands is parenthetically segregated in the text or is included, along with short biographies of the authors, in a section of notes at the end. In the introductory material they explain the principles of modern punctuation, which they use throughout.[58]

Needless to say, this kind of translation is a far cry from the kind of thing that Lu Hsün did back in 1903 in the Verne novels and "The Soul of Sparta." From this point in his life on, it would be characteristic of him to preserve differences and deny easy similarities. He would increasingly see traditional Chinese culture

---

France, and the United States; seven from Russia; three from Poland; two from Bosnia; and one from Finland. *HHL*, p. 232. The manuscripts were submitted to Chang T'ai-yen for editorial criticism. All the stories appeared under Tso-jen's name, though Lu Hsün translated three of them. Schultz, "Lu Hsün: The Creative Years," p. 98.

55. *LHYW*, I, 581-82.
56. Ibid., p. 149.
57. Ibid., p. 150.
58. Ibid., pp. 150-51.

as a great homogenizing machine. He, for one, would refuse to be blended in, and he would not allow this to happen to the foreign characters that he introduced. He would insist over and over again that "Mr. Smith" is not just like "Chang San," and that he himself is not just like this or that scholar from some long-fallen dynasty.

The rather difficult style of classical Chinese in which the translations were done makes it apparent that *Tales from Abroad* was addressed to the Chou brothers' intellectual peers rather than to any wider readership. Ts'ai Yüan-p'ei (1867-1940), a respected elder of Lu Hsün's and fellow native of Shaohsing, once commented that the style of translation employed in these two volumes was even more archaic than that of the famous Lin Shu.[59] Writing in 1920, Lu Hsün also expressed dissatisfaction with the rather stilted diction and opined that the stories in the collection ought really to be translated into the colloquial language so that they could be more widely read.[60]

With regard to Lu Hsün's peculiar relation to the colloquial language movement, Chou Tso-jen, writing in the 1950s, noted that both *Tales from Abroad* and "Remembrances of the Past" (Lu Hsün's first short story, written in 1911) were done in classical Chinese, and offered the following comments on his elder brother's participation in the new literature movement after 1918:

. . . his taking up his pen to write short stories was by no means for the purpose of promoting the movement for a colloquial literature; his main aim still lay in overthrowing the feudal society and its morality, that is to say it was a continuation of the literary movement [that he had hoped to spark with] *New Life*. The only difference was that this time, for convenience' sake, he used the colloquial language. Of course, he approved of the literary revolution, but he felt that it would not be very significant unless it were coupled with a revolution in thought.[61]

59. Ts'ai Yüan-p'ei, "Chi Lu Hsün hsien-sheng yi-shih (Notes on some odds-and-ends in the life of Lu Hsün)," *Yü Chou Feng*, XXIX (November 16, 1936), 266; hereafter cited as *LHYS*. A dedicated revolutionary, Ts'ai (1876-1940), was a Chekiang *landsmann* and one of the founders of the Restoration Society. Harold Z. Schiffrin, *Sun Yat-sen and the Origins of the Chinese Revolution* (Berkeley and Los Angeles, 1970), p. 341. He would become minister of education during the first year of the Republic; now he is remembered chiefly as the liberal and innovative chancellor (1917-23) of the prestigious Peking University.

60. *LHYW*, I, 582.

61. *HSJW*, p. 10.

In a lecture given at Fujen Universtiy in 1932, Tso-jen pointed out that during their years in Japan colloquial Chinese was viewed primarily as an instrument of communication to be used in establishing contact with the common people or laborers; for any serious literary enterprise one would use the classical language. "We may say that at that time the classical language was used [to communicate with] the master, while the colloquial was used [to communicate with] the servants."[62]

Here, of course, we are involved with Lu Hsün's attitude toward the masses. By the time he wrote "Remembrances of the Past" (1911), Lu Hsün had clearly cut himself away from any lingering hopes that he might have entertained regarding the possibility of transforming large masses of men through the kind of "new" didactic popular novel that Liang Ch'i-ch'ao championed. As we have seen in his attitude on popular superstitions, he no longer felt that it was the proper function of the intellectual to preach the masses out of their beliefs, however unscientific those beliefs might be: the function of the intellectual should rather be to understand their beliefs ("On Breaking through the Voices of Evil") or, in the style of the Mara poets, to give voice to their silent sufferings ("The Power of Mara Poetry").

After 1918, Lu Hsün wrote almost exclusively in colloquial Chinese. Back in 1909 (*Tales from Abroad*), or even 1911 (his first short story), such a choice would have meant that he was addressing a wide readership of the barely literate, rather than his own narrow, educated peer group. After 1918 it meant not that he had turned his attention away from that peer group, but rather that they had turned their attention (indeed, he was one of the leaders in the movement) to colloquial Chinese, which had thereby been legitimized as a means of serious expression for intellectuals. In other words, colloquial Chinese became the mode of choice not when intellectuals used it somewhat condescendingly for propagandistic or educational purposes, in the decade before the Republican Revolution, but rather when an increasing number of them began to use it to communicate with each other, in 1918 and afterward. Perhaps just as we speak of Han *fu* (prose poems) and Sung *tz'u* (song lyrics) to indicate the dominant mode of expression among the intelligentsia of those periods, so ought we to speak of Republican *pai-hua* (colloquial Chinese).

62. WHYL, p. 98.

The first volume of *Tales from Abroad* contained seven stories, two of which were translated by Lu Hsün: Andreyev's "The Lie" and "Silence"; of the nine stories in the second volume, one was translated by him, Garshin's "Four Days."[63] Instead of loosely slipping these stories into a long Chinese gown so as to make them less strange to his readers (the method he had employed in the Verne translations), now he attempted to translate word for word and to preserve all the strange foreign qualities of the original. A number of circumstances, however, prevented him from achieving his goal of precise translation (*chih-yi*). To begin with, there was already some distortion of the originals in the German translations from which he worked; furthermore:

A number of other inaccuracies in the translation result from the fact that the archaic classical style was not always capable of translating complex sentence constructions. There is no such thing as a subordinate clause in classical Chinese, so Lu Hsün found it necessary to break large passages into parts. For example, Lu Hsün divides L. Andreyev's sentence "And when I lifted up my eyes, I saw his profile—so white, austere, and upright, like some pensive angel over the grave of a forgotten man," into two, and the passage turns out as follows: "And when I raised my eyes, I saw his cheeks, as white as ivory, and his magnificent locks. I was sure that only an angel, kneeling beside a lonely grave and mourning a man forgotten by the world, could look like this." The pompous comparison of the cheek to ivory, which replaces Andreyev's terse epithet "white, austere, and upright," was borrowed from the German intermediary, but now the syntactical smoothness is lost in the transition from German to Chinese. Lu Hsün could not help feeling disturbed by this situation, and in a number of instances, attempting to capture the uniqueness of the original (i.e., the German translation), he breaks the rules of the classical language.[64]

What is important here, of course, is not the failure to reach the goal, but the attempt. "The principle of precise translation which Lu Hsün advocated from 1907 to 1909, was progressive and necessary for Chinese literature."[65]

Lu Hsün used German in much the same way that he used Japanese—as a passkey to other cultures. Mining bookstores for

63. *LHYW*, I, Introduction, p. 1.
64. Semanov, "Lu Hsün and His Predecessors," chap. 1, p. 26. Lu Hsün did, in a few cases, "adapt the translated text to his own tastes and sympathies" (ibid., p. 28).
65. Ibid.

the precious ore in old German magazines, the Chou brothers would occasionally find a story from one of their beloved oppressed countries. The best magazine from this point of view seems to have been *Aus Fremden Zungen*.[66] Yet the only German writers whom Lu Hsün found really appealing were Heine and Nietzsche. He was fond of quoting Nietzsche's words to the effect that "If you see a cart about to tip over, don't go prop it up—better go give it a push and help it on over!"[67] There was in this something of his own attitude toward traditional Chinese culture.

Tso-jen has said that Lu Hsün was especially fond of An-dreyev.[68] The significance of this remark is apparent when one reads the two Andreyev stories that he translated for *Tales from Abroad*. In both of these one senses the mood that would later be characteristic of Lu Hsün's own style. "Silence," in particular, reads very much like a story that he might have written during his mature years. Filled with images of alienation and loneliness, it is told in a gaunt, almost bony style that is moving precisely because of its lack of emotive words and the steadfast refusal of the author to comment on the action or the characters. He continued to read and to translate "aus fremden Zungen" the literatures of many countries right on through the peak of his creative years and afterward. As we shall see in the following chapters, while it is sometimes possible to say that he borrowed this or that device from the realm of non-Chinese literature, it is far less often that one can say which foreign author he took it from.[69]

The translation of these stories was Lu Hsün's last piece of literary activity before leaving Japan in 1909. Early in the spring Hsü Shou-shang told Lu Hsün that he was preparing to return to China, having accepted a position as dean in the Chekiang Normal

66. *KYLH*, p. 305.
67. *LHKC*, p. 207.
68. *KYLH*, p. 305.
69. Semanov notes that Lu Hsün's selection of Andreyev and Garshin among the various Russian writers available to him at that time in Japanese or German translation (Gogol, Turgenev, Chekhov, and Gorky) is significant in that these two writers are set apart from the rest by their pessimistic spirit. He feels that Lu Hsün was particularly drawn to them because he "saw no way out of the crisis" which faced China. "Lu Hsün and his Predecessors," chap. 1, pp. 25-26. Patrick Hanan discusses a number of specific borrowings in "The Technique of Lu Hsün's Fiction" *Harvard Journal of Asiatic Studies*, XXXIV (1974), 53-96.

School in Hangchow. Lu Hsün replied: "You're going back at just the right time. I have to return too. Tso-jen is getting married and that will increase expenses. I have to find something to do so that I'll be able to help out a bit." He asked Hsü to help him find a job. Upon returning to Hangchow, Hsü was able to obtain a position for his friend at the normal school, teaching physiology and chemistry.[70] Lu Hsün returned to China that summer, seven years after his arrival in Japan.

It looked, indeed, as though Lu Hsün were sacrificing his own interests for those of Tso-jen in much the same way that he had, a few years earlier, sacrificed those same interests for the sake of his mother in consenting to the marriage that she had arranged for him. His brother's marriage would eventually prove as painful for Lu Hsün as would his own, for Tso-jen's wife, Habuto Nobuko, would be partly responsible for the quarrels that caused the brothers to break up the common household that they shared in Peking between 1919 and 1923. If Lu Hsün's second wife, Hsü Kuang-p'ing, is to be believed (she is by no means a disinterested bystander), Lu Hsün said to his brother just before finally moving out in 1923, "You may say that I am wrong in several things, but when we were in Japan, because . . . you didn't have enough, I went home and took a job so that I could help you out." To which Tso-jen's cold reply was: "What's past, is past."[71]

When Lu Hsün first came to Japan he was generally committed to a career in science and, specifically from 1904 to 1906, in medicine. Yet most of his education up to that point had prepared him to read the classics and to compose prose and poetry—an education which, during the traditional period, held out the promise of a career as a scholar-official. That kind of career, however, had been threatened by the introduction of Western learning and the ever increasing need for specialists in the more

70. YHC, p. 31. The head of the school was Shen Heng-shan, a Chekiang landsmann (LHKC, p. 185), and many of the teaching positions were filled from the ranks of Chekiang students who had studied in Japan (HHL, p. 230), a large number of whom considered themselves students of still another Chekiang landsmann, Chang T'ai-yen (HHL, p. 217). After the revolution some of the Chekiang faculty followed Shen into the newly organized Chekiang Department of Education, while others—Lu Hsün among them—followed landsmann Ts'ai Yuan-p'ei into the national Ministry of Education.
71. Hsü Kuang-p'ing, Lu Hsün hui-yi-lu [Remembrances of Lu Hsün] (Peking, 1962;, p. 58; hereafter cited as HYL.

practical fields. When Lu Hsün went to Nanking in 1898 he was a young man educated for a position (that of the traditional scholar-official) that was doomed by the abolition of the examination system in 1905. While in Nanking, he attended the Naval Academy and the School of Mines and Railroads where the faculty and administration were, like Lu Hsün himself, steeped in the classical tradition of the humanities. They were, of course, only newly and imperfectly familiar with the applied sciences of the West which their schools were established to teach. And, given Lu Hsün's temperament, his education, even his extracurricular interests (novels, illustrations, sketches, and religious festivals), he might well have preferred a career in the humanities to one in the sciences had the choice been his to make with complete freedom.

In Japan, during the time in which he was preparing for a scientific career, he became increasingly aware of the possibility of a new vocation—that of creative writer and translator. It was a vocation that had attracted no small number of able people in the Japanese society in which he lived, a vocation that existed as an honored one in a number of the foreign cultures that were opened by his Japanese and German passkeys, and a vocation that had in effect been legitimized in China by Liang Ch'i-ch'ao's essay on the place of fiction in society and by the journalistic activities of patriotic men like Liang and Chang T'ai-yen. It was legitimized, too, by a long line of international heroes whom Lu Hsün identified as Mara poets. It was indeed a high calling, and it is not surprising that he was attracted to it. It was a vocation that, in his view, could help his fellow countrymen to see beyond the walls of China (translation) and beneath the surface of reality (creative writing). It was a vocation that he would eventually use to help push over a wobbling cart.

8

FIRST ATTEMPT AT THE SHORT STORY

The China that Lu Hsün returned to in 1909 was ripe ground for political revolutionaries who tended to think their way through difficult questions with the aid of a rifle, but it was not a good place for cultural ones with a bent for pondering questions of values over the soft tips of their writing brushes. Lu Hsün would spend the next few years in his native Chekiang Province; he would teach; he would take part in school administration; and he would cheer the arrival of the Republican Revolution in 1911. Around the time of the revolution he would write his first short story (in classical Chinese), leave it untitled, and toss it carelessly aside. A year or so later his brother Tso-jen would supply it with a title, "Remembrances of the Past (*Huai-chiu*)," and submit it to the *Short Story Magazine* (*Hsiao-shuo yüeh-pao*), where it would be published in 1913.[1]

Immediately upon his return from Japan, Lu Hsün proceeded to Hangchow to take up duties as a teacher of chemistry and physiology in the Chekiang Normal School. Like many other Chinese schools in that day, Chekiang Normal employed a number of Japanese instructors. In preparing lecture notes (copies were hectographed and given to students to help them follow the lectures) and in conducting classes, the Japanese often required the services of translators, who for the most part were Chinese

---

1. *HSJW*, p. 139. This magazine, a publication of the Commercial Press, Shanghai printed translations and original stories (in classical Chinese) between 1910 and 1920; from 1921 until its demise in 1932 (the result of a Japanese bombing) it was the leading Shanghai journal of the colloquial-language movement. Fairbank and Liu, *Modern China*, pp. 485-86.

students fresh back from Japan. This function Lu Hsün performed with characteristic competence: his translations (into classical Chinese) of the lecture notes for the biology and botany courses were much praised by the students.[2]

While teaching physiology, in response to student demand he added material on the reproductive system. In the rather staid Confucian China of his day, this was unprecedented. Hence, he set down one condition before beginning his lectures: no one would be permitted to laugh. Lu Hsün explained to a colleague that laughter would throw into chaos the serious classroom atmosphere requisite to giving such lectures. This part of the course was so well received that students from other classes asked for hectographed copies of his lecture notes. He told them that they were welcome to the notes, but he was afraid that they might not understand them: his notes were written in a very abbreviated and obscure style of classical Chinese in which such words as *vagina*, *penis*, and *semen* were expressed by characters whose significance would be understood only by those well versed in classical philology.[3]

Hsia Mien-tsun, another teacher at Hangchow, remembered him as a rather serious individual who smoked cigarettes heavily and read late into the night, and whose usual form of humor among colleagues consisted of satirically aping the manners of the contemporary official world.[4] According to Hsü Shou-shang, Lu Hsün was no more interested in sight-seeing at Hangchow than he had been in Japan. He visited the famous West Lake but once, and only because Hsü dragged him to it.[5] To be sure, he often did take students on trips into the countryside; the main purpose, however, was not sight-seeing but the collection of plant specimens. In Tokyo an excursion was worthwhile if it enabled you to buy a used book along the way; in Hangchow, if you could gather specimens. By precept and example, Lu Hsün encouraged students to collect, classify, and preserve plants. Whereas various kinds of costly equipment were necessary for other scientific endeavors,

---

2. *KMCLH*, p. 65.
3. Hsü Shou-shang et al., *Tso-chia t'an Lu Hsün* [Writers talk about Lu Hsün] (Hong Kong, 1956), p. 94; hereafter cited as *TCLH*.
4. Ibid., p. 95.
5. *YHC*, p. 33.

plant collecting provided students with an inexpensive and convenient way of making fresh contributions to knowledge.[6] On one occasion he made an unexpected trip down to Shaohsing to supervise burial arrangements for his Grandmother Chiang,[7] a trip that would later appear in fictionalized form at the beginning of a short story, "The Isolate (*Ku-tu-che*)." He was apparently much moved by the death of this lonely old woman, whose lack of prestige in the Chou family t'aimen was, as we have seen, partly the result of Grandfather Chou's having abandoned her there in favor of the sweeter meats to be found in Peking.[8]

At the beginning of the next school year, in the fall of 1910, Lu Hsün accepted a job as teacher and dean of studies in the high school at Shaohsing. The principal, Ch'en Tzu-ying, was a fellow Shaohsinger and friend of his student days in Japan; Ch'en had been one of the group that briefly studied Russian with Maria Konde. It is likely that the students at the high school romantically looked upon Ch'en and Lu Hsün as potential revolutionaries, though neither had ever openly said anything seditious. The students knew that they had been on friendly terms with revolutionaries in Tokyo, and probably considered it a forgivable bit of expediency when the two led them in paying respects to the ten-thousand-year tablet on Confucius's birthday.[9] Their esteem for Lu Hsün did drop suddenly, however, when he refused them permission to cut off their queues. Knowing that he had lopped off his own during his student days in Japan, they denounced him as inconsistent.[10] (He had cut off his queue about February 1903 and on a visit to Shaohsing in the fall of that year had sported an artificial one bought in Shanghai.) For his part, Lu Hsün seems to have felt that cutting off their queues would have pointlessly exposed the students to great danger; after all, the Manchus were still in power, and the place where Ch'iu Chin had met her death a few years earlier was there as a reminder, not far from the school.[11] The Manchus might make allowance for Lu Hsün's

---

6. *LHSC*, pp. 33-34.
7. *LHKC*, p. 43.
8. *HSJW*, pp. 185-89.
9. *LHC*, p. 73.
10. *KMCLH*, pp. 69-79.
11. *LHC*, p. 74. For more on Lu Hsün's own problems with the queue see *HSJW*, pp. 30-34.

pigtail-less state in view of his long sojourn in Japan. The cutting off of their queues by students who had never been abroad would have constituted an open declaration of revolutionary intent.

Apart from teaching, he occupied himself by collecting writings dealing with the history of Shaohsing, a labor that led eventually to the publication (1915) of *A Miscellaneous Collection of Traditions Related to the K'uai-chi District* (*K'uai-chi-chün ku-shih tsa-chi*).[12] He also gathered together and edited a number of pre-T'ang tales that were published (1912) in a volume titled *Fishing up Some Old Stories* (*Ku hsiao-shuo kou-ch'en*).[13] Since he was living at the family t'aimen in Tung Ch'ang Lane during this time, one cannot but wonder what was his relationship with his wife—a wife whom he would refrain from mentioning in his published writings, who was never to bear him children, and to whom he would later refer as "a gift from mother."[14] At the end of the summer of 1911 he quit his job at the high school, tried briefly to secure a position with a publishing house, and then decided to try his hand at running a newspaper.[15]

All of these plans were interrupted by the outbreak of the Republican Revolution in October. When news arrived in Shaohsing that the Manchu garrison troops in Hangchow had surrendered their weapons to the revolutionaries, a large meeting of townspeople was held, to determine what course of action to take. Lu Hsün was chosen chairman, an indication of his new prestige in Shaohsing as a teacher and returned student. He immediately suggested organizing a group of speakers who would circulate through the city and the suburbs, lecturing on the significance of the revolution and creating a climate of opinion favorable to it among the people.[16]

12. The collection was published under Tso-jen's name, though Tso-jen makes it clear that Lu Hsün did most of the work. Schultz, "Lu Hsün: The Creative Years," p. 146.

13. The *Miscellaneous Collection* and *Fishing up Some Old Stories* comprise vol. 8 of the twenty-volume *Lu Hsün ch'üan-chi* (Complete works of Lu Hsün), published in Shanghai in 1938 by a committee set up for that purpose; this edition is hereafter cited as *HCC-20*. Lu Hsün's compilations of old Chinese works are not included in *LHCC*, which is limited to creative works, essays, critiques, literary history, and letters; the 1938 edition includes these compilations and Lu Hsün's translations as well.

14. *LHPC*, p. 299.

15. *LHNP*, p. 33.

16. *LHSC*, p. 14.

As the revolutionaries came closer, things became increasingly unsettled: merchants boarded up their stores, refugees began to appear on the streets, and the city edged toward panic. Upon learning that this cloud of fear had been generated by a rumor of the imminent arrival of a remnant of the defeated Manchu garrison forces, Lu Hsün advised some concerned high school students to form a propaganda team and go out on the streets to calm the people. His advice was taken. Handbills were run off assuring the populace that the defeated-remnant rumor was groundless and reporting on the progress of the revolution to date. Lu Hsün went out with the young people and helped to distribute the information. In their attempts to calm the people, Lu Hsün and the students were quite effective—apparently "cultural" revolutionaries still had their uses.[17] The confused situation in Shaohsing at this time is reflected in "Remembrances of the Past."

Hard upon the rumor that Manchu troops were approaching, word came that Wang Chin-fa and his soldiers would soon arrive.[18] Lu Hsün and a group of students went out the west gate in high spirits that very night and prepared to greet the revolutionary forces. They waited long, but in vain. Little daunted, they went out again the next night (this time through the east gate) and before long Wang Chin-fa's forces arrived by boat.[19] The streets of Shaohsing were crowded with people of all ages and from every walk of life, carrying torches and lanterns. Standing on the street near a Christian church there was even a missionary with a white flag on which were written the two Chinese characters for "Welcome!" Despite their indifferent grooming, the troops were well ordered. They marched through the streets at a brisk and disciplined pace to the quarters that had been made ready for them. Soon after they had gone inside, people came bearing gifts of meat and drink in what was apparently a genuine atmosphere of enthusiasm.[20] Be that as it may, the tone of Lu Hsün's first short story would lead one to believe that he, at least, suspected that any armed group of invaders would have been feasted with similar cheer and good fellowship.

Wang Chin-fa was a native of Chekiang and in his early days had been a bandit pure and simple. Later he and the two secret

17. Ibid., pp. 15-16.
18. *KMCLH*, p. 94.
19. *LHSC*, pp. 16-17.
20. Ibid., p. 18.

societies he headed were brought into the ranks of the Restoration Society by the same T'ao Ch'eng-chang whom Lu Hsün had known in Tokyo. When the revolution came, Wang occupied Shaohsing, announced the establishment of a revolutionary government, and proclaimed himself *tutu* (civil and military commander).[21] A few days after his arrival, Wang called a mass meeting in order to assure the people that he would maintain order and to show them that he would not act arbitrarily without their advice. At this meeting Lu Hsün was appointed principal of the normal school under the new government.[22] It became quickly apparent, however, that the new regime was not really interested in doing much of anything except collecting taxes. People began to grumble. Some students suggested starting a newspaper to bring the pressure of public opinion to bear on Wang and his entourage. Lu Hsün and Ch'en Tzu-ying would serve as sponsors of the new periodical, along with Sun Te-ch'ing, an enlightened Shaohsing landlord who had been one of the earliest supporters of the anti-Manchu cause. The paper soon began to denounce Wang, who responded by sending the students a "gift" of 500 dollars. With a bit of clumsy sophistry as crutch, the students limped their way through an argument in favor of accepting the money as a contribution from a shareholder. Since Wang, by virtue of his generous donation, became a shareholder in their paper, the students felt that they were free, if not morally bound, to denounce his wrong-doings. Lu Hsün pointed out, to no avail, that the 500 dollars had been given for something far different from "shares." At this juncture, his old friend Hsü Shou-shang provided an escape from the sticky state of affairs. Hsü now had a position with the newly established Ministry of Education. Would Lu Hsün come to Nanking to accept a job in the new ministry, a job which Hsü had arranged with their *landsmann*, the new minister, Ts'ai Yüan-p'ei? Yes, he would. Thus he escaped from Shaohsing once more. A few weeks after he left, soldiers smashed up the newspaper office and Sun Te-ch'ing received a superficial bayonet wound. It was against this chaotic background of rumors and revolutionaries in late 1911 that Lu Hsün wrote his first short story and gave us his first fictional vision of reality.[23]

21. *LHCC*, II, 454, n. 6.
22. *LHSC*, p. 19.
23. *SWLH*, I, 416-18; *LHCC*, II, 282-84; *HSJW*, pp. 231-33.

Like many of Lu Hsün's stories, "Remembrances of the Past (*Huai-chiu*)," is strongly marked by visual qualities. It is as though Lu Hsün had walked about Shaohsing on the eve of the Republican Revolution taking mental pictures that he would later develop for his first story, mental pictures that he would juxtapose and contrast with images brought up from the depths of childhood memories. Working back from his stories to the mind of the man who created them, one has the strong feeling that Lu Hsün, more than most, created with the mind's eye. He uses words to conjure up images in the mind of the reader; however, he uses them sparingly and with design.

I rigorously avoided that superfluous verbiage sometimes associated with writing; so long as I felt that I had made my meaning clear, I preferred to do without frills. In the traditional Chinese theater there is no scenery and the New Year's cards sold to amuse children never show more than a few of the most important characters (although by now most such cards do have scenery). I was firmly convinced that this method was suited to my purposes too; therefore I never went out of my way to describe scenery and never allowed the dialogue to go on to any great length either.[24]

In "The Power of Mara Poetry" Lu Hsün speaks of literature as something that takes life and puts it directly into the hands of the reader. One might argue that any point made about the "imagistic qualities" of a writer's work is superfluous, for how could anyone write a story without in some way or other "imagining" the scenes he described, projecting them, so to speak, on his mind's eye? This objection is not without weight; however, what is being stressed here is that the frequency with which Lu Hsün's prose conjures up images in the mind's eye of the reader is unusual, and, no doubt, reflects a similar intensity of image-making in the mind's eye of Lu Hsün as he wrote that prose.[25]

24. From "How I Came to Write Stories (*Wo tsemma tso-ch'i hsiao-shuo lai*)." *LHCC*, IV, 393; *SWLH*, III, 230. My translation.
25. Perhaps those who use the eye more than the ear are creators; those who use the ear more than the eye, tellers of the tale. Lu Hsün creates a new view of China and shares it with his countrymen and the world at large through his stories. Lao She (1899-1966; best known to Western readers for his novel *Rickshaw Boy*), despite efforts to serve purposes higher than entertainment, remains a teller of the tale—and an unusually gifted one. He stands close to the traditional teashop storyteller, while Lu Hsün is a near cousin to the intellectual novelist of the West.

It is significant that Lu Hsün tended to remember the decisive events of his own life in imagistic form: he left Sendai because of a lantern slide showing apathetic peasants gathered about a Chinese who was about to be executed by Japanese troops as a Russian spy. Lu Hsün would use the main elements of that image in story after story: the oppressor, weapon in hand; the oppressed, woodenly waiting to be executed; and most important of all, the cold, indifferent masses of China standing almost catatonically aside—uninvolved, unsympathetic, and unloving.

In order to suggest something of the imagistic, almost theatrical, quality typical of so many of Lu Hsün's stories, it seems fitting to analyze his first work in this genre, "Rememberances of the Past," as thought it were a play. Since the story is presented as a reminiscence, the narrator stands as if on the apron of the stage, apart from the events which he is describing from memory. The story is set in the corner of a t'aimen in southeastern China. Stage right, we see part of the study; a door leads out into the yard. The main gate and part of the t'aimen's surrounding wall divide stage right from stage left, where we see a large, leafy tung tree with a few three-legged stools on the patch of ground shaded by its heavy foliage. On the extreme left we see a road that wanders off in the direction of upstage center, where it fades away into a painted continuation on a scrim. Whenever refugees or revolutionaries are being discussed, we hear crowd murmurs from behind this scrim.

Selected primarily to lend symbolic emphasis to the story, scenery and props are kept to a minimum. The plot itself unfolds almost as a morality play depicting the struggle between the forces of darkness and light. On the side of darkness there is the restrictive, pedantic atmosphere of the study; it is a walled room within a walled compound and symbolizes the alienation of traditional scholarship from both nature and society. Hence the lighting stage right is subdued; the props are books, benches, a thick-lensed pair of eyeglasses, and a pointer for disciplining recalcitrant students. On the side of light there is, stage left, the brightly lit area under the tung tree outside the gate; the props associated with this area are convivial stools on which to sit and swap tales, a bucket of water to damp down the dusty summer earth, and a long bamboo pipe for smoking.

Scene One: The curtain rises somewhat sluggishly. We see an old servant with a bucket of water wetting down the ground under a large tung tree. Every so often a refugee appears on the road only to disappear again; every now and then too, one is conscious of murmurs from behind the scrim. A boy of nine is seated at his desk in the study, racking his brains for the answer to some difficult question. His teacher, a bald-headed old man wearing thick glasses, paces back and forth, holding the book that he is reading so close to his face that his nose brushes against the page.

A spotlight now comes up on the narrator, a man in his thirties who stands on a small podium on the downstage right apron. He is short and wiry; he sports a small moustache. Reading from the diary on the lectern before him, he describes a typical day out of his nine-year-old boyhood, a day that now unfolds on stage. He begins by contrasting the heavy pedantic mists of the study with the clear air of freedom under the tung tree just outside the gate. The lights dim out as he tells of his joy in escaping from the study and expresses something of his remembered dislike for his old teacher.

Scene Two: The lights come up slowly on another day. The teacher, "Master Baldy" to his student, is explaining a passage from the *Analects* of Confucius. The bored lad squirms in his seat as the old man paces about. The heavy calm of the study is suddenly disturbed by the arrival of a middle-aged man in a long blue gown who bears exciting news: "The Long Hairs are coming!" The narrator identifies him as a rich neighbor, Chin Yao-tsung, a rather hapless fellow who has, since youth, been spoiled into a state of almost total incompetency by wealthy and doting parents. Nobody respects Yao-tsung except Master Baldy, and his regard, the narrator informs us, proceeds from very questionable grounds.

The Long Hairs were the Taiping rebels who had flooded through the area some three decades previously. It is apparent that Yao-tsung must have gotten things garbled; there simply could not be any Long Hairs around anymore. And yet rumors of rebellion are not to be treated lightly, for disturbingly often there is some substance to them. Master Baldy and Yao-tsung begin discussing what to do if the rebels, whatever they may be, do arrive. As the two lay their plans, it becomes increasingly obvious that they are equally unconcerned with whatever loyalty they may owe the established government, on the one hand, and with the politics of the rebel group that would replace that government, on the other. Their aim is not mere survival, but, rather, comfortable survival. Yao-tsung is prepared to ingratiate himself with the outlaws by giving them a welcome party. The learned Master Baldy approves, but sagely advises his old friend to at least take the precaution of having the festive arrangements made in the name of his underlings. Baldy points out that it would be less than prudent for Yao-tsung to have his own name associated with rebels who, after all, had not yet succeeded. The narrator, speaking as an adult, notes that Yao-tsung's plan of feasting the invaders was not his own invention, but rather a time-honored and tested stratagem taken from the very bedrock of experience of the scholar-official establishment. Yao-tsung exits to complete preparations for the feast. Thereupon Master Baldy dismisses class and exits through a door to the left into the interior of the house. The boy bounds exuberantly out to the yard.

Scene Three: The boy gambols about under the tung tree, then runs upstage left and begins poking at an ant hill with a long stick as Master Baldy reappears in the study, a bundle of clothes under his arm. With his free arm, the old man gathers up a few loose books, crosses through the yard, goes out the main gate, and, without a word, disappears down the road, making his exit downstage left. A few peasants appear briefly on the road, and the level of confused murmurs from behind the scrim rises. The boy stands and gazes off upstage into the distance as the old servant who damped down the earth in Scene One comes out through the gate and crosses to him. As Old Wang, for such is the servant's name, places a reassuring arm around the lad's shoulder, Amah Li, a woman in her fifties, comes running in from stage left. She begins prattling to Old Wang about a swarm of concubines that she has just seen over at the Chin family compound. The assiduous way in which she uses a part of her sleeve to rub a spot of dirt off the boy's forehead as she continues to chatter on about the Chin women makes it apparent that she is his amah. Finally, the boy pulls himself free and resumes his play at the ant hill. Amah Li goes on about the various kinds of cosmetics the concubines were packing in preparation for their flight; suddenly she remembers that it is about time to set out the supper and goes chattering her way into the house, followed by Old Wang. The boy continues poking at the ants as the stage darkens. After a few moments, Amah Li reappears at the door and calls him to his supper. The lights dim out.

Scene Four: The lights come up very slightly, leaving the stage quite dim. By the faint light of the night sky we see Old Wang seated on a stool beneath the tung tree, enjoying an evening pipe—a pipe whose glow on the darkened stage suggests the warm nature of the man himself. The boy is seated on a stool next to him. Old Wang has his arm around the boy's shoulder. Amah Li is seated on a third stool, on the other side of Old Wang. A group of a dozen or so local people form a semicircle about the trio; thoroughly bewildered about what is going on, they have come in hopes of picking up some news. There are more refugees on the road now, and the murmurs from behind the scrim have picked up in intensity too. Old Wang's dignified and composed demeanor provides the group with a center of stability. Between puffs on his long bamboo pipe he reminisces about the days when the long-haired Taiping rebels actually did invade the area several decades previously. During a long and rich life the old man has obviously acquired all the acting talents of a professional storyteller and manages to hold his audience so spellbound in the re-created world of that long-past rebellion that all thoughts of present danger are dispersed into the starry night. Master Baldy enters from stage left and goes through the gate into the house. His arrival jolts the group temporarily back to the present, but Old Wang dismisses its importance by telling them in knowing tones that it's too early for any news yet. He resumes his narration as Master Baldy comes back out and begins pacing back and forth before the gate.

The very anticlimactic climax of this scene, and of the story itself, occurs when Yao-tsung arrives with the news that the group reported heading in the direction of their town does not consist of rebels after all, but is only a motley collection of famine refugees. Reassured, the crowd now disperses as the local people head toward their homes in a rather lighthearted mood. Master Baldy and Yao-tsung exit, leaving Old Wang, Amah Li, and the boy still seated under the tung tree. The murmurs from behind the scrim gradually fade away.

Scene Five: Gathered about Old Wang's pipe, the three hold their relative positions in silence for a moment or so. Then in tones blended of nostalgia and sadness Old Wang says: "Eh, how many times have I heard people say, 'The Long Hairs are coming'? When the Long Hairs really did come, it was terrifying. But what did it amount to after all?"

The boy asks if Wang himself was ever a Long Hair, as the narrator explains from behind his podium downstage right:

I thought that if the Long Hairs came, then surely Baldy would have to go. In that case, the Long Hairs must be good people. Since Old Wang was so good to me, I reasoned, he must have been a Long Hair once himself.

No. Disappointingly, Wang was never one of them. He takes up again the thread of his interrupted narrative of those exciting and terrible days when the Long Hairs really *had* come. Soon the boy is totally enthralled by the old storyteller's magic. Just as Wang gets to the most exciting part, it begins to rain and Amah Li forces her young charge to go to bed. They all exit into the house.

Scene Six: The empty stage is still darker than in the previous scenes. The sound of rain increases. Voices are heard from offstage.

"Don't hit me, Master Baldy, I promise that I'll prepare my lesson next time . . ."

"Hey, what's going on in here? Are you dreaming? With all that shouting of yours you scared me right out of my *own* nightmare. What are you dreaming about?"

"Oh, it was just a dream. It didn't really happen. Amah Li, what were you dreaming about?"

"I was dreaming about the Long Hairs. I'll tell you about it tomorrow. It's almost midnight. Go to sleep now, go to sleep."

The lights fade as the final curtain falls.

Lest the foregoing analysis of "Remembrances of the Past" in theatrical terms should be confusing, the reader will perhaps find it useful to read my translation of the story (in the Appendix) before going on. At the risk of confusion, in any case, let us continue the theatrical analogy and examine the cast of the story. In this, Lu Hsün's earliest fictional analysis of Chinese society, what kinds of people do we find? Who are these people who inhabit his vision of traditional society? How does he divide people? Let us begin with Master Baldy. He is completely alienated from nature: we see him primarily in contact with books. The adult narrator remembers him as "so near-sighted that his lips almost touched the book, as though he were about to gnaw a few pieces out of it." Master Baldy's life was wholly devoted to books, and he delighted in them. "When he had been explicating the text for a long time, Baldy would wobble his knees in rhythm with the cadences of the text and nod his head in great sweeps, apparently enjoying himself immensely. I, on the other hand, was getting very bored." The closest that Baldy ever comes to nature in the course of the story is when he is concerned with the tonality of words like "flower" and "grass" for the purposes of poetic composition. One can imagine that for Baldy flowers exist primarily because the mythical creator of the Chinese written language, Ts'ang Chieh, once invented an ideograph to represent them. Master Baldy is the bearer of traditional culture—more specifically, traditional culture as contained in books. It is this "book culture" that Lu Hsün will spend most of his life attacking. As teacher, it is Baldy who will socialize—that is, poison—the younger generation through the imposition of ossified and unexplained rules.

Though it is apparent that Chin Yao-tsung is an utter lout with nothing to recommend him but his wealth, Master Baldy much admires him. We discover that in order to preserve his own position, Yao-tsung is fully prepared to toady to the rebels. Moreover, Master Baldy heartily approves of his friend's conduct; however, he advises him not to go about it too openly and hints at the dire punishment that Yao-tsung might expect from loyalist hands if the rebellion should fail. Thus, the crowning achievement of Master Baldy's "learning" is not to be found in his explication of the text of the *Analects*, but rather in the prudent advice that he gives Yao-tsung. The adult narrator comments:

From the time when P'an Ku created the universe on down through generation after generation of fighting and killing, through alternations of peace and war, through the waxing and waning of dynasties, Master Baldy's forbears had never laid down their lives to preserve a government, nor had they lost their lives by joining rebel causes. . . . If one were to explain Baldy's talent for survival on the basis of the modern theory of evolution, then one might attribute his talent to racial heredity. But in retrospect, as I see it today, his peculiar talent must have been gained entirely from books. Otherwise, how could you have explained the fact that neither Old Wang, Amah Li, nor myself had inherited this kind of talent?

Here, of course, we have the very core of Lu Hsün's message: what is wrong with China is embodied in the lackluster, hypocritical, opportunistic traditions of the establishment, traditions that have for untold centuries been the peculiar preserve of would-be-scholar-officials like Master Baldy. Both Master Baldy and his friend Yao-tsung are clearly in the camp of the oppressors; one has power and the other provides that power with ideological support. Baldy and Yao-tsung are the Japanese officer, sword in hand, of that lantern slide that so impressed Lu Hsün at Sendai, an image that precipitated his decision to embark on a literary career. Goodness lies with those who by virtue of age (the boy) or class (Amah Li and Old Wang) have only been imperfectly steeped in those traditions—traditions whose continuance is assured by the scholars and whose function is to justify the life-styles of the rich. Evil, then, lies within this book-tradition; it is not a given racial characteristic.

Baldy is cold and unfeeling; the old servant is warm and emotional. An uneducated man in his seventies, Wang is wise in the ways of the world and the heart. He is the only person on-stage for whom the boy seems to feel any genuine affection. He is also the only perpetually calm person on-stage and to that extent represents a kind of resigned stability and continuity (he is not a rebel). The Long Hairs touched his life, but they (like the Republican revolutionaries, Lu Hsün seems to suggest) did not really change anything. He would welcome something different, but seems convinced that it will not come: "Eh, how many times have I heard people say, 'The Long Hairs are coming'? When the Long Hairs really did come, it was terrifying. But what did it amount to, after all?"

The character of Amah Li, a woman in her late fifties, is not so well developed as that of Old Wang and serves primarily as a foil for his storytelling. The boy apparently approves of her, but does not have the same warmth of feeling for her that he does for Wang. Amah Li, Wang, and the boy are all, either by virtue of age or social class, in the camp of the oppressed; they are the kneeling prisoner in the lantern slide. The third element of that slide is also on-stage—the passive, spiritless masses. At Sendai they were the apathetic onlookers; here they are the local people gathered about Old Wang waiting for news as he recreates the harrowing days of the Taiping rebels. Lu Hsün comments most scoringly on their ignorance when Yao-tsung comes with the news that the imagined rebels are, after all, only refugees.

"Ha-ha! So it's only refugees! Ah . . ." Baldy laughed as though he were making fun of his own previous stupidity in having gotten so excited. He began to laugh at the idea of "refugees," for that was not frightening at all. The crowd of local people that had gathered began to laugh too; it wasn't that they had understood what was going on, but rather that, having seen an important person like Baldy laugh, they felt that it was their place to join in.

It is noteworthy that none of the roles onstage is highly individualized. Although Master Baldy and Yao-tsung are presented to the audience more vividly than the other characters, even they do not emerge as individuals. What Lu Hsün is about is not a study of separate characters but an analysis of groups. The division of the cast of "Remembrances of the Past" into two camps, oppressor and oppressed, bears the characteristic stamp of his later works; similarly, the rhetoric of the story, despite its being in classical Chinese, is distinctively that of the same Lu Hsün who would become famous with his colloquial-language short stories a decade later during the May Fourth movement.

Although the ancient warehouses of classical Chinese diction are sumptuously stocked with four-character clichés to ease the task of writers who have more memory than creativity, in "Remembrances of the Past" Lu Hsün avoids them. Given his excellent classical grounding, there can be little doubt that he was thoroughly familiar with the contents of such linguistic repositories, so that he would have known exactly where to go for, say, fifty ready-made expressions describing a tung tree. That he did not do so is an indication of his seriousness as well as his creativity. Here, as in his later works, he is concerned above all with content; it, and it alone, determines form. The style is economical, almost Spartan. Lu Hsün was a small and bony man, and readers of his colloquial short stories quickly discover that his sentences are as economically compact as was the man. His style in classical Chinese is even more lean and skeletal. The editor of the *Short Story Magazine* probably had this characteristic in mind when he said in criticism of "Remembrances of the Past":

When a writer has a solid subject, he can bring all of his powers into play; but if his topic is empty to begin with, he cannot—thus the importance of starting out on the right foot. . . . And yet I have noticed that when young people have just barely begun to learn how to write, they often turn immediately to an emphasis on style. The result is that their compositions have nothing to recommend them, and are often no more than mere showcases of rhetorical devices. The kind of writing exemplified in this story is just the thing for correcting that kind of defect.[26]

One can well imagine that the editor had in mind that style of Chinese which delights in piling up four-character clichés and antithetical couplets in empty displays of virtuosity. From this point of view, Lu Hsün's classical diction is indeed fresh and lively; the dominance of content over form is perhaps the distinguishing characteristic of the story.

Sarcasm plays a prominent role in the diction of "Remembrances of the Past." It is a weapon Lu Hsün was to use against his enemies again and again in later works. Here in his first story he employs it in naming the characters: Yao-tsung, for instance, can be translated roughly as "a credit to his ancestors," and Yang-sheng (the given name of Master Baldy) connotes one who admires the longs after sagehood. Sarcastic, too, is the narrator's general tone of voice, especially when he is describing the oppressors of his childhood. Consider the following passage in which the narrator explains Master Baldy's odd affection for Yao-tsung.

And yet, much to the amazement of Old Wang and the others, Master Baldy was very partial to him. In the privacy of my own mind I, too, sought out the logic for this odd affection. I remembered that in the past Yao-tsung, having reached the ripe old age of twenty-one without having sired a son, had taken three pretty concubines into his household. Baldy

26. In a note appended to the story when it first appeared in print.

had also started mouthing the saying "There are three things that are unfilial and to lack posterity is the greatest of these" as if to justify Yao-tsung's conduct. The latter was so moved by this that he gave Baldy twenty-one pieces of gold so that he too could buy a secondary wife. Thus, I concluded that Baldy's reason for treating Yao-tsung with such unusual courtesy was that the latter had shown himself to be thoroughly filial.

In summing up the character of Master Baldy, the narrator says:

People used to say that my teacher, Master Baldy, was the wisest man in all Wu Town. They really had something there, for he could have lived in any age of chaos and come through it without a scratch. [And now he] was an honored teacher who expounded to mischievous students like myself on the wisdom of Confucius, a man who had been able at the age of seventy to follow all of his heart's desires without exceeding the proper bounds of morality.

Thus, though written in classical Chinese, the sarcastic tone of the story's diction is quite similar to that of Lu Hsün's later colloquial-language stories.

In an article devoted to this story, Jaroslav Průšek has pointed out that it is sharply distinguished from the traditional Chinese short story in its treatment of reality.[27] The pre-modern fiction (both that written in classical Chinese and, to a lesser extent, even that in the colloquial language) saw reality as a conglomeration of discrete events; such fiction was primarily concerned with repro-ducing this or that set of events because of the intrinsic interest of the events themselves. It was a conception of reality that was a correlate to the commentarial tradition on the classics. The same kind of passion for the concrete was also clearly reflected in traditional historiography, which valued compilation over inter-pretation. In traditional fiction, too, reality for the most part remained uninterpreted. The event chosen for fictionalization was not selected because it helped to reveal new conceptions or interpretations of reality, but rather because it was something to interest a reader by virtue of its historical significance, bizarreness, spiciness, or supernatural elements. Neither the writer nor the oral performer was expected to give an individual interpretation. Průšek has well said of the traditional storyteller: "His private feelings and views do not interest the listener, and insofar as he

27. "A Confrontation of Traditional Oriental Literature with Modern European Literature in the Context of the Chinese Literary Revolution," *Archiv Orientalni*, XXXII (1964), 365-75.

expresses any judgment, it is a judgment of a general character, a
kind of *consensus omnium,* and not a personal opinion."[28] "Remembrances of the Past" is clearly distinguished from the traditional tale on almost all of these counts. It does not present the
reader with a *consensus omnium,* but rather with the author's
highly individual point of view, and it does not take as its material
an event whose intrinsic interest is guaranteed. Further, it makes
no attempt to impress the reader by a display of virtuosity in the
classical language.

Though presented ostensibly as a reminiscence of childhood,
"Remembrances of the Past" is fiction. Chou Tso-jen assures us
that Master Baldy, for instance, does not represent any particular
person out of Lu Hsün's childhood, but is, rather, representative
of all scholars and teachers. Yao-tsung was modeled on a neighbor
of the t'aimen, but only in the most general way.[29] As for old
Wang, there was no gatekeeper at the New T'aimen, a compound
so rambling that there was no single main gate for anyone to keep.
However, old Wang's stories, Tso-jen notes, are based on fact:
many such tales were told around the t'aimen when Lu Hsün was a
child. As we have seen, after having completed the story, Lu Hsün
apparently had mixed feelings about it, or about the China of
which he had written, for he tossed it aside. It was Chou Tso-jen
who submitted it to the *Short Story Magazine* some two years
later. It was as yet untitled; Tso-jen selected "Remembrances of
the Past," though he felt that the title was somewhat confusing.[30]

Leaving aside the question of the appropriateness of the title, we
may note that the story divides nicely into two stories, and in
these two stories we can see reflected the difference between the
traditional storyteller (old Wang) and the modern one (Lu Hsün,
the narrator downstage right). Old Wang speaks only of the most
extraordinary events connected with the rebellion—a bloody head
thrown by the Long Hairs into the arms of an old female servant,
the spooky atmosphere of the mountain that Old Wang fled to
during the troubles, and the business of gathering up the loot
which the Long Hairs were forced to abandon in their pell-mell
retreat when the rebellion died out. That Lu Hsün thought of
Wang's account of those bloody days in terms of traditional
fiction is made clear at the end of the story. The night growing

28. "The Realistic and Lyric Elements in the Chinese Medieval Tale," ibid., p. 11.
29. *HSJW*, p. 14.
30. Ibid., pp. 140, 143.

late, everyone else having left, Wang continues to reminisce about the Long Hairs:

"Ho Kou-pao, His Third Excellency's father, got back to Ho market at just about that time. When he got home he spotted a Long Hair who had tied up his hair into a large pigtail and was lying in wait in one of the broken closets. Then he—"

"Oh, oh, it's raining. We'd better go in and go to bed." Amah Li, seeing the rain, had decided to go in.

"No, no! Let's stay here!" I didn't feel at all like going in. I felt much as I did when I reached the end of a chapter in a novel. Just when the hero was in the most precarious situation, the novelist would close the chapter with the words: "If you want to find out what happened after this, then turn to the next chapter." I would usually not only turn to the next chapter, but would read straight through the whole volume. Amah Li was apparently not like me in this respect.

Old Wang's account of those terrible days, an exciting and detailed recording of shocking and surprising events without any attempt at overall interpretation, is, in effect, a traditional tale. The narrator-author's reminiscences are qualitatively different— as different as is the modern, foreign-influenced story from the traditional one. The events that Lu Hsün remembers are not simply factual (Wang's are) but also highly interpreted: the establishment will make peace with any revolution and seek to emasculate it while at the same time preserving itself. Through his "reminiscences" Lu Hsün shares with his audience a unique point of view, one that was strongly influenced by what he had learned from beyond the walls of traditional China. Old Wang's point of view, on the other hand, represents the *consensus omnium*. Within the frame of a modern story written in pre-modern language Lu Hsün has inserted a traditional tale.

As a whole, then, the story is modern in its content rather than its language. We touch here on something important: the literary revolution that occurred in China after 1918 was—when it was successful—a revolution not so much in language (colloquial over classical) as in content (an interpretive and individual point of view over the *consensus omnium*). As Chou Tso-jen emphasized in the remarks quoted toward the end of the preceding chapter, Lu Hsün participated in the literary revolution primarily because he wanted to change the content of the tradition, the substitution of colloquial for classical being of only secondary importance to him. Lu Hsün was a modern in the classical as well as the modern idiom.

9

HIBERNATION, CREATIVITY, AND CHANGE

For seven years after "Remembrances of the Past" Lu Hsün did not again turn his hand to creative writing. This period coincided with the childhood of the new republic established in the wake of the revolution of 1911—a revolution that Lu Hsün welcomed with enthusiasm. His initial zest, however, was soon washed away by disappointment with the developments he saw locally in Shaohsing.

Nationally, the situation was no better. Sun Yat-sen and a host of young enthusiasts had helped bring down the Manchus. Sun and his followers had youth, drive, and ideas; on the other hand, Yüan Shih-k'ai—the long-time Chinese servant of the Manchus and architect of China's first modern army—had the troops. Hence the capital of the new republic was shifted north to Yüan's seat of power in Peking, and Sun, the republic's first president, yielded that office to him. Little more than a year later, militant opposition to Yüan developed and a punitive expedition was launched against him with the blessing of Sun Yat-sen. When this "second revolution" (1913) failed, Sun was forced to flee to Japan. Thereupon Yüan increasingly ignored the republican principles upon which the new state was supposed to be based and in 1915 went so far as to proclaim himself emperor of a new dynasty. Disaffection in the provinces and his own death in 1916 ended his ill-fated plans; but meanwhile central authority had been seriously weakened. Local warlords now openly and bloodily competed for hegemony.

Bitter disappointment with the revolution and its chaotic aftermath contributed largely to Lu Hsün's retirement from the literary life for which he had renounced his medical studies several years earlier, and led to his almost total withdrawal from, and silence about, the political events that were exploding all around him. This lasted until 1918, when he again began to express himself through creative writing. With regard to his apparent political apathy, one biographer has pointed out that during fourteen years in the Ministry of Education, from 1912 to 1926, Lu Hsün remained sufficiently aloof to serve under no fewer than twenty-seven ministers. Such abillity is stereotypically attributed to wily Shaohsing men (Shaohsing *shih-yeh*). Lu Hsün seems to have been rather sensitive about letting people know specifically where he was from, preferring to introduce himself as a native of Chekiang Province. Throughout his life, the majority of his meaningful associations would be with fellow Chekiang-ers. "Place" was important to him, both in his friendships and as the source material of his creative work.[1]

As we have seen, it was immediate disappointment with the local effects of the revolution in Shaohsing that disposed Lu Hsün to relinquish his post as principal of the normal school and go to Nanking to accept a position in the Ministry of Education, headed by Ts'ai Yüan-p'ei. Since his old friend Hsü Shou-shang had recommended him for the job, it was natural that on arriving in Nanking he should move in with Hsü. They lived together, worked together, and in their spare time went together to the library, where Lu Hsün copied out examples of traditional Chinese stories that he would later use in his own anthology of stories (1927-28) from the T'ang and Sung dynasties.[2] In a sense, during this period he seems to have forsaken the interests he had acquired during his Japanese sojourn and to have reverted to those of his youth—copying and collecting old books.

When the new government, in recognition of the realities of power, shifted its seat from Nanking to Peking, Lu Hsün followed

1. LHC-1, pp. 15-22. Tso-jen has suggested that this sensitivity to the reputation of Shaohsing may account for Lu Hsün's abbreviated references to it as S City in his writings. As an alternate reason, he has suggested that his brother may have objected to "Shaohsing" as the pretentious year-title of the defeated Southern Sung court. LHKC, pp. 212-13.
2. YHC, pp. 34-35. The *T'ang-Sung ch'uan-ch'i chi* [Anthology of T'ang and Sung stories] is in two parts, the first published in December 1927 and the second in February 1928.

and moved into the Shaohsing Hostel, a combination club and boardinghouse established by Shaohsing men living in the Peking area. Here there were things that would tend to bring images of his youth sharply into focus while blurring his more recent memories of Japan. The characters on the gate-plaque, for instance, had been drawn by one of his father's friends, and the majordomo was an old man who remembered his grandfather, for the old bear himself had lived in the hostel for a while during his Peking days.[3] Much to Lu Hsün's chagrin, the majordomo would reel off anecdotes about the carryings-on of Grandfather Chou and his concubines.[4]

From his first days in Peking, Lu Hsün used his spare money to buy books and his spare time to repair and collate them. At the end of 1912, looking back over his purchases for the year, he noted in his diary:

I see that from May until the end of the year, a space of eight months, I have spent one hundred and sixty dollars on books, and yet I still have not obtained any really fine editions! Here in the capital old books are treated as antiques so that only someone with great buying power can afford them. [Since the examination system has been abolished] there is no need for people to read [traditional] books nowadays anyway. And yet someone like me, a man who does not have the money to afford them in the first place, still spends over twenty dollars a month collecting old volumes to please himself! It is enough to make one laugh and sigh at the same time.[5]

Given though he was to pursuits that belonged more to the monarchial past than to the republican present, Lu Hsün did not in any sense become a traditionalist. Yet, he did not openly rebel against elements of traditional culture of which he disapproved; he employed avoidance. His attitude toward the spring and autumn sacrifices in the Shaohsing Hostel is a case in point. There was a hall in the hostel in which the ancestral tablets of former Shaohsing men were kept; the hall was locked save for two occasions each year, one in the spring and the other in autumn, when it was thrown open so that sacrifice might be offered to the spirits of the departed. On the two Sundays of the year on which this was done,

3. *LHKC*, p. 213.
4. Ibid., p. 226.
5. *Lu Hsün jih-chi* [The diaries of Lu Hsün] (2 vols.; Shanghai, 1951), I, 37; hereafter cited as *LHJC*.

Lu Hsün got up especially early and escaped to Liu-li Ch'ang (the bookstore section of Peking) where he could admire examples of calligraphy on rubbings made from stone tablets and chat a bit with the store managers while his Shaohsing peers were engaged in more pious pursuits back at the Hostel. He followed up his browsing with tea and a snack, not returning until long after the ceremonies had ended.[6]

Lu Hsün was, at first, genuinely interested in his work at the ministry. Ts'ai Yüan-p'ei had a bold plan to substitute "esthetic education" for religion in the cultural life of the new republic and had, in part, engaged Lu Hsün because of the latter's interest in art. He made Lu Hsün chief of the First Section of the Division of Social Education; this section was in charge of libraries, museums, and art galleries.[7] At this time Lu Hsün still entertained hopes for the success of the republic and addressed himself to his new job with enthusiasm, giving talks on esthetics in the course of a summer lecture series sponsored by the ministry in 1912, and writing a "Proposal for the Dissemination of the Arts (*Ni po-pu mei-shu yi-chien shu*)," which was published in an official monthly publication of the ministry in February 1913. The lectures were poorly attended, and he was disgusted when he learned in July that the Provisional Committee on Education had decided to scrap esthetic education.[8] The "Proposal" is interesting for the light it throws on Lu Hsün's views of esthetics at the time. Noting that many of his contemporaries would emphasize the pragmatic aspect of art to the exclusion of everything else, Lu Hsün says that the real purpose of art is to develop true beauty; whatever utilitarian value it may possess is an incidental result of this purpose. Conceding, however, that public opinion is against him on this point, he goes on to list three pragmatic virtues of the arts: they are an expression of culture; they may be used as a prop to morality; and they can serve to improve the economy (if Chinese

---

6. *LHKC*, p. 213. A writer at the turn of the century said of the Liu-li Ch'ang: "They deal especially in curios, calligraphy and paintings, paper, books, and stone rubbings so that this is a place indeed where the man of letters may look around and enjoy himself." *Annual Customs and Festivals in Peking*, trans. Derk Bodde (Peking, 1936), p. 17.
7. *YHC*, p. 38. Later he was also given the position of secretary-adviser.
8. Semanov, "Lu Hsün and His Predecessors," pp. 41-45.

products are more artistic, they will be more competitive in the world market). Lu Hsün proposes to disseminate art by establishing museums, theaters (separate ones for the new foreign-influenced or translated plays), and concert halls, and by organizing art exhibitions and sponsoring conferences on literature and art.[9]

Ts'ai Yüan-p'ei, at loggerheads with conservative elements in the new government, left his post in July 1912 (the month in which esthetic education was abolished) and went abroad to study in Germany and France. (In 1916 he would return to become chancellor of National Peking University, which he would remold into a great institution of higher learning.)[10] The ministry was then headed by a dismal series of far less inspiring men, and Lu Hsün's work there no longer greatly occupied either his emotions or his time. After the failure of the "second revolution" in 1913, most bright young men seem to have resigned themselves to the fact that the republic was no more than a deceptive facade: outside, everything looked new (men no longer wore pigtails and now there was a president instead of an emperor), but on the inside, distressingly, things remained pretty much the same. In 1914, Lu Hsün withdrew even farther from the life around him as he began his study of Buddhist works; it is likely, however, that he did so more from scholarly than from religious motivation. This interest was no doubt influenced by Chang T'ai-yen, with whom he had studied in Tokyo. Chang had seen Buddhism as China's only path to salvation; Lu Hsün, while fully acknowledging its wisdom, considered it just as moribund as Confucianism.[11]

Most government offices in Peking at this time were rather relaxed places where clerks sat about drinking tea, smoking, reading newspapers and chatting. Lu Hsün once told a friend that there was very little office work to be transacted at the ministry, and that he utilized his spare time for translating from foreign tongues or collating old Chinese texts.[12] (His friend, Hsü Shou-shang saw Lu Hsün's superiority to other people as lying precisely

9. *LHCC*, VII, 273-75.
10. Boorman, *Biographical Dictionary of Republican China*, III, 295-99, and *LHNP*, p. 36.
11. *YHC*, pp. 46-48; *HYL*, pp. 33-48.
12. *LHC-1*, p. 76. The atmosphere in such government offices is clearly reflected in Lu Hsün's story, "Brothers (Ti-hsiung)."

in the ability to put spare time to constructive uses.)[13] The even rhythm of his daily life as an official of the ministry does not seem to have been appreciably different from that of his student days in Tokyo. His "levee" would occur sometime before ten o'clock. He would wash his face, have tea, and head out to the ministry. In the evening, he would have supper at the Shaohsing Hostel, chat until nine or ten o'clock, and then retire to his room, where he would go about whatever current project he had on the fire, not going to bed until one or two in the morning.[14] Obviously such a routine would hardly have been possible if he had been obliged to appear at the ministry at exactly eight or eight-thirty every morning.

According to Tso-jen, it was in 1915 that Lu Hsün took up in earnest the collecting of rubbings of stone and bronze inscriptions, and the reason was not entirely one of interest. Tso-jen notes that it was around this time that President Yuan Shih-k'ai set about the business of overthrowing the republic and having himself declared emperor. Yuan's agents were everywhere on the lookout for anyone who might possibly oppose his imperial ambitions. Many of his potential opponents disappeared, never to be heard from again. People were scared. One good way to escape the attention of Yuan's agents was to be utterly immersed in this or that hobby or pet dissipation. For instance, given enough money, one could become a gambling man, or a collector—antiques, paintings, or concubines would do equally well. A passion for mah-jongg seems to have been a particularly convincing way of proving one's harmlessness. Having neither interest in nor money for most of these ways of indicating one's ineptitude for more serious pursuits, Lu Hsün decided that the least expensive thing he could do (in keeping with his own interests) was to copy and collect monument inscriptions. In this fashion, Tso-jen asserts, he hoped to convince Yuan's agents that he was a simple antiquarian, totally innocent of political ambition.[15]

Even in transcribing stone inscriptions, a traditional scholar's avocation par excellence, Lu Hsün revealed his individuality. Whereas most of the literary men of the past had confined their interest to the calligraphy on the monuments of antiquity, he took a special interest in the art work also to be found there. Whatever

13. *YHC*, pp. 38-39.
14. *LHKC*, p. 223.
15. Ibid., p. 216.

his initial motivations in collecting inscriptions may have been (Tso-jen's explanation does sound a bit exaggerated), he continued with his hobby long after Yüan Shih-k'ai's death and it was finally displaced only by his creative writing.[16] Similarly, his interest in book buying was not restricted to literature, but included much in the realm of graphic arts:

A quick survey of the books Lu Hsün purchased [in 1912-19], the titles having been meticulously recorded in the appendices of his diary and occasionally scattered throughout the text itself, reveals his deep interest in Chinese art history. Many titles treating the Chinese painting are included in these lists and they suggest the reason for his reputation as a competent, careful critic of Chinese pictorial art, as well as his influential sponsorship and thorough study of Chinese woodblock printing.[17]

The interest in woodblock printing is of a piece with his childhood fondness for illustrated novels, sketching, and the pageantry of folk opera, the enthusiasm of his middle years for stone rubbings, and the interest of his declining years in the promotion of woodblock art. It is both instructive and important to note that the elements common to all these various forms of artistic expression are directness and simplicity. He disliked frills. He once pointed out, in an essay written for the house organ of the Ministry of Education, that though a man might, with care, duplicate a mulberry leaf in jade, or inscribe a thousand characters on a peach pit, neither would qualify as art, no matter how much skill was required for their execution.[18] As we have seen in our examination of "Remembrances of the Past," Lu Hsün showed a marked preference for simplification, for focusing on the essential, and a marked aversion to needless elaboration. It was a stylistic conception that united his interests in folk drama, art, and writing. The body of short stories that he was to write between 1918 and 1925 would exhibit these same characteristics.

Whatever talents and interests may have been incubating during these years of hibernation at the Shaohsing Hostel in Peking, from the plateau of his creative period he would later look back on this time and see it as a vast plain of loneliness:

. . . I had to drive away this loneliness, for it was too painful. Thereupon I used every available method of anesthetizing my spirit so that I might

16. Ibid.
17. Schultz, "Lu Hsün: The Creative Years," p. 148.
18. *YHC*, p. 39.

sink into the [general stream of the] Chinese people and so that I might go back into antiquity.[19]

This is indeed a statement of despair. It was as though he felt that looking beyond the walls of China had been an exercise in futility and that it would be better to sink comfortably back into the mass of his own people; it was as though he felt that all his modernity was not only painful but also mistaken, and that it would be better to renounce it.

The even tenor of his lonely existence at the hostel was briefly interrupted in 1916 by an event that would provide material for his first colloquial-language short story, "Diary of a Madman." Toward the end of October a maternal cousin arrived in Peking from Taiyuan, capital of Shansi Province, where—naturally enough, for a Shaohsing man—he had been employed as a confidential secretary. It seems that in Taiyuan he was suddenly stricken by something resembling paranoia and became convinced that everyone with whom he had any contact was plotting to do him injury. At this point he fled to Peking, but to no avail, for he felt that his enemies were fast on his heels. At first he stayed in a hotel where he constantly changed rooms in order to avoid his imagined pursuers. Finally, Lu Hsün gave him refuge in the Shaohsing Hostel. One morning he came knocking in great excitement at Lu Hsün's window. Asked what was the matter, he replied: "I'm going to be dragged off and beheaded today!" He then penned a farewell letter and begged that it be delivered to his family. Lu Hsün, realizing there was nothing he could do for the cousin, packed him off to a hospital. On the way, the sight of policemen at their posts terrified the sick man. When after a week at the hospital he still showed no signs of improvement, Lu Hsün got someone to escort him to Shaohsing, where the family might properly look after him.[20] After this exciting interlude, Lu Hsün's life resumed the relaxed rhythm of a government official's existence.

The loneliness of which Lu Hsün complained must have been somewhat relieved when Tso-jen came to Peking in April of the following year. It will be remembered that it was Tso-jen's

19. Preface to *Call to Arms*, dated December 3, 1922 (*LHCC*, 1, 6; *SWLH*, 1, 4). My translation.
20. *LHC*, pp. 85-86; *LHJC*, I, 234-35; also *HSJW*, pp. 10-11.

marriage to Habuto Nobuko in 1909 that prompted Lu Hsün to return to China and take a job in order to help finance this new branch of the Chou family. Tso-jen returned to China two years later, but for family reasons did not immediately take a position. In 1912 he became an English teacher at the Fifth Provincial Middle School in Shaohsing, where he remained until 1917.[21] Lu Hsün's diaries reveal that during this period he sent money not only to Tso-jen in Shaohsing, but also to Nobuko's family in Tokyo. In April 1917, at Lu Hsün's urging, Tso-jen came to Peking. The year before, Ts'ai Yüan-p'ei—the first minister of education and Lu Hsün's respected *landsmann*—had become the chancellor of National Peking University. Lu Hsün had apparently decided to avail himself of the opportunity thus presented to recommend his brother to Ts'ai, and, after a short delay, Tso-jen was indeed appointed to the faculty, to teach Greek, Roman, and Modern European literature. With one brief interruption in 1927, he was to remain on the faculty of the university until 1937.[22] Upon arriving in Peking, Tso-jen moved into the Shaohsing Hostel with his brother and experienced an exciting first year in the capital. The surface of life in the hostel itself seems to have been smooth enough—a calm only occasionally rippled by such things as copulating cats on the roof. Whenever that happened, Tso-jen and Lu Hsün would carry out a table and set it under the eaves; while Tso-jen steadied the table, Lu Hsün would climb up, armed with a broom, and drive the lovers away.[23]

In May 1917 an epidemic of scarlet fever struck the capital. Tso-jen took ill, and Lu Hsün borrowed enough money to call in a German doctor. Much to his relief, the doctor assured him that his

21. Ernst Wolff, "Chou Tso-jen: Modern China's Pioneer of the Essay" (Ph.D. dissertation, University of Washington, 1966), p. 6. This was the same school in which Lu Hsün had served as dean of studies in 1910. *HSJW*, p. 36.

22. Wolff, "Chou Tso-jen," p. 6. Established in 1898, National Peking University was, in its early years, little more than a playboy club for the sons of the wealthy and was "popularly known as 'the Brothel Brigade' (*t'an-yen t'uan*), 'the Gambling Den' (*tu k'u*), and 'the Fountainhead of Ribaldry and Bawdiness.' " In 1916, however, Ts'ai Yuan-p'ei took over the chancellorship and soon transformed the university into China's leading institution of higher learning, a center of the New Culture movement, and a preserve of academic freedom. See Chow Tse-tsung, *The May Fourth Movement* (Stanford, California, 1967), pp. 47-51.

23. *LHKC*, p. 218.

brother had nothing more than a mild case of measles. This incident would later provide the background for Lu Hsün's short story "Brothers (*Ti-hsiung*)," a psychological analysis of the subconscious hostility that can exist even between the closest of relatives. Then in the summer of that year an event occurred which probably did more than anything else to shock Lu Hsün out of the realm of his more antiquarian pursuits and bring him back into meaningful contact with the contemporary world.

On the first of July the servant who brought the morning basin of water for washing also brought the startling news that the imperial colors were once again flying in the capital.[24] In the course of one of the endless contests for power that wracked the young republic, Chang Hsün, military governor of Anhui Province, had marched into the capital and announced a Manchu restoration. The president at the time was Li Yüan-hung, who had served as vice-president under Yuan Shih-k'ai, but had not supported him in his imperial aspirations, and had succeeded him as president. President Li had invited Chang into the capital to help mediate a quarrel between himself and the warlord Tuan Ch'i-jui, whom he had just dismissed from the premiership. Tuan withdrew to Tientsin after his dismissal and subsequently led a coalition of warlords against Chang and defeated him. President Li was then forced to resign in favor of a puppet picked by Tuan, who thus wielded supreme power in Peking.[25] Friction with Tuan would eventually cause Lu Hsün to flee the capital in 1926, as we shall see.

During the contest between Chang (whose army still wore pigtails) and Tuan, the capital was plunged into confusion and some officials who were also natives of Shaohsing sought refuge in the hostel. On July 6 a Shaohsing man created a furor when he attempted to move in with a concubine in tow, for there was a regulation that expressly forbade bringing women onto the premises, seemingly because several years previously a concubine had hanged herself from a tree in the courtyard.[26] At last a compromise was reached and the couple was allowed to stay the night.[27]

24. Ibid., p. 219.
25. Latourette, *The Chinese*, pp. 404-6.
26. This was the second set of rooms that Lu Hsün had occupied in the hostel. He had been able to move into this very pleasant part of the compound precisely because of its inauspicious association with the suicide: no one else wanted to live there. *LHKC*, p. 214.
27. *LHKC*, p. 214.

On the morning of July 7, airplanes appeared over Peking, and one of them dropped a bomb on the Forbidden City. The Chou brothers, deeming the hostel unsafe, shifted their quarters to the New China Hotel, where they found many of their acquaintances already holed up. Two days later they sent a telegram to Shao-hsing assuring the family that they were all right, but by July 12 they were experiencing difficulty in finding anything to eat. Then, in a day or two, almost as quickly as it had begun, the whole thing blew over and they moved back into the hostel.[28]

The Chang Hsün incident had a profound effect despite its farcical aspects; people began to feel that China simply could not go on like this any longer. At this juncture Ch'ien Hsüan-t'ung (1887-1939), a *landsmann* and old acquaintance with whom the Chou brothers had attended lectures under Chang T'ai-yen in Tokyo, began visiting Lu Hsün at the hostel in an attempt to enlist his support in a cultural revolution which he and some other young liberals—staff members of the magazine, *New Youth (Hsin ch'ing-nien)*—hoped to spark. During August, Ch'ien came over several times in the evening and chatted for hours on end. He did most of the talking, Lu Hsün the listening.[29] The preface to *Call to Arms*, reproduced part of a conversation:

"What's the use of copying these?" he asked, probing one night as he leafed through my volume of inscriptions copied from ancient monuments.

"It's useless."

"Then what's your point in doing it?"

"It's pointless."

"I think it might be well for you to do some writing . . ." I knew what he had in mind. They were right in the midst of publishing *New Youth* and yet, at that time, it seemed that not only had no one come forth to

---

28. Ibid., p. 219; *LHJC*, I, 278-79.

29. *LHKC*, pp. 220-22. *New Youth* was published monthly at Shanghai and was devoted to cultural, literary, and political themes. It was the most influential publication of the New Culture movement in the years 1915-21. See Chow Tse-tsung, *Research Guide to the May Fourth Movement* (Cambridge, Mass., 1963), p. 29. Lu Hsün and Ch'ien Hsüan-t'ung eventually had a falling out, and in later years Lu Hsün avoided him, objecting to his garrulity as time-wasting. In 1932 he wrote a short satirical poem about his former friend. See Chao Ts'ung, *Wu-ssu wen-t'an tien-ti* [Fragments concerning the literary world of the May Fourth period] (Hong Kong, 1964), pp. 88-90; hereafter cited as *WTTT*. See also Chang Hsiang-t'ien, *Lu Hsun chiu-shih chien-shu* [Commentaries on Lu Hsün's old-style poetry] (Canton, 1962), pp. 105-10; hereafter cited as *CSCC*.

approve of what they were doing, but no one had come forth to oppose them either.

Lu Hsün went on to argue that, given the state of affairs in China, there was no chance that they could effect any change, anyway. Ch'ien appealed to the future and to the hope that they just might be able to change things in some way. Lu Hsün was won over, and the result was that *New Youth* published his first story in the colloquial language, "Diary of a Madman," in April of the following year.

> And after that, once things got started, there was no stopping. I kept on writing a series of short-story-like compositions . . . and in the course of time I had the ten-odd pieces [contained in *Call to Arms*].[30]

Between Lu Hsün's return to China in 1909 and his evening chats with Ch'ien Hsüan-t'ung in 1917, China had been embroiled in a vast drama of political change. Lu Hsün had neither the temperament, education, nor power to play a significant role on such a stage. He sat out front and watched the drama, but he did not participate. During his student days, he had lived in a Japan that was almost four decades distant from the beginning of its own great drama of political modernization in the Meiji Restoration of 1868; he had lived in a Japan that was feeling its way as a nation in the modern world, a nation that was examining and remolding its own cultural life. By temperament he felt very much at home on the boards of such a stage. It was not until the end of World War I, however, that China would turn away from an almost exclusive interest in political transformation to a broader range of concerns that would include such things as language and culture. It was at this point that Lu Hsün picked up his writing brush and shared his own vision of reality with his fellow countrymen through the short stories that were collected in *Call to Arms* (1923) and *Wandering* (1926). From the publication of *Wandering* until his death ten years later Lu Hsün wrote no more fiction.[31] During this

30. *LHCC*, I, 7; *SWLH*, pp. 5-6. I have altered the Yangs' translation.
31. Between 1926 and 1927 Lu Hsün completed a book of somewhat fictionalized reminiscences, *Dawn Blossoms Plucked at Dusk (Chao-hua hsi-shih)*, and in 1935 he completed a volume of even more fictionalized cultural reminiscences, *Old Tales Retold (Ku-shih hsin-pien)*. In the former, he reinterprets his own past; in the latter, he reinterprets a series of ancient myths and legends, often using them to score contemporary points. Both works are to be found in Vol. 2 of the *LHCC*. Lu Hsün wrote no more short stories after November 6, 1925, the date he completed "Divorce (Li-hun)," the last story in *Wandering*.

period he found short, vitriolic essays (*tsa-wen*) better suited to his increasingly political purposes than fiction. China was changing and so was he. To better understand the vision set forth in the stories, which will be analyzed in the following chapters, some further knowledge of Lu Hsün's life from the late 1910s onward is desirable.

In 1919 he bought a home at 11 Pa-tao-wan Lane, went down to Shaohsing, sold the family property there, and brought his wife and mother back to Peking. (The story, "Home Town [Ku-hsiang]," reflects this trip.) However, the sale of the Shaohsing property did not bring in enough to cover the purchase price of the new property and Lu Hsün was forced to borrow money from a Peking bank at a high rate of interest.[32] He liked that particular piece of property because it had many rooms and spacious yards, an important consideration since it had been decided that Tso-jen, Chien-jen, and their wives and children were to live there as well. Life on Pa-tao-wan Lane was not to be blessed with the big-family harmony that Lu Hsün had, no doubt, envisaged when he bought the property. For whatever reason, he and his Japanese sister-in-law did not get along, a circumstance that increasingly alienated him from Tso-jen.[33] Things came to a head in 1923, and the brothers split up. Lu Hsün, taking his wife and mother with him, moved out and took up temporary quarters in three rooms at 61 Chuan-t'a Lane.[34] In May of the next year, he took his wife and mother and moved into a more comfortable residence at 21 West Third Lane, a place that he had bought the previous October and remodeled in the meantime.[35]

It is difficult to ascertain the details of the quarrel between the brothers: neither Lu Hsün nor Tso-jen ever discussed it in print.[36]

32. *HYL*, p. 52.
33. *YHC*, pp. 60-61.
34. *LHJC*, p. 455. Lu Hsün's diary shows that during the months immediately following the move, his mother made several trips back and forth between Pataowan and Chuan-t'a lanes. Presumably she was arranging family affairs and perhaps also trying to patch things up between her sons. The first four stories in *Wandering* were written at the temporary address. One of them, "A Happy Family (Hsing-fu te chia-t'ing)," reflects the crowded living conditions there. *PHFH*, p. 35.
35. *HYL*, p. 57.
36. If the story "Brothers (Ti-hsiung)" reflects the psychological reality behind the quarrel, Lu Hsün's control of his younger brother's life and his slightly self-righteous role as the sacrificing elder brother may have been contributing factors.

Hsü Kuang-p'ing, the beloved common-law wife of Lu Hsün's later years, has much to say about the rift, but, understandably, she is highly partisan. It would be fair to summarize her testimony by saying that she blames everything on Tso-jen's wife, whom she describes as a spoiled female Japanese imperialist. According to Kuang-p'ing, Habuto Nobuko would only buy expensive Japanese products and felt that she was superior to everyone else because she was Japanese. She is said to have kept in close contact with the Japanese Embassy and to have run up the Japanese flag outside the Pa-tao-wan residence every time there was a rumor of trouble in Peking. Kuang-p'ing reports that Lu Hsün once told her that while he was living at Patawowan he used to turn over his entire check to Nobuko, but that she was so extravagant that, even with Tso-jen's salary thrown in, they did not have enough to make ends meet and were constantly forced to borrow. As we have seen, Lu Hsün came back to China in 1909 and took a job, in part, so that he could support Tso-jen and Nobuko; even after Tso-jen came back to China, most of his support continued to come from Lu Hsün, who was further expected to send financial aid to Nobuko's family in Tokyo. When Lu Hsün once returned to Pa-tao-wan Lane to pick up some of his things, he somewhat ungraciously reminded his brother of this debt. Tso-jen is said to have waved this aside with "What's past is past."[37]

His home life after moving away from Pa-tao-wan Lane was depressing. Life with Tso-jen, Chien-jen, and their wives and children may have been hectic, even quarrelsome at times, but at least it had been lively. By comparison his new restricted household consisted of a wife whom he did not love, a mother who adhered to old-fashioned family customs, and two amahs. Lu Hsün's wife, Chu An, paid ritual respects to her mother-in-law every morning and evening and was responsible for preparing all the meals. The sole responsibility of one of the amahs was to look after the needs of Lu Hsün's mother, while the other did the shopping for food, boiled the rice, and kept the house clean. The

Chou Tso-jen has said that Lu Hsün expressed his sorrow over their rift in the story "Remorse (Shang-shih)." According to Tso-jen's interpretation (which he concedes may seem wild), Lu Hsün in the guise of a first-person narrator writing about a lost love is actually mourning the death of their brotherly relationship. *HHL*, pp. 426-27.

37. *HYL*, pp. 49-64.

amahs were allowed to eat the plain rice if they wanted, but were paid enough so that they could take their meals out.[38]

By this time, in addition to his position at the Ministry of Education, Lu Hsün was teaching at several institutions of higher learning in Peking, including National Peking University and the Women's Normal School. He would put in an appearance at the ministry in the morning when he had classes in the afternoon, and in the afternoon if he taught in the morning. This round of daily life away from home was, no doubt, far more satisfying than life within it. According to one of the amahs, he seldom spoke to his wife. When she woke him in the morning, he would grunt; when she called him at mealtimes, he would also grunt; and when she asked him before going to bed (always much earlier than he) whether the gate was shut, he would say "It is," or "It isn't." When she asked him for household expense money, he would become even more wordy and ask how much she wanted or what it was that they had run out of. He was more talkative with his mother, often answering questions that she had about her reading. When at variance with her as to how the household should be run, he would always defer to her wishes, showing his displeasure only through silence.[39]

When a student movement erupted at the Women's Normal School in 1925, Lu Hsün took the side of the students and some of them began to visit him at home, bringing a bit of spring into an otherwise autumnal atmosphere.[40]

One of these students, Hsü Kuang-p'ing, a Cantonese who had looked upon him as a revered teacher since 1923, when she first attended one of his classes at the Women's Normal School, later became his common-law wife. Their son, Hai-ying, was born in 1929, Lu Hsün's only child. Kuang-p'ing first wrote to Lu Hsün in March 1925 and first visited him at home in April.[41] Interestingly, in October of the same year Lu Hsün wrote his only love story, "Remorse (Shang-shih)."

On March 18, 1926, students and ordinary citizens petitioned

38. Ching Yu-lin, Lu Hsün hui-yi [Remembering Lu Hsün] (Shanghai, 1947), pp. 68-69; hereafter cited as LHHY.
39. Ibid., p. 69.
40. Ibid., p. 71.
41. A selection of their correspondence, made by Kuang-p'ing, comprises vol. 9 of LHCC, under the title Liang-ti shu [Letters from two places].

the warlord regime of Tuan Ch'i-jui to show more resistance to the demands of foreign governments, demands which increasingly infringed on China's sovereignty. Shots were fired into the crowd. Among the dead and wounded were some of Lu Hsün's own students at the Women's Normal School. The outraged essays that he published at this time caused the warlord government to put his name on a list of persons to be arrested. At first he went into hiding in Peking. Then, toward the end of the summer, he and Kuang-p'ing took the same southbound train out of the city. She went to a teaching post at the Women's Normal School in Canton, and he to one at Amoy University that had been offered by Lin Yutang, then dean of the college of literature there and before long to become internationally known for his writings about China in English. After a short stint at Amoy, Lu Hsün went to Canton to accept a joint post as chairman of the literature department and dean of academic affairs in February 1927.[42] The year thus begun was to be very significant in Lu Hsün's life. For him, as well as countless other Chinese intellectuals, it was to be a turning point, and the turn would be to the left.

The year before, Lu Hsün had followed with enthusiasm the progress of the Northern Expedition, hoping that the Nationalist Party and its army would be able to clear away the warlords and reunite China. While he was teaching in Canton, however, the Kuomintang carried out its decision to purge itself of Communists (members of the Chinese Communist Party had been welcomed into the ranks of the Nationalists since 1924) and unleashed the White Terror, a bloodletting which drove the majority of decent literary men to the left. During the bloodshed some of the students who had followed Lu Hsün from Amoy to Canton were taken into custody. He did everything he could to obtain their release. When he failed, he resigned from Sun Yat-sen University in sorrow and disgust. While in Canton Lu Hsün came to admire the courage of the Communistis and he met a few of them; prior to that he had had no contact with the Communist Party. Before long, he and Hsü Kuang-p'ing left Canton and went to Shanghai. Except for two trips to Peking (1929 and 1932), he remained there until his death in 1936.[43]

42. *LHNP*, pp. 69-78.
43. Howard L. Boorman, ed., *Biographical Dictionary of Republican China* (4 vols.; New York and London, 1967-70), I, 420 (the articles on Lu Hsün and Tso-jen are by William Schultz); Mills, "Years on the Left," p. 92.

Lu Hsün and Kuang-p'ing began living together as man and wife in Shanghai. This change in their relationship is reflected in a charming reminiscence written by Ching Yu-lin, who had considered Lu Hsün as his teacher and literary mentor since 1924. He visited his teacher and Kuang-p'ing in late 1927, shortly after their arrival in Shanghai. One morning while he and Lu Hsün sat chatting, Kuang-ping brought in a letter and handed it to Lu Hsün saying, "See how dreadful those girls are. Chiang Shao-yuan has sent me a letter in which she says that she is going to have to change the form or address she uses with me. She says that we can't call each other sister anymore. She says that from now on she's going to call me *shih-mu* [literally 'teacher-mother,' wife of my teacher, whom I consider as a 'teacher-father' *(shih-fu)*]." Lu Hsün laughed and said, "Then go ahead and let her call you *shih-mu*. What's the difference?" At that point in the conversation, Ching Yu-lin observed that in that case he too would have to begin calling her *shih-mu*. Lu Hsün laughed again, this time so loudly that Kuang-p'ing blushed and said, "You're all dreadful, the whole lot of you!" Ching notes that Lu Hsün's life in Shanghai was at this point suffused with a warmth that had been sorely lacking in Peking, and suggests that Lu Hsün's writing style in Peking was influenced by his unhappy home life.[44]

After coming to Shanghai, Lu Hsün, who had heretofore been salaried, was forced to rely mainly on royalties (supplemented between late 1927 and the end of 1931 by a monthly stipend from the Academia Sinica arranged for him by Ts'ai Yuan-p'ei). His income was enough to live on. "However, his generosity, book collecting, support of publishing ventures, regular contributions for many years to his family in Peking, the drain of various periods in hiding, bad health, and the minor personal extravagances which Hsü Kuang-p'ing has described made him complain frequently that he had no money."[45]

Lu Hsün died of pulmonary tuberculosis in his fifty-sixth year, on October 19, 1936. *LHNP*, p. 152. Kuang-p'ing remained in Shanghai after his death, even under the Japanese occupation, during which she was imprisoned for two months. After the establishment of the People's Republic in 1949 she held a number of posts in the new government, but apparently never joined the Communist party. Much of her energy in later years went into editing Lu Hsün's works and writing reminiscences. Boorman, II, 131-32.

44. *LHHY*, pp. 72-74.
45. Mills, "Years on the Left," p. 194, n. 2.

During these Shanghai years, Lu Hsün moved farther and father left.[46] The White Terror of 1927 had shaken his faith in evolution —his belief that the next generation would be better than the last one. In Canton he had seen examples of heroism among the young Communists, but he had also seen other young people betray their peers to the authorities, even when such betrayal meant arrest and sometimes death. He said that he would never again trust young people unreservedly.[47] In 1928 he began reading Marxist criticism of literature and art, and during the next two years translated theoretical works by Plekhanov and Lunacharski into Chinese.[48] In 1930 he helped found the League of Left-Wing Writers.[49] In 1935, upon learning that the Red Army had weathered Chiang Kai-shek's repeated attempts to exterminate it and had successfully completed its epic Long March from central China to a new base area in the northwest, Lu Hsün together with the famous novelist Mao Tun sent a congratulatory telegram to Mao Tse-tung.[50] Although he never joined the Chinese Communist Party and had had his differences with it, he wholeheartedly supported the party "as the only effective opposition to the Kuomintang, and under the circumstances then existing in China, as the sole agent for national regeneration."[51]

In these final years, he continued to translate and to give unstintingly of his time in reading and improving the manuscripts of young writers. Lu Hsün had always been interested in the graphic arts and now, despite failing health, he launched a movement, almost single-handedly,[52] to revive the art of the woodblock print. During the final three years of his life he wrote essays at a furious pace and it was in these years that he "perfected

---

46. While Lu Hsün became increasingly radical and politically involved, Tso-jen became more and more retiring, so that, "during the early thirties particularly, he came to be regarded as playing the hermit to his brother's rebel." D. E. Pollard, "Chou Tso-jen and Cultivating One's Garden," *Asia Major*, n.s., XI, pt. 2 (1965), 181.

47. Huang Sung-k'ang, *Lu Hsün and the New Culture Movement of Modern China* (Amsterdam, 1957), p. 121.

48. Ibid., pp. 121-22. He based himself on Japanese translations.

49. *LHNP*, pp. 102-3.

50. Mills, p. 203.

51. Boorman, I, 421.

52. Shirley Sun, "Lu Hsün and the Chinese Woodcut Movement, 1929-36" (Ph.d. dissertation, Stanford University, 1974), Introduction.

his *tsa-wen* or essay style. These years were his brilliant finale."[53] After 1930 his hostility to the Kuomintang made him a marked man and he lived under the constant threat of arrest and possible execution, protected only by "his enormous personal prestige."[54] In Shanghai his life was vastly different from what it had been in Peking, in part because of political changes in China and also in part because of the love and intellectual stimulation that Hsü Kuang-p'ing brought into it. Still, none of the intellectual and emotional changes that Lu Hsün went through in the final decade of his life could contradict the vision of Chinese reality presented in his first short story, "Remembrances of the Past," in 1911 and in the twenty-five stories written between 1918 and 1925 and collected in *Call to Arms* and *Wandering*.

53. Mills, p. 191.
54. Boorman, I, 421-22.

10

A BESTIARY OF
LU HSÜN'S
FICTIONALIZED WORLD

Since we are approaching the stories from the standpoint of Lu Hsün's vision of reality, a useful way of determining the content of that vision will be to take up the stories as a whole and see what kinds of people inhabit Lu Hsün's fictionalized world. The majority of important roles go to intellectuals; women of all kinds come in a close second; third, we have various people in service occupations (boatmen, rickshaw men, and jacks-of-all trades); fourth, rebels, mad and sane; and last, one peasant, Jun-t'u in "Home Town." All these characters act out their roles against a human backdrop which we may appropriately label "ordinary people" and treat as a separate category.

We encounter three types of intellectuals: the traditional, the in-between, and the modern. They can be distinguished primarily by education: traditional intellectuals were trained in private tutorial schools (*ssu-shu*) which prepared them for the civil service examinations, in-betweens in Sino-Western academies (*hsüeh-t'ang*) which prepared them in modern as well as traditional subjects, and moderns in public schools (*hsüeh-hsiao*) which prepared them primarily in modern subjects, while often paying lip service to tradition. Hence, a traditional intellectual is one prepared exclusively for the civil service examinations, an in-between is one whose education prepared him equally for the examinations and for further studies in modern (Western) subjects, and a modern is one for whom the examinations were never an option (the system having been abolished in 1905) and for whom the classics upon which that system was based had lost much of their appeal. Each of the types correlates roughly with a historical period: the traditional intellectual with the Manchu dynasty, the in-between with the period of transition between the end of the dynasty and the establishment of the republic, and the modern with the Republican period.

TRADITIONAL INTELLECTUALS

The traditional intellectuals in Lu Hsün's stories are presented as either the oppressors or the oppressed; there is no middle ground. The first of them, of course, is Master Baldy in "Remembrances of the Past." To the little boy, as we have seen, he is merely an old pedant, but to the reader he exemplifies the sterile, restrictive, hypocritical aspects of a superannuated tradition whose chief protectors are scholars and rich men. Freedom, creativity, and fulfillment are to be found among the uneducated (Old Wang and Amah Li), among the criminal (Taiping and other rebels), or out in the unspoiled, burgeoning world of green grasses and chirping insects in the back yard. Indeed one gains the impression that the solution to all problems (perhaps human salvation itself) lies in remaining uneducated, in becoming a rebel, or in escaping to nature. The traditional intellectual fleshes out the accumulated evils of the learning and history of the past. The adult Lu Hsün was painfully aware of what was wrong with the traditions of the past, but, unlike the little boy in "Remembrances of the Past," he had lost the naiveté that would suggest joining the servants or escaping to nature as an alternative. Inability to find a viable alternative probably does much to explain the bittersweet pessimism of Lu Hsün's best work. It is significant that the analysis of the oppressive nature of traditional intellectuals in "Remembrances of the Past" is done primarily through the eyes of a boy who has not yet been assimilated into society: he has not yet fully realized that both birth and circumstances have irrevocably singled him out for the very adult pattern against which he rebels, a fact that is painfully brought to the attention of the narrator of another story, "Home Town," as we shall see.

Another memorable traditional intellectual presented as oppressor is Fourth Uncle Lu in "The New Year's Sacrifice (Chu-fu)."[1]

---

1. *LHCC*, II, 5-22; *SWLH*, I, 150-73.

The narrator of this story, written in 1924, tells us of a trip to his native place around the time of the New Year. Fourth Uncle is first introduced to us as a traditional scholar with a bent for Neo-Confucian studies; if we assume that we can deduce his rather unwholesome character from the fact of that predilection alone, we shall not be far from wrong. Upon the arrival of his nephew he immediately launches into an attack upon the "new party." The nephew, reform-minded himself, takes no umbrage at this, for he knows that his uncle still has in mind people like K'ang Yu-wei and the reform movement at the turn of the century—despite the fact that the year is now 1924![2] The atmosphere at Fourth Uncle's proves so very uncongenial that the narrator thinks of leaving as soon as possible.

The next day he meets Sister Hsiang-lin, a woman whom he had previously known and who has now become a beggar.[3] She recognizes him and, respecting his superior education, asks him about ghosts, spirits, and the afterlife. As a widow who was forced against her will to remarry, she is now terrified that when she dies the King of Hell will saw her body in two and present each of her former husbands with a half. The following evening the narrator overhears Fourth Uncle saying: "Not a bit earlier and not a bit later. She would have to pick just this time! You can tell from that alone what a rotten type she is!" He learns from one of the servants that Fourth Uncle is talking about Sister Hsiang-lin, who has "aged away." (At New Year's, especially, it would have been unlucky to use the verb, "to die.") The shock of the news puts him into a state of suspended animation, and events in the life of Sister Hsiang-lin are reenacted before his meditative eyes. He sees her introduced to the household of Aunt and Uncle Lu by Old Lady Wei. She is twenty-six, wholesome-looking and strong; Old Lady

2. Hsü Ch'in-wen has pointed out that six full years before the Republican Revolution Sun Yat-sen called K'ang a "supporter and loyal subject of the Manchus" and "traitor to the Chinese race." Yet Fourth Uncle still considers him terribly radical. *P'ang-huang fen-hsi* [An analysis of the stories in *Wandering*] (Peking, 1958), p. 11; hereafter cited as *PHFH*.
3. She is called Hsiang Lin-sao in Chinese. *Sao*, which I have translated as "Sister," means "elder brothers wife" and was used by extension as a general term of respect for married women. There was an element of class distinction in its usage: members of the gentry employed it amongst themselves and with inferiors; the common people also used it amongst themselves, but would not do so in addressing the gentry because of the undue familiarity it implied.

Wei recommends her highly as a servant. After learning that she is a widow, Fourth Uncle has some qualms about his wife's hiring her; there is something impure and unlucky about a woman who has had the temerity to survive her husband.

Sister Hsiang-lin proves an excellent worker. After a time, her mother-in-law shows up, claiming that she ran away without permission, and demands her back. This mother-in-law had originally bought Sister Hsiang-lin as wife for a child husband (her son, Sister Hsiang-lin's junior by ten years) and hence views her as a financial investment as well as a daughter-in-law. She is not going to lose that investment merely because her son died. Fourth Uncle opines, "Since it is her own mother-in-law who wants her back, what can we say?" Aunt Lu tallies up Sister Hsiang-lin's wages and hands the entire amount over to the mother-in-law. In order to get money enough to finance the marriage of her second son, the mother-in-law subsequently promises her in marriage, at a good price, to a man who lives far off in the mountains (it is difficult for mountain men to get wives, and they pay well). Sister Hsiang-lin refuses to go; she is tied and taken off to Ho village, where her new husband virtually rapes her. Within the year a son is born to her, and for a while it looks as though Sister Hsiang-lin will find some modicum of happiness.

A few years later, Old Lady Wei reappears at the Lu household with Sister Hsiang-lin in tow, explaining that her mountain husband died in a typhoid epidemic and her infant son was carried off by a wolf. Fourth Aunt is so moved by this recitation that she agrees to take her back. Uncle draws his wife aside to remind her that while it is true that Sister Hsiang-lin is to be pitied, still one ought to remember that a person like that exerts a noxious influence on morals; therefore it is all right to let her help with the housework, but she must on no account be allowed to touch any food or implement connected with the ancestral sacrifices. As a twice-married widow, Sister Hsiang-lin is, he is convinced, particularly impure, and thus he fears that the ancestors will not accept the sacrifices if she has any part in them.

Since Sister Hsiang-lin is judged unfit for such service, the Lus hire a certain Liu Ma as part-time help during the New Year's celebration, and it is Liu Ma who first puts the idea into Sister Hsiang-lin's head that her two husbands will fight over her in the afterworld so that the King of Hell will be forced to cut her in two—that is, unless she does something by way of atonement in the meantime. Liu Ma suggests buying an expiatory threshold in the local temple. (It will substitute for her body, and as people walk over it and trample on it, her sins will be wiped away.)

Sister Hsiang-lin finally saves enough to buy one, and thus on the occasion of the next ancestral sacrifice confidently begins to handle the sacrificial implements. Fourth Aunt sharply commands her to put them down. She is totally broken. Just after buying the expiatory threshold, she had begun to hold her head up again, for she felt that she had atoned for her sins, that she was clean, that she could make a fresh start. But now she is completely defeated. She goes from bad to worse; they let her go; reduced to begging, she dies in poverty as the Lu family prepares to invoke a New Year's blessing. Fourth Uncle's only reaction to her death, as we have seen, is to berate her for dying at such an unpropitious time: "You can tell from that alone what a rotten type she is!" Fourth Uncle, a traditional intellectual, appears before us as rigidly conservative, unfeeling, and superstitious—despite the rationalism of his avowed Neo-Confucianism. Thus he fleshes out the traditional Confucian morality that eventually destroys Sister Hsiang-lin. To be sure, the folk Buddhism of Liu Ma is actually no less frightening (indeed, perhaps it is even more so) than the rigid moralism of Fourth Uncle. However, it did at least provide an out: guilt, to be sure, but also expiation of that guilt, an expiation that Sister Hsiang-lin believed possible until Fourth Aunt destroyed even that illusion. The traditional morality woven into Fourth Uncle's Neo-Confucianism apparently recognizes guilt but does not recognize forgiveness, and provides no means of expiation. As Lu Hsün's old friend Hsü Shou-shang has well said, the tragedy "does not lie in the wolf's eating Ah-mao [her son], but rather lies in traditional morality's devouring of Sister Hsiang-lin."[4]

In this story, as in a number of others, Lu Hsün would have his readers believe that traditional society is a cannibalistic feast where the weak are served up for the delectation of the strong, where the oppressors take and the oppressed are taken. According to Chou Tso-jen, this view of traditional society and the Neo-Confucian ideology upon which it was based may have been suggested to Lu Hsün by Chang T'ai-yen's explication in Tokyo of the ideas of the eighteenth-century philosopher Tai Chen, who rebelled against

4. *WTLH*, p. 42.

Neo-Confucianism and regarded its so-called rational principles, *li,* as fearful killers. One may agree with Tso-jen that in such a story as "Diary of a Madman" Lu Hsün succeeded in giving Tai's rather abstract conception a very concrete form.[5]

Averring that to the best of his knowledge Fourth Uncle was not modeled on any particular figure at the New T'aimen in Shao-hsing, Tso-jen goes on to say:

This moralist does not occupy any particularly important position in the story. His function is merely to beat down Sister Hsiang-lin with [the concepts of] traditional morality, cause her to lose her position, and eventually starve to death. Therefore [Lu Hsün] simply does not go to any great pains to work him up as an individual.[6]

Given the abstract quality of the genesis of this character (and assuming that Tso-jen is right), it is a tribute to Lu Hsün's skill that he was able to put as much life into Fourth Uncle as he did.

Lu Hsün always feels much more at home with the oppressed, be they peasants or even intellectuals. Two of his most memorable

5. *HSJW,* p. 12. In this instance Tso-jen is talking about "Diary of a Madman," but what he has to say could be applied just as aptly to "The New Year's Sacrifice" and many others of Lu Hsün's stories. Tai Chen (1724-1777) believed that the Sung Neo-Confucians had done a disservice to Chinese philosophy and society (the two were inseparably linked) through their doctrine of "reason." Tai pointed out that etymologically, the Chinese character for reason, *li,* simply denoted the patterned lines on a piece of jade. The Sung Neo-Confucians, however, had reified *li* and made it into a weapon with which anyone in a superior position could bully those beneath him. Tai describes society in a manner that we see reflected in many of Lu Hsün's stories. Says Tai: "People in honored positions demand reason of those in humbler stations, elders demand it of their children, and those of high rank demand it of their inferiors. And yet when people of high station are themselves in violation of reason, they are still considered in harmony with the dictates of morality. Those in low and inferior positions strive to be reasonable, but even when they are, they are still considered in violation of the dictates of morality. Thus . . . superiors constantly demand reason of inferiors and there is no end to the guilt of those in lower positions. When a person is put to death by the law, there will be some who will pity him. But who will show any pity to those who are put to death by 'reason'?" *Chung-kuo li-tai che hsüeh wen-hsüan: Ch'ing-tai chin-tai pien* [A selection of Chinese philosophical documents throughout the ages: selections on the Ch'ing and modern periods] (Peking, 1963), p. 167, cited in the Bibliography as *CHWH.* Sister Hsiang-lin is clearly the victim of this big-tradition concept of reason which condemned the remarriage of widows (they had abandoned reason in favor of desire) and also the victim of the superstitions of the little tradition which tended to support big-tradition ideology.
6. *HSJW,* p. 164.

characters are oppressed traditional intellectuals, K'ung Yi-chi and Ch'en Shih-ch'eng. As the story "K'ung Yi-chi"[7] begins, an adult narrator reminisces about how things were when, as a teen-ager, he worked behind the counter of the Everybody's Happy wineshop in his native town. The narrator conjures up the image of a boy behind the open-air counter, making change for the customers, a ragtag lot of short-jacketed farm laborers. An atmosphere of gloom and ennui weighs broodingly over the shop, but all faces turn and light up in happy anticipation as K'ung Yi-chi makes his entrance. Old K'ung stands before the bar in a tattered scholar's gown (an anomalous contrast to the regular clientele of short-jacketed types) and orders some wine and beans. It would not be an unwarranted simplification to say that the people in this story (now all on stage) consist of oppressors and their common victim, the failed scholar K'ung Yi-chi. Although he wears the long robes of the traditional intellectual and interlards his conversation with rare gems from the classics, he has never passed a single examination, never held a single post. His only value to the community lies in his skill at drawing Chinese characters, whereby he ekes out a living as a scribe. Natural laziness, inordinate fondness for the bottle, and general dissatisfaction with his outcast state combine to harass K'ung into occasional drunken sprees, which he finances by stealing books from his clients[8] and pays for a second time with the humiliation and pain of public thrashings. Despite all this, he doggedly considers himself a scholar, a member of the establishment.[9] K'ung Yi-chi's real oppressors, of course, are his own blind acceptance of the establishment's norms (most concretely embodied in success in the examinations) and his unrealistic appraisal of his own position in society. Indeed, we quickly become aware that this traditional intellectual is probably the author of his own unsuccess and to that extent his own oppressor; and yet we cannot but be disturbed that everyone

7. *LHCC*, I, 20-24, *SWLH*, I, 22-28. The translations in the ensuing discussion are my own.

8. At the t'aimen in Shaohsing, Uncle Feng-t'ung had once behaved in a similar fashion.

9. HsüCh'in-wen remembers that there used to be a saying used around Shaohsing to describe someone like K'ung Yi-chi: "If he tries to squat, he can't get all the way down; if he tries to stand, he can't get all the way up." *Na-han fen-hsi* [An analysis of the stories in *Call to Arms*] (Peking, 1956), p. 22; hereafter cited as *NHFH*.

"I haven't got many left."

around him connives in this oppression and takes delight in taunting him: "K'ung Yi-chi, do you really know how to read? How is it you haven't managed to fish up even half a *hsiu-ts'ai* degree?" When they bait him for having been caught stealing again, and for having been publicly beaten by way of punishment, he denies it. They say that they saw him being trussed up and bambooed for stealing books. His answer is a classic of self-deception:

I merely "purloined" a few volumes and that certainly cannot be counted as "stealing" books. The purloining of volumes is, after all, well within the scope of the scholarly life. How can that be viewed as ordinary theft?

He ties up the conclusion of this indignant defense with a string of pompous quotations from the classics that sets the entire wineshop on a roar; even the teen-aged boy behind the bar joins in. Small children also use K'ung in much the same unfeeling manner:

There were a couple of times when the neighborhood youngsters heard all the laughing and ran over to get in on the fun. They'd trap K'ung Yi-chi in a circle and he would give them beans, one to each child. But having finished those, they wouldn't go away. They'd just stand there, eyes glued to his saucer. That would get him worried. He'd bridge his fingers defensively over the beans, bend down, and tell them, "I haven't got many left. They're almost gone already." Then he would straighten up, take another look at his beans, wag his head and comment in more learned fashion: "Few be my beans. Few be my beans. *Hath the gentleman many? Nay, nay, I say.*" Only then, amid gales of laughter, would the children scatter.[10]

Though in a crowd, emotionally, old K'ung is in total isolation; not one of the people who surround him shows so much as a glimmer of human sympathy. One is reminded of the conversations that Lu Hsün and Hsü Shou-shang had back in Japan when they decided that the Chinese people were most lacking in "love" and "honesty"—defects that had developed, they thought, during two periods of enslavement to foreign peoples (Mongols and Manchus). K'ung Yi-chi, a pastmaster at self-deception, is certainly lacking in honesty, and his tormentors seem devoid of the barest notions of sympathy and love. When his legs are rendered permanently useless by a particularly severe beating and he turns up again at the shop after a prolonged absence, dragging himself about on two dirty hands, his legs cushioned helplessly beneath him on a pad made of rushes—even then, the regulars of the shop simply mock him for having been beaten for stealing books again. After this last visit, K'ung disappears, and, as we have seen, the adult narrator only remembers him now because he had once provided him with a light moment or two.

K'ung Yi-chi was based on just such a person who used to be seen on Tung Ch'ang Lane in Shaohsing when Lu Hsün was still a boy. This person, surnamed Meng and sarcastically nicknamed "Master Mencius" by the local residents, was a frequent patron at

10. *LHCC*, I, 23; *SWLH*, I, p. 26. K'ung's words in italics are a play on *Analects* IX, vi. In his pompous use of language K'ung is reminiscent of the pedants satirized in the twenty-third chapter of Li Ju-chen's (c. 1763-1830) *Romance of the Flowers in the Mirror (Ching-hua-yuan)*.

the wineshop—the story retains its name—across the street from the t'aimen. It is likely that in his boyhood, as indeed is true in the fictionalized version of the events he penned as an adult, Lu Hsün was more struck with the callous way in which people treated Master Mencius than he was with Meng himself. Certainly, Lu Hsün treats his protagonist in the fictionalized "K'ung Yi-chi" with a compassion and sympathy that stands in inverse proportion to the cruelty and callousness shown by the patrons of the shop. Master Mencius must have made a great impression on the young Lu Hsün, for even the details of the rush pad and the use of "purloin" for "steal" were taken directly from him.[11]

Like K'ung Yi-chi, Ch'en Shih-ch'eng in "The White Light (Pai-kuang)" is a failed scholar.[12] Like K'ung, Ch'en is a victim both of the examination system and of his own ineptitude. In a sort of introductory scene, we find candidates thronging to the front of the examination hall to learn their fates from the list posted there. We see Ch'en still looking in vain through the extensive list of the successful, long after all the other candidates have gone home. The curtain opens (as one might say) on the corner of a large t'aimen. A number of young students are chatting and frolicking about in a dilapidated old room facing on a courtyard. When Ch'en Shih-ch'eng enters, they immediately take their places on a long bench, pick up their books, and begin reciting. This run-down family compound belongs to Ch'en, who gets a living by renting rooms and conducting a private school in his own quarters. Ch'en looks quite defeated as he comes in, and well he may: he has just failed the first of the civil service examinations for the sixteenth time.

He dismisses his students. Sensing his failure, they make no attempt to dissemble their disdain. To Ch'en it seems that now even the chickens in the courtyard despise him. In the past he had often fondly imagined how this general contempt would suddenly turn into groveling respect on that glorious day when he finally passed: the gentry would be eager to marry off their daughters to him and the common people would stand before him as if gazing on the countenance of a god, deeply repenting their former disregard. (Success for Ch'en would mean that he would then bully those who now bully him.) But that dream is empty. He has failed again.

---

11. *HSJW*, pp. 14-16.
12. *LHCC*, I, 124-29. This story is translated in *Silent China: Selected Writings of Lu Xun*, ed. and trans. Gladys Yang (London, 1973), pp. 59-64. The translation of the excerpt in the ensuing discussion is my own.

Having lost all appetite for supper, Ch'en paces about in the yard. He begins to hear voices directing him to a hidden treasure said to have been buried on his family property. He recalls hearing his grandmother tell him about it in his boyhood; its location is supposedly contained in a riddle: "Left turn, right turn, forward and back; / Gold and silver, sack after sack." While he is reminiscing over previous unsuccessful attempts to locate the treasure, a white glow appears inside his room. He goes in. The glow momentarily disappears, only to return, brighter than before, under a desk next to the wall. Ch'en draws the table aside and begins to dig.

He has failed the examinations so many times in the past that the people who rent rooms in his t'aimen, anticipating his strange behavior, go to bed early on those days when the results are posted. At first he digs cautiously, making as little noise as possible; but the unmistakable sound of metal against the earth, in inanimate disregard of Ch'en's embarrassment, rings out through the compound. He digs, and digs, and digs. In the end he finds only a rotting lower jawbone with a few teeth on it which seems to smile and say: "This time you're all washed up again!" He flees out into the courtyard in terror and lies down in the shadows under the eaves. Again he hears voices. Now they tell him that the treasure is not here. He must go up into the mountains. Ch'en gazes off toward the distant hills and before long a white light appears in that direction.

The next day, five miles from town, his nude body is found floating in a river. Not one of his neighbors takes the trouble to go to the authorities to identify him. Since there are no relatives to claim the body, after a perfunctory inquest, it is buried by the local constable.

As for the cause of death, there was of course no doubt about it. Stripping an abandoned corpse was really a common occurrence and insufficient grounds for suspecting foul play. Furthermore, the coroner had demonstrated that the deceased had fallen into the water alive by pointing out that Ch'en had, beyond any doubt, fought for his life in the water; river mud was embedded under every one of his fingernails.

As in the case of K'ung Yi-chi, we are probably justified in assuming that at least part of the reason for Ch'en's unsuccess lay within himself, though Lu Hsün chooses to leave this aspect of the

". . . and the body was nude."

tragedy undeveloped. We are not told, as we were in K'ung's case, that any of Ch'en's personal habits contributed to his failure. He is presented entirely as a victim of the examination system and of the cold, heartless society that surrounds him. His students, showing no sympathy for his plight, have only contempt for his failure. No neighbor will take responsibility for the body. Like "K'ung Yi-chi," "The White Light" indicts the entire society for its lack of warmth and love. Ch'en and K'ung are victims of the examination system, to be sure, but even more they are the frostbite victims of the emotional Arctic in which they live.

And what if they had been successful? K'ung Yi-chi is presented to us as a kind man, yet even in his case it is not inconceivable that, were he successful, he would treat other failures with an equal degree of cruelty. Certainly in Ch'en's case we are justified (given his imaginings of what it will be like when he passes the exams) in assuming that he would immediately become overweening and arrogant. One is reminded of the rather impressionistic sixth diary-entry in "Diary of a Madman" where the madman notes simply: "Pitch black. I do not know whether it is day or night. The ferocity of a lion; the timidity of a rabbit; the craftiness of a fox."[13] Lu Hsün viewed both individual and corporate Chinese personality in just such terms: men in superior positions (oppressors) are fierce as lions; men in inferior positions (oppressed) are timid as rabbits; and men who are not sure of their status in any given situation are crafty as foxes. In sum, Lu Hsün sees Chinese society as an arena of human intercourse where everything depends upon status—where a man will freely bully those under him while standing servilely in awe of those over him, a situation summed up in such common colloquial Chinese phrases as "fear the strong and bully the weak (p'a-ch'iang ch'i-jo)," or "bully the soft and fear the hard (ch'i-jo p'a-ying)."

Like K'ung Yi-chi, the character Ch'en Shih-ch'eng was closely modeled on a man whom Lu Hsün had known in Shaohsing. Here the model was Tzu-ching, the great-uncle who lived in the New T'aimen and, as we have seen, was for a time Lu Hsün's teacher. If Tso-jen's accounts are to be believed, Tzu-ching was even more extreme than the fictionalized Shih-ch'eng, so much so that had Lu Hsün described him directly, readers might well have rejected him as too farfetched. Tzu-ching's father, known around the New T'aimen as "Twelfth Old Master," had been a hsiu-ts'ai. He was, as has been told earlier, killed in the Taiping Rebellion, during which he had remained loyal to the central government; in posthumous recognition of that loyalty, the Manchus had granted him the lowest rank of hereditary nobility, a rank prestigious enough to be referred to in popular parlance as "half a future." As his son, Tzu-ching inherited this rank, and an official notice proclaiming that fact was posted in the main hall of the New T'aimen. Immediately next to this notice was a second one announcing that, in compliance with Tzu-ching's own request, his

13. *LHCC*, I, 14; *SWLH*, I, 14.

noble rank was hereby exchanged for the status of *sheng-yüan*—
a status which made him eligible to sit for the examination for the
second civil service degree, the *chü-jen*, right along with the
regular holders of the first degree (*hsiu-ts'ai*). Since the *hsiu-ts'ai*
was the usual prerequisite for this examination, Tzu-ching was
placed at a real advantage.[14]

It was an advantage that Tzu-ching failed to exploit. Apparently
out of a proud desire to prove that he was worthy of a *hsiu-ts'ai*
degree in his own right, he insisted on passing the examinations for
that degree before sitting for the *chü-jen* examination. He would
achieve his status rather than passively allow it to be ascribed to
him on the basis of his father's merit—on the face of it, a
commendable and reasonable stance. And he should have been
able to do so, for the first of the examinations for the *hsiu-ts'ai*
degree was not particularly difficult as long as one had read the
classics and could write an intelligible style of classical Chinese.
However, it turned out that Tzu-ching could not; his composition
was so disjointed and illogical that he failed to clear even this first
hurdle. Finally, one year the examiners told him that his composition was so bad that they never wanted to see him back there
again.[15]

As we have already noted in discussing Lu Hsün's childhood,
Great-Uncle Tzu-ching was a rather lonely widower whose two
sons had left home. He lived in a room at the New T'aimen whose
door faced out on a courtyard in which there grew an orange tree;
hence the children in the t'aimen referred to his quarters as "the
orange-tree room" or, from the color of the twin doors that led to
it, "the blue doors." On the threshold of his teens, Lu Hsün had
briefly studied Chinese composition and the *Mencius* with Tzu-
ching behind these doors. According to Tso-jen, the only possible
reason for letting his brother study with this inept old eccentric
was simply that Tzu-ching, who had at least some familiarity with
the Four Books, was available. At first only Tzu-ching's scholarship was suspect; later it was evident that the man was deranged.[16]

One afternoon while Tzu-ching was holding school behind the
blue doors, his old female servant burst into the room. A rather
disheveled and slovenly old girl who flew about the t'aimen higher

14. *HSJW*, pp. 122-23.
15. Ibid., pp. 123-24.
16. Ibid., pp. 124-25; *LHKC*, pp. 24-28.

than a kite much of the time, she was known to the family as the "Contented Old Dowager." She sat down on a chair in front of Tzu-ching's bed, weaving back and forth so much that he had to run over and prop her up to keep her from sprawling across the floor. In her cups, she began mumbling about a "white light." Tzu-ching became very excited and immediately dismissed his class. Then he left, coming back later with a stonemason who removed the flagstones by the bed in preparation for an excavation. Tzu-ching supervised the digging well into the night, and, unlike the character in "The White Light," apparently was clearheaded.[17]

When the hole was quite deep, he descended into it and began feeling around with his bare hands. Touching something that felt like the stones of an outer coffin, he became terrified and scurried out of the hole so quickly that he wrenched his back in the process and was not able to get out of bed for several days. After this he went from bad to worse and his school had to be disbanded. One night he began slamming his head against the wall while vilifying himself loudly for being an unfilial son (perhaps out of feelings of guilt because he had never gone to the town where his father had died during the Taiping Rebellion to fetch the body back to its proper ancestral resting place in Shaohsing).[18]

Before long he moved out of the t'aimen and for a while conducted another school in a neighboring temple. Then somehow or other he took it into his head that he ought to get married again; he obtained the services of a female go-between but in the end got no bride, for the go-between swindled him out of every penny that he gave her. Finally, during the hot part of the summer in 1896, he slipped his leash entirely. Going out onto a bridge,

he began by swearing at, and striking, himself. He followed this by taking up a pair of scissors, stabbing himself through the throat with them and then inflicting five or six small punctures in his chest. He then lit some paper that he had previously soaked in kerosene and lay on it for

17. *HSJW*, p. 126. There was a family legend that a treasure was buried somewhere in the New T'aimen. Its location was supposedly contained in a riddle: "A single pull away from the well, / And one straight line from the eaves will tell." *LHKC*, p. 128.
18. Ibid., pp. 29, 128.

a while as it burned. Finally he leapt from the side of a bridge into the river, shouting as he went: "The old ox has fallen into the water!"[19]

He was fished out by some neighbors and taken back to his old quarters behind the blue doors in the New T'aimen, where he died a day or so later.[20]

Considering the traditional intellectuals that have thus far been examined, it is apparent that Lu Hsün sees even members of this establishment group as either the oppressors or the oppressed. Master Baldy and Fourth Uncle Lu are at one extreme, K'ung Yi-chi and Ch'en Shih-ch'eng at the other.[21] Significantly, the middle ground is unoccupied. Nor do we find any traditional intellectuals who stand apart, clasping fast to their breasts the purer ideals of an antique age. For Lu Hsün, the society of traditional morality is a cannibalistic arena in which the strong eat and the weak are eaten, where the only hope of salvation lies in the liberation of the young. Given his own childhood, given the failure-ridden atmosphere of the New T'aimen, one would hardly expect him to envisage a middle ground or to entertain the possibility of the existence of other, more idealistic scholars of the traditional camp who might have a prescription for a decadent age.

The last character whom we shall examine under the "traditional intellectual" rubric is Ssu-ming, protagonist of "Soap (Fei-tsao)."[22] K'ung Yi-chi and Ch'en Shih-ch'eng were traditional intellectuals in a traditional society; Ssu-ming is more like Fourth Uncle in that he is a traditional intellectual living in the modern

---

19. *HSJW*, p. 127. My colleague, Professor Kung-yi Kao, has suggested that Tzu-ching meant by this: "I have served you faithfully as an ox that pulls the plow, but you have shown me absolutely no gratitude."

20. *LHKC*, p. 30; *HSJW*, pp. 126-27.

21. Chu T'ung remarks that the fate of men like K'ung Yi-chi must have been particularly poignant for Lu Hsün after his return from Japan. In an earlier period they might have comforted themselves with examples of scholars who achieved success late in life. The abolition of the examination system in 1905 removed that possibility. *Lu Hsün tso-p'in te fen-hsi* [An analysis of the works of Lu Hsün] (Shanghai, 1953), I, 95; hereafter cited as *TPFH*.

22. *LHCC*, II, 43-54; *SWLH*, I, 198-211. The first two quotations in the ensuing discussion are my own; the second two are the Yangs', with slight modifications.

society of the May Fourth period; like Fourth Uncle, he is a somewhat anachronistic hangover from an earlier day. The center of interest in "Soap," however, is somewhat different from that of the stories thus far examined. Here Lu Hsün directs his attention almost exclusively to the hypocrisy of traditional morality and the consequent disparity it engenders (in those who have drunk too deeply of it) between consciously held norms and subconscious desires. In this tale, written in 1924, the disparity is shown in sexual mores (in "Brothers," written the following year, the same disparity would appear in familial mores). Since for Lu Hsün it is only servants, women, and young people (those not included in the traditional system of education) who can manage to remain uncorrupted, he naturally uses people from these groups as instruments of his analysis. In "Soap" he uses a woman, Ssu-ming's wife.

The action of the story is triggered when Ssu-ming returns home from market with a cake of foreign soap ("Palmolive," from the description). He gives it to his wife, who immediately praises both quality and scent. Staring at the rough, unattractive skin on her neck, Ssu-ming enjoins his wife to use this kind of soap from now on. (Normally she picks pods from the so-called soap-tree and scrubs with them; now she concedes that this was probably a somewhat inadequate way of washing.)

Ssu-ming calls in his son, Hsüeh-ch'eng, whom he is sending to an academy where they teach English. He asks him the meaning of *o-tu-fu*, his approximation of the pronunciation of an English term. (It seems that while he was picking through several cakes of foreign soap one of a group of young students called him an *o-tu-fu*—"old fool.") Angry that his son does not immediately understand the word, he sends him off to look it up in a dictionary and then begins to criticize the modern educational system:

The students nowadays are a mess. As a matter of fact, back during the days of the Kuang-hsü period [1875-1908] I was one of the staunchest advocates of setting up academies [*hsüeh-t'ang*], but I never dreamt that they would become as corrupt as this. The students are forever talking of "liberation" and "freedom," but have no solid learning. They only know how to stir up trouble. And Hsüeh-ch'eng! I've spent more than a little on him. Wasted, all of it! It took me a great deal of trouble to get him into an academy where they struck a balance between Chinese and Western learning and where they touted their English program as "equally emphasizing speaking and understanding." You'd think that ought to work out fine, wouldn't you? Hah! Not a bit of it! He's studied for a whole year and can't even understand *o-tu-fu.* They must still be following the same old rigid ways that they used to . They call themselves academies of "learning," but what kind of products do they turn out? I say that we ought to close down every last one of them and be done with it!

His wife, dutifully joining in the spirit of his righteous feelings, agrees; emboldened by her support, he goes on to expatiate on the noxious influence that the education of women has had on the moral tone of society. His attitude in this regard too has apparently shifted as the years have slipped past. He tells his wife that in the past when Ninth Gramps opposed education for females, "I even attacked him; but looking at what's become of things now, I realize that the old people had the right idea after all." He interrupts this public-spirited peroration to call in his son, whom he berates again for his inability to understand the meaning of *o-tu-fu.* At this point the wife begins to exhibit an unanticipated degree of independence, a certain reluctance to go along with everything her husband says. She begins to defend her son just a bit.

As Hsüeh-ch'eng goes off again to see what he can find in the dictionary, Ssu-ming begins to describe a "filial" girl whom he saw at the market. There she was with her blind, white-haired old grandmother, begging from people. Many passers-by commented on her filial behavior, but very few people, notes Ssu-ming, gave her anything—a clear indication, as far is he is concerned, of the general depravity of contemporary society. Then people began to gather round and even make fun of them. One said to a friend:

"Ah-fa, don't be put off by the dirt on the goods. Just grab a couple of pieces of soap, wash her all over with a rub-a-dub-dub, and you'd have a pretty good piece there!"

Ssu-ming, of course, expresses to his wife his indignation at such low talk. Throughout the course of this dialogue, however, his wife becomes increasingly less tractable. She pulls away from her spouse's cozy indignation and asks him if he gave any money. Of course not! Because as he explains it, he only had a tiny bit of money on him at the time, and it would have been simply too embarrassing to take out such a paltry sum. This girl, he insists, was no ordinary beggar.

Subsequent developments reveal that Ssu-ming's wife is no ordinary wife, either. As the conversation proceeds, she exhibits an increasing independence of spirit; her reactions to his description of the beggar girl show that she has the psychological insight to realize the true—even if subconscious—nature of her husband's interest in this eighteen-year-old female incarnation of filial piety. She knows that a gift of money on his part to the girl would not have constituted alms, but rather a love offering; for that, a few paltry pennies would, indeed, have been "embarrassing." Hence that evening, when Ssu-ming begins berating Hsüeh-ch'eng again for not "understanding things" (i.e., being mature), she is fully cocked and set to fire:

"How can you expect him to understand the things on *your* mind? If he were really old enough to understand things, he would have long since set out with lantern or torch to search out that filial female for you. Luckily, you've already got one cake of soap here that you bought for her. Now all you have to do is buy one more and . . ."

One is amazed that such an obtuse clod as Ssu-ming should have so perceptive and sensitive a wife, a circumstance that is no doubt largely attributable to Lu Hsün's marked predilection in favor of women (along with servants and children). Ssu-ming denies her accusation, of course, and is probably sincere in doing so; not recognizing (or perhaps refusing to recognize) his motivations, he is unable to acknowledge the possible existence of subconscious drives. He may be a hypocrite, but not a conscious one. He lives among "names" (*ming*), and when "realities" (*shih*) do not fit those names, in traditional Confucian fashion he averts his gaze from all that is unseemly. His wife, not having been assimilated into the masculine Confucian tradition, is not nearly so fastidious. As she continues to force her husband's reluctant gaze in the direction of improper realities, he becomes increasingly uncomfortable and cries out in exasperation: "What kind of talk is this? You women . . ." Again she is waiting and ready:

"What about us women? We're a darned sight better than you men. If you men aren't cursing eighteen- or nineteen-year-old girl students, you're praising eighteen- or nineteen-year-old girl beggars. And there's nothing good on your minds in either case! 'Rub-a-dub-dub!' Why, you're absolutely shameless!"

Ssu-ming is rescued from this unpleasantly open encounter by the arrival of two friends, cosponsors with him of the "Literary League for Moral Renewal." The league, it seems, periodically sponsors a poetry and essay contest, announcing it (at their own cost) in a local newspaper. As the three friends discuss this project, it becomes apparent that the criticism which Ssu-ming's wife leveled at her husband applies equally to his two fellow pillars of morality. After finally seeing his friends out the front gate, Ssu-ming returns to the house. He still feels very uncomfortable in the presence of his wife and children. His eight-year-old daughter has the temerity to repeat her mother's words in a low voice: "Rub-a-dub-dub! Absolutely shameless." This is obviously no place for Ssu-ming. He retreats to the courtyard and the story draws to a close.

By virtue of age (apparently in his middle or late thirties in 1924), Ssu-ming would seem to belong to the generation of in-between intellectuals. It is clear, however, that both by education (he has apparently not studied any foreign tongues) and by sympathies he belongs much more in the traditional camp. Further, he is criticized mainly for hypocrisy, Lu Hsün's favorite accusation against traditional Chinese culture and its defenders.[23] Nominally a moral man of great rectitude, in reality Ssu-ming is a repressed bundle of lascivious middle-aged desires. His wife, conscious of this, denounces him for his moral hypocrisy. As the story closes we are told that Ssu-ming's wife continued to use the soap, and, after it was gone, bought another scented cake. In other words, rather than condemn her husband's desires as if she were a policewoman for traditional morality, she sought to concentrate those desires on her own person and give her husband an opportunity to express them in the flesh rather than go on fatuously and hypocritically sublimating them in pompous essays and poems on the subject of filial maidens. (The eighteenth-century thinker Tai Chen, whom we have previously mentioned,

---

23. While more evident in those stories dealing with traditional Chinese intellectuals, this theme is not absent in those tales which focus on in-between intellectuals. Most notably it is dominant in "Brothers (Ti-hsiung)," which describes a similar kind of hypocrisy (though not related to sex) in its protagonist, Chang P'ei-chün.

condemned the Sung Neo-Confucians, in part, for the dichotomy they created between "heavenly reason" (*t'ien-li*) and "human desire" (*jen-yü*), a dichotomy which provided ample garden space for the growth of hypocrisy. Tai would have understood Lu Hsün's story.[24]) Since readers often object to the somber atmosphere that broods over Lu Hsün's fictional world, let us note in passing that "Soap" is one of his most optimistic tales.[25] The wife has exposed her husband's hypocrisy and thus opened the way to change; and he, in turn, has made her aware of her diminishing sexual attractiveness, a loss for which, given enough soap and exotic scents, she may well compensate.

In his concern with the hypocrisy that results when one attempts to gloss over or ignore anything (reality) for the sake of maintaining appearances (name), Lu Hsün takes us back again to his student days in Tokyo when he decided that honesty (*ch'eng*) and love (*ai*) were the two things most lacking in Chinese society. The

---

24. The theme of moral hypocrisy is, of course, by no means new in China: more than two thousand years earlier the "Robber Chih Chapter (Tao-chih p'ien)" of the *Chuang Tzu* made a brilliant examination of it. More recently, and more relevantly in Lu Hsün's case, there was the eighteenth-century thinker Tai Chen (see n. 5 above), who believed that men's desires should be socialized instead of repressed. An enemy of the Neo-Confucian disjunction between "heavenly reason" and "human desire," Tai wrote: "The Confucian gentleman simply tries to bring human desires into accord with the right way. It is futile to try to control a river simply by blocking its passage. If you obstruct it on the east, it will flow out on the west; or worse, it will break your dam and create an ungovernable flood. Similarly, if one tries to control himself or to govern others simply by repressing the human desires, he may succeed in quieting them temporarily, but in the end the desires will inevitably outwit all attempts to restrain them. This is not what the Confucian gentleman does. Instead, he concentrates his attention upon the right way and merely seeks to cause men not to do those things that do not accord with it." See H. G. Creel, *Chinese Thought from Confucius to Mao Tse-tung* (Chicago, 1953), p. 231. Nor is it without significance that the same year that he wrote "Soap" Lu Hsün completed his edition of the works of Hsi K'ang, a Taoist philosopher of the Wei-Chin period who also emphasized the importance of freely expressing the feelings. The difference between someone like Tai Chen and Lu Hsün, of course, was that Lu Hsün considered traditional Confucian philosophy past all redemption; moreover, for the serious purpose of examining the problem, he used fiction rather than philosophical essay or classical commentary. But then, so did the "Robber Chih Chapter" of the *Chuang Tzu*.
25. The story "Brothers" closes on a similarly positive note.

word, *ch'eng*, of course, connotes openness and integrity. Repression or denial of desire (feigning to live up to *ming* while ignoring *shih*) destroys *ch'eng* and paves the way for hypocrisy. Refusal to pick up the surface of appearances and peek at the reality that lies beneath—this is one of the dominant themes in Lu Hsün's stories dealing with the traditional period. In "Diary of a Madman," the protagonist, during a period of madness that is actually a form of sanity, does glimpse beneath the righteous and moralistic surface of Chinese history and there discovers the reality of a bloody, cannibalistic feast where the strong butcher and the weak are butchered. Again the concern is a discrepancy between name and reality. Similarly, as we have seen, K'ung Yi-chi resolutely refuses to face reality and lives in a never-never-land of high-sounding phrases gleaned from the classics. Fourth Uncle in "The New Year's Sacrifice" is prepared to sacrifice the well-being of Sister Hsiang-lin without a second thought in order to preserve appearances; and Ch'en Shih-ch'eng in "The White Light" is so unable to face reality that he finally flees to the realm of true madness (as opposed to the seeming madness that is actually sanity in "Diary of a Madman"). It would seem that in Lu Hsün, himself, there was an unresolved conflict between the desire to look beneath the surface of reality and point out the ugliness there (call attention to the illness) and a profound sense of his own inability to do anything about that ugliness. (Would you wake suffocating people in a room from which there was no escape if you did not know how to get out yourself?) From that point of view the least tragic of the traditional intellectuals whom we have examined thus far is Ssu-ming: there is some reason to believe that both he and his wife will change in significant ways and perhaps be able, in part at least, to resolve the conflict that is at the heart of their story.

IN-BETWEEN INTELLECTUALS

Many of the people who appear in Lu Hsün's stories are readily identifiable traditional types with deep roots in Chinese society; their countenances would have been as familiar to a reader of 1720 or 1820 as to one of 1920. They are stock types, even though what Lu Hsün has to say about them is far from stereotypic. In the Chinese society of one or two centuries ago, however, one would not have encountered the cultural malcontent—a malcontent whom we may conveniently label the "in-between intellectual." The in-between intellectual, whether he be a returned student (fresh from a sojourn in Japan, America, or Europe) or the domestically produced result of a new system of education (represented by the *hsüeh-t'ang*), usually appears in Lu Hsün's short stories as a malcontent. His dissatisfaction is often more cultural than political. He is frequently as knowledgeable in such esoteric areas as Western logic as he is in the traditional Four Books and Five Classics. Culturally, he is "in between," and from the hindsight of the present we perceive that he is also temporally "in between" in the course of modern Chinese history: the old massive and monolithic orthodoxy of empire fades into the distance behind him as the new and equally massive and monolithic orthodoxy of the People's Republic looms up ever closer before him.

By virtue of generational position and education, Lu Hsün was one of the brotherhood of in-between intellectuals. He felt that the in-between intellectual's criticism of traditional Chinese life was eminently worthy of serious consideration, so much so that he often felt constrained to address such criticism directly to his readers. The most effective way to do this, especially in those pieces where the majority of the characters have been recruited directly from the ranks of traditional society, is, of course, through the role of narrator. By definition, a narrator stands outside the story he tells, and the role is peculiarly suited to the in-between intellectual who has been forced (by virtue of his education and unorthodox ideas) to stand apart from the traditional society in which he lives. Hence it is not at all surprising that the in-between intellectual appears so often in Lu Hsün's stories in this role.

The first in-between intellectual we encounter in Lu Hsün's two volumes of stories is the first-person narrator of a short reminiscence titled, "A Trifling Incident (Yi-chien hsiao-shih)."[26] This piece, dated June 1920, is presented as a recollection of an incident that occurred three years earlier on a Peking street. A rickshaw puller, in whose vehicle the narrator is riding, accidentally knocks down an old woman, apparently without doing her any harm. The puller, despite the narrator's insistence that he forget the

26. *LHCC*, I, 43-45; *SWLH*, I, 49-51.

whole thing and press on, takes time to comfort the old woman and then helps her to a police station where she will presumably report the accident and ask for medical aid. A minor event. Yet it was an event whose size was magnified on the screen of the narrator's mind against the background of the bleak and confusing history of the first years of the republic, a history of pointless and meaningless to him as "The Master said" (the conventional phrase introducing quotations from Confucius) and "The *Poetry Classic* states" (the similar formula for quotations from that classic). Contemporary history, the "now" of political rhetoric, has become as unreal to the narrator as the half-understood phrases of the classics that he memorized as a youth. Stimulated by the rickshaw man's act of unselfish benevolence, the narrator finds himself awakening to a new mode of being, more imbued with reality than any that he has previously known.

Almost in the twinkling of an eye, six years have passed since I came to the capital from the countryside. Were I to tally up the so-called great affairs of state that I saw or heard with my own eyes and ears during that time, the total would certainly not be small. And yet not one of them has left any trace in my mind and if you were to ask me to spell out the influences that these affairs had on me, then I would have to say that they only intensified an already vile disposition—to tell the truth, they taught me to despise my fellow men more and more every day.

Chou Tso-jen has said that "A Trifling Incident" is no story at all, and that if written at a later date it would have been filed away among his brother's random impressions (*tsa-kan*). He doubts that the incident ever occurred. The historicity may well be questionable (the pieces contained in *Call to Arms* and *Wandering* are, after all, fictionalized, whatever the number of autobiographical elements in them), and we cannot insist that the narrator is Lu Hsün. And yet, whatever the logic of facts may be, it is apparent that, judged by the logic of feelings, Lu Hsün was this narrator, an awakening in-between intellectual caught in the process of enlightenment. On the relationship of the narrator to Lu Hsün, the Soviet scholar I. V. Semanov has said:

Rare is the critic who misses the opportunity to mention that the narrator and author of a creative work are not one and the same person. This is not always true, and many stories by Lu Hsün . . . serve as proof. . . . Some critics without sufficient justification have, for example, deprecated the character of the narrator in "A Trifling Incident," forgetting that it was he who celebrated the rickshaw driver's nobility and condemned his own, essentially momentary, egoism. It cannot be overemphasized that the narrator in the majority of Lu Hsün's works is either a reflection of the author himself or, in any case, a man with similar convictions.[27]

I heartily agree. Furthermore, on the factual level, something of Lu Hsün's sympathy for rickshaw men may be gleaned from the following entry in his diary:

February 8, 1913.—Clear. Windy. Went to the ministry in the morning. The rickshaw man accidentally severed a rubber water-hose that was placed on the street. What appeared to be a policeman and a number of people in civilian clothes suddenly appeared and began pummeling him at random. In a decadent age human beings behave like wild dogs.[28]

Since the first four selections in *Call to Arms* all deal with China before the 1911 Revolution, "A Trifling Incident" is Lu Hsün's first piece set in the Republican period. It begins by recording the narrator's profound disappointment with the results of the revolution. Against this gloomy background of disenchantment with the new order, the ray of hope embodied in the rickshaw man's simple act of kindness and responsibility shines forth with doubled intensity and awakens the narrator to the possibility of a new mode of being and (were everyone to act in the same fashion) the possibility of constructing a different society. Of the various events that transpired in the wake of the revolution, only the memory of this "trifling incident" remains with the narrator, who says, "[It] makes me ashamed, constrains me to reconstruct myself, and increases my store of courage and hope." Lu Hsün was basically a literary man (a *wen-jen*), and it is perhaps for this reason that, along with an intense contempt for mere words, he had an admiration for action that bordered on worship. In evaluating various figures of Chinese antiquity in his *Old Stories Retold* (*Ku-shih hsin-pien*, 1922-35), for instance, he seems to have favored above all others the emperor Yü, who controlled the floods, and the philosopher Mo Tzu, who made an arduous journey to prevent a war. These two men had acted. Similarly, the

27. *Lu Hsün and his Predecessors*, pp. 157-58.
28. *LHJC*, I, 45-46.

heroism of this rickshaw puller is manifested not in anything he says, but through a simple, unpremeditated act.

"A Trifling Incident" was written in July 1920; three months later, on the occasion of the anniversary of the revolution, Lu Hsün wrote a piece for the October 10 supplement of a Shanghai newspaper.[29] He titled it "The Story of Hair (T'ou-fa te ku-shih)."[30] Like "A Trifling Incident," it is presented as a first-person reminiscence. It begins as the narrator tears a sheet off the calendar and discovers that the date is the Double Tenth—October 10, the anniversary of the revolution. A friend identified simply as "N" arrives, and the two men begin to reminisce over the revolution and to ponder its significance. It is apparent that, by virtue of age and education, both are in-between intellectuals. Says N:

"I really admire the way the Double Tenth is celebrated in Peking. In the morning a policeman comes to the gate and orders you to 'Hang up the flag!' 'Yes Sir, we'll hang up the flag!' From every home out steps a citizen—for the most part without any enthusiasm—and hauls up a tattered, faded bit of cotton cloth. It stays up until evening and then it is brought in and the gate is closed for the night. Once in a while a man forgets and then the flag is left up until the next day.

They've forgotten how to celebrate the anniversary, but then the anniversary has forgotten them too."[31]

For most people, the revolution which once promised so much has in the end not amounted to very much, has become something that one remembers out of government-imposed duty rather than any real affection. The two friends go on to recall how the graves of the young martyrs who died to bring about the new order are now

29. The *Shih-shih hsin-pao. LHCC*, I, 485, n. 1 at the bottom of the page.

30. *LHCC*, I, 46-51; *Ah Q and Others*, trans. Wang, pp. 59-64.

31. *LHCC*, I, 46. My translation. Tso-jen says that the content of much of N's speech is pure Lu Hsün, while his style of speaking is based on that of one of Lu Hsün's superiors at the Ministry of Education, Hsia Sui-ch'ing (1861-1924), head of the Division of Social Education, the division in which Lu Hsün was a section chief (see chap. 9); Tso-jen further states that his brother much admired Hsia. In effect, through the mouth of N (or Hsia), Lu Hsün recounts his own initial difficulties with the queue in Japan and later without it in China. As we have seen, while teaching in Shaohsing on the eve of the Republican Revolution, he advised his students not to cut off their pigtails and thereby earned their youthful contempt. *HSJW*, pp. 30-34.

caving in from neglect. Bravely attempting to push back some of the gloom that wraps ever more tightly about them, N gives himself a resounding slap on the back of his head at the spot where his pigtail used to be: "The thing that tickles me most is that after the first Double Tenth no one ever again mocked me or cursed me when I went out on the street."

Essentially, "The Story of Hair" registers the in-between intellectual's vast disappointment with the Republican Revolution—a revolution whose most profound effect was that of enabling men to lop off their queues. China was at this time, of course, a united republic in name only; the country was split into a number of competing spheres of influence under the control of various foreign governments and native warlords. It may well have been the case that the particularly bleak situation in Peking was largely responsible for the intensity of the pessimism expressed in this story. Hsü Kuang-p'ing, Lu Hsün's second wife, has pointed out, for instance, that in 1926, when he was in Amoy, Lu Hsün enjoyed the celebration of the Double Tenth there in a very positive manner. While the merchants in Peking put out faded flags and made a show of celebrating when ordered to, those in Amoy hung out flags and festooned their shops of their own volition and because of a genuine enthusiasm for the new order. Lu Hsün opined that this was because in Amoy the flag represented a revolution that carried hope with it, while in Peking it was simply another symbol of the warlords.[32]

Toward the end of this story N notes that hair is causing trouble again. Peking girls in 1920 were having trouble gaining admission to schools because they had taken to bobbing their hair.[33] The conversation dwindles away. As N takes his leave, he notes cynically: "Please excuse me for having disturbed you; luckily it won't be the Double Tenth any more tomorrow and then we can just forget the whole thing."

The antipathy of the narrator toward the establishment in "A Trifling Incident" and "The Story of Hair" is mild compared with that of the one in "Home Town (Ku-hsiang)."[34] Here the narrator

32. *HYL*, pp. 65-66.
33. Many schools had strict regulations against bobbed hair. *HSJW*, p. 37. Hsü Ch'in-wen says that this remark may refer to his younger sister, whom Lu Hsün helped to tiptoe around the regulations and into a normal school at about this time. *NHFH*, p. 41.
34. *LHCC*, I, 61-71; *SWLH*, I, 63-75.

tells of a trip from the city to the countryside, where, rather depressed, he has gone to sell his ancestral property to people of another surname. According to popular belief, only a very unworthy descendant of a t'aimen would ever be brought to such a pass. The scenery and the people have sharply deteriorated from what, in the idyllic fields of the narrator's memory, they were decades earlier. Thirty years ago the narrator had been the spoiled darling of a wealthy family. He recalls with particular lucidity of detail a year when his father was still alive and it was the family's turn to preside over an important clan sacrifice. It had been necessary to call in a part-time helper to aid with the preparations and stand guard over the sacrificial implements. The helper had brought his son, Jun-t'u, with him. It was Jun-t'u who made that wonderful boyhood winter especially memorable. The narrator's tone makes it clear that Jun-t'u was rare and precious precisely because he represented freedom—the lack of restraint of the lower classes as against the middle-class restrictiveness of the narrator's background and the freedom of the sea (Jun-t'u lives at the shore) as against the confinement of the land. Thirty years ago the narrator had been impressed, in the way only a boy a little over ten can be impressed, with this wonderfully romantic lad from the seashore.

Wow! Jun-t'u's mind was just chock full of all kinds of wondrous things, things that my ordinary, everyday friends knew nothing about. There were some things that they couldn't know, for while Jun-t'u was at the seashore, they—like me—could see only a rectangle of open sky from within a high-walled courtyard.[35]

Given such fond memories, the adult narrator looks forward with nostalgic anticipation to seeing his childhood friend once more. This explains the intensity of his disappointment when, a few days later, the friend appears at the t'aimen as a man in his

---

35. My translation. According to Tso-jen, it was in 1893 that Lu Hsün (then in his thirteenth year) met the boy upon whom Jun-t'u was based. On the occasion of an important sacrifice at the t'aimen, a man named Chang Fu-ch'ing (who did in fact have a watermelon patch close to the sea) was called in as part-time help. He brought with him a son, Yun-shui, and it was from this name that Lu Hsün derived Jun-t'u, substituting *jun* for *yun* (homonyms in Shaohsing pronunciation), and "earth" (*t'u*) for "water" (*shui*). Yun-shui's father was a rather bright man whom the children called Uncle Ch'ing and particularly admired for his skill in making toys out of bamboo. *HSJW*, pp. 50-52; *LHKC*, pp. 17-18.

forties, broken and prematurely old. The narrator greets him as "brother," to which his deferential response is "master," a response that makes the narrator realize in a flash the breadth of the barrier that has now come to separate them. The narrator's mother suggests that Jun-t'u continue to call her son "brother" as he used to when they were children together, but he demurs, pointing out that that was something belonging to those early years when he did not yet "understand" the ways of the world.

Soon after this, a woman of about fifty comes to the t'aimen to see if anything is for sale. At first the narrator does not recognize her. Then, as she gives him reminders, he begins to remember: this is Sister Yang-erh, who used to have the beancurd shop across the way. Strikingly pretty in her younger days, she had been known around the neighborhood as the "beancurd beauty." Much to the narrator's chagrin, she automatically assumes that he (as a member of the gentry) is wealthy and must have acquired a fair number of concubines by now. As she prattles on, it becomes increasingly apparent that the passing years have made her petty and mean besides taking her beauty.[36] Instead of the exciting peasant boy of his youth who used to call him "brother" there is a broken man of middle age who addresses him as "master"; instead of the pretty beancurd-shop proprietress, a greedy woman on the threshold of old age who treats him as a master and is convinced that he must be rich. As in "A Trifling Incident," we accompany the narrator at a moment of revelation. In "Home Town" it is a particularly painful one, a revelation of the distance that now separates him from the people of his youth. The qualitatively different life experiences of Jun-t'u and Sister Yang-erh have alienated them completely from the sphere of the narrator. During the visit his eight-year-old nephew and Jun-t'u's son strike up a friendship, and as the narrator prepares to leave this disappointing, you-can't-go-home-again atmosphere he can only hope that the two boys, as they move into adulthood, will remain as close as they seem to be now. At the same time he is poignantly aware that this hope lacks teeth and borders upon superstition.

36. Tso-jen has said that the Yang woman is not based on anyone in particular back in Shaohsing, though there may well be elements of one or another person in her. *HSJW*, pp. 54-55.

"It is just like a path . . ."

When I thought of hope, I suddenly became afraid. When Jun-t'u asked if he could have that set of candlesticks and the incense burner [to be used in making offerings] I had even laughed up my sleeve at him because I thought that he was forever worshipping idols and could not put them out of his mind for so much as a moment. And yet was not that thing which I now called "hope" also just such an idol, one that I had fashioned with my very own hands? It was merely that his hope was for something near at hand, while mine was for something rather vague and distant.

. . . I thought to myself, "Hope isn't the kind of thing of which you can say 'It exists' or 'It doesn't exist.' It is just like a path on the ground; for to begin with there are no paths on the ground. They are made when a number of people travel the same way."[37]

Apart from the various themes in Lu Hsün's writings that are rooted in particular times and attached to specific circumstances, there are others that are somewhat more transcendent. "Hope" or "the courage to be" is one such theme. The narrator of "A Trifling Incident" can draw such courage from the example of the magnanimous rickshaw man's act of kindness. It is an act that constitutes a revelation, a door opened out into the light. Jun-t'u's depressed condition and Sister Yang-erh's want of kindness constitute a further revelation, a door opened into darkness, a darkness and emptiness from which no spiritual sustenance can be drawn. Hence the narrator must turn in upon himself in search of hope and the courage to be. Once having found it, however, he suspects that it is simply another kind of self-deception and one that is not qualitatively different from that represented by Jun-t'u's superstitions. In the end he realizes that "hope" is justified by its own creation. It is created by those who, despite everything, can find the life and courage to create it, just as a path is made by those people who have enough life and initiative to move in a given direction across the land. The narrators of "A Trifling Incident," "The Story of Hair," and "Home Town" are all in-between intellectuals who are profoundly disappoined with the apparent failure of the 1911 Revolution to bring about any genuine changes in society. Despite their disenchantment, all three have the courage to keep on, though from a purely intellectual point of view they may occasionally suspect that such courage is virtually irrational.

Although (perhaps because) he was one of them, Lu Hsün did not have any great faith in the in-between intellectuals as a group. When those in-betweens who appear as narrators do have positive qualities, it is essentially because their stories are emotionally (if not factually) autobiographical, and this positive evaluation by no means applies to all of them. We have seen how, in Japan, Lu Hsün mistrusted the motivations of most of his fellow students, all

---

37. My translation. The second time that Lu Hsün met Yun-shui, the lad upon whom Jun-t'u was based, was in 1900. Yun-shui, by then a young married man, went to see a fortuneteller. Lu Hsün greatly embarrassed him by making fun of his trip to the fortuneteller's. *HSJW*, pp. 52–53. Perhaps that encounter is reflected in this passage.

of whom would, of course, belong to the camp of the in-between intellectuals.

The clearest indication of Lu Hsün's attitude in this regard is given in the most famous of his stories, "The True Story of Ah Q (Ah Q cheng-chuan)."[38] The story is set in a small village which is almost totally dominated by the prestige and power of His Honor Chao and His Honor Ch'en, two illustrious patriarchs who boast of two equally illustrious sons. His Honor Chao's son is a *hsiu-ts'ai*, while His Honor Ch'ien's sone is a returned student—hence an in-between intellectual. A beautiful section of the story describes the latter. Ah Q, the village roustabout, has just been beaten in a fight (as usual) and is standing stunned and aching on the road.

A man walked toward him from the distance. Another enemy had arrived! Here was another man whom Ah Q utterly detested—the eldest son of His Honor Ch'ien. Years back he had run off to town and entered one of those academies where they taught foreign subjects; after that somehow or other he went off to Japan. When he came back six months later, he had taken to walking straight-legged like a foreigner and his pigtail was nowhere to be seen. His mother had reacted with a dozen or so good rounds of wailing and his old lady had attempted three dives into a well. Wherever his mother went after that, she was always telling people: "Some lowdown people got him drunk and cut off his pigtail. Otherwise he could have been a big official but now he'll have to wait until it grows out again before he can think of that." But Ah Q didn't believe a word of it and insisted on calling him "imitation foreign devil" or "foreign sell-out." He would curse him under his breath whenever he saw him.

What most inspired Ah Q to play the righteous hero in "intensely abominating and bellicosely severing all bonds with such rank curs" was the phony pigtail. For a man to go so far as to get a false pigtail was nothing less than giving up any claim he might have to being human. And since his old lady hadn't tried a fourth dive into the well, she couldn't be a good woman either.

At this point we might well feel some sympathy for the poor returned "foreign devil" (and surely this section of the story does in part reflect Lu Hsün's own experiences with the pigtail). Later, when the revolution comes to Wei village, young Ch'ien forfeits all claim on our affections by revealing himself for the opportunist that he is.

38. *LHCC*, I, 72-114; *SWLH*, I, 76-135. The translations in the ensuing discussion are my own.

When the revolution first nears the village, the Chaos and the Ch'iens are terrified. The Chao lad, a *hsiu-ts'ai* and therefore a traditional intellectual, has always disdained the in-between Ch'ien lad; but adversity makes for strange bedfellows:

Chao Hsiu-ts'ai was always right on top of the news and as soon as he heard that the revolutionary party had already entered the town during the night, he immediately coiled his pigtail up on top of his head. At the crack of dawn he went to pay a call on Ch'ien, the imitation foreign devil, a man whom he had heretofore never considered his equal. But since now was a time for "everybody to join together in modernizing the country," they hit it off very well.

They join forces to "revolutionize" the local Buddhist convent where they beat up a nun, smash an imperial tablet, and make off with a valuable Ming dynasty censer—all in the sacred name of revolution. Both Chao the *hsiu-ts'ai* and Ch'ien the imitation foreign devil quickly win influential posts in the new government, in part no doubt because of the profound existential grasp of "revolution" they exhibited in their little foray on the convent. Ah Q, of course, is totally barred from the revolution and, much to the relief of the village's power structure, it soon becomes apparent that nothing has changed except perhaps a few titles. Where were the Chinese Mara poets that Lu Hsün had hoped for in Japan?

In "The True Story of Ah Q" Lu Hsün presented his audience with a scathing analysis of an opportunistic, self-serving in-between intellectual during the Republican Revolution. In "Dragon Boat Festival (Tuan-wu chieh)"[39] he turned to the position of the in-between intellectual in the corrupt warlord regime that ruled Peking a decade or so after the revolution. In the early 1920s the warlord government borrowed vast sums of money from abroad and gleaned taxes at home to carry on a civil war; hence it was often behind in the payment of its officials and teachers. Fang Hsüan-ch'o, the protagonist of "Dragon Boat Festival," is both a teacher and an official.[40] The festival, celebrated on the fifth day of the fifth lunar month, is traditionally a day when debts must be

39. *LHCC*, I, 115-23; Wang Chi-chen, trans., *Contemporary Chinese Stories* (New York, 1943), pp. 181-89. Wang titles his translation "What's the Difference?" The excerpts in the ensuing discussion are my own translations.
40. Chou Tso-jen has pointed out that much of the material for this story is autobiographical, many of the incidents being taken directly from contemporary events. On June 3, 1921, for instance, teachers demonstrating for

settled. Thus, given Fang's occupation and the title of the story, the die is cast: Fang is going to need money. And yet the story is as much concerned with how the Peking milieu during the early years of the republic has weakened Fang morally as it is with his difficulty in paying debts while receiving no salary. The opening paragraph makes this clear:

Fang Hsüan-ch'o had recently grown so fond of saying "It all amounts to just about the same thing anyway" that the phrase had virtually become his stock response to any situation. It was not just simply that these were *words* that he said; the fact was that the *idea* contained in the words had already moved into his brain and settled down for a long stay. At first he used to go around saying "It all amounts to the same thing anyway," but later, probably because he thought that this way of expressing it was a bit too extreme, he changed it to "It all amounts to *just about* the same thing anyway."

Fang Hsüan-ch'o takes his place in that long line of familiar figures found in Lu Hsün's stories composed of backsliding in-between intellectuals, ardently progressive in their youth, who had become ever more conservative with the passage of years and in the revolution's depressing aftermath of warlords and stagnant corruption.

When in the past he had seen elders lording it over the younger generation, he became indignant, but now his mind took a different tack and he would reflect that in the future when these young people had their own sons and grandsons, they would probably put on airs before *them* in much the same way. Thus he no longer felt any injustice in the situation. Similarly, when in the past he had seen soldiers beating a rickshaw puller he seethed with indignation, but now his thoughts took a different turn and he would consider that if the rickshaw puller were to become a soldier and the soldier were to pull the rickshaw, then the puller-become-soldier would do exactly the same thing. Thus he no longer worried about it. And yet, while thinking in this way, he would occasionally suspect that it was because he no longer had the courage to struggle against an evil society that he deceived himself into contriving such an escape route.

---

back pay were set upon by soldiers and beaten in front of the Presidential Palace in Peking. When this story was written in 1922, Lu Hsün, like Fang Hsüan-ch'o, was concurrently working as an official (in the Ministry of Education) and teaching at a university (National Peking University, where he taught the history of Chinese fiction). *HSJW*, pp. 114-22; Ou-yang Fan-hai, *Lu Hsün te shu* [The writings of Lu Hsün] (Canton, 1949), p. 204; hereafter cited as *LHTS*.

Though in need of money, he steadfastly refuses to join either of two groups organized (first by the teachers and later by the officials) for the purpose of doing something about getting paid:

Since he had already expressed his sympathy with the teachers' demand for their back pay, he approved, of course, when his colleagues demanded theirs. He, himself, however, remained comfortably ensconced in the yamen office as was his wont, instead of going with them to demand payment. And if some people suspected that he was loftily trying to be "above it all"—then of course that would be but a misapprenhension on their part. He explained it by saying that ever since he had come into the world people had always come to him to collect on debts, but he had never gone to dun anyone else; hence it was simply something that was "not one of his strong points."

Never really taking a stand, Fang behaves in a slippery, opportunistic manner somewhat reminiscent of Master Baldy or His Honor Chao.

Whether it was because of laziness or his own uselessness, he didn't know, but at any rate he felt that he was a person who didn't like to take part in movements and who was perfectly happy to keep his place and mind his own business.

On the evening of the fourth—it is the day before the Dragon Boat festival—he returns home early, still without his pay, or any part of it, and, much to his wife's disgust, announces that he will not be given any money until the eighth. Mrs. Fang, of course, is the one who will be left with the task of explaining this to the creditors who will dun them until then. Turning to alcohol for comfort, her husband sends out for a bottle of strong wine—on credit! He knows that he will not be refused, for a merchant who would refuse him on the eve of the festival might well bring down so much bad luck upon himself that not one of his customers would come to settle past debts the next day. Fang may be weak-kneed, but he is not dumb. Shades of Master Baldy and His Honor Chao!

"A book of verses underneath the bough, a jug of wine . . ."—it is all very idyllic for Fang, but his wife cannot forget their creditors and suggests that they buy a lottery ticket. Though the same idea had that very day floated to the surface of his own consciousness, Fang now puts down his wife's suggestion with outright fury. As the scene closes, he settles comfortably with a book of Hu Shih's new-style poetry and truly seems to be "above it all." There seems much justification for Professor William Schultz's characterization of the central theme of this story as "the spiritless acquiescence of man to corrupt, despotic government," and his observation that the implication of the story is that "so long as this deficiency in public spirit continues, so shall the existing government grind the populace under heel."[41] As an in-between intellectual, Fang Hsüan-ch'o has indeed been guilty of backsliding and losing courage (as he himself suspects) to the point of total capitulation to the status quo.

Since Lu Hsün was a member of the brotherhood, it is likely that in examining Fang (whose life situation so nearly paralleled his own) he was in good part analyzing himself. He stated that he often probed his own faults while ostensibly laying bare the foibles of others.[42] There is evidence that "Dragon Boat Festival" is a case in point. In "A Note on Payday," an essay written in 1926, Lu Hsün makes it clear that at least one of Fang's major complaints about the groups organized to demand payment of salaries was also his own.

In 1926, as was the case four years earlier when "Dragon Boat Festival" was written, the government was sadly in arrears in its payment of salaries. When Lu Hsün wrote his essay, the Ministry of Education had just declared a payday: it would give thirty percent of his full salary to any employee who showed up to request it in person within a three-day period. In the essay Lu Hsün objects to being treated in this rather cavalier fashion, as though in paying him the government were doing him a special favor, or even passing out alms to the needy. He notes (as did Fang Hsüan-ch'o) that his countrymen give themselves special airs whenever they are in control of money. Specifically mentioning his story, he aligns himself with Fang's attitude of being "above it all":

This business of drawing pay in person has a long history, and when Fang Hsüan-ch'o started complaining in the eleventh year of the republic I wrote a short story on this subject called 'Dragon Boat Festival.' But though history is said to move in cycles, it never repeats itself, and the present is slightly different from the past. In the good old days, the

41. "Lu Hsün," pp. 247-48.
42. *LHCC*, I, 362. (Cf. n. 60 below.)

advocates of drawing pay in person were the doughty leaders of the Assocation to Demand Back Pay—to save time I will not go into these special terms one by one; besides, it would be a waste of good paper. They rushed about day and night, appealing to the government or importuning the Ministry of Finance. But once they had the money they were loath to share it with those who had not helped to get it, and imposed this slight inconvenience on these undeserving people. Their idea seemed to be: we got this money, so in a way it is ours. If you want it, you must come here like mendicants. Look how clothing and congee are distributed—no one ever delivers them to the beggars' homes![43]

Noting that Lu Hsün seldom joined organizations, Ou-yang Fan-hai opines that he did not join the Association to Demand Back Pay because his personality would not allow it.[44] Like Fang Hsüan-ch'o, he might well have objected that joining was "not one of his strong points." Since it is precisely Fang's middle-of-the-road aloofness and lack of involvement that is criticized in "Dragon Boat Festival," one can assume that in the author Lu Hsün is dissecting himself. Ou-yang believes that in the Peking of 1922, with warlords and politicians battling and juggling for power, and righteous defenders of the "national heritage" trying to kill the colloquial-language movement, Lu Hsün became so discouraged that at times it did indeed seem to him that things all "amounted to about the same thing anyway." Ou-yang believes that this conclusion made him suspect that he was losing his courage to fight against a corrupt society, and that in writing "Dragon Boat Festival" he was in effect exorcising an evil spirit.[45] This seems likely.[46]

---

43. *SWLH*, II, 285. I have used the Yangs' translation, altering only the English rendering of the story title (the Yangs call it "The Double-Fifth Festival") and the romanization of the protagonist's name for the sake of consistency.
44. *LHTS*, p. 205.
45. Ibid., pp. 202-3.
46. This is not to say that, in creating the character Fang Hsüan-ch'o, Lu Hsün was merely analyzing himself under a pseudonym, but rather that, in criticizing one important aspect of Fang's personality, his *ku-kao*, Lu Hsün was in effect criticizing himself. In other ways, Lu Hsün was quite different from Fang. (This is a name, by the way, that may echo a nickname that Lu Hsün had for a while among his friends. See *HSJW*, p. 115.) Fang was a hack teacher; Lu Hsün's courses, on the other hand, were well organized and well taught. And, according to Tso-jen, these factors accounted for their popularity more than Lu Hsün's literary reputation and attracted students to his classes in great numbers despite his poorly pronounced Mandarin—never very easy for Northerners to

In "The New Year's Sacrifice (Chu-fu)," we examined Lu Hsün's presentation of a traditional intellectual (Fourth Uncle). Let us consider the story now from the point of view of the narrator, who is an in-between intellectual. During a visit to his home town the narrator encounters Sister Hsiang-lin. It has been five years since he last saw her, and he is shocked by her changed appearance. Though she is only forty, her hair is white; her face is so expressionless that it might have been carved from wood. Deferring to his superior knowledge, she asks if it is true that souls survive after death. Knowing that the people in his home town believe in an afterlife, the narrator wonders at the reason for her doubts and, to spare her pain, gives the answer that she wants: yes, they do. Then it must follow, she goes on to deduce, that there also exists a hell (*ti-yü*), a place where the dead are judged and punished.[47] The narrator is forced to admit that, logically, there ought to be some such place. Sister Hsiang-lin's mind runs on, past the timid pace of his reasoning, to wonder if families will be reunited there. As her questions increase in tempo and emotional intensity, the narrator becomes less and less confident and says that he is not sure about the business of families being reunited either. Backing off even further, he says that he is not certain about the survival of the soul after death. The next evening he learns that she is dead; he would like to get the details from Fourth Uncle, but dares not touch on such a subject on New Year's Eve. Later that night, as he sits musing by the light of an oil lamp, Sister Hsiang-lin's entire unhappy life passes before him in review. At dawn, he is finally aroused from this none-too-happy reverie by the sound of firecrackers announcing the New Year.

This is certainly one of Lu Hsün's gloomiest tales.[48] Even the joyous advent of the New Year does little to lighten the story's

---

understand. *HSJW*, p. 116; *NHFH*, p. 73. In the story, Fang's wife is apparently a rather traditional Chinese woman, more concerned with the practicalities of daily life than with the exciting topics of the May Fourth period. She is worried that her husband will consider her ignorant. His conversation with her rarely exceeds a limited number of grunts and signs. It seems likely that in this woman we see a reflection of Lu Hsün's own wife.

47. As we have seen, she is worried lest Yen Wang, who presides over hell, will split her body in two and give half to each of her former husbands.

48. The somber tone of "The New Year's Sacrifice" no doubt echoes Lu Hsün's spiritual depression at this time. He dates the story February 1, 1924, or two days after the lunar New Year. On the day before New Year's he had received

freight of sadness. The narrator is thoroughly depressed; he cannot even comfort himself with the feeling that with regard to Sister Hsiang-lin he, at least, has handled himself well. Describing the manner in which he broke off his unpleasant meeting with her, he notes:

Taking advantage of a lull in her questioning, I walked away and hastily retreated to Fourth Uncle's home, feeling very ill at ease. I mused to myself, "Perhaps my answer holds some danger for her. Seeing other people prepare to celebrate the New Year, no doubt she became doubly aware of her own isolation; but in asking that question could she have had anything else in mind? Had she perhaps had a premonition? If she did have something else in mind, and if because of what I said, something else should happen, then my words would in fact be partly accountable." But then I laughed at myself for perversely reasoning in such a hairsplitting fashion about a chance event of no great significance. No wonder that some educationalists have said that I am a neurotic. Furthermore, since I had clearly stated that I was not sure, I had already canceled out everything that I had said in my answer so that even if something untoward did happen, it would have nothing whatever to do with me.

That last statement moves the narrator perilously close to that none-too-illustrious crew composed of such men as Master Baldy, His Honor Chao, and Fang Hsüan-ch'o. Yet there is a difference. The narrator of "The New Year's Sacrifice" appears as a rather gentle, even poetic, person who is well aware of his defects and given to bittersweet self-criticism. His personality is clearly Lu Hsün's. Unlike Fourth Uncle, he feels genuine sympathy for Sister Hsiang-lin; unlike Fourth Uncle, too, he is self-aware—enough to realize that his sympathy is bootless. Self-awareness is a mark of many of the in-between intellectuals in Lu Hsün's short stories. They are awakened. Unlike Fourth Uncle, they have a keen sense

---

snips and snatches of his back salary from the Esperanto School (15 dollars of his December salary), Peking University (18 dollars of his July salary plus 8 dollars of August's), and the Ministry of Education (180 dollars—a windfall indeed—of his past April's salary). That evening the Esperanto School sent over his royalty on 97 copies of his *Brief History of Chinese Fiction*, which amounted to 23 dollars and 28 cents. He noted in his diary that he drank an unusually large amount of wine that night, and two nights later noted that he had been unable to get to sleep and had finished off an entire bottle. *LHJC*, p. 477. We have already seen that the back-salary situation in Peking bothered him and that he expressed some of his choler in "Dragon Boat Festival."

of what is wrong with society. Like this narrator, however, they are also aware of their inability to do anything about it. They are drugless diagnosticians pointing out diseases, but offering no cures. It is a distressing situation, to which they react in either of two ways: like Fang Hsüan-ch'o they may withdraw from any involvement, justifying themselves with rationalizations and comforting themselves with wine and poetry; or like the narrator of "The New Year's Sacrifice" they may continue to face reality, but with a bittersweet, self-critical—and guilty—awareness of their inability to change it.

The narrator of "Upstairs in a Wineshop (Tsai chiu-lou shang)"[49] is another in-between intellectual. He is somewhat reminiscent of the narrator of "The Story of Hair" in that he addresses the reader for no other apparent purpose than to tell of a chance meeting with an old friend. He has stopped at S-town[50] on a trip from northern China to his native region in the southeast. On a snowy night while he is having food and wine alone upstairs in a wineshop, the old friend, Lü Wei-fu, happens to come in. In the past they had been fellow students and, later, fellow teachers. The narrator has not seen Wei-fu in ten years and notes that he seems more haggard, less spirited, than at their last meeting. Wei-fu tells the narrator that now both he and his mother are living in a distant province where he is working as a family tutor. Taking advantage of the New Year's vacation, he has returned to S-town in order to shore up the grave of his younger brother, who died at the age of three. It seems that his mother has learned that water is encroaching on it, and is anxious lest it be swept away by the river. Wei-fu recounts how he hired workmen to dig up the grave, only to find the coffin rotted away and no trace of the body. He had then taken some of the soil from the spot where the body had been and placed it in a new coffin which he buried at the site of their father's grave. Conscious of the disappointed and searching look in the narrator's eyes (the old Wei-fu would have had the courage to face things head on and tell his mother that the grave had disappeared), he asks:

"What's this? Why are you looking at me like that? You wonder how I can have changed so much from the Lü Wei-fu you used to know. Yes, I

49. *LHCC*, II, 23-34; *SWLH*, I, 174-87. The translations in the ensuing discussion are mine.
50. An allusion to Shaohsing. *HSJW*, p. 166.

too can remember the times when we used to go to the city temple and pull the beards off the gods, how we would spend whole days arguing over ways to reform China and even come to blows over it. But now I am as you see me, a man who always takes the easy way out, a man who gets through things any which way he can. It sometimes even occurs to me that if my old friends were to see me now, they probably wouldn't accept me as a friend any more—but I am as you see me."

Wei-fu goes on to tell that before he set out on this visit to S-town, his mother had remembered that Ah-shun, the daughter of a boatman neighbor, once wanted some artificial flowers so badly that she cried for them until her father beat her; therefore Wei-fu's mother instructed him to buy a few sprays on the way. He notes in passing that he had visited the old man and the girl a year and a half before, on a trip to S-town, and had forced down a bowl of buckwheat cereal in order to please Ah-shun. Though they were rather poor, the father proudly considered it a mark of affluence that he was able to provide white sugar for Lü's cereal. Despite the fact that the resulting concoction caused him to have nightmares, Wei-fu continued to feel affection for the girl.

I still wished her a lifetime of happiness, and hoped the world would change for the better for her sake. And yet, realizing that these feelings were nothing more than the residual traces of those dreams I had in days gone by, I immediately laughed at myself and then forgot the whole thing.

Apparently in the days when he pulled the beards of the gods he had dreamt that something might be done for people like Ah-shun, but now, years later, he has given up the foolish dreams of his youth. Lü Wei-fu, like most of the other in-between intellectuals in Lu Hsün's stories, has become depressingly aware of the impotence of sympathy and of his inability to effect any change.

On the trip to S-town this time, Wei-fu has followed his mother's instructions and bought the artificial flowers for Ah-shun. That very afternoon, before meeting up with his friend in the wineshop, he had gone to deliver them. He was met by Ah-shun's younger brother, now considerably grown. When he asked about her, he was given such a hostile reception that he left without delivering the flowers. Going to the firewood shop near the boatman's house, he learned what had happened. Ah-shun, secretly long afflicted by tuberculosis (she did not want to worry her father), had become extremely depressed when an uncle, irked by her refusal to lend him money, gave her to believe that her father had betrothed her to a very undesirable man. Her depression caused her illness to take a sudden turn for the worse, and despite her father's repeated assurances of the high quality of her future spouse (assurances that were true, though she did not believe them), she died. Wei-fu asked the old lady at the firewood shop to give the flowers to a sister of Ah-shun, and decided that he would deceive his mother into thinking that Ah-shun was most pleased to have them.

As Wei-fu is about to take his leave, he tells the narrator that he is getting ready to return to his position as tutor in a household where he instructs the children in the Confucian classics. The narrator is astonished that his once progressive friend now stands in the traditional camp.

"Of course. Did you think that I was teaching ABCD?[51] At first I had two students, one reading the *Poetry Classic* and the other, the *Mencius;* but recently I've added a student, a girl, and she's reading the *Primer for Girls.* I don't even teach mathematics—it's not that I don't want to; it's just that *they* don't want it."

"I never expected that you would actually go and teach that kind of thing."

"Their old man wants them to read such things. I'm not part of the family, so it doesn't make any difference to me. What difference does such trivial stuff make anyway? If I just take things as they come . . ."

When the narrator expresses concern about his friend's future, Wei-fu replies:

"The future? I don't know. Think of it, not a single thing that we planned on in the old days has turned out as we would have had it. I don't know anything any more. I don't even know what tomorrow will bring, or even the next minute."

A number of noisy customers arrive, and the friends go their separate ways. Like so many of the in-between intellectuals in Lu Hsün's stories, Lü Wei-fu registers profound disappointment with what has happened in China (or failed to happen) in the wake of the Republican Revolution.

Lü Wei-fu is a broken, despairing man. And yet, what is it that has crushed him? Is it the course of Chinese history in the previous

---

51. ABCD (it appears exactly that way in the original Chinese text as well as in the translation) is simply a convenient tag for Western (and therefore modern) learning.

decade? Is it the perhaps natural world-weariness that many men take on with the years? Or is it perhaps the result of that unavoidable shift from the dreamy limbo of student days into one of the niches that every society lays out like traps for its youth? We do not know. We know only that, like Lu Hsün, Lü Wei-fu belonged to that in-between, transitional generation for whom schools like the Sino-Occidental Academy in Shaohsing provided a chop suey of ABCD and the Confucian classics. He would, no doubt, have preferred modern learning both for himself and for China, but he has been dragged back into a morass of traditional Chinese words and traditional Chinese morality. Lü Wei-fu belonged to a group that in the early 1920s could have justly called itself "a lost generation."

As is so often the case when Lu Hsün describes in-between intellectuals, much of the material in "Upstairs in a Wineshop" is autobiographical. On a trip to Shaohsing in 1919 to sell the family property, for instance, he supervised the removal of the graves of his sister (Tuan, born in 1887, who died of smallpox before a year was out) and his youngest brother (Ch'un-shou, 1893-1898) from their original locations (in danger of collapse) to his father's burial place.[52] Furthermore, the story of Ah-shun was based on a father and daughter who rented rooms in the New T'aimen when Lu Hsün was a lad. Like Ah-shun, this girl was very capable and a great help to her father. Like Ah-shun, too, she had a no-account uncle, Ah-kuei, who did in fact tell her out of spite, when she once refused to lend him money, that the man to whom her father had betrothed her was really not even on a par with Ah-kuei himself. Unlike Ah-shun, the girl at the New T'aimen had known better than to give any credence to her uncle's words. She died young, but, according to Tso-jen, it was because she was careless with her diet after a bout of typhoid fever. Her betrothed, no Adonis, but certainly better than her no-account uncle, came to her funeral and sincerely wailed his loss.[53]

Chou Tso-jen is of the opinion that the personality of Lü Wei-fu, though not modeled on any single individual, does to a degree remind one of Fan Ai-nung, a fellow student with Lu Hsün in Tokyo and later a fellow teacher at the normal school in

52. *HSJW*, pp. 166-68.

53. *HSJW*, p. 174. Lu Hsün's famous "Ah Q" was in part based on this uncle who eked out a living by hulling rice.

Shaohsing. Since Wei Lien-shu, the protagonist of "The Isolate," the next in-between intellectual whom we shall consider, was based in large part on Lu Hsün's friend, it is perhaps appropriate to say a few words here about him.

In a long reminiscence written in November 1926 and simply titled "Fan Ai-nung," Lu Hsün described his first meeting with this man.[54] It seems that in 1907, when the news reached Japan that the Chekiang revolutionaries Ch'iu Chin and Hsü Hsi-lin had been executed, a meeting of fellow provincials was called to mourn the dead and castigate the Manchus. The students were especially incensed by the barbarity of Hsü's execution: his heart had been torn out, fried, and eaten by the personal bodyguards of En-ming, the governor of Anhui Province, whom he had assassinated.[55] As Lu Hsün recalled it in 1926 (though his recollection is by no means a simple report of what actually took place), he had initially conceived an antipathy to Fan because at the meeting Fan had opposed the sending of protest telegrams to the Manchu government (considering this—and reasonably so, one would assume—pointless), even though Hsü had once been his teacher.[56] Lu Hsün did not see Fan again until they met in Shaohsing during the 1910/11 academic year when Lu Hsün was teaching and concurrently serving as dean of studies in the high school. Fan, looking rather seedy, reported that he was now eking out a living by teaching a few students in the countryside. He had run out of

54. *LHCC*, II, 278-85; *SWLH*, I, 410-21.

55. After studies in Japan, Hsü Hsi-lin (b. 1873) purchased an official post in Anhui Province as commission designate (*hou-pu tao*) in charge of police administration; concurrently he served as head of the Anhui Police Academy. When En-ming participated in a graduation ceremony at the academy, Hsü precipitously touched the spark that he hoped would set off the cannon of revolution. After the assassination, he and some of his students at the academy occupied the police armory and managed to hold off En-ming's troops for a while. Later in the day they were captured. Hsü was killed and his body was treated in the grisly manner described. Ch'iu Chin, his younger cousin and a co-founder of a revolutionary front organization called the Physical Education Society, was also executed in the wake of En-ming's assassination. The government's increasing suspicion of Hsü may have goaded him into his precipitous act. *LHCC*, II, 453, n. 1.

56. Chou Tso-jen, however, remembers that Lu Hsün's position at this meeting was really not so very different from Fan's; there are a number of minor discrepancies between the brothers' memories of Fan. *HSJW*, pp. 231-37. One must bear in mind that Lu Hsün's reminiscences are "works of art," not simple reports of what actually happened.

money in Tokyo and been forced to come home. Back in Shaohsing he felt so ostracized and persecuted (to a certain degree, a common experience for returned students) that he went into the countryside to teach. Once in a while, however, he came into town to get away from the depressing atmosphere of country life and to enjoy a few drinks. Fan and Lu Hsün now hit it off very well, and became frequent drinking companions. When Wang Chin-fa came into Shaohsing in the fall of 1911, he made Lu Hsün the principal of the new normal school. At the same time, he appointed Fan Ai-nung dean of studies.[57] Fan thereupon cut down on his drinking and seemed to take his job very seriously, but after Lu Hsün left to join the new Ministry of Education in Nanking, things went from bad to worse for him:

> By the time I moved from Nanking to Peking, the principal who was head of the Confucian League had contrived to remove Ai-nung from his post as dean of studies and he reverted to the old Ai-nung of pre-revolutionary days. I wanted to find something for him to do in Peking, which was what he wanted, too, but there was no opening. Later he went to live off a friend; I continued to hear from him often. As things went from bad to worse, the language of his letters became more and more bitter. At last he was forced to leave his friend's house, and then he drifted from place to place. Before long I heard from a fellow-provincial that he had fallen into a river and drowned.
>
> I suspected that he committed suicide. For he was an excellent swimmer. . . .

While there are certainly traces of Fan in Lü Wei-fu, the following résumé of "The Isolate (Ku-tu che)" should make it clear that the protagonist was based both on Fan Ai-nung and on Lu Hsün.[58] Like them, Wei Lien-shu is the product of a backwater childhood who breaks away from the conservative confines of his native area and out into a broader world of sophistication and new knowledge. Like Lu Hsün and Fan Ai-nung again, he is mistrusted for this very reason by his stay-at-home neighbors and relatives. And, much in the manner of Lu Hsün, he is a modern who advocates radical things without necessarily practicing them. For instance, he believes in destroying the traditional family

57. *HSJW*, p. 233.
58. *LHCC*, II, 84-107; *SWLH*, I, 212-37. The Yangs translate the title as "The Misanthrope." The translations in the ensuing discussion are my own.

system, but scrupulously fulfills all its obligations with dutiful and even submissive piety.

The narrator of "The Isolate" takes us back to a time when he is living in S-town. There he often hears the name of a local high school teacher, Wei Lien-shu. Wei comes from a small village off in the mountains where, orphaned at an early age, he was brought up by his grandmother. As the story opens, the grandmother has been stricken in a dysentery epidemic. Relatives and neighbors immediately send someone to S-town (two days each way) to fetch back Lien-shu to be with the old woman on what may be her deathbed and, if need be, to supervise the arrangements for her funeral and burial. Before the messenger is long on the road, she breathes her last. The relatives hastily meet in conclave to form a united front against the "modernized" grandson; because he has received his education outside the narrow confines of the village, they assume that he belongs to the "modern" group of reformers and that he will attempt to deviate from customary ritual in the matter of the funeral. In anticipation of such newfangled apostasy, they agree beforehand upon the funeral arrangements, which he will be forced to observe. When Wei arrives, he surprises everyone by accepting all the conditions imposed upon him and by supervising the funeral with conservative punctiliousness for the observance of ritually prescribed details. It will be remembered that Lu Hsün, while teaching in Hangchow in 1910, had to return home to oversee the burial of his Grandmother Chiang. According to Tso-jen, the words that Wei Lien-shu uses in ruminating over the unhappy lot of his grandmother are Lu Hsün's own poignant and intense reminiscences of the unfortunate lot of that poor Chiang woman.

Wei Lien-shu has deep sympathy for the oppressed, the down-and-out. For that very reason he finds it difficult to keep friends for very long. The world being what it is, people sometimes rise, things sometimes get better, and Lien-shu finds it impossible to remain on friendly terms with anyone who is rising. In his sympathy for the oppressed, of course, one sees a reflection of Lu Hsün. Like him, Wei smokes a great deal and, again, loves children and sees them as China's only hope. Unfortunately, Wei occasionally expresses his opinions in magazine articles that are considered radical, and these opinions provoke attacks on him in the local papers. Hostility mounts. Before long he loses his teaching job at the high school and things go from bad to worse. At this point the narrator loses track of his unusual friend.

After some time the narrator, who has left S-town and is now teaching somewhere else, receives a rather strange letter from Wei, still in S-town, saying that he has taken a position as adviser to a General Tu. The general tone of the letter is a bit mad: Lien-shu announces, almost ebulliently, that he is now doing all those things that he once despised. He wonders what his friend is going to think of him, and in the next line says that he does not really care. It is apparent that Wei has sold out to the establishment—has lost his ideals. He closes with:

> I shall probably not write you again after this; you have been long familiar with these quirks of mine. When are you coming back? If it's soon we should be able to see each other again—but when you come right down to it, I think that we're probably not walking the same road anyway. So why don't you just forget me? I thank you from the bottom of my heart for your frequent attempts to find me a livelihood. But now, why don't you just forget me? Besides I'm "all better" now, anyway.

Of course, in those warlord times, the position of adviser to a general gave one a rather high rank in society. As soon as Wei, by virtue of his association with General Tu, becomes powerful and prestigious, people stop bullying him and even begin to treat him with deference and respect. In this we have another vivid example of Lu Hsün's view of traditional society as a place where the strong are feared and the weak are bullied. Articles about Wei begin to appear in the papers again. This time they are favorable, and there is one story which even

narrated with fond relish a subject that had formerly been passed around as a joke on him, but was now called "an anecdote" with the connotation that "a man of outstanding capacity is bound to do a number of out-of-the-way things."

Preoccupied with his own troubles, the narrator loses track of Wei again, until during another visit to S-town he learns that his old friend has died of consumption.

Wei Lien-shu is unlike the other backsliding, in-between intellectuals that we have examined in that his fall, when it comes, is not gradual, but sudden, total, and virtually premeditated. (It is similar to the madman's return to "sanity" in "Diary of a Madman.") In joining General Tu's staff, he makes his leap into the mainstream of a corrupt society, and he does it with gusto.[59] Instead of being bullied, now he bullies. Instead of disdaining him, now society fawns upon him.

Wei is perhaps the closest to a self-portrait of all the intellectuals in Lu Hsün's stories. The people in his home town distrust him and regard him as a foreigner (a member of the "new party") because he has been away and has "eaten of foreign creeds." Like Lu Hsün, Wei considers children and down-and-outers superior to other people; he was close to his grandmother, and he supervised her burial; in the course of the story he tells how his relatives once tried to do him out of the family property, and Chou Tso-jen avers that the words used by Wei to describe this incident are the same that Lu Hsün used in explaining how Great-Uncle Chao-lan tried to do him out of the family property upon the death of his father in 1897.

Wei Lien-shu also closely resembles Fan Ai-nung, making one suspect that it was because Lu Hsün saw elements of himself in Ai-nung that the two of them got along so well when they met in Shaohsing. It seems probable that in creating the character Wei Lien-shu, Lu Hsün combined elements of himself and elements of Fan. The adult Lu Hsün was known as a fiercely independent person who was also a bit odd; one could take the title of the Wei Lien-shu story and apply it to Fan Ai-nung or to Lu Hsün with almost equal appropriateness. Lu Hsün once commented on his own writing:

Readers with a predilection for my works often say approvingly that my writing tells the truth. Actually this is too complimentary and they say it merely because of their predilection. Of course, I have no particular desire to deceive people, but I have never told all that was in my heart just as it was, either. For the most part when I had gone far enough to have a manuscript that could be turned in, I counted it as done. It is quite true that I often dissect other people, but even more often—and even more ruthlessly—I dissect myself.[60]

59. Hsü Ch'in-wen suggests (*PHFH*, p. 72) that Wei took this job in order to continue his resistance to the old society. The shame indirectly expressed in his letter gives the lie to that. Furthermore, after taking the job, he did not in fact wreak vengeance on anyone.
60. "Postscript to *Tomb* (Hsieh tsai *Fen* hou-mien)," dated February 2, 1926. *LHCC*, I, 362. *Tomb* (*Fen*), first issued in 1927, was a collection of Lu Hsün's essays written between 1907 and 1925.

This self-dissection is perhaps most striking in "Upstairs in a Wineshop" and "The Isolate."[61] In both stories one has the impression of overhearing a man in conversation with himself, a man trying to understand his own subjective motivations. It is as though the narrators of these two tales look at Lü Wei-fu and Wei Lien-shu and say to themselves: "There but for the grace of God go I." Through these characters Lu Hsün takes a close look at himself and perhaps exorcises evil spirits lurking just below the surface of his consciousness. If so, the difference between himself and the characters he created provides a good gauge of the success of that exorcism.

Like Lü Wei-fu, Lu Hsün was extremely disappointed with the results of the Republican Revolution; unlike him, he did not sell out to the old establishment and end up teaching the Confucian classics (though he did, it is true, for many years hold a sinecure in the Ministry of Education). Like Wei Lien-shu, he felt "different," isolated, perhaps even persecuted; unlike Wei, he did not suddenly join the oppressors (though he undoubtedly made his compromises). Lü Wei-fu is not what happened to Lu Hsün after the revolution; rather it is what could have happened to him and no doubt did happen to some of his contemporary in-between intellectuals.

The subject matter of "Brothers (Ti-hsiung),"[62] written in November 1925, a month after "The Isolate," is, if anything, even more intensely personal. It reflects the time, in 1917, when Tso-jen had a bout with measles. "Brothers" is centered on the conscious and subconscious life of Chang P'ei-chün, a petty bureaucrat in the Bureau of Public Welfare, an organization whose name satirically contrasts its function with the distinctly personal concerns of the men who work there. Around the office Chang P'ei-chün is famed for one thing, his exemplary fraternal devotion to his younger brother, Ching-fu. As the story opens, in a shabby office filled with desks and chairs, Ch'in Yi-t'ang, almost lost in a

61. The emphasis of the third story of this type, "The Story of Hair" (written to commemorate the Double Tenth), is on the objective history of China since the Republican Revolution; therefore elements of self-dissection, while not entirely lacking, are kept to a minimum.
62. *LHCC*, II, 130-141. My translation of the story is in *Renditions* (Hong Kong), no. 1, Autumn 1973, pp. 66-75.

cloud of smoke, sucks hard on the mouthpiece of his water pipe. Between spasms of coughing, he relates the latest family squabble that his sons have gotten into. In contrast, he and the others in the office admire the fraternal harmony and the selflessness that seem to characterize the relationship between Chang P'ei-chün and Ching-fu. In the course of acknowledging compliments on this admirable state of affairs, P'ei-chün attributes it to a total lack of personal competition over money or property. Another colleague, Wang Yüeh-sheng, inquires after Ching-fu's health, and when P'ei-chün announces that his brother is at home on sick leave with what is apparently a cold, Yüeh-sheng immediately warns him to be careful, for the city is in the midst of a scarlet fever epidemic. Greatly alarmed, P'ei-chün leaves work in the middle of the day in order to seek a doctor.

When P'ei-chün gets to the apartment building where he and Ching-fu share a set of rooms (their wives and children presumably are somewhere in the countryside—a situation which parallels that of Lu Hsün and Tso-jen), he telephones a German doctor at a hospital and, not finding him in, leaves a message. Failing to get in touch with the Western doctor immediately, he calls in a Chinese doctor who happens to live close by. Dr. Pai diagnoses the disease as *hung-pan-sha* and then sends a shiver down P'ei-chün's spine when announces that *hung-pan-sha* is what Western doctors call "scarlet fever." When asked if it can be cured, Dr. Pai opines that this depends upon the family's luck.[63]

Sinews tight as violin strings from worry, P'ei-chün calls the hospital again and presses them to send out the doctor whenever he gets back, regardless of the hour. As he keeps watch at Ching-fu's bedside during the night, he begins to worry about how he will take care of his brother's family (a wife and two children) if Ching-fu should die. Since P'ei-chün has a wife and three children of his own, things would be difficult. What if there is not enough money to pay tuition for all the children? Who should go to school? His own son is the brightest of the lot, but, he muses,

---

63. According to Tso-jen's diary (*HHL*, p. 321), no Chinese doctor was consulted when he had his bout with the measles. One suspects that Dr. Pai's rather gratuitous introduction into the story is designed mainly to afford Lu Hsün an opportunity to "get in his licks" at a lifelong enemy—traditional Chinese medicine.

people will be critical if he chooses this boy. At that point the German doctor arrives and, much to P'ei-chün's relief, finds that Ching-fu has nothing more than a good case of measles.

P'ei-chün sleeps then, but the next morning, as he gets dressed, disturbing dream-images float through his mind and, try as he will, he cannot thrust them back beneath the surface of consciousness. (a) A little girl, face all bloody, is standing before his bed; he is getting ready to hit her. (b) He is back in his native district, carrying his brother's casket on his back; people stand about and praise him. (c) He sends his own three children to school as his brother's children, wailing, beg to be allowed to go too. Conscious of his own power, he strikes out at the face of his brother's child. (d) His brother's child, face all blood and tears, leads a group of people in to accuse him. P'ei-chün finally finishes getting ready for work and heads off to the office at the Bureau of Public Welfare.

Lu Hsün makes it strikingly clear to his readers that, having been exposed to the specters of his subconscious, having recognized their existence, P'ei-chün can no longer take for granted the moral rectitude of his relationship to his brother. Now as we look in on the office, we see a reenactment of the scene of yesterday; nothing has changed—except Chang P'ei-chün. As he enters, Wang Yüeh-sheng takes note of him and remarks that he looks a bit different from the way he did yesterday.

P'ei-chün also seemed to sense that both the office and his colleagues were somewhat different from what they were yesterday—somehow or other unfamiliar, even though everything else in the office was familiarly the same: a broken coat-hook, a spittoon with a chunk chipped out, a chaos of dust-covered case records, a rickety reclining chair with a missing leg, and Ch'in Yi-t'ang seated upon the chair, water pipe cupped in his hands, coughing and sighing as he shook his head and said: "Just like always they fought all the way from inside the house right out to the front gate."

"And that's just why," chimed in Yüeh-sheng, "I think you ought to tell them about P'ei-chün and get them to copy him and his brother. Otherwise, they'll be the death of you yet, old man."

This is, of course, a stock scene that has often been acted out in the office, but today it occurs against the background of Pei-chün's experience of having peeked beneath the surface of reality into his subconscious. Therefore all the talk has, for him, a hollow, almost surrealistic ring.

"Number Three says that the loss that Number Five took on public bonds cannot be counted as their joint responsibility and that Number Five ought to—ought to—ought to—." Yi-t'ang was doubled over coughing.

"Well as the saying goes, 'people are different,' " said Yüeh-sheng as he turned away to face P'ei-chün. "Well then there's nothing really seriously wrong with your brother anyway."

"Nothing serious. The doctor says it's measles."

"Measles? That's right. Come to think of it, I've heard that it's rampant among the children roundabouts. Three kids living on the same court-yard with me all have it. Absolutely harmless. And to think that you got so excited about it yesterday that even we outsiders couldn't help but be moved by your concern. As the saying goes, 'There is nothing like fraternal affection.' "

"Did the bureau chief check in yesterday?"

"As the saying goes, he made himself 'as scarce as hens' teeth.' All you have to do is go and sign in for yesterday and nobody will be the wiser."

"Said that Number Five ought to make it good himself," said Yi-t'ang as much to himself as anyone else. "These public bonds really do great harm to people. I can't make head or tails of them myself, but it seems that anyone who has anything to do with them ends up taking a beating. And yesterday by the time evening rolled around they were at it again. Fought all the way from inside the house right out to the front gate. Number Five said that since Number Three has two more children in school than he does, that means that Number Three has gotten more out of the public funds too. Got so mad . . ."

"The whole thing is getting more muddled all the time," said Yüeh-sheng in despair." And that's why when I see brothers like you, P'ei-chün, I respect you so much that, as the saying goes, I 'put you on a pedestal.' It's the straight truth. I swear it. It's not just something I say to your face to flatter you."

P'ei-chün didn't say anything, but, spotting a messenger who had just entered the office with a piece of official business, he rushed over to him and took the documents. Yüeh-sheng followed P'ei-chün, stood behind him, and read aloud from the document in his hands.

" 'In order to maintain public health and promote the general welfare, Citizen Ho Shang-shan and others hereby petition the Bureau of Public Welfare to immediately order its branch office to arrange a casket for and bury the body of an unidentified male who dropped dead in the eastern suburbs.' You let me take care of that," said Yüeh-sheng. "Why don't you take off a bit early. I know that you must be worried about your brother. You two are as affectionate as 'pied wagtails on the moor,' as the saying goes."

"No." P'ei-chün held onto the document. "I'll take care of it myself."

Yüeh-sheng did not make a point of it. P'ei-chün was apparently in a very calm state of mind as he proceeded silently to his own desk where, his eyes still on the petition, he reached out and removed a somewhat corroded brass cover from the top of an ink box.

A beautifully composed (in the original, at any rate) passage from an equally well-built story, the scene is almost like a ballet or painting. It is, also, cut down to bare essentials: Ch'in Yi-t'ang repeating his old tale like a Greek chorus; Yüeh-sheng filling the air with his garrulous clichés—clichés which embody the accepted norms of traditional familial morality; and, painfully conscious of the contrast between the pretty names that cover the expectations of traditional morality and the reality of his own feelings, P'ei-chün himself.

We can treat Chang P'ei-chün as an in-between intellectual on a chronological basis. We are also aware that immediately behind him lurks the figure of Lu Hsün. There is no real indication, however, of what kind of education he has received or what views he holds on various issues of the day, though we see that he has a marked preference for Western medicine and views native practitioners with contempt. In sum, in this story more than in most of the others, we are interested in the protagonist rather as an individual than as a representative type; the thrust of the story is psychological rather than sociological. One cannot really say that Chang P'ei-chün is a representative of traditional, in-between, or even modern intellectuals, for the focus of interest is on the disparity between his conscious and subconscious life.

In Lu Hsün's first colloquial-language short story, "Diary of a Madman," at one point the madman begins to read between the lines of Chinese history—lines which are studded with high-sounding phrases about righteousness and morality. Between the lines, the madman begins to see the real message: "Eat people." Fear the strong and bully the weak, oppress those whom you can and fawn upon others, eat people—but take care to dress up this "reality" in the "names" of traditional morality. As we have seen, such anti-traditionalism is a characteristic of Lu Hsün's stories, and it often appears in the disparity between the pretty names and the ugly reality which they gloss over. In "Brothers," for the first time we see this theme and this method of presentation applied to an individual rather than the spatial and temporal sweep of Chinese society and history.

In so far as P'ei-chün is an individual, rather than a representative type, Lu Hsün moves away from the concern with Chinese society or history in general that is displayed in the earlier stories in *Call to Arms*. The use of Yüeh-sheng's clichés strung out on a clothesline as a wash of "names" to serve as background for the "reality" of P'ei-chün's feelings is rather clever. Yet in this story one senses a certain reduction in social significance and political involvement, a turning away from the public to private. The autobiographical elements are very strong. Speaking of the plot, Lu Hsün's old friend Hsü Shou-shang has said:

Most of it consists of experiences that Lu Hsün went through himself. It was probably sometime around the end of spring or the beginning of summer in 1917. He and his younger brother, Tso-jen, were both living in the Pu Shu Study of the Shaohsing Hostel. Tso-jen suddenly developed a temperature. There was an epidemic of scarlet fever going through Peking at the time. More than that, one of our colleagues at the Ministry of Education had died during just such an epidemic the year before. All this made Lu Hsün especially apprehensive and he called in a German doctor by the name of T'i-pu-erh for a diagnosis. Only then did he discover that actually it was nothing more than a case of measles. The next day when he came to the ministry he was in exceptionally good spirits and recounted to me in great detail how slow the doctor had been in coming and how quick he had been in making his diagnosis. And then he said, "To think that Ch'i-meng [Tso-jen], as old as he is, had never had measles."[64]

Hsü also states that Ching-fu is based on Tso-jen both in speech and in mannerisms (shown in passages which are not discussed here) and that the Bureau of Public Welfare is in fact the Ministry of Education as it was in Peking during those days. Hsü maintains, however, that the dream fragments are manufactured out of whole cloth.[65] In one of his reminiscences, Tso-jen says that the part about his illness is accurate enough, but that about the dreams is probably poetry. Curiously, in the same passage Tso-jen notes that once when he was very ill Lu Hsün did in fact say to him: "The thing that I'm afraid of is not that you may die, but rather the business of having to take care of your wife after you are gone."[66] In a somewhat later reminiscence of the same event, Tso-jen states

64. *WTLH*, p. 62. According to Tso-jen's diary, this all occurred around the middle of May 1917. *CNST*, p. 91.
65. *WTLH*, pp. 63-65.
66. *CNST*, pp. 90-91.

that after his recovery Lu Hsün said that what had worried him most was the responsibility of taking care of Tso-jen's family in case he died. This, says Tso-jen, is reflected in the dream sequence in "Brothers": "[Although the actual event and the composition of the story] were eight years apart, Lu Hsün still hadn't forgotten it. I've never understood the reasons for this; perhaps one would have to go to the theories of Freud to find an answer."[67]

It seems certain that in examining the disparity between conscious and subconscious levels in Chang P'ei-chün's character, Lu Hsün drew heavily on his own experiences. In almost everything written about his relationship with Chou Tso-jen, he is presented in the role of the strong, self-sacrificing big brother and it is very probable that he saw himself in this light, much as P'ei-chün viewed himself as the ideal, concerned, unselfish, self-sacrificing elder brother in the opening part of the story. Lu Hsün's second wife, Hsü Kuang-p'ing, in discussing her husband's relation to Tso-jen, heavily emphasizes just this type of selfless devotion. She reports an occasion when, after moving out of Pa-tao-wan Lane, Lu Hsün returned to pick up some things and went so far as to remind Tso-jen that he had quit Japan and returned to China in order to make money to support him. Tso-jen reportedly waved this aside with the words: "What's past is past."[68] Given all this, it seems quite likely that the psychological part of "Brothers" was largely autobiographical.

It is precisely this personal emphasis of the story that makes it difficult for Lu Hsün's fellow-provincial and friend, Hsü Ch'in-wen, to fit it to the simplistic image of Lu Hsün as patriotic knight in the battle against feudalism at home and imperialism abroad. Hsü is uncomfortable with the story. He manages rather ingeniously (indeed, almost convincingly) to divert attention away from the individuals in the story to the society around them. Emphasizing the decadence of a government office dedicated to public welfare in which there is so little to do that the clerks spend their time sitting about discussing their highly personal affairs, Hsü sees the subject matter of the story as primarily political and economic:

The main function of Chang P'ei-chün's bad dreams is to point out the evil that lies in the omnipotence of money, an evil that destroys love and

67. *HHL*, pp. 322-23.
68. *HYL*, p. 58.

affection in the world of men. Whether one explains these bad dreams in terms of "selfishness" or "hypocrisy," the fact still remains that they were brought to completion by the economic system of the times.[69]

In discussing the symbolism of the dream fragments, Hsü uses a similar explanation:

"All by himself carrying a casket on his back, carrying it all the way from outside the front gate right into the house." Is not this dream image simply a symbol for the weight of his [P'ei-chün's] burden? From this we can see that the affection between the brothers is genuine, but that [it] cannot withstand the heavy pressures of economic problems.[70]

This interpretation seems plausible enough, but it does violence to the general tone of the story and points away in a direction toward which Lu Hsün's thought showed no marked inclination: total denial of individual responsibility and complete despair of the individual's power to do anything to change himself. Lu Hsün's phrasing in the dream image that Hsü quotes is not intended to point up P'ei-chün's burden, but rather to contrast with the stock line of Ch'in Yi-t'ang, "Fought all the way from inside the house right out to the front gate," and thereby emphasize the comparison of the open (conscious) hostility between the other set of brothers and the hidden (subconscious) hostility between P'ei-chün and Ching-fu.

As "Brothers" draws to a close, we do see a change in P'ei-chün; there is some hope for him. His hypocrisy of the previous day in holding up the relationship between himself and Ching-fu as an example to Ch'in Yi-t'ang was not conscious. His "ideal" relationship with his brother could be described by any one of the clichés from the stockpile of traditional morality (just as Yüeh-sheng had depicted it), but it was a relationship that had never been tested. The possibility of his brother's death did test it, and proved it to be less idyllic than it had seemed the previous day. When P'ei-chün returns to the office, he is more aware of his true feelings. It is a mark of his honesty that he refuses to accept any more tributes to his fraternal virtue.

Since "Brothers" was written a good two years after Lu Hsün's breakup with Tso-jen, there can be little doubt that it was informed at a psychological level by that experience, though it is not necessarily a direct reflection of his mental state during that

69. *PHFH*, p. 3.
70. Ibid., p. 91.

period.[71] One of Lu Hsün's lifelong concerns was the discrepancy between name and reality; he had a tendency that bordered on compulsion to look beneath the surface of things. In "Diary of a Madman" the object of this compulsion is nothing less than the whole of traditional China; in "Brothers" it is a single individual vis-à-vis the traditional expectations of fraternal relationships (embodied in the clichés that Yüeh-sheng is forever mouthing at the office). Lu Hsün understood his experiences not as idiosyncratic happenings but rather as threads in the whole fabric of Chinese society and culture. His transformation of experience into fiction is a function of his peculiar ability to understand the general situation of the Chinese people in terms of his own life. It is this ability, in part, that makes him an artist.

MODERN INTELLECTUALS

Each of the three groups of intellectuals that we examine in this chapter has its own characteristic problem: with the traditional intellectual the problem is the examination system; with the in-between, backsliding; and, as we shall see, with the modern intellectual, a certain superficiality. Modern intellectuals are those who were educated largely after the examination system was abolished and for whom "sitting for the examinations" was never a real possibility. Some of them will attempt to preserve the "national essence" that disappeared along with the examinations, while others will attempt to suplant it with a new "foreign essence" imported from America and Europe. The leading character in "A Happy Family (Hsing-fu te chia-t'ing)"[72] is just such a young intellectual in search of a foreign essence.

71. It is tempting to speculate that Lu Hsün may, in part, have written "Brothers" in hopes of a reconciliation with Tso-jen by giving evidence of his own heightened understanding of what was wrong with their relationship.
72. *LHCC*, II, 35-42; *SWLH*, I, 188-97. Just below the title of this story Lu Hsün notes: "in the manner of Hsü Ch'in-wen." When the story was first printed, in vol. X, no. 3 (March 1, 1924;, of *Women's Journal (Fu-nü tsa-chih*— a Shanghai monthly), he appended a more complete explanation: "Last year when I read Hsü Ch'in-wen's 'An Ideal Mate (Li-hsiang te pan-lü)' . . . I suddenly got the idea for the present story. Moreover, I thought it would be well to tell it using the same technique that Hsü had employed; but it remained just an idea. Then yesterday I suddenly thought about it again and, having nothing better to do, wrote my story as you see it here. However, *my* story seems to go gradually off track at the end and to become somewhat too

The story introduces us to a struggling author living in cramped, noisy quarters with a wife and young child.[73] He is trying to compose a short potboiler for which he chooses the title "A Happy Family." By selling it to *Happiness Monthly* he hopes to earn enough to pay at least some of his bills. Given his age, background, and interests, we can safely classify him as a modern intellectual: we learn, for instance, that he and his wife were not brought together by their parents in a traditionally arranged match; they had freely determined to establish their own household five years before, despite all obstacles. Essentially, "A Happy Family" recounts the frustrated and, in the end, unsuccessful attempts of the young husband to write his story. Thwarted by the delivery of firewood, the delivery of cabbages, the nagging of his wife, and the bawling of his three-year-old child (slapped by her mother for knocking over the kerosene lamp), he finally gives up, wipes away his daughter's tears with the first page of his manuscript, and then resignedly tosses it all into the wastebasket. One

---

somber. Generally speaking, I believe that the endings of Hsü's works are not so solemn. But even so, on the whole, I cannot but say that my story is still 'in the manner of.' " *Lu Hsün ch'üan-chi pu-yi hsü-pien* [Pieces left out of the complete works of Lu Hsün, continued] ed. T'ang T'ao (Shanghai, 1952), p. 255; hereafter cited as *PYHP*.

Hsü Ch'in-wen thinks that by "using the same technique" Lu Hsün has in mind the sarcastic tone of Hsü's original story. He had written "An Ideal Mate" to satirize what he saw as the ridiculous way of thinking represented by an announcement of an essay contest in *Women's Journal* on the subject of the ideal mate. *PHFH*, p. 29. Hsü's story, told in the first person, begins with the arrival of a friend who tells him about the contest; the narrator then suggests that the friend describe *his* ideal mate. Hsü presents his story as a record of what the friend says. *Hsü Ch'in-wen hsiao-shuo hsüan-chi* [A selection of Hsü Ch'in-wen's stories] (Peking, 1956), pp. 19-22; hereafter cited as *CWHS*. It would seem that Ch'in-wen's story merely inspired Lu Hsün to write on a similar theme.

73. Lu Hsün moved into rather restricted quarters at 61 Chuan-t'a Lane during August 1923 following his breakup with Chou Tso-jen and remained there until May of the next year. Sun Shih-k'ai, *Lu Hsün tsai Pei-ching chu-kuo te ti-fang* [The places that Lu Hsün lived in Peking] (Peking, 1957), pp. 4-5; hereafter cited as *LHTPC*. The first four selections in *Wandering* were written during this period. When Lu Hsün wrote "A Happy Family," his mother had moved into the easternmost of the three rooms he occupied on Chuan-t'a Lane, while he (and presumably his wife) occupied the western room which served as both bedroom and study. The middle room was used as combination dining room and storage room. *PHFH*, p. 35.

of the central themes of the story is this ludicrous contrast between the reality of the young writer's environment and the hollow unreality of a series of castles in the air that he considers, one after the other, as possible subjects for his story. Hsü Ch'in-wen has said that this particular kind of satire was quite timely in China in the 1920s:

By no means did Lu Hsün take up this central theme idly, as an archer without a target might aimlessly loose his arrows. He rather took it up because at that time there were many young people who, instead of attacking their problems realistically through the reform of society, simply indulged themselves in empty dreams of having a happy home; this was especially the case since those in power and their cohorts were engaged in lofty discussion of such things as the "ideal mate" in order to delude young students and make them lose interest in politics and grow increasingly corrupt. Therefore, he wrote this kind of piece to remind everyone of what was actually going on.[74]

Though Hsü's explanation was written from the hindsight of 1958, it does make the valid point that Lu Hsün was warning the young intellectuals of the period away from romantic and unrealistic ideals and was trying to get them to focus their attention back on near-at-hand realities.

The real subject of Lu Hsün's satire in "A Happy Family," however, is not so much the young author as the young couple whom he creates for his story-within-a-story. They are modern returned-students (apparently having studied in America or England, since they speak English to each other). The husband wears foreign clothes; the wife does her hair in foreign style, though she wears a Chinese dress; and in most things it is possible to be foreign (and thus superior to their stay-at-home compatriots) they are. They deviate sharply, however, in the matter of food: the cuisine in their home is Chinese (foreigners have praised Chinese cooking).

Lu Hsün, as we have seen, had long loved and studied Russian literature. It must have been galling to him that in the China of the 1920s there were many people who objected to Russian literature on the rather frivolous grounds that it was not cheerful enough. In this regard Hsü Ch'in-wen has said:

---

74. *PHFH*, pp. 30-31.

At that time there were some people, so-called high-class Chinese, who, having superficially studied a bit of the gentry-style culture of the West, considered themselves superior and elegant, and were ardent lovers of literature and the arts—although they opposed Russian novels, which often described the lower classes.[75]

Hence the young couple of the story-within-a-story do not read Russian novels. Their author briefly considers the possibility of having them read Byron and Keats, but in the end decides that these two are also unsuitable. From the point of view of Lu Hsün, this is highly significant, for the implication is that somehow Byron and Keats are as potentially dangerous as those Russian authors who write about the lower classes.[76] In sum, Lu Hsün views the couple, along with the entire segment of the May Fourth intelligentsia for whom they stand, with hostile eyes. They are out for themselves, unrelated to society and irresponsible where it is concerned; above all, they are superficial.[77]

"Schoolmaster Kao (Kao Lao-fu-tzu),"[78] written about three months after "A Happy Family," continues the criticism of May Fourth intellectuals. Again the main charge is superficiality—a superficiality disguised this time under the deceptively dignified mantle of nationalistic, albeit conservative, slogans. As the story opens we learn that Kao Kan-t'ing, a young wastrel, has recently distinguished himself by having an essay printed in one of the local papers; it is called "On Every Citizen's Duty to Reconstruct Our National History." The essay is pompous both in its title and because Kao has written it primarily to impress people with the

75. Ibid., p. 32.
76. Lu Hsün's Byron, of course, is Byron the Mara poet, the rebel. It was not a view that was universally shared. In a poem titled, "The Romantic Age" (1929), for instance, the young leftist writer Yin Fu (b. 1909, executed by the Nationalists in 1931) said that the days of Byron and his "noble ladies and nightingales" were over. *Yin Fu hsüan-chi* [Selected writings of Yin Fu] (Peking, 1951), p. 34; hereafter cited as *YFHC*. The relevance of Keats is not apparent to me.
77. They are not very different from the young couple that Lao She (1899-1966) so effectively satirized in his short story "Neighbors (Lin-chü-men)," written in the 1930s.
78. *LHCC*, II, 73-83; "Professor Kao," trans. Wang Chi-chen, *The China Journal*, XXXIII (July-December 1940), 11-17. *Lao-fu-tzu* translates more accurately as "schoolmaster" than as "professor."

righteousness of his stand and the breadth of his learning (he primps before mirrors, too). The reader is soon made aware that Kao's knowledge of history goes little beyond the bits and snatches that everyone picks up through popular culture (operas, novels, poems). And yet this pompous little essay is enough to win him an invitation to lecture (four hours a week at thirty cents an hour) at the School of Virtuous Maidens, an institution in whose director's eyes the only apparent criterion for the selection of faculty is that their minds shall be as reactionary and confused as his own. Before receiving this offer, Kao has been known among his friends by a nickname. The letter of engagement from the school, however, addresses him with a high-sounding epithet, School-master Erh-ch'u Kao. (In violation of Chinese custom, the surname is given last; the whole name is a play on the Chinese transliteration of "Gorki.")[79]

When Huang San (a gambling, drinking, theater-going, and woman-chasing companion) drops by to pay a call, Kao is somewhat irked by his excessively relaxed and carefree manner, for it bespeaks a lack of respect for the honored schoolmaster. Having glanced over the letter of engagement from the school, Huang opines that society has deteriorated enough since the opening of modern boys' schools, and exhorts Kao not to get mixed up in such an unseemly frivolity as a girls' school. Furthermore, it turns out that Huang has come on serious business: a country-fresh bumpkin has arrived in town with a large sum of money, and Huang has organized a mah-jongg game to help relieve him of it. Huang informs Kao of the time and place, and asks him to be sure to be there. Kao finds Huang's visit increasingly distasteful (as "Schoolmaster Kao" and the author of a well-known essay, Kao now feels quite superior to this low-life friend). What is more, not knowing a great deal about Chinese history, he needs the time to bone up before going to his first lecture. He finally gets rid of Huang by giving him a set of clearly marked mah-jongg tiles, particularly good for cheating a bump-kin. Leaving, Huang enjoins Kao to be on hand that night for the fleecing. Kao hurries off to the school, hoping to get there early enough for a little cramming before his lecture.

79. Kao has substituted the *ch'u* in the Chinese word *chi-ch'u* (foundation) for the *chi* which is used in the accepted transliteration, "Kao Erh-chi," for Gorki.

The scene shifts to a "green room" at the School of Virtuous Maidens (though academic rather than theatrical, the room is a place where instructors prepare themselves before going onto their various classroom stages). Kao is received by Wan Yao-p'u, dean of studies. It seems that Wan has made something of a reputation for himself by publishing a series of poems exchanged between himself and a goddess. They were published in the same paper that printed Kao's famous essay, which Wan says he has read, though he remembers the title somewhat inaccurately as "On China's Responsibility to Its National Quintessence." Kao does not correct him with regard to the title, perhaps because the spirit is the same though the words may vary, or, more likely, because he was not paying attention. He is still trying to work in a little time for preparation before class. Wan, insensitive to this, prattles on and on. Finally he leads Kao into a classroom and introduces him to a sea of female heads. He recites Kao's background for the girls, getting the title of the essay right this time (he has notes), and then leaves. As Schoolmaster Kao reads nervously from an open textbook, he keeps imagining that the girls are giggling at him. Becoming increasingly nervous, he reads so rapidly that he finishes too soon with the material that he has reviewed. Not being familiar with the next part of the text, he is somewhat humiliatingly forced to dismiss the class. Kao, stalwart defender of the national past and staunch advocate of the national quintessence, does not know enough about either to fill a single lecture period without intensive review and preparation.

After this unfortunate initiation to lecturing, Kao decides that he will resign. The scene now shifts to Huang San's place and a table of mah-jongg players. Before the game begins, Kao announces: "I have no intention of continuing. I really don't know what girls' schools are coming to. It is definitely not worthwhile for respectable people like us to get mixed up in the mess . . ." Kao's spirits, however, improve markedly as tiles begin to pile up before him and the story closes.

During the late 1910s and early 1920s, Lu Hsün was firm in his opposition to any attempt to turn the clock back in China. Exceedingly well read in the traditional literature himself, he was vehemently opposed to burdening young people with its study and was therefore an implacable critic of those people who would revive the old learning or attempt to preserve the "quintessence of the national tradition." He expressed himself perhaps most clearly in this regard in an essay written in 1918, "A Record of Things as I felt Them, No. 35":

How about a man with a tumor on his face or a boil on his forehead? Now, since such things certainly mark him off from the common herd and give him a distinctive appearance, they may be considered as his "quintessence." The way I see it, it would be far better to have this "quintessence" amputated and be as good as everyone else.

Now, if you want to argue that China's national quintessence is *good* as well as distinctive, then how is it that we have gotten into the mess we are in? Not only do those of the new school shake their heads, but those of the old school also sigh.[80]

"Schoolmaster Kao," though written seven years after the above statement, is a fictionalized version of the same theme in the form of an *argumentum ad hominem:* here is an example of what those who support the traditional culture and advocate its preservation are really like.[81]

While writing in defense of the national essence, Kao also changes his name, as we have seen, to something resembling the Chinese transliteration of Gorky, indicating to those of his compatriots "in the know" that he considers himself a desciple of the Russian author.[82] Yet he probably knows no more about Gorky than he does about the Chinese "essence" that he purports to defend. Basically, he is a frivolous, dishonest, and opportunistic individual. Lu Hsün focuses in on him, however, not as an individual, but as a typical representative of the "national essence" supporters and would have us believe that they are equally frivolous, dishonest, and opportunistic. One might be tempted to think that Lu Hsün viewed the mordern young intellectuals disdainfully because by 1924 he was a middle-aged man, and the middle-aged sometimes view young people in their twenties as inferior to what they were at that age. But this is not the case. As we have seen, even as a young man during his student days in Japan he similarly suspected that many of his compatriots advocated this or that righteous program of reform for China with

80. *LHCC,* 1, 383; *SWLH,* II, 28-29. My translation.
81. For more on Lu Hsün's essay attacks on both national (Chinese) and foreign "essences" see the valuable discussion in Huang Sung-k'ang, *Lu Hsün and the New Culture Movement of Modern China* (Amsterdam, 1957), pp. 81-82.
82. *PHFH,* p. 62.

selfish and opportunistic motivation. Throughout his life he displayed a strong tendency to be as interested in *why* a man said something as in *what* the man said.

A third story in which Lu Hsün deals with modern intellectuals, "Remorse (Shang-shih),"[83] gives almost equal weight to a male and a female protagonist (and provides a transition from the consideration of intellectuals in Lu Hsün's stories to his treatment of women). "Remorse" stands in a revealing contrast to "Schoolmaster Kao" in that it is concerned primarily with "foreign essence" rather than the national variety. It examines the lives of a young couple in love during the high tide of the May Fourth movement. The story is presented in the form of notes written by Chüan-sheng, a young government clerk who lives in one of the hostels established for fellow-provincials in Peking and puts in six days a week working in a government bureau. Chüan-sheng's life is rather bleak until Tzu-chün, a modern young woman full of the liberal ideas of the May Fourth period, brightens it up. Eventually they decide to live together, whereupon Chüan-sheng leaves the hostel to set up house on Good Omen Lane with his love. A year later he is back in the hostel, living again in the room that he had vacated, and there he pens the reminiscences that comprise "Remorse."

During the halcyon days when Tzu-chün first entered his life, he could hardly contain himself as he awaited her visits. When she arrived at his room in the hostel, he would discourse at length on the despotism of the family system and the need to destroy old customs, on equality between the sexes, and on Ibsen, Tagore, and Shelley. (We have here, of course, a virtually total rejection of "national" essence and a consequent acceptance of a "foreign" one.) It is obvious from the beginning that the uncle with whom Tzu-chün lives strongly disapproves of her relationship with Chüan-sheng; despite this, six months after their first meeting she announces: "I belong to myself. None of them has any right to interfere with me." Chüan-sheng is absolutely elated by this show of independence, for—he later confides in his notes—it made him realize that Chinese women were not so hopeless as pessimists would have one believe. One cannot but be startled by the abstract quality of Chüan-sheng's elation—elated not because she

83. *LHCC*, II, 108-29; *SWLH*, I, 238-61. The second quotation in the ensuing discussion is a modification of the Yangs' rendering; the rest are my translations.

loves him, but rather because through her he realizes that Chinese women in general have more independence than the pessimist would have one believe! Nonetheless, at this point Chüan-sheng is sharply brought up against social realities, realities with which he may well disagree, but which he cannot ignore with impunity:

> When I saw her out the gate, as usual we maintained a distance of more than ten paces between us. As usual too, the old fogy with catfish whiskers pressed his face so hard against his dirty window pane that he flattened his nose into a little pancake. And when we reached the outer courtyard, from behind a sparkling clean windowpane there appeared, as usual, the face-cream plastered visage of the little dandy who lived there. Walking proudly, looking neither to the right nor left, Tzu-chün saw none of this . . .

Society, in the persons of a lascivious old man and a foppish young one, is watching them; and through the person of the uncle with whom she lives, Tzu-chün's family is watching them. Even in the liberal atmosphere of the May Fourth period, society and family are not lightly to be denied.

Encouraged by her show of independence, Chüan-sheng proposes that they set up house, and she blushingly accepts. In a China where marriages are traditionally arranged by the families of the bride and groom, there is, of course, little precedent for this kind of proposal. Hence the only model that Chüan-sheng has is a foreigner he once saw in a movie; like that foreigner, he now goes down on one knee as he proposes to Tzu-chün. Here we have perhaps Lu Hsün's most striking image of what he sees as the fatuous, mindless imitation of foreign models regardless of their applicability to the Chinese situation: Chüan-sheng awkwardly down on one knee, asking Tzu-chün to live with him. Later on in the story he is often embarrassed as Tzu-chün fondly recalls every last detail of his proposal.

Their first days together are idyllic, although there are some clouds on the horizon: Tzu-chün is disowned by her uncle, and Chüan-sheng breaks up with some of his friends who in one way or another disapprove of his unconventional liaison. Tzu-chün soon becomes so busy with her household chores that she doesn't have time to read or go for strolls any more. (Reality is creeping in on the couple in still another guise.) Even her hands begin to get a bit rough as she busies herself with cleaning the rooms and taking care of the chicks and dog they have bought. At last the clouds gather into a storm: on the eve of the Double Tenth, Chüan-sheng receives notice from his bureau that he has been dismissed, a move that he has half expected all along. He has known for a long time that the foppish dandy who is forever smearing cold cream over his face is a gambling companion of the bureau chief's son; hence, he has anticipated that sooner or later rumors about his situation would be reaching his boss from that direction. Much to Chüan-sheng's surprise, Tzu-chün seems unusually disheartened by the news. He, on the other hand, bravely decides to put an ad in the paper for a position as a copyist or teacher; he will also try to make some money by translating. In order to get his translations done, he soon finds it necessary to tell Tzu-chün, much to her displeasure, that she will have to adjust their meal schedule to his work instead of interrupting him whenever it is time to eat.

When finances become even tighter and he takes their pet dog outside the city and abandons it, Tzu-chün makes no attempt to mask her feeling that he has behaved most callously. She becomes increasingly cold and distant. It is winter now, and the house is cold too. In search of warmth, Chüan-sheng escapes to the public library. While he is sitting there musing over his life, this thought occurs to him:

... during more than half a year for the sake of love alone, blind love, I had neglected every last one of the other important things in life. The first and foremost of these was livelihood: a man must make a living before love can have a place wherein to dwell.

The danger of blindly accepting imported foreign ideals in complete disregard of social and personal realities becomes painfully clear.

Chüan-sheng now becomes increasingly indifferent to Tzu-chün, and she, fearing that she has lost his love, forces him to give constant (and therefore false) proofs of his regard. In compliantly assuring her of his love, he is in fact lying, and here we have another of Lu Hsün's favorite themes—hypocrisy.

At this point she resumed that business of making me repeat the things that I had said when I first fell in love, and even began requiring new proofs of my affection, wringing from me a series of affectionate, though hypocritical, replies. At the same time that I exhibited affection to her on the outside, within I was writing a rough draft of hypocrisy on the pages of my heart. Gradually those pages were so filled that I no longer had breathing space. In the midst of my suffering I often thought that a man must really have the greatest courage to tell the truth; if he lacks this courage and hides for the moment in hypocrisy, then he is a man who will never be able to open up a new road for himself.

Chüan-sheng notices that Tzu-chün no longer uses the rebellious and idealistic phrases that were such a normal part of her vocabulary before their marriage. She does not even read any more. Instead of advancing together with him, she now hangs on his coattails. He decides that they ought to break up. He will tell her the truth.

I began by chatting with her, deliberately bringing in our past life together. I touched on literature and art and went from there to foreign authors and their works, to *Nora* [the title given Ibsen's *A Doll's House* in Chinese translation] and *The Lady from the Sea*. I praised Nora's decisiveness. . . . It was nothing more than the kind of thing that I had said in that dilapidated room back in the hostel the year before, but now it was all empty. As the words came out of my mouth and entered my ears, I kept suspecting that there was an impish child behind me mimicking every thing that I said.

Tzu-chün asks him for the whole truth: has he changed? He has:

. . . you want me to be honest. That's as it should be. People shouldn't be hypocritical. Let me be honest then. It's because I no longer love you! But this is really much better from your point of view, for now you can go your own way without the slightest anxiety.

She is hurt. She is shocked. But she does not immediately leave him; he continues to frequent the library as a means of avoiding her.

In the public library I often glimpsed flashes of hope: a new life lay open before me. With courage she would come to her senses and resolutely leave our ice-cold home and, moreover, without the slightest degree of rancor. Then I should be light as a cloud drifting across the sky . . .

As winter is giving way to spring he returns home one day to find her gone. His eventual reaction is relief. Then he begins to wonder what life will be like for her now, and it occurs to him that perhaps he should not have told her the truth, after all. To her, he reflects, the truth could hardly have been as attractive as the lie.

I had thought that if I presented the truth to Tzu-chün, she could, without so much as a single glance back, move forward again with pluck and determination in much the same way that she had handled herself when we initially decided to live together. But I am afraid that that was my mistake, for then her courage and fearlessness had been born of love.

Lacking the courage to shoulder the heavy burden of hypocrisy myself, I had not scrupled at giving her the still heavier burden of truth. After having fallen in love with me, she had been forced to shoulder this heavy burden as she went down the so-called road of life in an atmosphere of intimidation and cold stares.

I even imagined her death!

Soon afterward he learns through a family friend that Tzu-chün has, in fact, died. He is filled with remorse and loneliness, yet he knows that he will go on living, and senses that there are still roads open before him, things that he can still do. He even hopes that there really is a hell filled with ghosts and spirits so that he may someday go there and seek Tzu-chün's forgiveness. But in the meantime he resolves to forget her and to go on with his own life.

I am going to take the first step down a new road of life. I shall take truthfulness and secrete it in the wounds of my heart as I walk silently forward, taking forgetfulness and falsehood as my guide.

As we have noted before, Lu Hsün was not in his own life a particularly adventurous soul, nor did he ever counsel those close to him to take a dangerous path. As a student in Japan he did not actively participate in revolutionary groups though the opportunities were there; teaching in Shaohsing, he advised his students not to cut off their pigtails and needlessly court danger. Similarly, during the May Fourth period he often worried that radical young people would imitate foreign life-styles without proper assessment of the possible consequences. He had, in fact, been long concerned with the problem of blind worship of and adherence to foreign ideals, the main theme of "Remorse." In 1923, two years before writing this story, he dealt with the same problem in a speech given to the Literary Club of the Peking Women's Normal School. He titled his talk "What Happened after Nora Left?" and discussed Ibsen's plays, *A Doll's House* and *The Lady from the Sea*, the Chinese translations of which were very popular at the time—so popular that Lu Hsün, assuming familiarity on the part of his audience, did not other to recapitulate them in any detail. He did, however, almost immediately warn the girls against taking Ibsen too seriously:

But in the end Nora left. What happened after she left? Ibsen doesn't answer and he is already dead now. And even if he were alive, he still wouldn't take responsibility for answering the question because Ibsen was actually writing a poem; he was by no means responding for the benefit of society to a problem that had arisen in that society. He was like an oriole who sings because he wants to sing and not because he wants anyone to derive pleasure or benefit from listening to his song. Ibsen was not at all wise in the ways of the world. It is said that at a party that some women gave in his honor, a spokesman for them got up and thanked him for writing *A Doll's House* and thus presenting the mind of man with a new revelation regarding such things as feminine self-consciousness and emancipation. He surprised everyone by saying "When I wrote that, that's not what I had in mind at all. I was simply writing poetry.[84]

Lu Hsün went on to point out that as far as he could see, Nora only had two alternatives after leaving her family: to fall into prostitution or to go home. In general the thrust of his talk was to warn the girls against accepting foreign ideals uncritically or trying to apply them to Chinese conditions regardless of whether or not they fit. He does not want the girls to get hurt. (Do not cut off your queues!)

Though blind and romantic espousal of foreign ideals in disregard of Chinese realities is the dominant theme of "Remorse," the story also has a very important secondary theme: feminism, or, if you will, the conflict between the concrete and the abstract. Chüan-sheng is a modern intellectual, and—he is a male. As a male intellectual, Chüan-sheng falls in love not so much with the concrete Tzu-chün as with the abstract idea of free love. When Tzu-chün boldly announces that she is her own woman, he is less impressed with the individual woman, Tzu-chün, than with the idea that her plucky announcement shows that there is some hope for Chinese women in general. Only after he breaks up with her does he realize that the courage she exhibited at that point in her life was not derived from some abstract ideal or ism, but rather from the love that she bore him. She did as she did out of feeling; he did as he did out of intellect. Representing feeling, however, she also represents an impure world of compromise—compromise with existing conditions, compromise with reality. A man of intellect, Chüan-sheng accepts no compromises, but rather insists on an unconditional war against hypocrisy in the name of intellectual integrity. When he thinks that he no longer loves

84. *LHCC*, I, 269; a translation of this talk (not included in *SWLH*) is to be found in Gladys Yang's *Silent China: Selected Writings of Lu Xun*, pp. 148-54.

Tzu-chün, he simply says so and then deludes himself into believing that he has done her a favor by not dissembling. He is an absolutist and an intellectual prude.

These were also qualities that distinguished Neo-Confucianism, a system of thought which systematically denied equality to women and often maltreated them in the name of "reason" (*li*), that abstract principle which was the foundation of all mores. Though a modern intellectual, Chüan-sheng is not so very different from Fourth Uncle in "The New Year's Sacrifice." Fourth Uncle's definition of reason is, of course, quite different from the abstract set of foreign ideals to which Chüan-sheng subscribes, as different as the May Fourth period was from traditional China. But in their preference for abstract principles over concrete individuals Chüan-sheng and Fourth Uncle are not very far apart.

MIDDLE-CLASS URBAN WOMEN

The modern young woman Tzu-chün of "Remorse" provides a link between the analysis of Lu Hsün's intellectuals and the analysis of his women. Tzu-chün is herself a modern intellectual, but her feelings determine her life. With few exceptions, Lu Hsün is much more favorably disposed toward the women in his stories than he is toward the men. If the world is divided into two camps, the oppressors and the oppressed, women clearly belong to the latter group and therefore, given Lu Hsün's way of seeing things, are good. Lu Hsün always sided with the underdog—hierarchically (wives over husbands) and temporally (the young over the old). Those in subordinate ranks have the advantage of not having to justify their positions in society on the basis of religion, morality, or what have you; women, precisely because they occupy such a subordinate status, can afford to see things as they are, free from hypocrisy and without the aid of a pair of distorting glasses borrowed from this or that ideology. They are wholesomely concrete; their men are often hypocritically abstract.

The couple who occupy center stage in "Dragon Boat Festival (Tuan-wu chieh)"[85] clearly exhibit this contrast.[86] Lu Hsün sums up the essential nature of their relationship when he first brings

85. *LHCC*, I, 115-23; under the title "What's the Difference?" in Chi-chen Wang's *Contemporary Chinese Stories*, pp. 181-89.
86. In discussing this story earlier we noted that in analyzing Fang Hsüan-ch'o, Lu Hsün was, no doubt, in part dissecting himself. In Mrs. Fang, a rather

them together before the reader. The bureaucrat husband, Fang Hsüan-ch'o (whom we have already discussed at some length) gains his wife's attention, and signals to her that a conversation is about to begin, with the salutation "Hey!" Lu Hsün explains:

They had not received a modern education and hence the wife had no school name or elegant sobriquet; there was really nothing else that he could call her. Of course, he might have followed the old custom and simply have addressed her as "wife," but he didn't want to be considered behind the times either and hence came up with "Hey!" His wife didn't even have so much as a *hey* to use on him, but in accordance with the couple's customary way of doing things, he knew that when she issued forth words while facing in his direction, they were meant for him.

Similarly, when Fang Hsüan-ch'o is about to terminate one of these conjugal colloquies he communicates his intention simply by turning his face in another direction. Obviously, conversation between the Fangs seldom strays beyond the bounds of the absolutely necessary. As we have seen, the steady equilibrium of their less-than-passionate and intellectually unredeemed relationship is thrown somewhat off center by the government's consistent, almost diligent, failure to issue salaries to its employees.

The longer that the authorities procrastinate, the more independent and unawed Mrs. Fang becomes vis-à-vis her spouse. When he returns home for lunch the day before the Dragon Boat Festival, she even goes so far as to thrust a stack of unpaid bills under his nose: "Altogether it will take a hundred and eighty dollars to cover them. Have you been paid?" As the story goes on, she presses him repeatedly to come up with some way of meeting their debts; perhaps he could write an article and submit it to a magazine or newspaper. One after another he manages to side-step every suggestion with which she booby-traps the road between himself and an escapist land of bliss (Hu Shih's poetry). As a last resort, she hesitantly suggests that he might at least purchase a lottery ticket. Fancying himself an educated man,

---

traditional wife, there may be glimpses of Lu Hsün's first wife. Tzu-chün in "Remorse" may reflect the image of his common-law wife, Hsü Kuang-p'ing. "Remorse" was written in October 1925. Miss Hsü, who initiated the relationship, first wrote to Lu Hsün (as humble student to revered teacher) in March of the same year and first visited him in April 13; between then and October they exchanged a fair number of letters and often met. See *LHCC*, IX; *LHJC*, I, 527; *LHNP*, p. 66; *RJNP*, p. 18.

above superstition and pie-in-the-sky schemes to get rich, Fang is beside himself with anger: "What nonsense! How could you possible think of such an uneducated . . . !" His anger flares all the more because he has himself resisted that very temptation earlier in the day. Fang enjoys righteously identifying with those "educated people" who do not engage in such superstitious claptrap. (A similar kind of above-it-all pride prevented him from taking any part in the salary negotiations). The truth of the matter is that he couldn't afford to risk what little he had left on a lottery ticket. He does not come out and say so, however, but rather condemns his wife for being "uneducated" because of her suggestion.

Similarly, Ssu-ming in "Soap" denied his wife's suggestion that he was sexually interested in the filial girl whom he had seen begging on the street, the hypocritical vehemence of his response being in direct proportion to the herculean effort that he had had to make in order to wrestle that thought down into the cellar of his subconscious. Since she was not part of the superordinate masculine establishment, Ssu-ming's wife had not had to worry about whether her every act was in accordance with the dictates of Confucian morality; her husband, considering himself an upright man and faithful guardian of traditional mores, was forced to avert his eyes from the obvious, and thus composed a paean to the filial piety of a beggar girl while buying his wife a cake of soap. With the realism of the underdog, with the insight of the oppressed, his wife saw through his subterfuges to the psychological reality beneath. And despite her own judgment as to the propriety of his erotic preferences, she was canny enough to please him by using the soap. When it was gone, she bought more, on her own.

LOWER-CLASS COUNTRY WOMEN

While "Dragon Boat Festival" and "Soap" present Lu Hsün's readers with the wives of town-dwelling intellectuals, "Storm in a Teacup" and "Divorce" introduce women from the countryside, a step or two down the social scale. In comparison with their urban sisters, they are a bit more aggressive and somewhat coarser.

"Storm in a Teacup (Feng-po)"[87] introduces us to the wife of a boatman. The story is set against the turbulent background of the 1917 attempt of the loyalist "pigtail general" Chang Hsün to

87. *LHCC*, I, 52-60; *SWLH*, I, 52-62.

restore the last Manchu emperor. Imperial restoration implied
hirsutial restoration, and it was understood that anyone who had
failed to retain his pigtail badge of loyalty during the Republican
"rebellion" would be in for it once Chang had suppressed that
rebellion and restored order. A rhymed saying in the countryside
at the time pointed up the dilemma that every man faced regarding
the disposition (or non-disposition) of his queue: "A man without
a pigtail's got no way to hack it / But General Chang'll get 'im if
he happens to lack it."[88]

In a setting of cottages facing a river, Sister Seven-Pounder is
setting out supper on a table that she has placed outside to take
advantage of whatever cool air there is from the river on a sultry
summer's night. She has just spotted Seven-Pounder, her boatman
husband, returning late down the river, and hurries to finish
setting out the rice and vegetables while doing her best to ignore
the incessant chatter of her grandmother-in-law, Old Lady Nine-
Pounder, who keeps insisting that the family is going to pot—the
evidence being that each generation at birth weighs one pound
(*chin*) less than the preceding one. (The custom in the village, to
which we have referred previously, is to name children on the
basis of their weight at birth. Hence the odd names, which in
verification of Old Lady Nine-Pounder's observation, serve also as
marks of generational status.) Saucy Sister Seven-Pounder, however, argues that the discrepancy lies in the scales used rather than
in any difference in the babies. As her husband approaches, she
greets him: "How come you're home so late, you dead corpse?
Where did you croak off to? Didn't you care that we were waiting
supper for you?" With a worried expression, Seven-Pounder tells
of the rumor that the emperor has been restored and that every
man must have a pigtail—which he does not. She replies, shoving
a bowl of hot rice at him, "Why don't you just hurry up and eat
your rice as usual! You think that putting on a face that belongs at
funerals is going to grow you another pigtail?" While they are
eating, she notices Seventh Master Chao down between the tallow
trees, lumbering in their direction over a plank bridge. He is the
proprietor of a wineshop in a neighboring village and has a
reputation of sorts for learning, based on his knowledge of a
novel, the *Romance of the Three Kingdoms*. Because of this

88. *HSJW*, p. 41.

"But where is Seven-Pounder's pigtail?"

roundabout connection with classical learning, Seventh Master Chao identifies with the big tradition of the scholar-officials and often goes about with the air of a survivor of a fallen dynasty. Sister Seven-Pounder sees that he is wearing his blue cotton gown and has let his pigtail down. (He had coiled it on top of his head after the revolution.) This is the third time that he has donned the blue cotton robes of the establishment in the past two years: the first was when an enemy of his took ill; the second, when another enemy died. Sister Seven-Pounder now recalls with a start that two years ago her husband once got drunk and cursed out Chao.

Upon his arrival, Seventh Master Chao makes it immediately plain that he has come to exult in his enemy's pigtailless state. He reminds them that back in the days of the Taiping Rebellion it was a case of "keep your hair, lose your head; keep your head, lose your hair."[89] This bit of historical lore is lost on Seven-Pounder and his wife, who are thoroughly frightened nonetheless. She objects that they all depend upon Seven-Pounder and therefore it would be unjust to punish him. "That won't make any difference," gloats Seventh Master Chao. "The punishments for people without pigtails are written out in a book, item by item, as plain as the nose on your face! It has nothing to do with how many people there are in his family." Sister Seven-Pounder, upon hearing that it is written down somewhere in a book, gives up every last shred of hope. Angrily pointing her chopsticks at her husband, she yells: "This dead corpse got into this himself; let him suffer the consequences himself." She continues to rail at him for having been so foolish as to go into town and get his pigtail cut off. A young widow who lives in the neighborhood, Sister Pa Yi, breaks in and tries to make peace between the quarreling couple. Six-Pounder, Seven-Pounder's little girl, thrusts her bowl in her mother's direction for another fill-up of rice. Her mother, however, cracks her across the top of the head with her chopsticks while bawling out Sister Pa Yi: "Who told you to butt in anyway, you man-hungry young widow!"

The blow from the chopsticks jars the rice bowl loose from the child's hand. A piece chips out as it hits the ground, giving Seven-Pounder an excuse to vent some of the anger that had welled up inside while his wife was scolding him. He downs Six-Pounder with an angry slap across the mouth accompanied by "motherfucker (*jih-niang-te*)!" Seventh Master Chao, angered that the young widow does not seem properly intimidated by the prowess of General Chang Hsün, now vividly describes the ferocity of that doughty gentleman. The assembly breaks up with everything still up in the air. The next morning Seven-Pounder takes his boat into the city as usual.

One evening about ten days later, as Seven-Pounder returns from his daily trip to town, his wife tells him that she passed the wineshop and noticed that Seventh Master Chao was sitting inside with his pigtail coiled up on top of his head again and was not wearing his long gown. She concludes with relief that the emperor

89. Chou Tso-jen states that this saying actually dates from the early days of the Ch'ing dynasty, not from the time of the Taiping Rebellion. *HSJW*, p. 44.

is not really going to be restored after all. The storm has finally passed, and Sister Seven-Pounder and the other villagers begin to treat Seven-Pounder with the more respectful attitude that was their wont before the rumor of the restoration. Going along with whatever opinion is prevalent, cursing out her husband before the neighbors, Sister Seven-Pounder is certainly not a very attractive woman— memorable, but not particularly engaging. And yet one cannot say that she is bad, either. After all, she depends on Seven-Pounder exclusively for her support, and the position of a widowed mother in traditional Chinese society was less than enviable. Though far less awed by her spouse than her city sisters married to scholars or officials, she is nonetheless just as dependent on him.[90]

In "Divorce (Li-hun),"[91] his last short story, Lu Hsün presents still another peppery young woman from the countryside, Chuang Ai-ku. Although no details are given on the occupations of Ai-ku's husband or her father and brothers, the context makes it apparent that her social class is roughly that of Sister Seven-Pounder.

Two or three years before the action of the story, Mr. Shih, Ai-ku's husband, took up with a young widow and turned his proper wife out of the house. Since that time Ai-ku has been living with her father and brothers. They have tried repeatedly to get her husband and his father to take her back. Both the old and the young man (Ai-ku consistently refers to them as the "Old Beast" and the "Young Beast") have refused. Old Mr. Shih wants his son and Ai-ku to dissolve their marriage and has offered a cash settlement which Ai-ku and her father, Chuang Mu-san, have refused, the daughter proving even more recalcitrant than the father.[92]

90. Writing from the perspective of the People's Republic of China in 1956, Hsü Ch'in-wen is somewhat less gracious in his assessment. He says that traditional society has dulled Sister Seven-Pounder so that she has no mind of her own, though with proper leadership even such a woman might be inspired to take a better path in life. *NHFH*, p. 44.

91. *LHCC*, II, 142-52; *SWLH*, I, 262-73. The quotation in the ensuing discussion is my own translation.

92. Hsia Chih-ch'ing points out that Ai-ku's refusal to accept the dissolution of the marriage stems from the fact that as a divorced woman in traditional society she would be thoroughly disdained. Therefore, despite disclaimers, she would prefer to remain Young Beast's wife—better an unloved wife than a castoff woman. *History of Modern Chinese Fiction, 1917-1957* (New Haven, 1961), p. 45.

As the story opens, Chuang Mu-san and Ai-ku get into a boat[93] bound for P'ang village where they have an appointment with Old Gentleman Wei, who is trying to serve as peacemaker between the Chuangs and the Shihs. So far, old Chuang has never agreed to his terms. Since this is a rural area where everyone knows everyone else's business, the other passengers immediately begin discussing the affair. A man who identifies himself as Wang Te-kuei tells that he has heard how Chuang and his six sons went and tore down the kitchen stove of Ai-ku's husband and the young widow he had taken up with.[94] Wang says that everyone who heard about this said that Chuang was in the right. Elated by this apparent show of support, Ai-ku begins prattling out all her private affairs into the eager ears of Wang until her father silences her with a curse. Wang Te-kuei gets off at Wang's Cove and the boat moves on in silence to P'ang village, where father and daughter debark and head for Wei's house.

At the Wei house, the Shihs are present, but attention is focused on a man who is more expensively dressed than the others and seems to command great respect among them. This is Seventh Gentleman, a prestigious city-based relative who is in town for the Wei's annual New Year's reunion. It seems that this Seventh Gentleman is something of a scholar and antiquarian (throughout the negotiation he scratches his nose with a Han dynasty anus-stop —a jade piece thrust into a corpse to keep it from decaying); furthermore, he is said to be on friendly terms with the local magistrate; hence his prestige is great indeed.

Wei announces that since he has not himself had enough "face" to persuade Chuan Mu-san to accept the terms of a divorce, Seventh Gentleman has now agreed to take a hand in it. Wei states that, on the whole, Seventh Gentleman sees things the same way as he does but has generously stipulated that the Shihs are to add another ten dollars to the settlement. Ai-ku waits confidently for her father's rejection of this latest proposal. It does not come. She is a bit surprised that her father, who is respected and feared by

93. Travel by boat, of course, recalls the "water-country" (*shui-hsiang*) of Lu Hsün's home area. Tso-jen has noted that many of the characters, incidents, and even the swear-words in this story come out of Lu Hsün's childhood memories (*HSJW*, pp. 200-201).

94. According to Tso-jen, in that area it was common during the course of a village or family feud to pull down an opponent's stove; the stove symbolized the entire family and its destruction represented final victory. *HSJW*, pp. 200-201.

the local people, can find nothing to say in this situation. In desperation, she speaks for herself:

From the day I married him I was always humble, respectful, and stuck to every rule of a proper wife. But they had it in for me and every last one of them acted as fierce as a tiger. And the year that that weasel chewed up the big rooster it wasn't I who left the chicken coop open. It was that damned mangy dog who pushed it ajar when he stole in to eat some of the feed. But Young Beast there clouted me across the face without ever bothering to get at the facts.

She goes on to say that the real reason for Young Beast's hostility was that he had fallen for that "damned little widow" and was looking for excuses to get rid of his proper wife. She appeals to Seventh Gentleman for justice. Mr. Wei suggests that she calm down a bit and prepare herself to go along with Seventh Gentleman's decision, whatever it is. Ai-ku finishes by saying that unless justice is done, she will appeal the case to the highest authorities in the land and ruin both families if necessary.

Seventh Gentleman breaks in to remind her that the young ought to be more compliant, for "compliance brings wealth." He says that he has already given her an extra ten dollars in the new settlement, and reminds her that since the in-laws have given her her walking papers, she will have to go anyway, settlement money or not. Ai-ku expresses surprise that even a man of the stature of Seventh Gentleman seems so taken in by them. Young Shih avails himself of this opportunity to point out to Seventh Gentleman that if Ai-ku is like this even before him, he can imagine what she was like at home as a wife, forever calling his father Old Beast, and calling himself Young Beast and sometimes even "bastard." Hearing this, Ai-ku is indignant and immediately responds: "What son of a ten-times-ten-thousand-man whore ever called you a bastard?" Furthermore, she says, he was forever calling her "bitch," or worse, and had even started in on her ancestors after taking up with the widow.

At this point Seventh Gentleman gives a piercing, trailing cry: "C-o-m-e i-n!" All is silence. Everything comes to a stop. Ai-ku is taken completely aback. A servant dressed in blue gown and black velvet vest comes in and walks over to Seventh Gentleman, who gives him an order that no one can hear. The man answers "Yes, sir" and leaves. Now, fearful that something terrible is about to take place, Ai-ku blurts out: "I always meant to accept Seventh Gentleman's decision." Mr. Wei is thoroughly delighted that she has finally come round. The families exchange wedding certificates and money. And then Seventh Gentleman sneezes on the snuff that his servant—the man in blue gown and black velvet—has just brought him. (That was the whispered order!) As the story closes, Chuang Mu-san and his daughter leave, refusing a parting cup of New Year's wine.

By virtue of their general uncouthness and peppery speech, both Sister Seven-Pounder and Ai-ku make a strong impression on the reader. Chou Tso-jen has remarked that although such women were often beaten and generally maltreated, some were still very tough and frequently used oaths.[95] Ai-ku, in particular, swears with the fluency of someone who has thoroughly mastered the art. While accepting the traditionally subservient role of women, neither Sister Seven-Pounder nor Ai-ku is particularly awed by men. Sister Seven-Pounder reads out her husband before the neighbors with complete license and Ai-ku swears at her husband with equal abandon. In the end, however, both women are cowed by the power structure of traditional society—and cowed by inferior representatives of it at that. For although Seventh Gentleman may have read the classics and is something of a connoisseur of antiquities (anus-stops), and although he exchanges visiting cards with the local magistrate, he is not, after all, in an official position himself. Similarly, in "Storm in a Teacup," Seventh Master Chao is nothing more than the proprietor of a wineshop whose relation to the scholarly tradition is based only on his passion for, and knowledge of, a long-famed popular novel, the *Romance of the Three Kingdoms.* Yet when he dons the robes of a scholar and spouts the lore he has picked up, he seems identified with the establishment—an identification strong enough to cow poor Sister Seven-Pounder, whose mind is put at rest only when she sees that he has taken off his scholar's robe and has wound up his pigtail on top of his head again. Both Seventh Gentleman and Seventh Master Chao identify upward in order to lord it over those below them, another instance of Lu Hsün's *p'a-ch'iang ch'i-jo* ("fear the strong and bully the weak") analysis of traditional Chinese society.

Women of the middle and lower social levels acknowledge their inferiority to men; in that acknowledgment, however, there are differences of degree—the differences being in proportion to the

95. *HSJW,* p. 48.

extent to which their men are identified with the power structure of scholar-officialdom. In the oppressor-oppressed continuum on which Lu Hsün placed most relationships, Sister Seven-Pounder and Ai-ku clearly stand among the oppressed. And yet, as Tso-jen has pointed out, oppressed though they may be, they retain a certain strength and resilience. Precisely for that reason they become objects of our fascination (or even admiration) more than objects of our pity. These women have been bent somewhat by the weight of the burdens traditional society imposes on them, but they are far from broken. In that respect, they contrast starkly with two of the most memorable women in Lu Hsün's fictional world: Sister Shan-ssu in "Tomorrow (Ming-t'ien)"[96] and Sister Hsiang-lin in "The New Year's Sacrifice (Chu-fu)."[97]

As "Tomorrow" opens, Sister Shan-ssu,[98] living in a village and widowed for two years, is barely managing to support herself and a three-year-old son by spinning cotton yarn. Her difficult situation is further complicated in that her son is seriously ill.[99] Although she has given him the usual folk-cure and has made a vow at the temple (promising the gods this or that in return for his health), the boy shows no improvement. On the contrary, his condition continues to deteriorate. Finally, in desperation, she consults a traditional doctor who makes a mumbo-jumbo diagnosis and gives her an expensive prescription to be filled at the herb shop from which he receives a kickback.[100] The boy dies, and Sister Shan-ssu goes heavily into debt for his funeral.[101] Throughout his illness and the preparations for his burial, the community shows no sympathy or concern; people relate to Sister Shan-ssu primarily for what they can get out of her. The passive victim of a

96. *LHCC*, I, 35-42; *SWLH*, I, 40-48.

97. *LHCC*, II, 5-22; *SWLH*, I, 150-73.

98. I have translated Shan-ssu sao-tzu as Sister Shan-ssu. *Sao-tzu* is the same as *sao*, discussed in n. 3.

99. Tso-jen says that the description of the illness suggests pneumonia, and that Lu Hsün probably had in mind his youngest brother, Chou Ch'un-shou, who died at the age of six when Lu Hsün was at home on vacation from Nanking in the winter of 1898. *HSJW*, p. 26.

100. The doctor may be based on one of those who treated Lu Hsün's father; doctors were in the habit of sending one to a particular herb shop with which they had connections. *HSJW*, pp. 26-27.

101. According to Tso-jen, the funeral of a three-year-old in the countryside would not have been at all elaborate and hence would not actually have been so costly. *HSJW*, pp. 27-28.

heartless world, she reveals more about the society around her than about herself.

Sister Hsiang-lin, in "The New Year's Sacrifice"[102] bears her suffering with the same kind of helpless passivity. Twice married (the second time against both traditional morality and her own will) and twice widowed, she is generally considered as impure, tainted, defiled, and, therefore, unlucky. As we have seen, at the climax of the story (and her life), she is briefly roused from her spiritual torpor and goaded into doing something positive to cope with her environment. Even then, the stimulus comes from without. Liu Ma, who has been hired as part-time help for the occasion of the New Year's sacrifice in the Lu family (impure Sister Hsiang-lin cannot be allowed to defile the ceremonial implements with her tainted hands), has just listened to the woman recite the unhappy details surrounding her forced second marriage.

"Sister Hsiang-lin, you know, you really got the worst part of that deal," said Liu Ma ominously. "If you'd fought harder, or just battered yourself to death against that table and made an end of it, you'd have been much better off. But now? Since you didn't even live with your second man for two full years, you've really gotten yourself into a big sin. Just think of it! When you die and go to the land of the shades, the ghosts of those two men are going to fight over you. Which one will you give yourself to? The Great King down there will simply have to cut you in two and give one half to each man! I think . . . ."

A look of terror appeared on Sister Hsiang-lin's face; she had never heard anything like this back in the mountain village.

"I think you ought to do something to make up for it as soon as possible. Go to the village temple and buy a threshold to represent your own body. Then thousands and thousands of people will step over it and that will atone for the sins that you've committed in this life so that you won't have to suffer for them after you die."

She did not respond in any way at the time, but there was no doubt that she was exceedingly depressed, for when she got up the next morning, there were large black circles around both of her eyes. After breakfast she went to the Earth God Temple at the west end of Lu village and asked to be allowed to purchase an expiatory threshold. The keeper of the temple remained adamant in his refusal right up until Sister

---

102. The plot of this story is outlined in the discussion of Fourth Uncle in the section on traditional intellectuals. The long excerpt from the story is my own translation.

"... and give one half to each man!"

Hsiang-lin was on the verge of tears, and then he grudgingly gave in. The price was set at twelve thousand cash.

Sister Hsiang-lin had stopped conversing with people a long time ago, for everyone was sick and tired of her tale of the tragic death of her son, Ah Mao. Ever since her talk with Liu Ma, however (and news of that conversation seemed to have spread almost immediately), a number of people began to take a new interest in her and even went out of their way to look her up and coax her into conversation. The former topic of these talks, of course, was exchanged for a fresh one centering on the scar on her forehead.

"Sister Hsiang-lin, I ask you, why did you finally give in to him that time?" one would ask. "Ah, what a pity you bashed that hole in your head for nothing," another would chime in, looking at the scar.

She probably knew, too, from their smiles and the tones of their voices, that they were making fun of her and so she always stared at them without saying anything; and later on she no longer even turned her head when they addressed her. She would remain tight-lipped the livelong day, and, bearing that scar on her forehead that everyone considered a mark of her disgrace, would run her errands, sweep the floor, prepare the vegetables, and wash the rice. It wasn't until a year was almost out that she asked for the wages that she had told Fourth Aunt to hold for her. She exchanged the cash for twelve silver dollars and then asked for some time off. Before the time it would take you to eat a meal was out, she was back. She appeared very relaxed and there was an unaccustomed look of life in her eyes. She seemed downright happy as she told Fourth Aunt that she had already bought an expiatory threshold at the Earth God Temple.

When the time of the ancestral sacrifice arrived with the winter equinox, she began working even harder. When she saw Fourth Aunt arrange the sacrifice on a table which she then moved to the center of the main hall with Ah-niu's help, Sister Hsiang-lin confidently walked over to fetch the wine cups and chopsticks.

"Sister Hsiang-lin, put those down!" shouted Fourth Aunt with alarm.

She drew her hand back as though she had touched a hot poker, and at the same time her face turned ashen; she did not even try to offer her help with the candlesticks, but just stood there as if lost. It wasn't until Fourth Uncle came to light the incense and told her to get out of his way that she finally moved. The change that came across her this time was enormous. The next morning not only were her eyes sunken in, but all trace of life was gone from them too. Furthermore, she became very timid: not only was she afraid of the dark, afraid of shadows, but even when she saw people—even her own employers—she was always very skittish, a bit like a mouse that comes out of its hole in broad daylight. Other than that, she just sat totally immobile, like a lifeless wooden doll.

After this, of course, she goes from bad to worse: her hair turns white, her memory fails, and the Lu family lets her go. She becomes a beggar and dies on the streets. In this description of the downfall of Sister Hsiang-lin, Lu Hsün has given us one of the best pieces of prose written during the fiction explosion of the May Fourth period. It is characteristically careful and competent. And yet we learn far less about this unfortunate widow than we do of the people around her. Her passivity is extreme; she is a piece of litmus paper with which Lu Hsün tests the feelings of those around her for acid, and the bitter acid of a loveless society is not found wanting.

The mirror that Lu Hsün held up to Chinese society was a devil's mirror, the mirror of a Mara poet which reflected the hitherto unnoticed and silent sufferings of oppressed groups. In this mirror, women, not men, are morally superior, in that they have never been assimilated into that massive and corrupt body of words which perpetuated the oppressive tradition of the scholar-official and which was the exclusive preserve of men. In this mirror, the further distanced one is from the Confucian high tradition, the less likely is one to justify behavior in righteous formulaic phrases that have long since ceased to command real belief, the less likely is one to be hypocritical, and thus the more likely is one to be capable of sincerity (*ch'eng*) and even love (*ai*). Thus women have the apartness and objectivity that, for instance, enables Ssu-ming's wife to see through her husband's sexual hypocrisy to the psychological reality beneath.

Mrs. Fang and Ssu-ming's wife are both spouses of intellectuals, men who identify with the establishment; Fang Hsüan-ch'o is a connoisseur of modern poetry and considers himself to be above the ignorant habits of ordinary people who do such things as buy lottery tickets; Ssu-ming is a professed defender of traditional morality who denies any sexual interest in the filial maid of the kind expressed by the lower-class pair on the street whose vulgar conversation he repeated to his wife. Whatever the hypocrisy of the husbands, both wives are, of necessity, realists. Mrs. Fang knows that she must face their creditors and that she needs money; she does not worry about "how it would look" if the Fangs bought a lottery ticket. Ssu-ming's wife knows that her husband was erotically stimulated by the image of a nude eighteen-year-old filial maid, all scrubbed up with fragrant soap, waiting to receive him. She attempts to displace that repressed erotic image with her own person. The wholesomely concrete way of thinking of both Mrs. Fang and Ssu-ming's wife stands in sharp contrast to the hypocritical abstractions of their husbands. Neither wife uncritically accepts the norms of her husband; both women attempt to manipulate their men. They may not always succeed, but they are both strong, capable women and tomorrow is another day. Sister Hsiang-lin and Sister Shan-ssu, on the other hand, are hopelessly (and rather helplessly) oppressed. It is, of course, significant in this regard that both are widows as well as mothers. The intensity of the oppression that they suffer is heightened by the fact that they both uncritically accept the norms of society: Sister Hsiang-lin attempts suicide to retain her status as "chaste widow" and Sister Shan-ssu makes vows, draws lots, and, eventually, goes into debt to give her son a proper funeral. Neither of these women can fight back. Tomorrow will bring them nothing. Ai-ku in "Divorce" also accepts the norms of society, but she demands that her husband's family live up to them. When it becomes obvious that her in-laws have the power and the prestige to flout those norms with impunity, she bows to the inevitable, and yet one feels that, given her youth and resilience, there is still some hope. Sister Seven-Pounder, in "Storm in a Teacup," is very strong too, but alarmingly conformist.

In Lu Hsün's stories, middle- and lower-class women are oppressed, but not (with the exception of widows) totally defeated. Given their disadvantaged positions, what more might one reasonably expect these women to do? On the conservative side, one could suffer helplessly like Sister Shan-ssu or Sister Hsiang-lin, or fight back futilely like Ai-ku. Given a more liberal view, one could attempt to manipulate things to one's advantage in the manner of Mrs. Fang or Ssu-ming's wife. Or from a radical position, one might rebel like Tzu-chün. And yet, dissatisfied as he was with the position of women in Chinese society, Lu Hsün refused to sanction open rebellion. He seemed to feel that in the absence of the protection of a powerful feminist movement, the individual rebellion of an occasional enlightened female was pointless. However admirable the freedom of foreign women might appear at a distance, Lu Hsün was well aware that freedom always exists in the concrete reality of a given society. Even Ibsen's Nora, the personification of feminine rebellion during the May Fourth period, lived in a well-defined social context and her "freedom" too, as Lu Hsün reminded the lecture audience of young women, must have been subjected to severe, if not crippling, limitations subsequent to her romantic attempt to be her own woman.

SERVICE OCCUPATIONS

After intellectuals and women, the third-largest group to be found in Lu Hsün's short stories consists of those people who provide services to the community at large, be it as managers (wineshop

"Brother Jun-t'u, you've come!"

and teashop proprietors) or menials (rickshaw men, boatmen, and jacks-of-all-trades). With the exception of Ah Q (the most successful of Lu Hsün's characters), such people play relatively minor roles. The wineshop manager in "K'ung Yi-chi," for instance, does little more than individualize society's generally callous attitude toward the failed scholar, K'ung Yi-chi. Seventh Master Chao (another wineshop manager), in "Storm in a Teacup (Feng-po),￼" serves primarily as a manifestation of the general trend of all groups in society to accept the status quo, toadying to those in power while bullying the weak. In the latter story the boatman Seven-Pounder does not disclose much about himself, but he does show us quite a bit about the people who surround him. As we have seen, when news arrives that the monarchy has been restored, he is in great trouble. His wife and the villagers cease to show him the respect that was their wont. When it becomes apparent that the restoration was only a rumor, they resume their former deferential attitudes (another instance of *p'a-ch'iang ch'i-jo*).

In "Home Town (Ku-hsiang),"[103] it will be recalled, the narrator is a middle-aged intellectual of gentry origin who describes his profound despair at discovering that the peasant Jun-t'u (whom he remembers as a lively boyhood friend) has become a broken and prematurely old man who now addresses him as "Master." Their first meeting after the lapse of many years is, of course, strained.

"Brother Jun-t'u, you've come!" I had a whole string of things that I wanted to talk about—woodcocks, jumping fish, shells, and that odd animal called the *ch'a*, and yet at the same time something seemed to hold me back so that these topics of conversation merely swirled about in my brain without my being able to spit them out.

At first he stood there perfectly still; his face expressed a mixture of joy and sadness. Then his lips moved as though he were on the point of saying something, but no words came forth. Finally he began to assume a very respectful attitude and addressed me quite clearly:

"Master—."

A chill ran up and down my spine as I realized what a lamentably high dividing wall had risen between us. Nor could I find anything to say in return. He turned his head and said, "Shui-sheng, kowtow to the master," dragging out a child who had been hiding in back of him, an exact copy of what Jun-t'u had been himself twenty years earlier—a bit thinner and paler perhaps, and there was no silver ring about his neck,[104] but otherwise he was the same. "This is my fifth; he hasn't been around much and that's why he's so bashful."

Mother and Hung-erh [the narrator's nephew] came downstairs, probably attracted by the sound of our voices.

"Old Mistress, I got your letter quite a while back and you'll never know how happy it made me to hear that the Master was coming home," said Jun-t'u.

"What's this talk of 'Master'? Why the formality all of a sudden? You used to call each other 'brother,' didn't you? Call him 'Brother Hsün' as you used to," my mother said happily.

---

103. *LHCC*, I, 61-71; *SWLH*, I, 63-75. The excerpt from the story is my own translation.
104. A talisman which bound the boy fast to life.

"The Old Mistress is really too—what kind of manners would that be? Back then we didn't know any better."

Jun-t'u is primarily important as a means to self-insight on the part of the narrator, like the rickshaw puller in "A Trifling Incident," who even more serves this purpose. In "Tomorrow," Sister Shan-ssu remains almost totally undeveloped. We see what society does to her, but we never find out how she sees the world,[105] or what idiosyncratic factors in her background might account for her fate. Similarly with Sister Hsiang-lin, we see that she accepts the prevalent folk mores, but we do not enter into her consciousness and see the world as she does. We preserve a similar distance in the case of K'ung Yi-chi, though we do draw close enough to realize that he has an unrealistic appraisal of his relationship to the society in which he lives. In fact, many of Lu Hsün's characters are essentially litmus strips dipped into society to test for acid. This is especially true of those people in service occupations, with the notable exception of the most successful of all Lu Hsün's characters, Ah Q.

AH Q

Ah Q is singularly successful as a character because he is an almost perfect balance of self-revealing (psychologically analytic) and other-revealing (sociologically analytic) elements. "The True Story of Ah Q (Ah Q cheng-chuan)"[106] begins with Lu Hsün addressing his readers directly in the uncharacteristic diction of a popular storyteller. By stating that he doesn't know what Ah Q's surname is, he immediately universalizes his protagonist. It seems that Ah Q once laid claim to "Chao"—when Honored Master Chao's son passed the *hsiu-ts'ai* examination. He even basked comfortably in the reflected glory of his "relative's" success until Honored Master Chao slapped him across the face for such presumption. Since Ah Q's given name was not important enough to be widely recorded, Lu Hsün confesses to his readers that he does not know how to write it; he settles for a common prefix to given names, the Chinese character "Ah," and adds to this the letter "Q" (Lu Hsün was fascinated by the resemblance between

---

105. A very moving passage in "Tomorrow" tells how Sister Shan-ssu saw her own room in an entirely different way after the death of her son, but this is done more for poetic effect than to allow her an occasion to reveal herself to the reader.

106. *LHCC*, I, 72-144; *SWLH*, I, 76-135.

"Q" and a head with a pigtail hanging down).[107] Ah Q has spent so much of his time away from Wei village (the setting of the story) that Lu Hsün cannot even make so bold as to identify him as a Wei villager. In other words, Ah Q is to be taken as an everyman.

And what of Ah Q's own testimony? It too provides little about his background. To be sure, in arguments he occasionally taunts an adversary with "Our family used to be much richer than you!" and asks contemptuously, "Who in the hell do you think you are anyway?"[108] But he never goes into detail. A combination roustabout and rural jack-of-all-trades, he lives in the temple of the local tutelary god and does whatever odd jobs he can find around the village. He looks down on everyone, including the educated sons of the two local rich families, the Chaos and the Ch'iens. As a *hsiu-ts'ai*, Honored Master Chao's son is representative of the old learning. The eldest son of the Ch'ien family, as a returned student, stands for the new learning:

After studying in a foreign school in the city, it seemed he had gone to Japan. When he came home half a year later he walked straight-legged like a foreigner and his pigtail was gone. His mother cried bitterly a dozen times, and his wife tried three times to jump into the well. Later his mother told everyone, "His pigtail was cut off by some scoundrel when he was drunk. He would have been able to be an official, but now he will have to wait until it has grown out again before he thinks of that." Ah Q did not, however, believe this and insisted on calling him "Imitation Foreign Devil" and "Traitor in Foreign Pay."

Ah Q's disdain for his fellow villagers is made possible, in part, by his conviction that his sons may well rise higher in the social scale than any of them. Ah Q, it will be noted, effectively absents himself from the present: his family *used to be* and his sons *will be* much better off than he is now. (Actually, of course, he knows nothing of his family and will never have any sons.) When temporal escape is impossible, he has at his disposal another effective device—psychological victory. This consists of rationalizing defeats into victories, something he accomplishes by pathetically looking on the bright side of the ugliest situations and,

107. The use of the letter Q instead of a Chinese ideograph was a frivolity that Lu Hsün allowed himself, according to Tso-jen, because the piece was written for the Sunday supplement. *HSJW*, p. 64.
108. At a time when, internationally, China was not much to be reckoned with, Lu Hsün's readers drew parallels between Ah Q's stance vis-à-vis Chinese society and the stance of China toward other nations.

occasionally, by schizophrenically dividing his conscious personality into two roles—superior and inferior, oppressor and oppressed, winner and loser. Ah Q, of course, identifies with the superior-oppressor-winner half, at one point going so far as to slap himself in the face while identifying with the slapper rather than the slapped. In the event that these methods should fail, as a last resort he has one other escape route—forgetfulness, and he manages to forget failures very quickly indeed.[109]

Ah Q is a compulsive competitor. He will compete in almost anything. When he runs into Whiskers Wang, who happens to be picking lice at the time, Ah Q sits down next to him and makes a match of it. When he loses (he cannot find as many as Whiskers Wang and when he does pop a rather measly one between his teeth the sound is not nearly so loud or impressive as the little explosions that issue triumphantly one after another from between Whiskers Wang's lips), he picks a fight. Much to Ah Q's surprise, Whiskers Wang, whom he has heretofore never considered his physical equal, wins the fight also. Two consecutive defeats notwithstanding, Ah Q manages a psychological victory by mouthing a piece of classical lore while being beaten: "A gentleman uses his tongue, not his hands." Immediately following this encounter, he bumps into young Ch'ien (son of Honored Master Ch'ien) and taunts him for his artificial pigtail (like Lu Hsün, the Ch'ien lad had cut off his pigtail while a student in Japan). The predictable result is that Young Ch'ien gives Ah Q another good drubbing. Nevertheless, Ah Q comes up with a psychological victory: when the beating is over, he heads off to the wineshop and by the time he gets there has managed to forget the whole thing. Despite these victories, however, it has been a rather bad day for Ah Q.

At the wineshop there is a Buddhist nun out front. Ah Q spits and blames all his bad luck that day on the fact that he was destined to run into an unlucky nun on the road.[110] He goes on to insult, tease, and bully her for the amusement of the customers in the wineshop, a clear indication that he shares the *p'a-ch'iang ch'i-jo* mentality of so many other characters in Lu Hsün's stories,

109. Similarly, readers could reflect, China tended to forget national disgraces.
110. According to Tso-jen, when people met a nun on the road, they would spit to avoid bad luck; two men walking together would split up and let her pass between them to achieve the same result. *HSJW*, p. 78.

regardless of class.[111] The hapless nun's only response is to curse Ah Q and hope that he shall remain without sons. In China this is indeed a potent curse, a curse that turns Ah Q's will-o-the-wisp thoughts in the direction of sex and procreation.[112]

At this point Lu Hsün addresses his readers directly again, to report Ah Q's belief that all nuns carry on with monks, that a woman alone on the street must be looking for a man, that a man and woman talking together must be arranging a rendezvous.[113] Stimulated by the nun's curse, Ah Q makes a stupid and unwelcome pass at a widowed female servant in the Chaos' household, where he is temporarily employed grinding rice. He is then beaten and thrown out of the house as the Chaos try to persuade Amah Wu that the smirch on her chaste-widow reputation is neither large enough nor dark enough to warrant suicide. News of the furor in the Chao household soon spreads through the village, with the result that no one is willing to employ Ah Q for odd jobs any longer. Livelihood cut off, he flees to the city to make his fortune.

When, after a prolonged absence, Ah Q returns to Wei village, he looks down on his fellow villagers as provincials who have never beheld the wondrous and curious sights that he has enjoyed in the city; he especially delights in regaling them with a juicy description of the decapitation of a revolutionary that he witnessed. After a while it comes out that he was affiliated with a group of burglars: he lets a few things slip out in conversation and it becomes known that he has odds-and-ends for sale that he could have acquired in no other way. His new reputation as thief does nothing to diminish his prestige in Wei village, and leading families compete with each other in buying the booty that he has brought back. His prestige suffers a severe drop, however, when it is discovered that within the band of burglars he was merely the

111. Writing in 1935, Tso-jen noted that early leftist critics had attacked Lu Hsün for ridiculing the peasantry through his unflattering portrayal of Ah Q, but after he turned to the left this sort of criticism dwindled away and Ah Q was even hailed as a representative of the proletariat. *K'u-ch'a sui-pi* [Bitter tea jottings] (Shanghai, 1935), pp. 283-85; hereafter cited as *KCSP*.

112. Ah Q's escapade in this regard reflects an episode in the life of Lu Hsün's grand-uncle Tzu-ching, in the Shaohsing t'aimen.

113. Tso-jen has said that his brother is here criticizing, through Ah Q, the gentry's philosophy toward women. When writing poetry, they saw women as beautiful toys; when writing history, as dangerous nymphomaniacs capable of ruining a family or toppling a state. *HSJW*, pp. 79-80.

man who stayed outside the house and received the stolen goods as they were passed out.

Rumors of revolution reach Wei village, and Ah Q has mixed reactions. Basically a conformist, he has always disliked revolutionaries and thought of them as people who were creating trouble for him personally as well as for society at large. Nevertheless, when he discovers that the village's modest power-elite is terrified of them, his attitude changes dramatically. He begins to imagine all the differences that a revolution will make in his life. Heretofore he has always been a loner. The revolution will bring him group membership and brotherhood; it will bring him new prestige; it will bring him an opportunity to avenge the past slights that he has suffered; it will provide him with sex. Yes, Ah Q, too, will become a revolutionary! Having determined to revolt, he carries out his "revolution" on the most defenseless of people—the nuns at the Convent of Quiet Self-Improvement. Much to his dismay, however, he discovers that others have already "revolutionized" them: the two sons of the Chao and Ch'ien families came by earlier in the day, smashed an imperial tablet (despised symbol of the Manchus), stole an antique censer, and beat up an old nun.

It occurs to Ah Q that he might do better as part of a group; consequently, he seeks out the revolutionaries. The "revolutionaries," of course (and here we have Lu Hsün's view of the Republican Revolution), turn out to be just like the existing elites, indeed, some are the same people. When Ah Q is audacious enough to try to join them, they simply throw him out. Apparently the revolution was much ado about nothing:

The people of Wei village became more reassured every day. From the news that was brought they knew that, although the revolutionaries had entered the town, their coming had not made a great deal of difference. The magistrate was still the highest official, it was only his title that had changed; and the successful provincial candidate also had some post—the villagers could not remember these names clearly—some kind of official post; while the head of the military was still the same old captain. The only cause for alarm was that there were also some bad revolutionaries who were making trouble and had started cutting off people's pigtails the day after their arrival. It was said that the boatman Seven-Pounder, from the next village, had fallen into their clutches, and that he no longer looked presentable.[114]

114. Although Lu Hsün used a new pen name for this story, he could not resist giving knowledgeable readers a hint that he was also the author of "Storm in a

Despite the fact that the old establishment, in its new "revolutionary" guise, remains intact, Ah Q still hopes that the actual arrival of the revolutionary troops in their white helmets and armor will bring some improvement in his lot. One night, returning home late from the wineshop, slightly inebriated, he is attracted by the sound of a disturbance. He follows the sound to its source and discovers a group of soldiers in white helmets and armor ransacking the Chaos' house. Mindlessly he watches for a while and then returns home to the temple, absolutely furious that they did not ask him to join them.

After the Chao family was robbed, most of the people in Wei village felt pleased yet fearful, and Ah Q was no exception. But four days later Ah Q was suddenly dragged into town in the middle of the night. It happened to be a dark night when a squad of soldiers, a squad of militia, a squad of police, and five secret-servicemen made their way quietly to Wei village and under the cover of darkness surrounded the temple, posting a machine gun opposite the entrance. . . . The captain . . . offered a reward of twenty thousand cash. Only then did two militiamen summon up the courage to jump over the wall and enter.

Ah Q is arrested for the robbery and forced to sign a confession. He objects that he cannot write. They tell him that they will settle for a circle. As he picks up the unfamiliar writing brush, he decides that he shall at least be able to save some face if he can draw a perfect circle—but the brush tip goes awry just before he closes it. If nothing else, Ah Q has, at least, brought to jail with him his psychological apparatus for winning victories, and he soon consoles himself with the thought that only a jackass would be able to manage a perfect circle in the first place.

Throughout this new ordeal, Ah Q comforts himself with the observation that at some time or other it is probably everyone's fate to be arrested and forced to sign a confession. When he is dragged from the jail to be paraded through the streets as a public example, it finally dawns on him that he is to be executed. After the initial terror has subsided, he similarly calms himself with the thought that now and then it is probably also everyone's fate to be paraded through the streets and executed. As he nears the execution ground, Ah Q tries to think of a defiant snatch of opera

---

Teacup (Feng-po)"—published under the pen name Lu Hsün—in which Seven-Pounder appeared.

that he might sing (something stereotypically expected of bold and brazen cutthroats) but cannot. A heroic phrase traditionally recited by condemned criminals comes to Ah Q's mind: "In another twenty years I'll be a strapping man again" (through reincarnation the man executed will come back in another body and avenge his death). Ah Q manages to recite almost the entire sentence. The crowd is well pleased and gives him a loud "Hao (Bravo)!" Throughout his life Ah Q has been able to hold reality out, but in these final moments the crowd's *hao*, sounding to him very much like the howl of a wolf, finally cuts through all his walls of defense and brings in reality with all its terror.

Ah Q took another look at the people who were shouting "Hao!"

Thoughts spiraled around in his mind like a whirlwind and whisked him back to a time four years ago when he had encountered a wolf at the foot of a mountain. It had stuck to his trail, always maintaining the same distance, looking for a chance to devour his flesh. Ah Q had been scared half to death, but fortunately he had had an ax in his hand at the time and it had given him enough courage to make it back to Wei village. He had never forgotten that wolf's eyes—ferocious and timid at the same time, sparkling like two ghostly fires that seemed to burn through him from the distance. But now he saw eyes that were even more terrible, eyes that he had never seen before—eyes that were dull and sharp at the same time, eyes that had already devoured his words and now wanted to consume something that lay beyond skin and flesh, eyes that had stuck to his trail, always keeping the same distance.

And then it was as though all those eyes came together into some single thing that tore at his soul.

"Help—"

But Ah Q never said that. Blackness had already covered his eyes. He heard the shots ring out and felt his body scatter like a heap of dust.[115]

Throughout the story, Ah Q moves in a world of well-defined roles; the play of life has long since been written, has long since gone through its final revisions. All that is required is that a man play his role. Ah Q's difficulty, of course, lies in being dissatisfied

---

115. I have taken great liberties in translating this passage in order to convey its feel as well as its substance. The description of the eyes as fierce and timid at the same time is reminiscent of the sixth entry of the diary by Lu Hsün's madman: "The ferocity of a lion, the timidity of a rabbit, the craftiness of a fox." Here at the climax of Lu Hsün's greatest story the crucial Sendai slide incident that determined him to become a writer is dramatically reenacted.

with the relatively minor part that he is accorded in the play. This leads him to attempt a series of different roles, from roustabout rural handy-man to lover, thief, would-be revolutionary, and finally condemned criminal. But what of the distinction between role and actor? Roles are generalized, but actors are individual. In traditional China too, one man might in his life "play many parts," and yet one might still expect some sort of continuity in the actor who plays them. After all, the actors behind the roles are individual human beings. The world of traditional Chinese society as presented in Lu Hsün's stories, however, is not interested in individuals. It is a society which prefers, and is most readily able to deal with, readily identifiable types: nuns, condemned criminals, and so on. Similarly, in thought it prefers, and is most readily able to cope with, stereotypes; Ah Q believes that all nuns carry on with monks, and the crowd that follows him to the execution ground believes that condemned criminals will say heroic things.

Since life is a play whose script has long since been set, it follows that any degree of self-consciousness—wonder about the continuity of the individual actor behind the roles—is potentially dangerous, for it might lead one to change a gesture or ad-lib a line, and that will not be permitted. All the characters in "The True Story of Ah Q" are fundamentally concerned with playing their proper roles. The wife of the imitation foreign devil, as the disgraced mate of a man who has lost his pigtail, attempts suicide; and Amah Wu makes a similar attempt when she concludes that she has been disgraced by Ah Q. Or take the example of the imitation foreign devil himself (opportunistically gone over to the revolutionary side) when Ah Q goes diffidently into his courtyard in a silly and foredoomed attempt to join the revolution:

Ah Q tiptoed inside. . . .

He wanted to get the imitation foreign devil's attention, but he didn't know what to call him. Of course, it wouldn't do to just call him "imitation foreign devil." Nor did "foreigner" sound quite right. "Revolutionary" wouldn't do either. Perhaps he should simply call him "Mr. Foreigner."

But "Mr. Foreigner," who was gazing into the sky, discoursing with great fervour, hadn't even noticed him.

"I'm the kind of person who's always chafing at the bit and so whenever we met I'd always say 'Hung, old friend, let's get on with it!'

but he'd always say 'Nein'—that's a foreign word you wouldn't under-stand. If he hadn't kept saying no, we'd have succeeded a long time ago; that just goes to show you how careful he is. He's tried I don't know how many times to get me to go to Hupeh, but I still haven't agreed to it. Who wants to work in a little district town anyway?"

"Um . . . this . . . ah . . ." Ah Q had waited for a pause in the conversation and now summoned up all his courage and began to speak, but for some reason or other he didn't address him as "Mr. Foreigner" after all.

The four men who had been listening gave a start and turned to stare at Ah Q. Mr. Foreigner too caught sight of him for the first time.

"What do you want?"

"I—."

"Get out!"

The Ch'ien lad is clearly on stage, playing a part. Revolutionaries are aggressive and want to get things done. "I'd always say, 'Hung, old friend, let's get on with it!' " They understand foreign tongues: "But he'd always say 'Nein'."[116] They are expansive people who (like the scholar-officials of the empire) get important assignments all over the country: "He's tried to get me, I don't know how many times, to go to Hupeh." The imitation foreign devil has found a new role to play, a new model to imitate. Ah Q himself is no more and no less serious about playing a "revolutionary" than is the Ch'ien lad. When he decides to join the revolutionaries, he signals that fact by singing martial songs and swaggering along the street. Later on, when it is clear that he is going to be executed, he tries to emulate the braggadocio of the fearless condemned man. As we have seen, bullets bring his ill-starred life to an end just as he is about to discard his masks and cry out for help.

One of the best discussions in Chinese of Ah Q's character is that which Chou Tso-jen wrote in 1922:

This man Ah Q is a summation of all the "roles" a man may play in Chinese society. He is a man with no will of his own: his consciousness consists of the accumulated customs handed down by society from one generation unto another. For that reason Ah Q cannot be said really to exist in contemporary society, and yet he exists everywhere at once. Mr. Shen Yen-ping [better known by his pen-name, Mao Tun] has stated in the *Short Story Monthly*: "If you try to walk through society and point out an Ah Q in the flesh, you will be doomed to failure. And yet as I was

116. The original has the English "no."

reading the story Ah Q's face struck me as very familiar indeed. Of course he is familiar! He is a distillate of all the traits of Chinese character." Mr. Shen is perfectly right in saying this. The protagonist of Gogol's novel, *Dead Souls*, Chichikov, is also like that: we cannot find an actual Chichikov traveling about buying up dead agricultural serfs, but among various types of opportunistic enterpreneurs we can perceive his shadow (as Kropotkin has pointed out). However, there is this difference between them: whereas Chichikov is an international type, Ah Q, on the contrary, is a national type. He is just like Pandora of the Greek myth.[117] Heir of the collected patterns of the totality of roles that four thousand years of nightmarish experiences had created in traditional society, Ah Q is the condensed summation of all these patterns—patterns that include attitudes toward love, happiness, reputation, and morality —redrawn so as to be presented as a single, individual mask. Therefore, Ah Q is actually a "composite photograph" made up of all the weak points of Chinese character. Of these, the most trenchantly described are a Chinese lack of will to seek life and a lack of respect for human life; I personally feel that these two defects are the major causes of China's present illness.

In sum, no matter how childish this story may be from an artistic point of view, the very fact of the author's willingness to openly display his antipathy in such an honest and objective way is, in a very real sense, nothing less than a long-needed dose of bitter medicine for Chinese society. Thus, the existence of this story in China, to my way of thinking, is not without profound significance. The only fault that one can find is that while the author's original intention seems to have been to roundly castigate Ah Q, as the reader approaches the end of the tale he begins to feel that the only really lovable person in all of Wei village is Ah Q! He is certainly the most upstanding person in town, and it is precisely for that reason that he is cut down in the end. (Tolstoy said something very similar in criticizing Chekhov's "The Darling.")[118] Lu

117. Apparently Tso-jen has in mind that version of the myth which presents Pandora carrying a box that she brought down from heaven as the first woman on earth—a box containing all possible human ills.
118. "The Darling" tells of a woman with no mind or life of her own; she is merely an extension of her husband. In an afterword to the story printed in 1906, two years after Chekhov's death, Tolstoy wrote: "Chekhov intended to curse, but the god of poetry commanded him to bless, and he unconsciously clothed this sweet creature in such exquisite radiance that she will always remain a model of what a woman should be in order to be happy herself." See David Magarshack, trans., *Anton Chekhov: Lady with Lapdog and Other Stories* (Penguin Books, 1964), Introduction, p. 13.

Hsün wanted to knock Ah Q down, but by focusing all of his attention on him, contrary to his own expectations, he helped raise him up instead! Perhaps this is one respect in which the author failed. As for the fact that some people may feel that the satire is exaggerated to the point that it detracts from the credibility of the story—I cannot agree at all, for in this world it is often the case that "fact is stranger than fiction." Indeed, in the drab vicinity of my home town I personally saw the models upon whom this kind of character is based. Among them there was even one shrunken, real, and lovable Ah Kuei who is still living even today.[119]

The international success of Ah Q in translation belies Tso-jen's point that Ah Q, in contrast to Chichikov, is a national type. While Ah Q's peculiar defects may have been more pronounced in the China of Lu Hsün's day than they are in other cultures, they are by no means limited to China. And what are those defects? Cowering before the strong while bullying the weak (something that probably occurs in every complex social group this side of paradise—its inimical effects being particularly magnified in China by the intensity of Chinese concern with hierarchy), forgetfulness (what man, Chinese or not, can afford to dwell on his most humiliating moments, to cherish them in his memory?), and psychological victory. As we have seen, Ah Q wins psychological victories by various means. He sometimes comforts himself with pipe dreams of the great power and prestige of his family in the past or the possible greatness of his posterity in the future; he sometimes consoles himself by asserting moral superiority over his opponent: "A gentleman uses his tongue, not his hands." When all else fails, he resorts to schizophrenic bifurcation of his personality into winner and loser halves, identifying always with the former. This last technique is no doubt the most dangerous; it could remove Ah Q so far from reality that he would be truly insane. All of Ah Q's methods, however, lend him a certain psychological resilience which makes him admirable in a bittersweet way. We may object to *Ah Q ching-shen* ("Ah Q spirit") when it is taken too far, but we have to admit that it is spirit: we never see Ah Q completely dejected. Like a rubber ball, the harder he is thrown against the wall, the farther he bounces back. He may not be morally upright, but he is psychologically tough.

119. *CNST*, pp. 114-15.

Addressing himself to Russian readers in the preface of a Russian translation of the story in 1925, Lu Hsün chose to emphasize the sociological rather than the psychological elements:

Although it is what I have tried to do, I am still rather uncertain as to whether I have succeeded in taking the soul of one of my contemporary countrymen and setting it down on paper. I do not know how others may feel, but I, personally, have always felt as though there were a high wall here in our midst, separating each of us from the other so that communication becomes impossible. This state of affairs was brought about by our intelligent men of antiquity—our so-called sages and worthies—who divided the people into ten classes and proclaimed each class hierarchically different from the others. Although the nomenclature they employed to distinquish those classes is no longer in use, its ghost still lingers on and has become still more frightful than its original, so that by now hierarchical distinctions even exist in a single individual—so that a hand cannot help but look down upon a foot as lower-class and a member of the out-group. Now when the creator made men he was extremely crafty to begin with and arranged things so that it was impossible for one man to feel the physical suffering endured by another; our sages and their disciples, however, improved upon this and added a refinement that the creator had overlooked: they arranged it so that henceforth it was impossible for one man to feel even the spiritual suffering endured by another.

Piece by piece, our ancients also created written words of a difficulty that is truly frightening. And yet I don't blame them entirely for that, for I don't feel that they did it on purpose. Whatever their intent may have been, however, it was nonetheless true that a good many people could not begin to utilize such a difficult writing system to express themselves. That difficulty was subsequently increased by the high wall of commentaries and glosses thrown up [around the classics], so that the common people wouldn't dare so much as dream of becoming literate. And thus it is that today the only voices that we hear out of our antiquity are those of a few disciples of the sages, mouthing their own opinions and maxims for their own benefit. As for the common people, they grew, withered away, and died in total silence like so much grass pressed under a large stone—and things have already been going on that way for four thousand years!

It is most difficult in China even to attempt to depict the soul of such a silent people; as I have said, we Chinese are in effect the citizens of a still unmodernized ancient state and therefore we remain divided and out of contact with each other even to the extent that it seems that one's own hand does not understand one's own foot. Although I have made every effort to re-create the rough outline of the soul of our people, I have often been made conscious of the existence of some barriers that still stand between us. In the future it will probably occur that the masses who are at present shut in behind such high walls will become conscious of themselves, step outside, open their mouths and speak—but as of this moment that seldom occurs. Therefore the only thing that I can do is to rely on my own observations and for the time being, in my apartness, write them out as a representation of human life as experienced in China from my point of view.[120]

It may be that Lu Hsün emphasized the sociological aspects of the world of Ah Q because he was addressing a Russian audience. What he says about giving a voice to the silent masses of China is, however, entirely in harmony with his belief that his function as a writer ought to be like that of the Mara poets whom he had so admired earlier—warriors of the spirit who gave voice to the silent suffering of entire peoples, warriors who broke the silence with their articulate cries.

The critic Ou-yang Fan-hai has remarked that in the treatment of Jun-t'u in "Home Town" we can find traces of the positive kind of sympathy that Lu Hsün felt for Ah Q.[121] His methods of dealing with the two men, however, are radically different. In the case of Jun-t'u both Lu Hsün and his readers remain on the outside; we see Jun-t'u as a figure in a painting and never move inside his psyche to see, feel, and experience the world as he does. In the case of Ah Q, Lu Hsün invites us inside the labyrinth of his protagonist's psyche and shows us around, pointing out this and that in a fashion that occasionally causes us to realize with a flash that some of the back corridors of our psyches are not totally dissimilar from what we find in Ah Q.

As we have seen in the preface to the Russian translation, Lu Hsün strongly doubted his credentials as a guide to the mind of Ah Q. He feared that the barriers thrown up between classes in China made it virtually impossible for one class to be at all aware of the mentality of another. Such doubts may have been justified, but they are probably not so important as Lu Hsün would lead us to believe. Ah Q is successful primarily because psychologically he is a Chinese everyman, not because he is a member of the voiceless masses to whom Lu Hsün, as Mara poet, is lending speech. It is possible, of course, that Lu Hsün emphasized the class aspect of

120. *LHCC*, VII, 77-78.
121. *LHTS*, pp. 180-83.

Ah Q's character because he was addressing himself to a Russian audience living in the midst of a recently established experiment in achieving a classless society.

The models for Ah Q were of mixed class origins. A pair of brothers who lived at the New T'aimen in Shaohsing were, like Ah Q, rural jacks-of-all-trades. The elder, Hsieh Ah-yu, was a stable and responsible person; the younger, Hsieh Ah-kuei, was a part-time worker and part-time thief.[122] Ah Q got his name and occupation from Ah-kuei and was, to that extent, of lower-class origin. And yet he was based in part on Lu Hsün's Grand-Uncle Tzu-ching, who lived at the t'aimen and was, as we have seen, the model for Ch'en Shih-ch'eng in "The White Light"; Tzu-ching provided material for a significant part of Ah Q's personality.

Early in the story Lu Hsün recites a list of Ah Q's "victories." Each of these, of course, is in fact a defeat that Ah Q transforms into a victory through this or that psychological mechanism. After a succession of such "victories," Ah Q goes to the gambling tables at the village fair. Surprise of surprises, he finds himself winning a great deal of money! Suddenly a scuffle breaks out; when it is over and the confusion dies down, Ah Q discovers that his big pile of silver is nowhere to be seen. He returns dejectedly to the local temple where he sleeps, feeling *almost* defeated. Try as he may, he just seems incapable of turning this defeat into a victory, even in his own mind. Then, when every other psychological device at his command fails, he splits his personality into superordinate and subordinate halves and, needless to say, casts himself in the superordinate role.

> But he immediately turned his defeat into a victory. Raising high his right hand, he slapped himself across the mouth twice, as hard as he could. His face stung and began to ache a bit. But immediately afterward he was able to calm down and relax; it was as though the one who had struck him across the mouth was *one* self, while the one who had been struck was *another*. Still later, it seemed almost as though he had struck someone else entirely—although his own face still stung a bit. Totally satisfied now—victoriously, he lay down.

Tzu-ching, upon whom Ah Q was in part based, died in 1896 when Lu Hsün was in his sixteenth year. Tzu-ching had slipped his leash many times before his final fit of madness and suicide: it

---

122. For more on the Hsieh brothers see *HSJW*, p. 65; *LHKC*, pp. 107-9; and *CNST*, pp. 103-4.

would happen late at night usually, and he would begin by castigating himself for being an unfilial offspring; then he would slap himself and slam his head against the wall.[123]

Such behavior may seem extreme, be it actual (Tzu-ching) or fictional (Ah Q), but it reflects one of the most fundamental problems of traditional Chinese culture—hierarchy. To be born Chinese, in the Han dynasty or in the time of Lu Hsün, meant to have a strong interest in prestige-graded relationships: ruler to subject, father to son, elder brother to younger brother (a distinction maintained even in the case of twins), and so on. From such a central problem neither Lu Hsün nor his readers could stand aloof. Ah Q's problem was theirs; it was part of being Chinese. Had it been the problem of an enemy or an out-group, Lu Hsün and his readers might possibly have felt no sympathy for Ah Q, might even have been glad to see him destroyed. Ah Q, however, did not exclusively represent one class or calling; he was an everyman, hence it was impossible to view him with indifference. Perhaps not everyone felt sympathy for Ah Q in the superior, uninvolved way that one can luxuriously experience pity for a member of the out-group, but it is likely that most people felt some empathy with him. As the short-story writer and novelist Chang T'ien-yi has pointed out, Lu Hsün in creating Ah Q, took common psychological defects of his countrymen and wrapped them all together in a single package which he then exhibited for all to view:

Ouch! "The True Story of Ah Q" really hurts people! It makes a public exposure of the very scabs that Ah Q taboos; what's more, it even makes a public exposure of Ah Q's very defect of tabooing defects! Those people who suffer from this fault thus no longer have any place to hide.[124]

This was so much the case that some readers began to suspect that the story was a fictionalized exposé of their own affairs. They began wildly guessing the identity of the author (Lu Hsün had used a new pen name, Pa Jen) in order to determine whether he was someone who might be privy to their secrets.

Ou-yang Fan-hai's reference to "sympathy" and his comparison of Ah Q to Jun-t'u are both provocative; yet, as we have shown, a

123. *HSJW*, p. 126.
124. Chang T'ien-yi et al., *Lun Ah Q* [Discussing Ah Q] (Shanghai, 1947), p. 21; hereafter cited as *LAQ*.

distinction needs to be maintained. Lu Hsün *sympathized* with Jun-t'u (perhaps as a member of the gentry, even felt somewhat guilty about him), but he *empathized* with Ah Q. As early in life as his student days in Japan, he had believed that China's main problem lay in the area of psychology or, to use a more traditional term, morality (*tao-te*), and that what was wrong with China—a lack of love and honesty—could not be easily or quickly remedied through political or institutional change. He saw clearly the contradiction immanent in the circumstance that contemporary critics of Chinese society (himself included) had been formed by the very system that they criticized. If they were to have any hope of transforming it, they would have to begin with themselves. This is the point made in "Diary of a Madman," his (and modern China's) first colloquial short story. The diarist, during his brief excursion into the land of "madness," sees Chinese society (and the history that produced it) as cruelly despotic and irredeemably unjust, a cannibalistic feast where the strong eat the weak; yet he begins to realize that his own generation has been formed by the society which he condemns; hence his final plea is to "save the children," for they alone have not yet become cannibals.[125]

125. Lu Hsün's emphasis upon youth is probably as much a function of this recurring idea as it is of his penchant for Darwinism. Believing in evolution, in 1919 he wrote:

"To me the continuation of the species—the perpetuation of life plays an important role in the animal kingdom. Why this continuation? For the sake of evolution naturally. But to have evolution the young must supercede the old. Thus the new should advance joyously towards death. When all tread this path, that is evolution." (*SWLH*, II, 42; *LHCC*, I, 412).

It is important to remember that in this context what he meant by "evolution" was actually closer to "revolution"—a revolution that could be brought about when adults totally liberated their children from the rules of the adult society in which the parents themselves had been raised. Writing in the same year, Lu Hsün said in "What Is Required of Us as Fathers Today":

". . . we of this generatin should start to emancipate all coming after us. The emancipation of children is something so natural that it should need no discussion, but the elder generation in China has been too poisoned by the old customs and ideas ever to come to its senses. . . . Burdened as a man may be with the weight of tradition, he can yet prop open the gate of darkness with his shoulder to let the children through to the bright, wide-open spaces, to lead happy lives henceforward as rational human beings." (*SWLH*, II, 54; *LHCC*, I, 246.)

Had Lu Hsün been of a temperament to decide that China's main problems were political (to be resolved by the substitution of one form of government for another), it is likely that the characters in his stories would have readily, and perhaps simple-mindedly, sorted themselves out into two propagandistic bins: the good guys (progressives) and the bad guys (conservatives). Since he saw the problems as psychological or moral, no easy resolution was possible. He did not look at Ah Q and say, "Your problem is that you are oppressed; rise up and be free!" Rather, he looked at Ah Q and said, "You are your own worst problem; it is what you have become within, as well as the oppressive forces that prey on you from without, that makes you suffer so." The assignment of responsibility for China's ills to both the individual and the group is not limited to Ah Q; Lu Hsün makes it in a number of his stories; but it is here that he most even-handedly divides his barbs between the individual and society. Precisely for that reason, Ah Q is the most powerful and memorable figure to appear in any of them.[126]

"The True Story of Ah Q" is one of the two stories in Lu Hsün's output that take their titles from their protagonists, the other being "K'ung Yi-chi." Incident largely determines the parts of K'ung Yi-chi's personality that are brought into focus and we see only those aspects that are revealed by the young clerk in the shop, the manager of the shop, the other patrons, and the children. We move from society to individual. With Ah Q the emphasis is somewhat different: we begin with him and move out into the society which surrounds him, and here, much more than

---

It is clear that Lu Hsün's commitment to social Darwinism was a commitment to a revolutionary evolutionism by means of which the young would transform China. As we have seen, he began to shift away from this belief when he saw young people informing against each other during the bloody White Terror of 1927.

126. Hsü Ch'in-wen has caught something of this in describing Lu Hsün's attitude toward Liu Ma in "The New Year's Sacrifice":

"With regard to workers of this kind among the people who have developed faults because they have lived so long under feudal control, Lu Hsün expresses his sympathy for their unfortunate plight but at the same time he detests their willing submissiveness and inability to stand up and fight back. In other words he pities them in their misfortune, but is angry with them for not resisting." (*PHFH*, pp. 8-9.)

in the case of K'ung Yi-chi, we are made aware of the interdependence of group and individual, and the interrelatedness of environment and ego.[127] The society in which Ah Q lives is in many senses wrong, and as a product of that society Ah Q is in many ways individually wrong. His individual defects, are, as we have seen, a compendium of what Lu Hsün saw as the psychological shortcomings of Chinese personality. If there is a "wrong" kind of personality, it would seem that there should also be a "right" one. This may well be, but Lu Hsün never spells out what that "right" kind of personality is. He claimed no more than to be a diagnostician who could, with luck, identify the disease.

Ah Q's personality defects do not fall into a bin that we can simply label bad, wrong, undesirable. Upon closer examination they turn out to be his strengths. He constantly rationalizes his defeats into victories, a process which, to be sure, is totally unrealistic. Yet it gives Ah Q great psychological resilience: hurl him against a wall of disgrace and defeat and he will not break, but rather bounce back ready to take another throw; disgrace and defeat him in such a humiliating way that not even the most subtle of his psychological acrobatics will enable him to interpret the experience as a victory and he will simply forget it. His is a prodigious psychological shield, one that is pierced only at the very end of his life. In this sense, Ah Q is not only a summation of Chinese psychological defects; he represents some Chinese psychological strengths as well. And since disgrace and defeat are among the "thousand natural shocks that flesh is heir to," Ah Q's experiences and his devices for coping with them are not limited to China. Indeed, Ah Q is an international everyman; hence it is that he is lovable, even in translation. There are probably few people in any culture who would not prefer Ah Q to a man who masochistically dwelt upon his defeats or interpreted his share of the "thousand natural shocks" in a self-defeating and paranoid manner. Imagine a lovable Cyrano, if you will, over in a corner brooding disconsolately over his ugly nose. Perhaps a degree of Ah Q-ism is a necessary element in every man for the preservation of life itself. A partial deception of oneself (optimism) may be necessary to guard against a morbid desire to see the truth in its naked entirety, a desire that may well camouflage a bent toward self-destruction.

This discussion may read into the story meanings that Lu Hsün did not intend. They are, however, meanings that are well within his *weltanschauung* as he revealed it when he spoke to the Literary Club of the Women's Normal School in Peking in 1923, two years later:

The most painful experience of human existence is to awake from one's dreams to find that there is not a single road left open. If a person has not yet spied out a road that he can take, it is most important that you not wake him. Take the T'ang dynasty poet, Li Ho [790-816]. Was it not a miserable life that he led? And yet when he was about to die, he said to his mother: "Mom, God has finished building a white jade palace and has called me to write something to commemorate its completion." How was that anything else but a painfully obvious bit of deception, a dream? And yet, there they were, a youth and an old woman, one dying, the other living—the one who died, died content, and the one who was to go on living was able to set her heart at rest and go on with the business of life. At such times, lying and dreaming reveal their magnificence. And so I think that if we cannot spy a road to take, then what we really need is dreams.

Under no circumstances, however, are we to dream of the future. In one of his novels Artsybashev once called on the carpet an idealist who was dreaming of the golden world of the future.[128] In order to create that world, the idealist had first brought suffering on a number of people by awakening them. [Through the novel] Artsybashev says to him: "You are preparing a golden world for their sons and grandsons, but what do you have to give to them, themselves?" [The idealist] did have *something* —hope for the future. But the price was too great. For the sake of this hope, he would intensify people's sensitivity so that they might experience with even greater intensity the depth of their own suffering; he

---

127. Ou-yang Fan-hai has suggested that Ah Q's dreams of revenge and his hatred for those over him are new elements in Lu Hsün's stories, and opines that this new understanding of the peasantry may have been influenced by his reading of Gorky and Artsybashev. *LHTS*, p. 185.

Chu T'ung, writing from the perspective of 1954, gently chides Lu Hsün for not having understood the true revolutionary potential of Ah Q because Lu Hsün's thought had not yet been expanded by the works of Marx and Lenin; he chalks up a point for him, however, for showing that the Republican Revolution had failed to involve the peasantry. *Lu Hsün tso-p'in te fen-hsi* [An analysis of Lu Hsün's works] (2 vols.; Shanghai, 1953-54), I, 37, 43; hereafter cited as *TPFH*.

128. In 1921 Lu Hsün translated one of Artsybashev's novels from a German translation. The passage mentioned here is in *LHCC*, I, 534-35.

would awaken souls only to have them personally preside over the dissolution of their own bodies. But at times like these only lying and dreaming appear as truly magnificent. And so as I see it, if we can't find a road to take, then what we really need are dreams—not dreams of the future, but rather of the immediate present.[129]

Obviously, Lu Hsün did not approve of those psychological characteristics which he saw at the heart of China's failure in the modern world and which he concentrated in the person of Ah Q. However, admirable in the abstract, Ah Q's psychological resilience is carried to an extreme—an extreme which makes it material for satire rather than emulation.[130] While a maudlin brooding over the reality of his weakness would probably do little to change Ah Q, the same can be said of his blithe indifference to basic reality. And it was that kind of avoidance of reality that Lu Hsün saw as the characteristic defect of traditional Chinese culture.[131] A more realistic appraisal of himself and society could provide the conditions, at least, through which an unexamined and meaningless existence might possibly be invested with a modicum of consciousness of its own direction and perhaps even a degree of real significance. For above all else, the character Ah Q satirizes mindless conformity to the past and mindless conformity to social norms: it is this mindlessness against which Lu Hsün's sharpest satirical barbs are directed. Ah Q stands in a complex critical relationship to both the individual and society, and his complex psychological shortcomings, extreme though they be, imply compensating strengths. All of these complexities, however, exist in a context of total mindlessness and it is this that is Lu Hsün's true enemy.

REBELS

The rebels against society, though numerically not the most representative, have perhaps the most important role in Lu Hsün's

---

129. *LHCC*, I, 270.
130. K'ung Yi-chi also employs Ah Q's device of putting negative experience in the most favorable light, but in a far more pitiable manner; having been caught stealing books, he excuses himself by drawing a pedantic distinction between the colloquial word for steal (*t'ou*) and its more literary-sounding counterpart (*ch'ieh*); having had his legs broken in a beating which he received as punishment for a theft, he vainly insists that they were broken in a fall. *SWLH*, I, 24, 27; *LHCC*, I, 21, 24.
131. "On Looking Facts in the Face," *SWLH*, II, 185-91; *LHCC*, I, 328-32.

stories. When Lu Hsün addresses his readers directly, in the guise of narrator, more often than not, he does so as social critic or rebel.[132] Characteristically, the narrator is an avatar of the Mara poet whom he lovingly described in the essay on "The Power of Mara Poetry" in 1907, and to that extent Lu Hsün takes his place in the line composed of such men as Byron, Shelley, Pushkin, Mickiewicz, Petöfi, and Gogol.

Given the basic mindlessness of the traditional society which Lu Hsün presents to his readers, it is not surprising that anyone in that society who questions its structure or basic norms is adjudged mad. Given, too, his realization that the critics of Chinese society were formed by the society whose defects they purported to see, perhaps "madness" was in a sense necessary in order to obtain the objective clarity of an apart observer.

The first rebel we encounter is the madman in "Diary of a Madman (K'uang-jen jih-chi)."[133] He sees traditional China as a cannibalistic arena in which the strong devour the weak. He is interested in changing that society—in converting people from cannibalism to a higher level of humanity: hence he is considered mad. To question what is, is to be in the wrong. In his diary the madman describes a conversation he had with a young man of twenty.

. . . I simply asked him, "Is this business of eating people right?" He went right on smiling and said, "Unless it were in a famine year, how could it ever come to eating people?" I realized at once that he too was one of them, one of those who like to eat people; my courage multiplied a hundredfold and I determined to press my question no matter what.

"Is it right?"

"What do you want to go asking about that kind of thing for? You're really too fond of . . . making jokes. Great weather we're having."

"The weather is nice; there's a nice moon out too, but I still want to know if it is right."

He seemed very put out with me and began to mumble, "It's not—"

"It's not right? Then how come they're still eating people?"

"No one's eating anyone."

"No one's eating anyone? They're eating people in Wolf Cub village this very minute. And then it's written out in all the books too, in bright fresh blood!"

132. Though certainly not in such a story as "Village Opera (She-hsi)."
133. *LHCC*, I, 9-19; *SWLH*, I, 8-21. The story excerpts in the ensuing discussion are my own translations.

His expression changed and his face turned grey as iron. He opened wide his eyes and said, "Perhaps they are, but it's always been this way in—."

"Is it right just because it's always been this way?"

"I'm not going to discuss such things with you. Anyway you shouldn't talk about them. If you talk about them then you're the one who's in the wrong."

Even if a man clearly sees that something is wrong, he is to remain silent. He must not only refrain from doing any analytic thinking about the problem; he is not even to mention it. In this story, naturally enough, the madman is cured when he turns his eyes away from unseemly realities and prepares to join the mindless mass of officials who govern the country.

In a short essay in 1919, Lu Hsün made a similar point about the lack of criticism of the traditional marriage system. Despite the fact that many people suffered from the inequities of the system (as we have seen, Lu Hsün was one of them), few dared to complain. The sufferers were silent, and Mara poets who might break the silence were very rare:

> . . . in the past we heard no outcries in the wake of this suffering. Even if one were suffering, if he cried out, he was immediately considered to be in the wrong, and old and young alike would shake their heads and castigate him.[134]

Physical suffering and mental anguish are also to be borne mindlessly; even an outcry will not be tolerated, not to mention an analysis.

The diarist's extended detour from the highway of sanity starts when he begins to notice the way that people watch him on the street: the Chao family dog gives him a funny look, and rich old Mr. Chao eyes him queerly, as though he feared him and would like to do him violence. All along the road he is conscious of an odd look in people's eyes. The madman wonders:

> What grudge is there between me and rich old Mr. Chao? Or for that matter, what grudge is there between me and the people on the road? The only thing that I can think of is that twenty years ago I once stepped on Mr. Antiquity's running account book of many years standing[135] and

134. *LHCC*, I, 397; *SWLH*, II, 35.

135. That is to say, the classics and the traditional morality that they contain. Wang, *Ah Q and Others*, p. 205, identifies this phrase as "an allusion to the classics, which have been characterized by their critics as of no more value and no more edifying than the account books kept by shopkeepers."

Mr. Antiquity was quite displeased. Although rich old Mr. Chao doesn't know him, he must have gotten wind of it and felt like taking Mr. Antiquity's side. And so he's gotten the people on the road to be my enemies.

He further wonders why the children seem equally hostile and concludes that it must be the influence of their parents. At a loss to explain the intensity of the general hostility that surrounds him, the madman attempts to ferret out an answer. He opens a history book and finds it chock full of concepts of benevolence, righteousness, and virtue. After pouring over the book at great length, suddenly he sees through the manifest level of the high-sounding phrases to the hidden reality that lies just beneath. Line after line, page after page, the message is the same: "Eat your fellow man!"[136] The traditional morality of the past is but a cynical cloak of respectability thrown over a festering social mass where every man either eats or is eaten. (We may note in passing that here, as in "Remembrances of the Past," instead of seeing books as storehouses of a revered tradition Lu Hsün tends to view them as repositories of corruption.) The only way to put an end to the cycle of cannibalism and create a new way of life is, of course, to "free the children"—the madman's final and passionate plea before returning to the dubious realm of sanity.

Wei Lien-shu, the protagonist of "The Isolate," a story already discussed in a different context, is in many respects similar to the madman.[137] Though a severe critic of society, Wei punctiliously observes many of the conventions that he believes ought to be reformed, if not abolished. At odds with his environment, though perhaps not insane, he is certainly highly neurotic. Like the madman, he is able to look beneath the surface of things to a reality that others cannot see and thereby becomes aware of the need to liberate the young and to be kind to the oppressed. Like

---

136. As we have seen, this view of traditional society and the Neo-Confucian ideology upon which it was based derives from the ideas of the eighteenth-century thinker Tai Tung-yuan, who regarded the rational principles (*li*) of Neo-Confucianism as fearful killers. *HSJW*, p. 12.

137. The madman diarist, as was noted in the discussion of Lu Hsün's early life, was modeled on a maternal cousin of Lu Hsün's who ran away from his post as a confidential secretary in T'ai-yuan when he was stricken by a kind of paranoia; he briefly visited Lu Hsün in the fall of 1916. It may be that the experience of this cousin figures also in "The Isolate," for Wei Lien-shu toward the end of his life accepts a similar kind of position and becomes adviser to a warlord, a rather traditional kind of occupation for bright young men from Shaohsing.

the madman, too, he is cured at that moment when he gives up this perspective and joins the establishment. Wei takes a job with a warlord and writes to his friend that he is "well" now.

Perhaps Lu Hsün sometimes suspected that he was himself such a marginal rebel, one who like Wei Lien-shu had not ventured all the way out into the extreme land of open rebellion and madness, but rather had lingered in the in-between stretches of discontent, criticism, and near-neurosis. During the period when he wrote the stories in *Call to Arms* and *Wandering* he was, after all, a respectable government clerk holding down a sinecure in the Ministry of Education—a political moderate who sought to improve society through exhortation and persuasion.

"The Eternal Lamp (Ch'ang-ming teng)"[138] introduces a young rebel who is more symbol than flesh. The story opens in Fifth Auntie Hui's teashop, where the customers are discussing him. One of them, Square Head, announces that the rebel has threatened to blow out the lamp in the local temple—the lamp after which the village, Lucky Light, has apparently been named. Another, K'uo-t'ing, explains:

"If he blew out the eternal lamp what kind of village would our Lucky Light village be? There just wouldn't be a 'lucky light' village anymore, that's all. And don't all the elders say that that lamp was lit by Emperor Wu of the Liang dynasty and that the flame has been handed down to us from that time without ever going out—not even during the times of the Long Hair disturbances?"

"Have you ever noticed"—he clicked his tongue in admiration—"the beautiful emerald glow of that flame? Why, all the strangers who come our way make a special point of stoppin' off to see it. They all praise it."

Here, of course, are set up as targets two notions for which Lu Hsün reserved his most bitter ire: (1) traditional Chinese culture as a precious and unique heritage passed down from ancient times and therefore ought to be continued, and (2) traditional Chinese culture should be preserved because even foreigners have praised its value and attractiveness. Nor does Lu Hsün pass up this opportunity to criticize the big tradition of the past as a special preserve of the upper classes. Unlettered Fifth Auntie Hui hears "Emperor Wu of the Liang Dynasty" homophonously as "the fifth younger brother of the Liang family":

138. *LHCC*, II, 55-66. The excerpts in the ensuing discussion are my own translations.

". . . after all, the eternal lamp was first lit by the fifth younger brother of the Liang family, wasn't it? Don't they say that if that lamp ever goes out, this here tract of land we're on will turn to sea and we'll turn into fish?"

In mindless conformity to the values of the dominant big tradition, though it is a tradition of which she is not really a part, Fifth Auntie Hui, like her patrons, condemns the temerity of anyone who would change things. As Chou Tso-jen has pointed out, the teashop people and the rebel's uncle, Fourth Master, are the centers of interest in this story. The rebel is primarily a device to reveal them.

Eventually the customers go over to the temple and have a look around; they find the rebel outside the locked temple, vainly trying to persuade the gatekeeper to let him in. He explains that he is trying to get inside to put out the eternal lamp and thus save the village from plagues and epidemics. When he threatens to burn the temple down, they leave to warn the villagers and to enlist the aid of his uncle, Fourth Master. After the scene shifts to Fourth Master's, it soon becomes obvious that the rebel's uncle takes no interest in anything save his own personal affairs. He suggests locking his nephew up in a spare room in the temple. This is done, and as the story ends, children are playing outside the spare room. Their riddle-guessing game is interrupted by the sound of a voice:

"I'll set it on fire!"
The children suddenly remembered the madman. They all focused their attention on the west room and saw one hand latched onto a window bar and the other clawing away at the wood. From between the bars there flashed a pair of fiery eyes.
The silence lasted only an instant before it was broken by the mangy-scalped child who suddenly let out a yell, broke into a run, and headed for the gate. The other children all ran out too, shouting and laughing as they went. The bare-chested lad again pointed the reed he was carrying back in the direction of the madman and from his panting, cherry-like little mouth there came forth a crisp cry: "Pow!"[139]

139. Hsü Ch'in-wen has commented with reference to this passage: "In the beginning Lu Hsün always thought the next generation would invariably be better than the one before it and that young people are always better than old. From this bit of description, however, we can see that he was beginning to have his doubts about the 'theory of evolution.' " *PHFH*, p. 54. If this is true, the year in which "The Eternal Lamp" was composed (1925) would certainly herald an important turning point in Lu Hsün's thought. The evidence, however, seems too skimpy to warrant such a conclusion. To be sure, the image of a small child

If one can measure roles in proportions of "flesh" and "symbol," then the rebel who is executed in "Medicine" on the eve of the Republican Revolution is similar to the one who is determined to put out the eternal lamp in that he is more symbol than flesh. Even his surname, Hsia, is symbolic. Prefixed by Hua, the surname of the teashop manager who pays the executioner to soak bread in Hsia's blood (as a cure for his tubercular son), it forms the compound, "Hua-Hsia," an ancient designation for China.[140] Furthermore, the rebel's surname and given name taken together, Hsia Yü (the character for "summer," followed by a character with the "jade" radical) call to mind the famous female revolutionary who was executed in Shaohsing while Lu Hsün was a student in Japan and whose name was Ch'iu Chin (the character for "autumn," followed by a character with the "jade" radical).[141]

In "Medicine," K'ang Ta-shu, the executioner, comes into the Huas' teashop and boasts of how lucky it was for the Huas that he thought of using the blood-soaked roll to cure their son's tuberculosis.[142] We gather, between the lines of his loud and self-important monologue (he is feared and respected by the patrons of the shop and deferentially treated to tea and an olive by the Huas), that having failed to squeeze anything at all out of his prisoner (Hsia's clothes went to Red Eye, the jailer), he thought of the Huas' consumptive son and thus came up with this way of getting a little something out of the young revolutionary's death. K'ang is totally unaware of the discomfort that the word "tuberculosis" occasions poor Mrs. Hua, who has obviously tabooed the word, and is

holding a reed in play warfare and shouting "Kill!" or "Pow!" at an adult seems to have fascinated Lu Hsün (it appears again in "The Isolate"), but it was an image that had been in Lu Hsün's mind since early childhood when Eight-Pounder Shen used to run around the t'aimen in Shaohsing, spear in hand, shouting "Kill!"

140. C. T. Hsia, *A History of Modern Chinese Fiction 1917-1957*, p. 34.

141. *HSJW*, pp. 21-22, and *PHFH*, p. 26. The person who was said to have turned her in, Hu Chung-sheng, was subsequently assassinated by Wang Chin-fa, the militarist who had appointed Lu Hsün principal in the wake of the revolution.

142. According to Hsü Ch'in-wen, it was the custom to split the steamed roll (*mant'ou*) and hold it open over the neck as the blood came spurting out when the head dropped. *Yü-wen-k'o chung Lu Hsün tso-p'in te chiao-hsüeh* [The teaching of Lu Hsün's works in classes on language and literature] (Shanghai, 1961), p. 9; hereafter cited as *TPCH*.

equally unconcerned when the Hua boy comes out from a back room and sits at one of the tables, accompanying most of this loud monologue with fits of coughing. While the boy coughs, K'ang keeps repeating that he has provided the lad with a sure cure.

When K'ang goes on to how young Hsia even tried to get the jailer to revolt, a young man sitting in the back of the shop explodes in indignation, and when K'ang tells of how the jailer cracked Hsia across the mouth, Hunchback Wu Shao-yeh (a local character who spends most of his days sitting about the Huas' teashop) gleefully reflects on how much that must have hurt, Red Eye being a skilled boxer.

"The worthless wretch wasn't afraid of being beaten. He even said, 'Pitiful, pitiful!' "

A greybeard in the shop said, "What's 'pitiful' about beating the likes of someone like that?"

K'ang Ta-shu took on a condescending expression and smiled coldly as he said: "You didn't hear me right. The way he said it was that Red Eye was to be pitied!"

A dazed expression appeared in the eyes of those who heard this last remark; all conversation stopped. Hsiao Shuan [the Huas' consumptive son] had already finished his bowl of rice. He had eaten so much that he was sweating all over and his head seemed to be steaming.

"Red Eye was to be pitied—crazy talk, he must have taken leave of his senses," said the greybeard, as though the truth had just dawned on him.

"Must have taken leave of his senses," the young man in his twenties said, also as though the truth had just dawned on him.

At this point, the atmosphere of the shop livened up and chatting and laughter were heard again. Hsiao Shuan took advantage of the hubbub to cough his head off. K'ang Ta-shu came up to him, patted him on the shoulder, and said, "A guaranteed cure! Hsiao Shuan, stop coughing that way. A guaranteed cure!"

"Crazy," Hunchback Wu Shao-yeh observed, nodding his head.[143]

143. My translation. Huang Sung-k'ang has called attention to a statement by Sun Fu-yuan on Lu Hsün's motivation in writing "Medicine." " 'Medicine' describes the ignorance of the masses and the sorrow of the revolutionaries caused by the ignorance of the masses. To put it in a more direct way, revolutionaries sacrificed their lives in the struggle for the ignorant masses, but the latter did not even know for whom it was that the former had sacrificed their lives." The statement is doubly significant in that Sun says that it is based on what Lu Hsün told him personally. (Quoted in *Lu Hsün and the New Culture Movement of Modern China* [Amsterdam, 1947], p. 38. The translation is Dr. Huang's; for the original see *ESS*, p. 14).

"A guaranteed cure!"

Again, insanity is the only possible explanation for rebellion or revolution. It is for these ordinary people in the teashop—the greybeard, the young man in his twenties, and Hunchback Wu Shao-yeh—that Lu Hsün reserves the greatest part of his venom. They represent what he long saw as the greatest defect of Chinese society: passive acquiescence to a cannibalistic hierarchy. These ordinary people remind one of the madman's observation about "the ferocity of a lion [vis-à-vis the revolutionary]; the timidity of a rabbit [vis-à-vis the executioner]; and the craftiness of a fox [in knowing whom to despise and whom to fear]."

ORDINARY PEOPLE

When ordinary people appear in Lu Hsün's stories, either in minor roles or as members of a crowd surrounding the main action, they are of two kinds: (1) unspoiled or (2) mindlessly conformist. The unspoiled have retained their basic goodness because they have not been corrupted by assimilation into the big tradition; they have remained uneducated and are therefore good. The mindlessly conformist simply reflect general opinion and therefore symbolize all that is wrong with Chinese society. They fear the strong and bully the weak; they mindlessly affirm all that is supported by authority, superstition, or public opinion. The people who sit about the teashops are prime examples; the "sensation of inconsolability in Lu Hsün's work is . . . intensified by the fact that the hero is surrounded neither by sadists nor scoundrels, but by ordinary people."[144]

Predictably, the unspoiled kind usually appear in stories where we find Lu Hsün nostalgically reminiscing over his early youth. We have seen how in his first story, "Remembrances of the Past," two unspoiled ordinary persons dominate the stage: the narrator's kindly amah and Old Wang, who tells him exciting tales about the days of the Long Hairs. At one point, a crowd of the other, mindless kind appears briefly in the background, moving along the road in unreflecting response to a rumor:

I noticed that there were more people on the road than ants on an ant hill. They all seemed frightened and were wandering about as if they couldn't decide which way to go. Most were carrying things, though a few were empty-handed. Old Wang told me that they were probably preparing to flee the impending difficulties. I noticed that among them were quite a few people from Ho market who were apparently fleeing to Wu town; the residents of Wu town, on the other hand, were obviously fleeing in the direction of Ho market.[145]

This is perhaps as close as we shall come to actual peasants in Lu Hsün's stories, for the ordinary people whom he knew in his youth were not real peasants. Even the famed Jun-t'u in "Home Town" is a part-time farmer who spends the off-season as a handy man.

144. V. I. Semanov, "Lu Hsün and His Predecessors," p. 117.
145. See Appendix.

For the most part "the people" in Lu Hsün follow occupations other than farming; they are teashop and wineshop managers, clerks, jacks-of-all-trades, boatmen, servants, and amahs. They stand somewhere between the peasantry and the ruling class, to which Lu Hsün belonged. (As we have seen, in his preface to the Russian translation of "The True Story of Ah Q," Lu Hsün was very conscious of the difficulty inherent in an attempt by anyone of his class to understand the mentality of those further down the social scale.) The description of Jun-t'u in "Home Town" shows how close Lu Hsün felt in early youth (before education and occupation had yet created their walls) to this middle group; this theme is also emphasized in "Village Opera (She-hsi)."[146]

Really not a story at all, "Village Opera" is an essay which opens with a vitriolic attack on Peking opera and closes with an extended reminiscence of a visit that Lu Hsün made with his mother to her native village when he was eleven or twelve, during which he saw an opera performed in the open air.[147] He presents most of the children with whom he played almost as relatives, for the village was a one-clan place where everyone had the same surname and was at least what we would call a "kissin' cousin." Lu Hsün tells us, not without a trace of pride, that ninety-nine out of a hundred of the children at the village could neither read nor write—hence, given his love for the unlettered, they are unspoiled; they are good. He spends much of the visit in their company, idyllically fishing and frolicking about the countryside.

. . . another thing we did was to take the buffaloes out together, but, maybe because they are animals of a higher speicies, oxen and buffaloes are hostile to strangers, and they treated me with contempt so that I never dared get too close to them. I could only follow at a distance and stand there. At such times my small friends were no longer impressed by the fact that I could recite classical poetry, but would hoot with laughter.

The above passage makes it clear that the narrator and his young friends belonged to different worlds, to different social classes. Throughout the reminiscence, these country lads treat their town cousin with great warmth, but this obviously arises as much from

---

146. *LHCC*, I, 139-49; *SWLH*, I, 136-49.
147. Lu Hsün viewed Peking opera as bedlam suffered in the stuffy confines of unattractive theaters.

"... I never dared get too close to them."

their respect for the "young master" as from their innate, unlettered goodness.

In the opening paragraphs of "Storm in a Teacup" Lu Hsün very effectively satirizes the traditional scholar's propensity for romanticizing the carefree lives of ordinary peasants from a safe, sanitary distance:

The old folk and the men sat on the low stools, fanning themselves with plantain-leaf fans as they chatted. The children raced about or squatted under the tallow trees playing games with pebbles. The women brought out steaming hot, black dried vegetables and yellow rice. Some scholars, who were passing in a pleasure boat, waxed quite lyrical at the sight. "So free from care!" they exclaimed. "Here's real idyllic happiness."

The scholars were rather wide of the mark, however. And that was because they had not heard what Old Lady Nine-Pounder was saying. Old Mrs. Nine-Pounder was in a towering temper . . .[148]

In presenting his unspoiled little friends, the narrator of "Village Opera" comes perilously close to this same kind of romanticism.

From his point of view as adult narrator, Lu Hsün tells us that what he looked forward to most on these visits to his mother's native village was the possibility that he might get to go see an opera at Chao village. The one that he describes in "Village Opera" is being performed there in conjunction with the celebration of a religious festival. Somehow or other his immediate family fails to make a reservation early enough and all the boats that day (Chao village, like his mother's native village, is a river settlement) are taken, and hence they cannot go. He is terribly disappointed.

That evening, however, after returning from the opera, several village boys around his own age suggest to his mother and grandmother that they be allowed to take him back to the performance (which is, of course, continuous) in a boat that has come back which they can now borrow. Once his mother and grandmother have been talked around, his friends whisk the young master downriver to see all the fun. The opera itself, which is played on a stage on the river bank and which they watch from the boat, does not amount to very much, but Lu Hsün remembers with warm nostalgia the boat trip, the comradeship of his friends, and the business of roasting some beans in the boat on the way back—beans which they pick (without permission) along the way. For this theft they are taken to task the next day when they run into Liu Yi, from whose field they got last night's beans:

"Shuang-hsi, you young rascals stole my beans yesterday! And you didn't pick them properly, you trampled down quite a few." I looked up and saw old Liu Yi on a punt, coming back from selling beans. There was still a heap of leftover beans at the bottom of the punt.

"Yes. We were treating a visitor. We didn't mean to take yours to begin with," said Shuang-hsi. "Look! You've frightened away my shrimp!"

148. *LHCC*, I, 52; *SWLH*, I, 52.

When the old man saw me, he stopped punting, and chuckled. "Treating a visitor? So you should." Then he asked me: "Was yesterday's opera good?"

"Yes." I nodded.

"Did you enjoy the beans?"

"Very much." I nodded again.

To my surprise, the old man was greatly pleased. He stuck up a thumb and declared with satisfaction: "People from big towns who have studied really know what's good. I select my bean seeds one by one. Country folk can't tell good from bad, and say my beans aren't as good as other people's. I'll give some to your mother today for her to try . . ." Then he punted off.

Even as raconteur of a lyrical reminiscence, Lu Hsün seems somewhat insensitive here to the social distance that separates him from Liu Yi. There is nothing to indicate that the lot of these people may not have been equally as miserable as that ascribed to Jun-t'u in "Home Town." In the latter story, however, the idyllic world of childhood reminiscence is brought up hard against the world of adult realities when the narrator returns to his native place as an adult and rediscovers the world of his childhood friend from an adult point of view. Since "Village Opera" was written more than a year after "Home Town," how does one explain this apparent flight into sentimentality?

What seems the only possible explanation is that during this period Lu Hsün was strongly under the influence of Vasily Eroshenko. This blind Russian poet, born in the Ukraine, was also a scholar of Esperanto, musician, and teller of children's tales. Before coming to China, he had lived in India, Burma, and Japan. Upon deportation from Japan in late 1921 (on suspicion of being a spy or, perhaps, an anarchist) he came to China. Eventually, someone introduced him to Ts'ai Yuan-p'ei, the chancellor of Peking University, and Ts'ai invited him to teach Esperanto. Since Eroshenko spoke no Chinese, Ts'ai was worried about how he would get along in Peking. Discovering that Eroshenko spoke fluent Japanese, he decided that the Chou household would be the ideal place for him. For Lu Hsün, Chou Tso-jen and his wife (Habuto Nobuko), and Chou Chien-jen and his wife (Nobuko's younger sister), Japanese was a household language, and at Tso-jen's invitation, in the spring of 1922, Eroshenko moved into Pa-tao-wan to live with them. On July 3 he left to travel through

Russia to attend an interational conference on Esperanto in Finland. On November 4 he returned to Peking and remained there until April 1923 at which point he left for good.[149]

When Eroshenko began a series of lectures at the university, the hall was packed. (Lu Hsün's translation, from the Japanese, of his fairy-tale drama "The Rosy Clouds" had already appeared serially in the supplement to the *Morning Post*, and hence Eroshenko was well known in Peking.) The Russian spoke in Esperanto, which Tso-jen translated into Chinese. Later on, when the Chinese translation was dispensed with and the initial fascination of the man began to wear off, attendance dwindled.[150] The last three pieces in *Call to Arms*—"A Comedy of Ducks," "Some Rabbits and a Cat," and "Village Opera"—were written in October 1922; it seems likely that the uncharacteristic sentimentality of "Village Opera" and the other two resulted from the lyrical Russian's having struck a responsive chord in Lu Hsün's heart.[151] Eroshenko seems to have tempted him in the direction of a temporary retreat from the reality of China in the 1920s to the more soothing realms of nature and childhood. Consider, for example, this passage describing the narrator's return from the opera:

> The boat seemed like a great white fish leaping through the foam with a freight of children on its back. Some old fishermen who fished all night stopped their punts to cheer at the sight.

It reads like something that Lu Hsün might satirize. This lyrical mood may also have moved him to present all the ordinary people

149. *HHL*, p. 413; *LHC*, pp. 123-24; *HSJW*, pp. 129-30.
150. *HHL*, p. 414.
151. Berta Krebsovà, while acknowledging the influence of Eroshenko on "A Comedy of Ducks" and "Some Rabbits and a Cat," sees "Village Opera" as a natural step forward in Lu Hsün's art: "Dans ses premiers contes—gravures fines de types humains et de milieux sociaux—il se révèle observateur sobre et précis. Aucun motif personnel ne vient alors altérer l'impassibilité de son réalisme souvent âpre. Plus tard, sa conception change: la lumière et la sympathie pénètrent dans ses récits pour en adoucir l'austérité originale (cf. Le Théâtre du Village)." *Lu Sün: sa vie et son oeuvre* (Prague, 1953), pp. 86-87.
One could accept this judgment were the high lyricism of "Village Opera" continued in the stories contained in Lu Hsün's second collection, *Wandering*, but this is by no means the case. Krebsova also thinks that the idealistic Russian did not influence Lu Hsün's realism: "Les contes 'Le Lapin et le Chat' et 'La Comédie des Canards' sont d'un caractère différent. Ils sont nés sous l'influence du poète russe Yaroschenko. . . . Les contes de Yaroschenko témoignent d'une philosophie un peu naïve de leur auteur idéaliste. . . . L'influence de Yaroshcenko n'a aucunement affécté le réalisme sobre et précis de Lu Sün." (Ibid.)

in this reminiscence as unspoiled, forgetting for a while even the existence of the other kind.

Ordinary people of the other kind, the mindless conformists of adulthood, are perhaps best exemplified by the wineshop idlers in "K'ung Yi-chi." Since the narrator is reminiscing about a period as a teen-ager when he had already been assimilated into the work force, it is only natural that the world that unfolds before us is not part of any idyllic garden of youth, but rather a corner of the arena of traditional adult society whose cold ways he has already learned to ape. The people who frequent the wineshop use old K'ung as a butt for their jokes; they humiliate him without mercy; and the attitude of the teen-aged clerk is but a reflection of theirs. Like the customers who engage Fifth Auntie Hui in conversation in "The Eternal Lamp," the people at the Everybody's Happy wineshop are a mindless lot who accept society's norms and live entirely in terms of the fear-the-strong-and-bully-the-weak pecking order. K'ung Yi-chi, clearly belonging to the camp of the hopelessly oppressed, is fair game for bullying. Weak and broken in spirit themselves, these ordinary people mindlessly reflect the norms of their "betters."

The two kinds, the unspoiled and the mindlessly conformist, are symbolic of two life-stages: childhood and adulthood. For Lu Hsün the movement from childhood to adulthood seems to imply a transformation of the ego from unspoiled naturalness to mindless conformity—a move from a Taoist garden of Eden, as it were, to the corrupt Confucian world of adult society and its manifold hypocrisies. The Taoist realm of the natural belongs to the children, and to the women. Those assimilated into the world of adult male society become conformists and take their places in the hierarchical pecking order. What choices, then, are left open to a person in Lu Hsün's fictional world? Not many. One can really retain a childhood innocence only so long as he remains a child; if he insists on retaining this purity in the adult world, he can do so only by refusing to be assimilated, by remaining on the borders of society as an isolate, an oddball, a rebel. This was the path taken by Wei Lien-shu in "The Isolate"; it will be remembered that Wei remains faithful to his ideals during the early part of the story but sells out toward the end and becomes a mindless conformist. There would seem to be no middle ground. To move from unspoiledness into corrupt conformity is to ruin one's life, and also to perpetrate an evil system. Hence the madman's desperate plea that at least the children be freed from this vicious cycle, a cycle that constitutes an endless drama whose roles are divided between the oppressed (children, women, the lower classes) and the oppressors (adults, men, the upper classes).

Where does Lu Hsün himself stand? It is no accident that the majority of his important male protagonists belong to the world of the in-between intellectual. Significantly, these characters often appear in the role of narrator ("A Trifling Incident," "Home Town," "The New Year's Sacrifice") or are presented as intimates of the narrator ("The Story of Hair," "Upstairs in a Wineshop," "The Isolate"). This was the group that Lu Hsün knew best and to which he belonged. When he presents traditional intellectuals, he preserves a certain distance and contents himself with merely showing them as pedantic, unfeeling, and hypocritical (Master Baldy, Fourth Uncle Lu, Ssu-ming) or, in a more sympathetic mood, as victims of the examination system (K'ung Yi-chi, Ch'en Shih-ch'eng). On the whole, he stays outside these characters and does not engage in psychological analysis. Since he had first-hand knowledge of the mentality of the in-between intellectuals, however, he often takes his readers on explorations of their minds ("Brothers," "The Isolate," "Upstairs in a Wineshop," and so on). Theirs is a frame of mind best characterized by the title of his second collection of stories—*Wandering;* many among them are aware of what is wrong, but are unable to find any way out, condemned to a life of "wandering" between the old culture and the yet-to-be-born new one. Nor can they look to the modern intellectuals for guidance, for the latter are faulted by shallowness and hypocrisy ("A Happy Family," "Schoolmaster Kao," "Remorse"). The only bright spots in the dreary crowd represented in Lu Hsün's vision of reality are provided by women (Mrs. Fang, Ssu-ming's wife), children (Jun-t'u as a boy), and those rare people outside the establishment who have not been corrupted by their environments (the rickshaw puller in "A Trifling Incident," Ai-ku in the early part of "Divorce").

As a young student in Japan, Lu Hsün maintained in "The Power of Mara Poetry" that literature is as necessary to human beings as food and clothing, for it takes up life and, in a way denied to the academic disciplines, places it directly in the hands of the reader for his contemplation. This is what he does in his stories.

11

AN ARCHITECT OF STORIES AND A CARPENTER OF WORDS

I

Discussing the "art" of a writer who works in a language other than one's own is beset with difficulties, but then, what isn't? In this part, I shall attempt to point out what it is that is good about Lu Hsün's works. For, whatever may be said of his position in the sweep of modern Chinese history or in the context of modern Chinese literature, Lu Hsün is well worth reading—not because he was important, but because he was a fine writer. In the following pages I hope to suggest something of Lu Hsün's artistry both as an architect of stories and as a carpenter of words.

In structure, Lu Hsün's short stories are quite varied; they range from the informality of anecdotes told over a cup of tea to the strict formalism of a classical ballet—from "The Story of Hair" to "A Warning to the People." If we take the stories as a whole, within this diversity a few characteristic structural devices emerge. These are:

Repetition—repetition of phrases, props, and even characters in an incremental, ballad-like fashion as a means of building up the underlying framework of the story.

Use of envelopes—a special instance of repetition in which the repeated elements serve as the opening and final curtains of the entire story or of scenes within it.

Contrasts of sound and silence—contrasts in which sound breaks upon silence to signal a beginning and is returned into silence to signal an end.

Contrasts of stillness and action—contrasts that occur in the
mind's eye of the reader so that people and things are jarred
into action as the story opens and then are returned into the
quiescence from which they came as it ends

One cannot claim that these elements are present in all of the
stories, but they do occur, with modifications, in the majority and
can, therefore, be considered as typical. Nor can one claim that
the presence or absence of these devices is an absolute gauge of
any individual story's worth. In the best of the stories, however,
they provide structural clarity, create a certain theatrical quality,
and lend poetic overtones. One is again reminded of Lu Hsün's
characterization of literature in "The Power of Mara Poetry" as
something that takes human existence and places it directly in the
hands of the reader.

Discussion of "A Warning to the People" has been reserved for
this chapter because it provides such an excellent example of these
structural techniques, techniques which the careful reader will find
repeated (with modifications) in the majority of Lu Hsün's stories.
As "A Warning to the People"[1] opens, the reader is immediately
conscious of two things, silence and the heat.

At this time of morning on a certain street in the western part of the
Realm of Optimum Good[2] [Peking] there was not even the slightest bit of
hubbub. Even though the blazing sun was not yet shining straight down,
the gravel on the road already seemed to glitter brightly under its rays;
the oppressive heat was thoroughly diffused through the air and everywhere proclaimed the dominion of midsummer. Several dogs lolled out
their tongues, and even the black crows in the trees had their beaks open,
gasping for air. And yet, there were, of course, some exceptions. From
the distance there came the faint metallic sound of two cups being struck
together—the hawker of chilled prune juice reminding people of his
presence, and making one feel almost cool. And yet, that lazy, inter-
mittent, tinny sound also served to underline the lonely silence of the
street.

Now came the sound of footsteps as silent rickshaw men rushed
headlong down the street as though trying to escape the fiery sun above.

"Hot meat dumplings! Fresh out of the steamer . . ." Eyes squinted
against the sun, mouth awry, a fat lad of eleven or twelve shouted out his
call in front of a small stand by the side of the road.

1. *LHCC*, II, 67-72 Wang Chi-chen's translation, to which I am indebted,
appears in *China Journal*, XXXII, no. 6, (June 1940), 247-51.
2. This is an old epithet for the capital, but Lu Hsün's use of it is, of course,
sarcastic.

In the original (I dare not vouch for my translation) this is truly a fine piece of writing. Lean, graceful, and strong, it immediately sets the stage with a minimum number of words and props. The scene opens in a silence punctuated by the clink of tin cups being struck together; hard upon this comes the sound of rickshaw men's feet, and then the call of the boy hawking dumplings.

The action proper does not begin until the vignette on stage is jarred completely awry when, "like a rubber ball that has been thrown hard against a wall and bounces back again," the young dumpling-hawker bounds over to the other side of the street, attracted by the spectacle of a seedy-looking policeman with a prisoner on the end of a rope. Lines of Chinese characters are written on the white vest which has been thrown over the prisoner's blue cotton gown. The characters spell out the details of his offense and explain that he is now being paraded about the streets as a "warning to the people."

The prisoner has an identifying prop, a new straw hat with the brim turned down on all sides so that no one can see his eyes. Before long a semicircle of people forms around the policeman and his prisoner. Lu Hsün makes much of having some of the people try to peek under the brim to get a good look into the fellow's eyes. Among the later arrivals are a bald-headed old man and a bare-armed, red-nosed fat man who gets close enough to the prisoner to examine the writing on the vest. Perhaps conscious that others are waiting to hear what's written there, the fat man murmurs a series of unintelligible sounds. A nursemaid, with a child clasped in her arms, crowds in behind the old man and almost does him out of his place. We may note in passing Lu Hsün's predilection for striking visual characteristics to distinguish minor characters: the fat man is red-nosed and bare-armed; the old man is bald; the nursemaid has a child in her arms.

A primary-school student bounds up to see the fun "like still another rubber ball thrown hard against a wall" (the whole phrase is repeated—Lu Hsün is firming up the body of the story by adding bone to the skeleton beneath the flesh.) This boy also has a prop, a cotton cap which he presses down on his head with one hand as he scurries around, trying to worm his way into the crowd. As people in the semicircle shift about, trying to get a better view, a rough-looking fellow, probably a workman, suddenly asks the bald-headed old man what crime the prisoner has committed. The old man pops wide his eyes and stares down the audacious workman; others in the crowd soon join the old man in directing cold stares at the workman, who finally becomes so nervous that he begins to feel as though *he* had committed the crime and, crestfallen, slips away.

At this point, the dumpling-hawker's boss comes onto the scene, slaps the boy on the cheek, and swears at him for goldbricking, whereupon the boy breaks free of the crowd and runs back across the street to his post before the food stand. His return to this spot marks the end of the primary action of the piece, action that began when he first bounded across the street and ends now as he goes back. Thus the dumpling-hawker serves as an envelope for the main action and adds another rib to the body of the story. The main action having ended, Lu Hsün prepares to draw the story to a close. Having opened the story with such elements as dogs lolling out their tongues and rickshaw men hurrying along as though trying to escape the heat of the sun, he brings these elements back together to fashion his ending:

> On the other side of the street was the fat boy, head cocked to one side, breathing heavily, as though taking a nap; on the road itself were the silent rickshawmen, rushing headlong down the street as though trying to escape the fiery sun above them.

The people now begin to be restless, until their boredom is relieved somewhat by a bit of excitement down the street: a rickshaw man has taken a spill. But it is apparently not very serious, for he immediately picks up the shafts of his rig and prepares to continue on.

"Are you all right?" his passenger inquired as the rickshawman prepared to pull his vehicle again.

The man merely nodded his head and pulled the rickshaw along its way as everyone blankly followed him with their eyes. At first they could tell which rickshaw it was that had just taken a spill, but later, as it mixed in with the other rigs, they could no longer be sure.

Then the street was hushed again; a few dogs stuck out their tongues and panted. The fat man stood in the shade of a locust tree and watched the belly of a dog rise and fall with great rapidity.

The nursemaid held her child and scurried off under the eaves. The boy, cocking his head to one side, squinted his eyes into little slits, and raised his voice to call out in sleepy tones, "Hot meat dumplings! Hey ho! . . . Fresh out of the steamer. . . ."

Lu Hsün ends with that line. At the beginning of the story, he presents us with a relatively quiet and sleepy scene, which he jars about in presenting the main action and which he returns to its original relative stillness at the end. Clearly, the theme of the story is the people's mindless craving for excitement and their heartless indifference to the suffering of others, themes that we often encounter in the works of Lu Hsün. However, Lu Hsün's condemnation of these psychological defects, frailities to which he had hoped to draw curative attention, is so artistically and classically understated that one wonders whether the story could have made a strong impression on many readers. This would seem highly doubtful, for it reads like a poem so skillfully made that one is likely to be as much taken with its form as with its substance. Such doubt may have had a part in Lu Hsün's giving up the writing of stories, after the publication of *Wandering*, in favor of the more direct means of expression afforded by the essay form.

If, from a structural point of view, we ask what kinds of stories Lu Hsün wrote, we find that an obvious division can be made between the stories that employ a first-person narrator and those that do not. The former may be divided again into two groups: stories whose narrator is a fictional construct, and those whose narrator can be taken to represent the feelings, thoughts, and experiences of Lu Hsün himself. The stories with Lu Hsün as narrator divide further into those which present him in a polemical frame of mind and those (rather atypical and written somewhat under the influence of Eroshenko) which present him in a basically sentimental mood. The various groupings can be exemplified as follows:

Stories told by a fictional narrator—"Diary of a Madman," "K'ung Yi-chi," and "Remorse"

Stories told by Lu Hsün—(i) in a polemical mood: "A Trifling Incident," "The Story of Hair," "Home Town," "The New Year's Sacrifice," "Upstairs in a Wineshop," and "The Isolate"; and (ii) in a sentimental mood: "Some Rabbits and a Cat," "A Comedy of Ducks," and "Village Opera"

Of the polemical stories, properly speaking only "The New Year's Sacrifice" and "The Isolate" are true "short stories" in the sense that they have beginnings, middles, and ends and are not (as is the case with the remaining four) simply reminiscences of the narrator and his friends. In all six stories Lu Hsün is recognizably himself: an in-between intellectual, disillusioned by the aftermath of the Republican Revolution, and disheartened by an increasing realization of the distance, both in *weltanschauung* and life experience, that separates his class from the peasantry. To some degree, in all these stories Lu Hsün editorializes on his times, something he was to do increasingly in the latter part of his life—especially after 1933—when he turned almost exclusively to the essay form and penned so many "miscellaneous reactions (*tsa-kan*)" to contemporary events that his enemies gave him the somewhat contradictory epithet of "specialist in miscellaneous reactions (*tsa-kan chuan-chia*)."[3]

Twelve of the twenty-five stories in *Call to Arms* and *Wandering* are presented from the third person point of view. In five of these the mind of the protagonist is thoroughly analyzed and fully revealed to the reader; hence they may be further characterized as individual-centered and psychological. In the remaining seven, Lu Hsün preserves such esthetic distance from his central characters that we may further describe these as group-centered and sociological. Thus divided, the stories are as follows:

Individual-centered—psychological: "Dragon Boat Festival," "A Happy Family," "Soap," "Schoolmaster Kao," and "Brothers"

Group-centered—sociological: "Medicine," "Tomorrow," "Storm in a Teacup," "The White Light," "The Eternal Lamp," "A Warning to the People," and "Divorce"

In the first group the center of interest is an individual who is at the same time the object of a probing psychological analysis. Since each is an "in-between intellectual," it is apparent that Lu Hsün took a more intimate, less objective approach when dealing with people of his own generation and background than when dealing with traditional society.

The protagonists in these five stories are in large part morally responsible for what they have become and, to that extent, are capable of change. Those who are the centers of interest in the remaining seven are, on the other hand and without exception, victims of society and the real object of analysis is not the

---

3. Hsü Chung-yü *Kuan-yü Lu Hsün te hsiao-shuo tsa-wen chi ch'i-t'a* [On Lu Hsün's stories, miscellaneous reactions, and other things] (Shanghai, 1957), p. 59; hereafter cited as *CCT*.

individual who stands center-stage but, rather, the society around him. In the first set of stories the individual is at once the center of interest *and* the object of analysis; he is presented not so much as a victim of society as a victim of his own hypocrisy ("Soap" and "Schoolmaster Kao"), cowardice ("Dragon Boat Festival"), preference for dreams over reality ("A Happy Family"), or failure to perceive psychological depths beneath surface appearances ("Brothers"). In these cases it would be possible for the individual to make significant changes in his life without having first to destroy or reweave the whole fabric of society. In two of the stories, "Soap" and "Brothers," there is a fairly strong element of hope at the end, indicating that the protagonist may in fact be on the road to changing in some significant way. In contrast, the protagonists of the second set belong exclusively to the world of traditional China, and in this world Lu Hsün does not hold individuals responsible for what they have become; in the first set—individual-centered (psychological)—he does.

In order to consider in some detail Lu Hsün's use of the structural devices outlined earlier, let us take an example from each of the categories just noted and one that is in a category of its own: (*a*) fictional narrator ("Diary of a Madman"), (*b*) Lu Hsün as narrator—polemical mood ("Storm in a Teacup"), (*c*) Lu Hsün as narrator—sentimental mood ("Village Opera"), (*d*) individual-centered—psychological ("Soap"), (*e*) group-centered—sociological ("Medicine"), (*f*) in a category of its own ("The True Story of Ah Q").

FICTIONAL NARRATOR ("DIARY OF A MADMAN")[4]

Structurally, "Diary of a Madman" consists of a preface and thirteen serially presented diary entries. We see the madman in various stages of his malady and in his developing awareness that he himself is part of the cannibalistic society against which he rebels. This society, by which he has been formed, is so much a part of him that there can be no escape from it—hence the cry of desperation in the last line of the last entry: "Save the children . . ." The implication is that the madman will now return to the "sane world." This is clearly foreshadowed in the fictional narrator's prologue, which also provides the piece with a typical Lu

4. *LHCC,* I, 9-19; *SWLH,* I, 8-21.

Hsün envelope. Written in classical Chinese, the prologue contrasts sharply with the colloquial-language diary entries; accordingly, I translate it into rather stilted English:

There was once a pair of male siblings whose actual names I implore
your indulgence to suppress. Suffice it to say that we three were bosom
companions during our school years. Subsequently, circumstances con-
trived to keep us asunder so that we were gradually bereft of intelligence
regarding each other's activities. Not too long ago, however, I chanced to
hear that one of them had been sorely afflicted with a dire illness. This
intelligence came at a time when I happened to be returning to my native
haunts and, hence, I made so bold as to detour somewhat from my
normal course in order to visit them. I encountered but one of the
siblings, who apprised me that it had been his younger brother who had
suffered the dread disease. However, by now, the younger brother had
long been sound and fit again; in fact he had already gone someplace else
to await a substantive official appointment. The elder brother apologized
for having needlessly put me to the inconvenience of this visitation.
Concluding this disquisition with a hearty smile, he showed me two
volumes of diaries which he said would reveal to me the nature of his
brother's disorder during those dread days.

Because of the envelope, when the reader comes to the plea for
saving the children at the end of the story, the obvious inference is
that the madman is preparing to return to the "sane" world of the
traditional establishment where he will await appointment to the
bureaucracy.

As the entries proceed, the madman becomes ever more aware
that everyone, from the Chao family dog up, will abuse—or even
eat—those who are lower (and therefore weaker) in the social
structure and at the same time will stand in servile fear of those
who are higher. The diary entries show the process of reasoning
by which the madman relates his individual affliction to a broader
scope of social issues: through reading and meditation, he discovers that this type of cannibalism has long and deep roots in the
history of his culture. We observe his bootless attempt to change
it: if only he can convert his brother from the eat-or-be-eaten
ideology that supports the social structure, he feels, he can work
his way back to normal life by helping to create a sane society.
Finally we witness his eventual despair of ever being able to attain
sanity and we grasp the implication of that despair: he will now
rejoin the ranks of the *truly* mad. He is reduced to the desperate

hope that the children of future generations, at least, may be able to escape the madness that he now goes to embrace.

In structure, "Diary of a Madman" has a definite beginning from which the scenes proceed and a definite end toward which they move. One can view Entry Six, with some justification, as a middle point. It consists of but two lines, and yet, given the context in which they are set, it provides a midway pause in the progress of the action (besides contributing heavily to the macabre mood):

Pitch black, can't tell if it's night or day. The Chao family dog has begun yowling again.
The ferocity of a lion, the timidity of a rabbit, the craftiness of a fox . . .

The latter sentence summarizes the madman's descriptions and interpretations of the expressions in the eyes of the people who surround him; it is a capsule judgment of the psychological state of those who live in a cannibalistic society.

As in most of his stories, Lu Hsün holds scenery and props to a significant minimum: at the beginning of Entries One and Two, where a diarist might normally note what kind of day it was, the madman tells what kind of moon there was; in Entry Four, when the elder brother brings in a doctor to examine the madman, the doctor wears glasses and the madman records that the doctor surreptitiously peered at him sideways over the frames with a murderous look in his eyes. Further, the separate entries are all threaded together by the interest the diarist takes in the expressions in people's eyes. In Entry One he calls attention to the funny look given him by the Chao family's dog. In Entry Two he says that rich Old Chao has looked at him on the street that day as though he were afraid of him and, at the same time, as though he would like to do him violence. He refers to the dog's look again in Entry Seven, where he compares it to the ghastly stare that a book he has read attributes to the eyes of the hyena—a look which he subsequently relates back to wolves and then, through wolves, to the doctor in Entry Four. The eye theme is significant in that, no matter what people say to him, the madman is able to see through the smoke-screen of their words to the real cannibalistic intent in their hearts revealed by the expression in their eyes; it is invariably this that betrays their true psychological state—the state he summarized in "The ferocity of a lion, the timidity of a rabbit, the craftiness of a fox."

In Entry Three a tenant farmer reports that his fellow villagers banded together to kill a local badman and then ate the badman's heart and liver. This report is mentioned also in Entries Five, Eight, and Ten. In addition to repeating themes and phrases from one entry to another, Lu Hsün occasionally uses repetition with a single entry. The second sentence of Entry Three, for instance, "You must study anything before you can understand it," is repeated verbatim toward the end of the same entry. Taken as a whole or in its parts, "Diary of a Madman" is tightly structured.

LU HSÜN AS NARRATOR—POLEMICAL MOOD
("STORM IN A TEACUP")

"Storm in a Teacup"[5] is presented by an omniscient narrator whose personality is conformable to that of Lu Hsün in his more polemical mood. A few opening paragraphs of description set the stage: a river village; women setting out the evening meal on the strand between their homes and the river; children playing; men and old folks gossiping while they wait for the food; and idle scholars passing by in a pleasure boat, waxing poetic over the idyllic scene. The story closes with a final descriptive paragraph in which the omniscient narrator returns things to normal after the "storm" has passed. The action of the story, enveloped between the opening and closing descriptive passages, falls into five scenes. (i) Seven-Pounder arrives home with the news that the emperor has ascended the throne. (ii) Mr. Chao, proprietor of a neighboring wineshop, arrives wearing the long blue gown of the old scholar-gentry with whom he has always upwardly identified (he has come to gloat over Seven-Pounder's pigtail-less state). (iii) When Mrs. Seven-Pounder castigates her husband for having lost his pigtail, Sister Pa Yi attempts to put a word in for him. Angered out of control by Sister Pa Yi's remarks, Mrs. Seven-Pounder cracks her own daughter on top of the head with chopsticks when she thrusts out her bowl and clamors for rice. The little girl drops the bowl and a piece is chipped out of it. (iv) Seven-Pounder returns home the next evening with the repaired rice bowl. (The high cost of the repair gives his mother occasion to repeat the tag line she has been intoning with unpleasant frequency from the

5. *LHCC*, I, 52-60; *SWLH*, I, 52-62.

beginning of the story: "Each generation is worse than the last. I've lived long enough." (v) A week or so later, when Seven-Pounder comes home his wife tells him that Mr. Chao has once again coiled his pigtail up on top of his head and is no longer wearing his blue gown. She happily concludes that there has been no restoration of the emperor and hence her husband is safe. In "Storm in a Teacup" we encounter almost the entire range of structural devices that Lu Hsün employed in building up his stories: formal envelope (in the opening and closing descriptions), distinguishing props to identify the characters (Seven-Pounder and his long bamboo pipe are inseparable), repeated lines to lend rhythm and give bone to the story ("Each generation is worse than the last"), and use of characters in a structural fashion (the costume changes of Mr. Chao).

LU HSÜN AS NARRATOR—SENTIMENTAL MOOD ("VILLAGE OPERA")

It will be remembered that "Village Opera"[6] (like "Some Rabbits and a Cat" and "A Comedy of Ducks") was written during the period when Lu Hsün was influenced by the blind Russian poet Eroshenko. It consists of little more than a loosely structured first-person reminiscence in which the personality of the narrator is roughly conformable to what we know of Lu Hsün—save for the sentimentality. It begins with the author's exceedingly low evaluation of Peking opera. In fact, since more than a third of "Village Opera" is given over to criticizing Peking opera, Hsü Ch'in-wen has plausibly suggested that much of this material may reflect conversations with Eroshenko in which Lu Hsün explained and critized Peking opera for the benefit of his foreign guest.[7] The remarks on Peking opera lead the narrator to reminisce (by way of pleasant contrast) about the village opera that he saw as a boy on the brink of his teens while accompanying his mother on a visit to her home town. Even to the most casual reader, however, it is apparent that the narrator, or we might as well say Lu Hsün, remembers the visit not so much for the opera as for the pleasant and pastoral business of getting there by boat, mooring in the river, and watching the opera at a distance in the company of country lads his own age while roasting beans under the stars.

6. *LHCC*, I, 139-49; *SWLH*, I, 136-49.
7. *NHFH*, pp. 85-86.

Throughout the reminiscence Lu Hsün seems, uncharacteristically, to enjoy thoroughly his position as educated-young-master-from-the-city back among the unlettered farm boys, who are very knowledgeable about oxen and not particularly impressed by his own familiarity with the *Poetry Classic*. Throughout his stay in the village the boy is treated with deferential, almost obsequious courtesy by young and old alike. And yet the boy (not to speak of the adult Lu Hsün who re-creates the experience for his readers) seems blithely unaware of the class distance that separates him from these country folk. He poetically attributes the gracious treatment they accord him to the unspoiled goodness of simple, uneducated, country people. Apparently Eroshenko beguiled Lu Hsün away from the arena of social problems and led him into a rather romantic and very stereotypic conception of the cool, green, and comforting fields of pastoral reminiscence—and perhaps Lu Hsün sorely needed the respite.

As in many of the best stories, in "Soap"[8] Lu Hsün establishes structure through ballad-like, incremental repetition. The dominant repeated elements are two props and a line of dialogue. The story opens as Ssu-ming comes home and presents his wife with a cake of scented soap; it closes with a description of her washing with a second cake of scented soap which she has, apparently, bought on her own. These two cakes of soap provide the typical Lu Hsün envelope, and the cake of soap bought by the husband serves to tie the many incidents of the story together in a thematic unity.

After Ssu-ming's return home, we learn that while he was fussily picking over various cakes of soap in the store, a young student swore at him in English: "Old fool!" Ssu-ming calls his son (who is studying English) to his side, approximates the pronunciation of the foreign epithet, and orders him to look it up in a dictionary. Throughout the story, Lu Hsün uses the soap and the dictionary as his two primary structural props; the third is provided by a line of dialogue.

Ssu-ming bought the soap after hearing a roustabout on the street look at an eighteen-year-old beggar girl and observe to his companion: "Ah-fa, don't be put off just because the goods is a bit

8. *LHCC*, II, 43-54; *SWLH*, I, 198-211.

dirty. All you gotta do is get a couple cakes of soap, and then with a few *rub-a-dub-dubs* all over that little body you'd have yourself quite a piece there." Ssu-ming, unaware that it was the subconscious effect of this remark that prompted him to buy soap for his wife, repeats it to her in public-spirited tones of righteous indignation. He is outraged to think that anyone could think such a low, vile thought about a young girl whom *he* sees as a praiseworthy model of filial behavior! (She immediately handed over any alms she received to an aged grandmother at her side.) Repeated at key intervals in the story, the *rub-a-dub-dub* remark firms up its skeleton and lends it thematic clarity. Ssu-ming's wife is the first to make the connection between the remark and her husband's purchase of the scented soap. It is she too who gradually comes to realize that her husband's excessive praise for the beggar girl's filial behavior is but the sublimation of a sexual fantasy. Thanks to his wife's sensitivity, Ssu-ming is a wiser man as the story ends, and as the last *rub-a-dub-dub* is repeated he is even self-aware enough to be shamed.

The Chinese critic Pa Jen (pen name of Wang Jen-shu), as previously noted, singled out "Soap" as a particularly good example of the qualities of concision and theatricality so often encountered in Lu Hsün's stories. Pa Jen also observed that in revealing his protagonist through fragments of his life enveloped within the confines of a single evening, Lu Hsün moved very close to the techniques used in writing for the theater.[9] At the beginning of this chapter I mentioned "contrasts of stillness and action" as one of Lu Hsün's typical structural devices—something that is also quite common in the theater. It is natural then that such contrasts should serve an important function here in "Soap," one of the most theatrical of the stories.

In "Soap" plot progression is clearly modulated by alternate stretches of silence and sound, stillness and action. The story opens in silence as Ssu-ming's wife and daughter sit in the house pasting paper money for the dead while his son practices a form of Chinese boxing in the courtyard. The plot builds to a crescendo as Ssu-ming expatiates to his wife on the decadence of society in general and the perfidy of the *rub-a-dub-dub* roustabout in

9. Pa Jen (Wang Jen-shu), *Lu Hsün te hsiao-shuo* [Lu Hsün's stories] (Shanghai, 1957), p. 38; hereafter cited as *LHSS*.

particular, then it dwindles into silence again as the family wait for mother to serve the evening meal.

A second crescendo builds when Ssu-ming's wife, angry at the way her husband has been carping at their son, suddenly comes to the boy's defense and, at the same time, lets Ssu-ming know that she thinks *his* attitude toward the filial beggar girl was no different from that of the *rub-a-dub-dub* roustabout. The arrival of Ssu-ming's literary friends (they have formed a club for the improvement of social mores through literature) diminishes this crescendo.

A third crescendo builds as one of Ssu-ming's literary friends is so amused by the *rub-a-dub-dub* remark (Ssu-ming has repeated it for them) that he cannot control his thundering laughter. The crescendo diminishes as Ssu-ming, increasingly indignant at his friend's unseemly behavior, finally silences him; it continues to diminish as Ssu-ming sees his friends out the gate, and the story ends in the same silence in which it began.

GROUP-CENTERED—SOCIOLOGICAL ("MEDICINE")

Lu Hsün divided "Medicine"[10] into four numbered parts. In the first half of part one we are introduced to a teashop manager, Hua Lao-shuan, his wife, and his tubercular son; the second half takes us out with Lao-shuan onto the early morning streets toward a spot where a crowd is gathering. As readers, we are kept guessing why the crowd is there until an ominous figure approaches and gruffly exchanges a blood-soaked *man-t'ou* (steamed bread-roll) for a packet of Lao-shuan's money. The title of the story appears as someone in the crowd wonders who this "medicine" is for. It seems that the crowd must have been watching a decapitation, but we cannot be sure.[11]

10. *LHCC*, I, 25-34; *SWLH*, I, 29-39.
11. The critic, Ou-yang Fan-hai, has claimed (*LHTS*, p. 150) that "Medicine" loses much of its effectiveness because Lu Hsün teases the reader; Ou-yang scores this technique as one of the defects of the "psychologism" of Leonid Andreyev, whose influence on the story Lu Hsün himself acknowledged. Essentially, Ou-yang is carping at Lu Hsün for not fulfilling the expectations of readers of traditional fiction. It is precisely this sort of indirection, of course, that gives "Medicine" a modern touch. A traditional author might well have presented the execution directly to the reader. Lu Hsün, assuming that fiction had a higher purpose than entertainment, expected active participation from his readers. For his acknowledgment of Andreyev's influence see *Chung-kuo hsin wen-hsüeh ta-hsi* [Encyclopedia of the new Chinese literature] (reprint of 1935 edition; Hong Kong, n.d.), p. 1476; hereafter cited as *HWHTH*.

In the second part the Huas cook and serve the bloody roll to their tubercular son, hearts filled with hope and trepidation, and a regular patron of their shop, hunchbacked Wu Shao-yeh, arrives early, as usual, to while away another meaningless day there. The third part is set somewhat later in the same day and a few more patrons are gathered in the shop. When an old graybeard comments on the dark circles around Lao-shuan's sleepless eyes, Hunchback Wu begins to explain, only to be interrupted by the arrival of the executioner, K'ang Ta-shu, who swaggers in and brags to the Huas about how fortunate they are to have a friend like himself who is well posted on the neighborhood news. He assures them that this is a guaranteed cure, talking so loudly that he awakens the son, Hsiao-shuan, sleeping in the next room, whose wracking cough provides an ironic contrast to K'ang's glib confidence. The graybeard asks about the particulars of today's beheading. While K'ang is answering, Hsiao-shuan comes in from the next room and sits at a table. He accompanies the executioner's monologue with fits of coughing.

K'ang relates that the condemned was the son of Fourth Mother Hsia (we have already noted that the combined names of the two families, Hua-Hsia, constitute an ancient name for China) and had been turned in as an anti-Manchu revolutionary by his own uncle. He goes on to tell how young Hsia even tried to get his jailer to revolt. At this point in the story, Lu Hsün again exhibits his fondness for the contrapuntal use of sound and activity against a background of silence and stillness. K'ang states that the Hsia boy was not intimidated by beating but merely said, "Pitiful." The graybeard asks rhetorically what there is pitiful in beating the likes of someone like Hsia. K'ang, with a knowing air of superiority, points out that Hsia meant that the jailer was to be pitied. Again Lu Hsün gives the reader a sound-silence contrast: dumbfounded by this unexpected revelation, the patrons of the teashop freeze into total immobility, and action returns to the group only when the graybeard leads them toward the truth that instantly clears away the fog—Hsia was mad! They all come to life again as they express their common agreement with this conclusion.

Part Four is set in a graveyard just outside the west gate of the city. Paupers are buried to the right of a path through the middle of the graveyard, criminals to the left. (The grave mounds, harking back to the bloody "medicine" Hsiao-shuan was given, are described as resembling piles of *man-t'ou* set out for a rich

"... make that crow fly onto your grave."

man's birthday.) It is the time of the Ch'ing-ming festival when people traditionally pay respect to the dead. Mother Hua appears, offers a sacrifice, and burns some paper money before a grave on the right-hand side of the road. She continues to sit there as if in a stupor. Another woman appears on the path with offerings and paper money; she sets out the sacrifice, weeps for a while, and then burns the paper money. Her son's grave is on the left-hand side of the road, directly across the path from that of Mother Hua's son. Suddenly the woman lurches back a few steps and points to the grave. Fearing that the woman is about to take leave of her senses, Mother Hua crosses the path that separates them and comforts her. "Look! What's that?" the woman says, pointing to some flowers arranged in a wreath on her son's grave. Interpreting this as a sign that her son is trying to communicate with the world, she addresses him directly and by name. (Now the reader knows as fact what he has known intuitively since the woman arrived: it is young Hsia's grave.) Mother Hsia asks that her dead son give her a sign by making a crow perched on a nearby limb fly to his grave. The women wait. More people begin to arrive at the graveyard. Finally Mother Hua urges the Hsia woman to leave. The two mothers walk away and the story ends as the crow stretches out its wings and flies off to the horizon. This is surely one of Lu Hsün's gloomiest tales: the blood of a martyr offered up as a superstitious cure for a tubercular boy.

Here in "Medicine" we see still another example of Lu Hsün's fondness for modulation from inaction to action and then back to inaction again: the story opens in silence, builds steadily to a crescendo in part three (the teashop during the busy part of the day) and then softens to a dimuendo as the story closes. Typically, too, minor characters are identified by strking physical traits (red-eyed Ah-yi, Hunchback Wu, the graybeard), and props are held to a minimum (the bloody *man-t'ou*, the wreath of flowers—the latter a sop to hope which Lu Hsün threw in to please others, not himself, according to his preface to *Call to Arms*).

The wreath of flowers, despite Lu Hsün's own disclaimer and similar opinions on the part of critics,[12] does serve an essential function in the last part of the story in that it affords Lu Hsün an opportunity to reveal something of Mrs. Hsia's folk beliefs to the reader. She interprets the appearance of the flowers not as most readers would (a hopeful symbol that there were others who

12. Ou-yang Fan-hai has objected that Lu Hsün has added a needless note of mystery by failing to explain where the flowers came from (LHTS, p. 150). Hsü Ch'in-wen (following Sun Fu-yüan) has observed more helpfully that there would have been nothing strange about the appearance of the flowers since Ch'iu Chin, upon whom Hsia Yü was in part based, had many admirers who might well have gone to her grave (*TPCH*, pp. 11-12). Tso-jen, on the other hand, has pointed out that the use of such flowers constitutes an anachronism; it is a custom that dates from the 1930s. Hsü Ch'in-wen approves the flowers but opines that the crow merely serves to heighten the mood of desolation without symbolizing anything. To insist upon giving it a symbolic value, he believes, would be tantamount to seeing Lu Hsün as a symbolist who simply did not even grasp the basic tenets of realism. (*NHFH*, p. 32.)

remembered the young revolutionary and would carry on his work), but rather as a sign from her son protesting the injustice of his execution. From the viewpoint of the Manchu government, of course, his beheading was just: he was an avowed revolutionary who would not change his ways even on pain of death. His mother, no revolutionary herself, undoubtedly thought that he had been wronged only in the sense that he had not committed the crime for which he had been executed. She believed that he had taken a traditional way of protesting this injustice, even from the grave, by causing the flowers to appear. Furthermore, it is the appearance of the flowers that moves Mrs. Hsia to say: "They murdered you. But a day of reckoning will come. Heaven will see to it. Close your eyes in peace—If you are really here, and can hear me, make that crow fly onto your grave as a sign." Lu Hsün ends the story by having the crow "fly like an arrow toward the far horizon." Had the crow flown to the grave, as Mrs. Hsia wished, then the story would have ended on a note of despair: it would have directly validated the superstitious beliefs of Mrs. Hsia and, indirectly, it would also have reinforced the superstitious set of medical assumptions to which the Hua boy was sacrificed. Hence the flight of the crow is a second symbol of hope.

The story is group-centered in that the Hsia boy remains undeveloped and is little more than a piece of litmus paper with which Lu Hsün tests society for acid. All the characters in the story, including the executioner, are victims of an evil social system. Unaware of their own roles in society, they blindly play their parts. This is, of course, opposite to the situation in "Soap," an individual-centered story in which Ssu-ming's Neo-Confucian hypocrisy is the acid and the characters around him are the litmus paper strips.

IN A CATEGORY OF ITS OWN
("THE TRUE STORY OF AH Q")

In various ways, "The True Story of Ah Q"[13] is unlike any other of Lu Hsün's stories. Except for its great length[14] and rambling, episodic structure, it could be classed with those stories in which

13. *LHCC*, I, 72-114; *SWLH*, I, 76-135.
14. Excluding "The True Story of Ah Q," the other 24 stories in *Call to Arms* and *Wandering* average about 11 pages in the *LHCC* edition; "The True Story of Ah Q" runs to 42.

Lu Hsün appears in the role of polemicist narrator. Quite evidently the narrator is not Lu Hsün in a sentimental mood, and in personality he is too close to Lu Hsün as we know him "in the round," so to speak, to be considered a fictional narrator.

The story is famous for its unmasking of an alleged general characteristic of the Chinese psyche—a form of self-deception whereby "psychological victories" (*ching-shen sheng-li*) are substituted for victories in the world of reality. One might therefore regard "The True Story of Ah Q" as a psychological tale. It will not fit that category, however, and for a most revealing reason: all the protagonists of the psychological tales could conceivably improve themselves without having to remake the society in which they live. Ah Q is wholly a product of the society which surrounds him, and his spiritual reconstruction is inconceivable without a total revolution in the social order. In other words, in the individual-centered stories the protagonist can be held responsible for what he has become; Ah Q cannot. Nor can "The True Story of Ah Q" be properly classed with the group-centered stories, for in all of these (with the possible exception of "Storm in a Teacup") the protagonists are presented solely as the victims of society. Thus, the reason for not classifying it among the group-centered tales reveals another striking characteristic about the story: Ah Q, as protagonist, is *victimizer* as well as *victim*. To be sure, he is bullied and maltreated, but whenever given the opportunity he bullies and maltreats those in positions inferior to his own, and his dream of revolution, further, is narrowly limited to notions of exploitation and revenge.

The fact that "The True Story of Ah Q" appeared serially on a weekly basis (occasionally skipping a week) in the Peking *Ch'en Pao* (Morning Post) obviously had much to do with the character of the story.[15] It was originally intended for a column titled *K'ai-hsin Hua* (Cheerful anecdotes), but after the story began to

15. Before 1921 no newspaper had a supplement, although the fifth page of the *Morning Post* did include some literary odds-and-ends that lent the paper a fresh and lively air. Sometime in late 1921, P'u Po-ying developed the idea of adding a Sunday supplement to the paper, under the editorship of Sun Fu-yüan, a former student of Lu Hsün's at the San Hui Normal School (the school in which Wang Chin-fa had installed Lu Hsün as principal in 1911). P'u wanted to supplement to be varied and rather relaxed in tone. Sun asked his old teacher to contribute something and the result was the famous "*Ah Q cheng-chuan.*" Sun says that Lu Hsün agreed primarily in order to help his former student do well in

appear, Lu Hsün and his editor agreed that it was hardly appropriate for this column, and it was moved to the "New Literature"
section.[16] The story is a ramblingly narrated series of incidents
about the people of Wei village and their reaction to the Republican Revolution. Throughout, the presence of the narrator is
dominant. He is a person of high intelligence and wry humor,
whose manner at first is lighthearted; as the story goes on,
however, his tone becomes increasingly somber and his manner is
presentation, ever more serious.

Installment I, the introduction, consists largely of the narrator's
monologue, and does little to forward the plot. The material for
this sarcastic and rambling discourse is taken largely from traditional Chinese culture and the doings of those modern intellectuals
who see themselves as the preservers of that heritage; barbed satire
is aimed at such diverse targets as the stereotyped biographies
written by traditional historians and the various contemporary
critics and enemies of the New Culture movement.[17] Ah Q, a
roustabout who holes up at the temple in Wei village, appears and
we see Mr. Chao slap him across the face for his temerity in laying
claim to the Chao surname after the Chao boy passed the first of
the civil service examinations.

Installments II and III present Ah Q's life-style and psychology
through a series of incidents which also bring out the broad
outlines of society in Wei village. Repeatedly, we are shown Ah
Q's peculiar way of winning psychological victories by either
rationalizing his defeat or belittling the victor. When everything
else has failed, we even see him slap himself across the mouth
while identifying with the "slapper" rather thatn the "slapped."
We get to know the venerable Chao and his son, the local
hsiu-ts'ai, as well as the venerable Ch'ien and *his* son, a Western-
dressed student who has recently returned pigtail-less from studies
in Japan and even sports the Westernized young gentleman's

---

a new job. Mao Tun (Shen Yen-ping), et al., *Yi Lu Hsün* [Remembering Lu Hsün]
(Peking, 1956), pp. 6-8; hereafter cited as *YLH*. For dates of publication see Chou
Shu-jen (Lu Hsün), *Na-han: chu-shih pen* [*Call to Arms:* annotated edition]
(Hong Kong, 1958), p. 155, n. 1; listed in the bibliography as *NHCSP*.

16. *LHCC*, II, 281-82; *SWLH*, II, 307-9.

17. Chou Tso-jen has pointed out that his brother wrote about Ah Q at precisely
that time when scholars like Ku Hung-ming were praising pigtails, bound feet,
despotism, and polygamy. *HSJW*, pp. 67-68.

walking stick. Ah Q enters and loses a contest (finding lice and popping them between the teeth) with Whiskers Wang, and we see him pick a pointless fight with Wang, only to receive still another drubbing. Ah Q attempts to unburden himself of part of his choler by directing insults at the Westernized young Ch'ien, and the result, of course, is a painful beating with the walking stick. Having been bullied himself, Ah Q becomes a bully in turn, humiliating a helpless Buddhist nun to gain the plaudits of a few wineshop idlers.

Installments II and III do nothing for the story's plot movement, which is not initiated until Installment IV, when Ah Q's clumsy attempt at seducing the Chao's maidservant, Amah Wu, results in his losing his means of livelihood and getting into trouble with the local authorities. In the course of this action the narrator, much in the fashion of a traditional storyteller, digresses to present the audience with a satiric disquisition on the traditional Chinese male's attitude toward women.

Installment V furthers the plot by relating how the evil reputation that Ah Q gained as a consequence of the Amah Wu incident causes him to forfeit all possibility of employment at odd jobs. Misreading the situation, Ah Q blames his ill luck on another roustabout and picks a fight with him. Of course, he loses. Denied all employment, he has no choice but to leave Wei village and go to try his luck in town. Installment VI depicts the tremendous change that takes place with regard to Ah Q's position in the village when he returns from town some months later, obviously having prospered. Wealth and the prestige that travels in its train are, of course, honored above all else in Wei village, and the *p'a-ch'iang ch'i-jo* (fear the strong, bully the weak) mentality of its inhabitants ensures everyone's respect for Ah Q's newly acquired wealth—respect that is not lessened when it comes out that he became prosperous by joining a band of burglars. The villagers' respect declines only when they learn that Ah Q was not an aggressive thief (the kind that breaks into a house and hence is to be feared) but merely a passive one (who waited on the outside for the stolen goods to be handed out to him). Structurally, the action in this installment is of the revelation type and does little to move the plot ahead.

In Installment VII, rumors of revolution arrive and there is a further satirical revelation of Wei village's *p'a-ch'iang ch'i-jo* ethic.

At first hostile to the idea of revolution, Ah Q identifies with the revolutionaries and pretends to be one of them as soon as he discovers what fear and awe the idea of "a revolutionary" inspires in the rich and powerful. When, however, he goes to carry out the revolution in a local convent (i.e., loot it), he is, as we saw in the last chapter, dismayed to find that he has been preceded by the *hsiu-ts'ai* of the Chao family and the returned student of the Ch'ien household. Obviously, both the traditional and progressive elements of the local power structure, heretofore mutual enemies, have decided to ally themselves in common bond with the "revolutionary" cause so that the class structure of Chinese society will remain unchanged despite the Republican Revolution. Such complexities, of course, are far beyond the mentality of Ah Q, who merely "feels" disappointed.

In Installment VIII, irked that the revolution, now apparently successful, has brought so few changes to Wei village, Ah Q decides that the trouble is that he has failed to enlist formally with the revolutionaries. With ludicrous incongruity he goes to the Ch'ien family compound to join up, and in the courtyard approaches young Ch'ien, who now sports the insignia of the revolution. Predictably, Ch'ien drives him out with repeated blows of his walking stick, much as when old Chao slapped him across the mouth for trying to identify with the traditional establishment when Chao's son passed the *hsiu-ts'ai* examination. For a time Ah Q wanders listlessly about the village and mindlessly lingers near the Chao home to watch "revolutionary troops" looting the place. He observes this all the more appreciatively since he himself had served an apprenticeship in this line of work while in town. He returns to the village temple and in retrospect is furious that the looters did not ask such an expert as himself to join them.

An Installment IX opens, local police and militia surround the temple. At length they drum up enough courage to enter Ah Q's lair. Captured, taken to town, and forced into a confession, Ah Q is executed before a firing squad (a Republican refinement over the headsman's axe). As the scene unfolds, some attention is drawn to Ah Q's peculiar psychology, but the real focus of interest is the cold, indifferent, passive society that surrounds him. (Perhaps Lu Hsün is recalling the slide incident at Sendai that decided his choice of a literary career.)

As the story approaches an end, the narrator's sarcasm and irony are unrelieved by any of his earlier flippancy; he seems almost despairing:

As for public opinion in Wei village, there was no disagreement: naturally everyone said that Ah Q was bad; the very fact that he had been executed stood as clear proof of that. If he hadn't been bad, then how could he have gotten himself shot? The talk around the town where the execution took place was, on the other hand, downright critical. Most people were unhappy because a shooting wasn't nearly as much fun to watch as a head-chopping. Furthermore, think of how poorly Ah Q had done in the role of condemned criminal—paraded around the streets all that time as a warning to the people and he hadn't even managed to sing a single snatch of opera! They had wasted their time following him.

The greatness of Ah Q, as a character, lies in Lu Hsün's having combined in him the personality traits of both "victim" and "victimizer." Similarly the high artistic quality of the story lies in its combination of techniques that would seem mutually exclusive: those of the traditional Chinese storyteller and the modern Western short-story writer. The former was interested primarily in plot and sought to perfect himself in entertaining ways of presenting his plot to his audience—a "fun" attitude toward fiction which Lu Hsün himself elsewhere disdained. Interested primarily in the story itself, the traditional storyteller had a loose and rambling idea of plot and would often link incidents together in carefree fasion to make a "long fiction" (*ch'ang-p'ien hsiao-shuo*—a term sometimes translated simply as "novel," but which John Bishop has more accurately rendered as "accretive novel").[18] Lu Hsün had turned to fiction not to entertain, but to make serious and individual comments upon Chinese society (as opposed to what Průšek has characterized as the "common opinion" presented by the storytellers). Hence, familiar though he was with traditional techniques (as is evidenced by his *Brief History of Chinese Fiction*), he avoided those techniques in his typical stories, which are clearly foreign-influenced in form.

Bishop has faulted traditional Chinese fiction for its "monotonous occupation with 'story'" and for its attempt to "reproduce the

18. "Some Limitations of Chinese Fiction," in John L. Bishop, ed., *Studies in Chinese Literature*, Harvard-Yenching Institute Studies, vol. 21 (Cambridge, Mass., 1965), p. 240.

social macrocosm rather than explore the human microcosm."[19] Similar considerations mark off the modern Western short story from its traditional forms:

> The modern story-teller, then, has not dispensed with incident or anecdote or plot and all their concomitants, but he *has* changed their nature. There is still adventure; but it is now an adventure of the mind. There is suspense, but it is less a nervous suspense than an emotional or intellectual suspense.[20]

The modern writer, in order to accomplish his aims, cannot dispense with plot or incident:

> . . . some incident is, of course, necessary: one of the best definitions ever given of the technique of fiction is that action reveals character, and that character demonstrates itself in action—and action is another word for incident. But incident now is merely a trigger—a tiny piece of mechanism which explodes a projectile that smashes some façade, or explodes some concentration of laughter, fancy, tragedy, or delight.[21]

In "The True Story of Ah Q" the incidents are often entertaining, but they also reveal something about the characters of Ah Q and those around him. Yet the story retains much that is reminiscent of traditional storytelling. Structurally, it is a happy combination of Chinese and Western modes.

Lu Hsün's well-known statement that he took advantage of his editor's absence from town to finish what could have been an interminable series of installments by executing Ah Q, however disingenuous, does point to the fact that like many colloquial tales of the serially chaptered (*chang-hui*) variety, it could have been spun out to almost any length. Moreover, in the introductory installment Lu Hsün indicates that he had this type of tale in mind and that he borrowed the "true story" of his title from the stock phrase of the traditional storyteller: "enough of this digression, now let's get back to the true story (*hsien-hua hsiu-t'i yen-kuei cheng-chuan*)." Lu Hsün's story further resembles the traditional colloquial fiction in that he spends a good deal of his introduction on a rambling digression in which he takes pot shots at a number of favorite enemies before getting into the story proper. Were he actually to tell the tale in a teashop, this device would serve as a

19. Ibid., pp. 242-43.
20. Sean O'Faolain, *The Short Story* (London, 1948), p. 64.
21. Ibid., p. 65.

good filler while waiting for customers to come in; one could even enter the shop as he began on Installment II and still get one's money's worth, losing very little of the story proper. Perhaps, in consenting to write such a serial in the first place, Lu Hsün was intrigued by the scope it would afford him to experiment with the techniques of traditional Chinese ficiton. Indeed, "The True Story of Ah Q" does not exhibit many of the structural devices that he used in his shorter and more foreign-influenced stories. He does not, for instance, employ to any great extent such devices as poetic repetition, envelopes, or the rhythmic pacing achieved through the contrapuntal use of action and quiescence. And of course, given the serial nature of the story, we cannot logically expect it to be characterized by scene economy, though, like many Lu Hsün stories, it is marked by an economy of significant characters and props.

We have had occasion before to refer to Lu Hsün the acid-tongued polemicist, Lu Hsün the sentimentalist, and Lu Hsün the artist. The polemicist negates, the sentimentalist affirms, and the artist attempts to hold both the modes of his creative personality to a higher, more objective esthetic standard. One is reminded of Yeats:

> The rhetorician would deceive his neighbors,
> The sentimentalist himself; while art
> Is but a vision of reality.[22]

The worth of "The True Story of Ah Q" as story lies in its being "but a vision of reality." Certainly Lu Hsün and much of his audience disliked a great deal of what they saw in Ah Q, but in the privacy of their own consciences they were no doubt forced to admit that these same tendencies existed within themselves. It would not have been possible for them to sit back and righteously condemn Ah Q as they could have condemned, for instance, a character like Schoolmaster Kao. Lu Hsün—perhaps despite himself—approached Ah Q with a great deal of compassion. Ah Q is more rounded than many of Lu Hsün's other characters in that he

22. *The Collected Poems of W. B. Yeats* (New York, 1933), p. 184. Three lines from Yeats's poem "Ego Dominus Tuus" are taken from *The Collected Works of William Butler Yeats* (copyright 1918 by Macmillan Publishing Co., Inc., renewed 1946 by Bertha Georgie Yeats) and are used by permission of the publisher and M. B. Yeats, Miss Anne Yeats, and Macmillan of London and Basingstoke.

is presented as responsible, though not totally responsible, for what he becomes. A fully human type, he is an object of our sympathy as well as a target of our scorn.

II

In Taoist fashion, one might say that the language of the stories in *Call to Arms* and *Wandering* achieves the level of excellence that it does precisely because it is so very unimportant. As Lu Hsün himself has indicated, his aim in writing these stories was not to be an artist but to point out the disease he saw in Chinese society, hoping that some abler spiritual physician would attempt to cure it. For him, Chinese realities were of overriding importance, and *language* was only secondary. However, having gotten his priorities straight, he proceeded to present the substance of what he had to say in carefully wrought sentences and phrases that were not equaled by any of his contemporaries. What is more, he said his piece in a language that he was helping to fashion as he wrote—a new colloquial form of writing that was to be the chief vehicle of all intellectual products of the May Fourth period. Lu Hsün's colloquial style was strongly influenced by his wide reading in foreign literatures and by no means a mere continuation of the diction of traditional vernacular literature.[23] Paradoxically, however, the terseness of his style was strongly indebted to the classical diction that the new colloquial language revolution sought to overthrow. Lu Hsün's diction, by no means the language of everyday discourse, was highly literary, despite its being based on colloquial rather than classical Chinese.

23. Jaroslav Průšek says that even the novels of exposure which appeared in the late Ch'ing did not significantly depart from traditional fiction of the storyteller variety in either technique or diction. On the problem of diction in modern Chinese literature he says:

"Il me semble que nous touchons ici à la différence fondamentale existant entre l'ancienne et la nouvelle littérature. Les moules et les clichés artistiques dominent souverainement dans l'anciene littérature et l'auteur qui leur adapte son sujet se voit bien souvent obligé de malmener ce dernier pour satisfaire à ces regles. La tradition littéraire est plus forte que les relations avec le réel. Et si nous voulions donner une forme positive à nos affirmations, nous pourrions dire que ce n'est que lorsque la volonté d'exprimer la réalité influe fortement sur la forme de l'oeuvre au point de lui donner une valeur qualitativement nouvelle que l'oeuvre en question représente un nouvelle conquête dans l'histoire de lettres." ("Quelques remarques sur la nouvelle littérature chinoise," in *Mélanges de Sinologie offerts a Monsieur Paul Demiéville* [Paris, 1966], p. 211.)

The essential qualities of his diction were noted in an essay, "On Reading *Call to Arms*," written in the 1920s by someone using the pen name Y-sheng:

The first thing that strikes our attention is the simplicity and clarity of the sentences. Dialectical words are not thrown in. There is not a single wasted sentence, nor even a wasted word. Moreover, it is so pleasantly fluent that it seems to take on a rhythm of its own.[24]

Contemporary Chinese readers, having grown more accustomed to fiction whose style closely approximates ordinary speech, are likely to disagree with the last sentence.

Three decades later, the critic Chu T'ung also emphasized linguistic care as a contributory factor to the success of Lu Hsün's works. In an essay of 1957, "The Artistry of Lu Hsün's Language," Chu selects "appositeness" as the outstanding characteristic of Lu Hsün's language:

The most important quality of language art is "appositeness" which is the mother of all literary language. "Appositeness" implies the unity of content and linguistic form; moreover, it is from this very unity that artistry is born. Separation of form and content, even the slightest crack, brings with it damage to the artistry and thought of a story. And it is this which explains Lu Hsün's painstaking care—one might even say downright fussiness—in the selection of his vocabulary, a care that went to such great lengths that he would weigh and consider the use of a single word over and over again. To express each individual bit of content he would use *this* and no other linguistic symbol.[25]

Given Lu Hsün's preference for Spartan simplicity in life-style as in writing, one might expect that the ornaments of language would not hold a particularly important place in his short stories, and such is the case. Metaphors and similes do occur, but not in great frequency; when used, however, they have telling effect. Consider the following metaphor describing the emaciated appearance of Hsiao-shuan (the tubercular boy in "Medicine") as viewed from behind: "His two shoulder blades stood out prominently and printed there the Chinese character for the number 'eight'." This, of course, defies translation. It has been ingeniously rendered as "his shoulder blades stuck out so sharply, an inverted 'V' seemed

24. In T'ai Ching-nung, ed., *Kuan-yü Lu Hsün chi ch'i chu-tso* [On Lu Hsün and his works] (Peking, 1926), p. 67; listed in the bibliography as *KYLHCT*.
25. In *TYPC*, p. 83.

stamped there,"[26] but some of the visual force is lost and the metaphor becomes a simile. Unfortunately, many of Lu Hsün's most telling similes and metaphors are similarly difficult to translate. When Schoolmaster Kao sets out with the purposeful strides to take up his duties as a teacher, for instance, Lu Hsün says: "As soon as he stepped out the gate he strode off, his shoulders rising and falling like the crossbar of a carpenter's hand drill, and soon left Huang San [his mah-jongg-playing crony] out of sight."[27] Though virtually untranslatable into the languages of countries where geared drills are employed by carpenters rather than the bow-and-string arrangement usual in China, the image is particularly effective; in addition to being visually striking, it immediately suggests the ordered and purposeful activity of honest work contrasted to the playboy life of Huang San.

In "The White Light," Lu Hsün describes the feelings of Ch'en Shih-ch'eng when, already middle-aged, he has just failed the civil service examinations for the sixteenth time: "But now, the future, which he ordinarily so beautifully envisaged for himself, suddenly collapsed once again like a sugar pagoda that has gotten wet, leaving nothing save a pile of debris."[28] During religious festivals large sugar pagodas were placed before the gods in sacrifice while small ones were glumped down by children in a single mouthful. The simile is particularly felicitous in that just a few sentences earlier, Ch'en has imagined how, after he passed the examinations, "people would treat him with all the respect and deference usually reserved for the gods." Now that dream, like a sugar pagoda placed before the gods but melted by a sudden shower, collapses before him.[29]

Not surprisingly, some similes and metaphors center on the difficulty of breaking out of the old into the new. In "Upstairs in a Wineshop," Lü Wei-fu reflects upon his return to his home town with an extended simile that points to his failure to break away

---

26. *LHCC*, I, 26; *SWLH*, I, 32.

27. "Professor Kao," trans. Wang Chi-chen, *China Journal*, XXXIII (July 1940), 13.

28. *LHCC*, I, 124.

29. I am indebted to Professor David Ch'en and Chang Eh-feng of The Ohio State University for this explanation. Mr. Chang also told me how the small ones were made: two wooden blocks hollowed out in the form of a pagoda were placed together as a mold; syrup was blown into the mold; after cooling, the pieces of wood were separated and the small, brittle pagoda was removed.

from the darkness of his intellectual home town to the light of that new society which he had hoped to create as a youth.

"As soon as I got back, I saw how ridiculous I was." He picked up his cigarette with one hand, took his wine cup in the other, and said to me with a bittersweet smile: "When I was a boy, sometimes I'd see a bee or fly light someplace. Then he'd be scared off by something or other and fly away. But after making a small circle, he'd come back and light down in the very same place again. I thought that this was stupid and even pitiful. I certainly never foresaw then that I myself would fly back after making nothing but a small circle. I didn't expect to see you come back either. Couldn't you have flown a bit farther?[30]

Lu Hsün often uses similes simply to enliven his descriptive prose. In "A Warning to the People" a fat little boy abandons his station in front of the shop where he works and bounces over to the other side of the street to see what all the excitement is about, "like a rubber ball that had been thrown hard against the wall and bounced back again."[31] And in "Some Rabbits and a Cat" Lu Hsün uses another striking simile to describe rabbits defending their berries against raiding birds:

When crows or magpies would try to come down for their share of the berries, the bunnies would arch their backs, suddenly extend their powerful hind legs and, sinews crackling, leap straight up into the air like a wind-blown spiral of snow taking off into the sky.[32]

In "Brothers" Lu Hsün describes the heroic, albeit futile, efforts of the elder brother in trying to banish from his mind subconscious feelings of which he has only recently become aware:

He wanted to suppress these dream fragments, to forget them, but like goose feathers that one may try to stir down into the water, they would invariably surface after a few turns.[33]

Despite his skill and resourcefulness in employing the ornaments of language, one cannot stress too much that Lu Hsün was not lavish in using them.

In the use of adjective and adverbs there is a similar Spartan tendency. The aim was to intensify through concision. In 1931, in

30. *LHCC*, II, 26; *SWLH*, I, 178. My translation.
31. *LHCC*, II, 67; *China Journal*, XXXIII, 247.
32. *LHCC*, I, 130; Appendix.
33. *LHCC*, II, 138-39. My translation.

a letter to an editor, Lu Hsün presented several suggestions on creative writing, among which were these:

Read your story through at least twice after finishing it, and ruthlessly cut out all words, phrases, and sections that are not essential. It is better to compress the material for a story into a sketch than to stretch the material for a sketch into a story. . . .

Don't make up adjectives and things like that which no one else can understand.[34]

In "How I Began to Write Short Stories" (1933) he says:

There were no sets on the stage of the old Chinese theater; similarly, the New Year's pictures sold to children showed but a few main characters (though nowadays most of them have backgrounds drawn in too). I was thoroughly convinced that this method was perfectly suited to my own goals in writing; hence, I never went in for extended descriptions of scenery, nor did I ever allow the dialogue to run on for any great length.[35]

Lao She faulted traditional Chinese vernacular fiction for its failure to integrate characters and plot with scenery; he objected that, with few exceptions, scenery was described (often with the aid of poems) as a fixed backdrop for the action that unfolded before it and was, seemingly, independent of it.[36] Similarly, C. T. Hsia notes that:

By and large, the Ming and Ch'ing novelists [a period that covers the years 1368 to 1911] pay little attention to mood and atmosphere, so that narration, dialogue, and description are rarely integrated into an organic whole. To introduce a new scene, the novelist may describe a place quite elaborately, but in the subsequent narration few of the descriptive details will again be hinted at, so that the characters in that scene go about their business virtually detached from their setting.[37]

Lu Hsün, in the opening paragraph of his first story, "Remembrances of the Past," already shows his ability to fuse scenery and story:

Outside the gate at our house there stood a tung tree which was about thirty feet tall. Once a year fruit would cover it like stars spread out on

---

34. *LHCC*, IV, 289; *SWLH*, III, 138.
35. *LHCC*, IV, 393; *SWLH*, III, 230. I have been loose and interpretive in the translation.
36. Lao She (Shu Ch'ing-ch'un), *Lao-niu p'o-ch'e* [An old ox and rickety cart] (Hong Kong, 1961), p. 18; listed in the Bibliography as *LNPC*.
37. *The Classic Chinese Novel* (New York and London, 1968), p. 14.

an evening sky and the children would try to knock them down with small stones—stones that often continued in flight until they came through the open window of my family study and occasionally landed on my desk. Whenever that happened, my teacher, Master Baldy, would run outside and scold the children.[38]

Lu Hsün repeatedly refers to the tung tree, using it as a symbol of freedom from the dull authority of Master Baldy. Another example in the same story describes Master Baldy's pedantic manner in explicating the *Analects of Confucius:*

I didn't follow his explanations of the text because most of the words were so obscured by the shadow of his nose that I couldn't even see them. The only thing that I was conscious of was that the title *Analects* was capped by the Master's bald head—so glittering and bright that I could see my face in it, albeit somewhat indistinctly, not nearly as clearly as in the old pond out in the backyard.[39]

Of his colloquial-language stories, "Upstairs in a Wineshop" comes closest to "Remembrances of the Past" in using nature both to reflect the feelings of the narrator and as a structural device to sharpen the outline of the story. Throughout this piece, crimson camellias blossoming in the snow occur as an image of hope and at the same time as a symbol of home for both the narrator and his old friend Lü Wei-fu: one would see this sort of thing only here in their native south (to which both have returned for a visit), not in the north country to which they have, for various reasons, removed. There are references to snow in the opening part of the story and a final reference at the end when the narrator, having just experienced a bittersweet reunion with a friend who has failed in life, finds the snow and wind invigorating in that they help him to wash away remembrances of the past and his unfortunate friend:

As I walked alone toward my hotel, the cold wind and snow beat against my face, but I felt refreshed. I saw that the sky was already dark, woven together with houses and streets into the white, shifting web of thick snow.[40]

While, generally, Lu Hsün was never one to "allow the dialogue to run on for any great length," he used it far more than his

38. *LHCC*, VII, 257; Appendix.
39. Ibid., 258.
40. *LHCC*, II, 34; *SWLH*, I, 187.

statement would lead one to believe. "The Story of Hair" is largely a monologue interrupted here and there by the occasional remarks of a first-person narrator;[41] the same holds for "Upstairs in A Wineshop," and the plots of "The Eternal Lamp" and "Divorce" are revealed almost entirely through the dialogue of the main characters. Much of the movement of "Remembrances of the Past" is powered by dialogue.

In characterizing people through speech mannerisms Lu Hsün often succeeds in making them memorable. Consider the pedantic K'ung Yi-chi, whose speech often lumbers along in classical cadences and is chock-full of classical allusions. Ridiculed at the wineshop for having been caught stealing books again, K'ung defends himself with a humorously irrelevant distinction: "I merely purloined a few volumes, and that certainly cannot be counted as 'stealing books'; the purloining of volumes is, after all, well within the scope of the scholarly life. How can it be viewed as ordinary theft?" Later, defending himself against children who are about to eat all his beans, he tells them, "I haven't got many left. They're almost gone already." Immediately after, he straightens up and comments to himself in more learned fashion, "Few be my beans. Few be my beans. *'Hath the Gentleman many? Nay, nay, I say.'* "[42] K'ung's fondness for speaking in classical Chinese calls to mind Wang Yüeh-sheng in "Brothers," who is distinguished in a similar fashion by his love for four-character classical clichés.

In "Brothers," the relationship between Chang P'ei-chün and his younger brother, at the manifest level, fulfills the moral ideals of Confucian society. At a deeper, subconscious level, there are many elements of hostility. In the office, Ch'in Yi-t'ang is forever reciting the details of the fights that occur between his sons and constantly praising Chang P'ei-chün for the good relationship he has with his younger brother. Wang Yüeh-sheng, another member of the office force, also praises P'ei-chün at every opportunity.[43] Lu Hsün individualizes Wang Yüeh-sheng and at the same time exposes the shallowness of his thought by having him speak in four-character clichés (*ssu-tzu-t'zu*—which may, of course, translate into more words in English). When he hears some more details

41. See *HSJW*, pp. 30-31, for more on the relationship of "K" and the narrator.
42. *LHCC*, I, 23; *SWLH*, I, 26. The words in classical Chinese are a play on *Analects* IX, vi.
43. I add "as the saying goes" whenever translating one of Wang Yüeh-sheng's four-character clichés; the phrase does not appear in the Chinese text.

of the continuing battle between the Ch'in lads, thinking of the contrast offered by the ideal relationship that is assumed to obtain between P'ei-chün and his younger brother, Yüeh-sheng comments: "Well as the saying goes, 'the hearts of men differ.' " Soon after this, addressing P'ei-chün directly, he says: "As the saying goes, 'There is nothing like fraternal affection.' " Toward the end he tells P'ei-chün: "You two are as affectionate as 'pied wagtails on the moor,' as the saying goes." Apart from serving to characterize Wang Yüeh-sheng, the four-character clichés also serve to contrast traditional ideals of fraternal relations with the reality of a modern pair of brothers.

In "Medicine," the executioner, K'ang Ta-shu, is a man quite unlike K'ung Yi-chi or Wang Yüeh-sheng; he is brusque, aggressive, with a touch of the bully about him. As soon as he sets foot in the teashop, he says to Lao Shuan: "Has he eaten it? Is he better? Lao Shuan, you're lucky, really lucky. If I hadn't been so up on local news . . ."[44] The shorthand of speech reveals that K'ang Ta-shu, knowing about Lao Shuan's tubercular son, saw an opportunity to turn a quick profit and initiated the transaction involving the bloody roll as medicine for the boy. The concision to be obtained through the summary of dialogue was attractive to the word-frugal Lu Hsün. Another example of dialogue shorthand occurs in the opening scene of the same story. Just before Lao Shuan goes out to purchase the roll, he looks in on his son and says: "Hsiao Shuan . . . Don't get up. . . . The shop? Your mother will set things out."[45] These few words of dialogue save Lu Hsün from having to narrate that Hsiao Shuan thought his father was coming to tell him it was time to get up and get the shop ready for the day's business, and that he helped his parents there.

Another example of concision through dialogue is found in the story "Divorce," when Chuang Mu-san and his daughter have just boarded a small passenger skiff. Chuang Mu-san's announcement that they are going to P'ang village shrouds the boat in silence as all the other passengers turn to look at father and daughter.

"Is it Ai-ku's business again?" asked Pa-san at last.

"It is. . . . This affair will be the death of me. It's dragged on now for three years. We've quarreled and patched it up time after time, yet still the thing isn't settled. . . ."

"Will you be going to Mr. Wei's house again?"

44. *LHCC*, I, 29; *SWLH*, I, 34.
45. *LHCC*, II, 25; *SWLH*, I, 29.

"That's right. This won't be the first time he's acted as peacemaker; but I've never agreed to his terms. Not that it matters. Their family's having their New Year reunion now. Even Seventh Master from the city will be there. . . ."

"Seventh Master?" Pa-san opened his eyes very wide. "So he'll be there to put in his word too, eh? . . . As a matter of fact, since we pulled down their kitchen range last year we've had our revenge more or less. Besides, there's really no point in Ai-ku going back there. . . . He lowered his eyes again.[46]

Lu Hsün, at variance with the conventions of traditional (and much modern) Chinese fiction, dispenses with further references to who is saying what. The great prestige of Seventh Master is revealed through Pa-san's momentary fumbling for words, a fumbling which is followed by his unstated opinion that it would be best to avoid all further trouble and go along with whatever Seventh Master decides. Pa-san's use of "As a matter of fact" shows that he is opposed to doing anything more for fear of incurring the displeasure of Seventh Master, though he obviously does not want to offend Chuang Mu-san by saying so openly. His lines also show that he is on Mu-san's side. Was this sort of concision possible only because Lu Hsün was writing in the colloquial language? No. That it was also possible in the classical language is evident in "Remembrances of the Past." The household has been thrown into chaos by a rumor of revolution; the old Taiping rebels seem to have risen again. It is now evening and Old Wang is regaling the boy narrator and Amah Li with hair-raising tales of the Long Hairs. Suddenly the news arrives that the talk about rebels was nothing but a rumor after all:

Old Baldy paced around for a long time and then announced that he was going home with the news in order to reassure his own family. Saying that he would be back in the morning, he gathered up his volumes on how to write the eight-part essay and headed for the gate. Just before leaving, he looked at me and said: "Since you haven't studied the live-long day, how do you expect to have the text memorized well enough to recite for me in the morning? Hurry and get back to your books and stop being so mischievous." Feeling more and more depressed, I fixed my eyes on the glow of Old Wang's pipe in order to avoid having to answer him. Old Wang continued smoking. The flickering light of his pipe reminded me of an autumn firefly fallen into a pile of grass; then I remembered the summer before how I had fallen into a pond of reeds

46. *LHCC*, II, 142-43; *SWLH*, I, 262-63.

while trying to catch one. Thinking about these things, I managed to put Baldy completely out of mind.

"Eh, how many times have I heard people say 'The Long Hairs are coming'? When the Long Hairs really did come, it was terrifying. But what did it amount to after all?" Old Wang stopped smoking and sat there slowly nodding his head in reminiscence.

"Old man, did you ever really see the Long Hairs? What were they like?" There was a sense of urgency in Amah Li's voice.

"Were you ever a Long Hair yourself?" I asked hopefully. I thought that if the Long Hairs came, then surely Baldy would have to *go*. In that case, the Long Hairs must be good people. Since Old Wang was so nice to me, I reasoned, he must have been a Long Hair once himself.

"Ha, ha. No, I wasn't. By the way, Amah Li, how old were you at the time? I must have been twenty-some myself."[47]

Jaroslav Průšek has pointed out that, unlike the case in traditional fiction, dialogue in "Remembrances of the Past" is not used simply to forward the plot, but rather to evoke a certain atmosphere and to reveal social relationships.[48] Old Wang's silence as Master Baldy lectures the boy is followed by his meditative "But what did it amount to, after all?" The implication is that at one time Wang felt vague longings for some sort of change, but that he has long since made his own peace with the fact that it will not come. To be sure, this sort of thing was more difficult in the classical language —a language restricted to the written page and not used as a means of oral communication—but it was by no means impossible.

As Hsü Ch'in-wen has pointed out, Lu Hsün was particularly successful in reproducing the flavor of lower-class women's speech.[49] Consider Fifth Auntie Hui in "The Eternal Lamp." While she is describing to the patrons of her wineshop how the local madman had once before been tricked out of his obsession with putting out the eternal lamp, one of them interrupts her to ask how it is that he doesn't remember any such goings-on. She replies:

"How would you know about it? You were still a small fry then who only knew how to drink your milk and shit your drawers. Even I was somethin' different back in those days. You should have seen my hands then; they were soft and tender, so soft—"

"You're still all soft and tender even now," said Square Head.

47. *LHCC*, VII, 263; Appendix.
48. "Lu Hsün's Huai-chiu: A Precursor of Modern Chinese Literature," *Harvard Journal of Asiatic Studies*, XXIX (1969), 174-75.
49. *PHFH*, p. 16.

"Blow it out your ass!" said Fifth Auntie Hui, the smile on her lips belying the angry expression in her eyes. "Don't talk such nonsense; we're dealin' with serious business here."[50]

The use of "small fry (*hsiao pa-hsi*)" and "drink your milk and shit your drawers (*ho-nai la-shih*)" adds the right amount of pungency to her talk. One can almost see the old girl blushing as she smiles and says, "Blow it out your ass! (*fang ni ma-te p'i*)."

The most striking element of Lu Hsün's style is its tone, which is hardly ever neutral. It ranges from hatred to love, from satire to lyricism. One is aware of his tone of voice, and one senses whether he loves or hates the subject at hand. Even in the most objectively presented of his stories, "A Warning to the People," his tone is not neutral.

His satire is usually directed at the gap between the reality (*shih*) of Chinese society and the pretty names (*ming*) of its classically established ideals.[51] Naturally enough, much of his satire involves the satirical use of classical Chinese. This is usually accomplished by the incongruous insertion of a classical expression into a descriptive passage (or piece of dialogue) set in a contemporary scene. Yet, while the ludicrous effect is intensified by the colloquial surroundings, this contrast is not in fact vital. As a case in point, there is a humorous application of a classical expression in Lu Hsün's first short story, which was, as we know, composed entirely in classical Chinese. Old Wang is telling how Fifth Uncle Chao, the gatekeeper at the t'aimen back during the days of the Taiping Rebellion, assumed that he should stay at the family homestead when the rebels came, so that he could protect the property of his well-to-do employers, who themselves had fled.

"At that time the gatekeeper here was Fifth Uncle Chao. That guy was really thick. When the master of the house heard that the Long Hairs were on the way, he ordered everyone to flee for his life. And what do you think Chao said? 'But if the master leaves, then there won't be anyone here to look after things. I'll have to stay so that those ruffians don't take over the house.' "

50. *LHCC*, II, 56-57.
51. There are exceptions. In "Schoolmaster Kao" his satire is directed against the superficial hypocrisy of a contemporary hack, but does not carry with it any such anti-classical overtones. Nor is the classical tradition directly involved in "Brothers," where the gap between the *ming* of P'ei-chün's conscious life and the *shih* of his subconscious is the real object of Lu Hsün's attack, although the classical tradition of familial morality is indirectly involved too.

"Wow, what a stupid lout!" Amah Li suddenly cried out in dismay as she roundly castigated the shortcomings of a "former sage" like Fifth Uncle Chao.[52]

There can be little doubt that when Lu Hsün says "She roundly castigated the shortcomings of a 'former sage' (*li-ch'ih hsien-hsien chih fei*)," his words carry satirical overtones. He is not making fun of Amah Li; he sympathizes with her and uses her to underscore the ludicrous incongruity of Fifth Uncle Chao's mindless loyalty to the gentry with his own position in society.

In the same story, Master Baldy's pedantic and useless friend, Yao-tsung, is characterized by Amah Li:

Moreover, Amah Li once told me that, from infancy to manhood, Yao-tsung had been tied so close to his parents that you would have thought he was their prisoner. He never got out of the house to meet people, and hence was a very clumsy conversationalist. If the talk turned to rice, then he would say something about rice, but he didn't know the difference between ordinary rice and the glutinous kind; if the talk turned to fish, then he would manage to say something about fish, too, but he didn't know the difference between a bream and a carp. Sometimes when he didn't understand, you would have to give him several pages of the kind of commentary that the scholars do on the classics. Even then there would probably be much in the commentary that didn't get through to him, and you would have to provide him with a sub-commentary. But even in the sub-commentary there would, no doubt, still be words that would prove too difficult for him and in the end you would have to drop the subject without his having gotten any of it. Since that's the kind of fellow he was, none of us really liked to talk with him.[53]

The use of "commentary" and "sub-commentary" (vitally important words in the tradition of classical scholarship) is clearly satirical. Thus, even in a classical-language story, Lu Hsün was able to use classical words and expressions in a satirical manner. The use of colloquial language during the May Fourth period, however, greatly facilitated the presentation of this sort of incongruity by furnishing a contrasting background which made classical words and expressions seem even more out of place.[54] (There is a similar contrast in Peking opera, where almost all the

52. *LHCC*, VII, 261; Appendix.
53. Ibid., 258-59.
54. In *Old Stories Retold* (*Ku-shih hsin-pien*), Lu Hsün had scope to play with colloquial-classical incongruities both ways, since he could also put contemporary expressions into the mouths of such historical figures as Lao Tzu or Po Yi

important roles are sung or done in recitative, using the classical language, while the clowns speak in the everyday language of the streets.)

Lu Hsün's satirical use of the classical language creates a certian tone of jocular irreverence toward the verities of the past (the clown's vernacular often creates a similar effect as he poses his own take-it-as-it-comes life-style against the more straight-laced morality of his superiors). It is no accident that we find the highest density (Chang T'ien-yi has noted at least a dozen instances) of this in "The True Story of Ah Q," which begins in a downright flippant tone.[55] Unfortunately, almost all of these colloquial-classical contrasts defy close rendering in translation, so that whoever reads the story in English misses the subtleties and rich aftertaste of Lu Hsün's prose.

For satirical tone, he did not, of course, rely exclusively on colloquial-classical incongruity. Most of the satirical overtones of his colloquial-language stories are achieved through context. An effective instance occurs at the end of "The True Story of Ah Q," in the narrator's comments beginning "As for public opinion in Wei village," already quoted.[56] It is one of the bitterest passages to be found in any of the stories. Every word seems fanged.

Lu Hsün once said that only five of his books could, by any stretch of the imagination, be regarded as literature: *Call to Arms, Wandering, Wild Grass, Old Tales Retold,* and *Dawn Blossoms Plucked at Dusk.*[57] When one thinks of a lyrical Lu Hsün, the two books that come to mind are *Wild Grass,* with its sometimes indecipherable prose-poems, and *Dawn Blossoms Plucked at Dusk,* with its poetic reminiscences. *Old Tales Retold,* a compilation of reinterpreted myth and history, contains little that is lyrical. *Call to Arms* and *Wandering,* on the other hand, have a great deal, despite their dominantly somber tone. By "lyrical," I refer to those poetic sections of Lu Hsün's prose in which we can hear a voice singing in the background, alternately joyous and

---

and his brother, Shu Ch'i. Berta Krebsová has observed in this regard that "the insertion of archaic expressions into the ordinary spoken language gives a humorous touch to the narrative, in the same way as the anachronistic insertion of expressions contemporary with the time of writing into the historical context helps to bring out the irony or ridiculousness of the situation." "Lu Hsün and His Collection *Old Tales Retold,*" *Archiv Orientální,* XXVIII (1960), 654.

55. *LAQ,* pp. 64-65.
56. *LHCC,* I, 114; *SWLH,* I, 135.
57. *LHCC,* IV, 247-49; *SWLH,* III, 172-74.

sad. Whenever that lyrical voice is heard, the subject is likely to be childhood, remembered friends, the Chekiang countryside, or family life. Homeland and youth inspired him to the joyous lyricism of "Village Opera," where he posed the sophistication of Peking opera against the unlettered simplicity of festival plays in the Chekiang of his youth. His more typical lyricism appears in stories such as "Upstairs in a Wineshop" and "The Isolate," where the voice of the narrator is meditative and melancholy. It appears also in stories which he tried to present as impersonally and objectively as possible. In "Tomorrow" we get the impression that we are onlookers, free to judge as we will. Yet toward the end of the story we are increasingly aware of the presence of the maker of the tale, aware of his personality. Sister Shan-ssu has returned to the loneliness and emptiness of her room after burying her son:

Now she knew that her Pao-erh was really dead. She didn't want to see her room anymore. She blew out the light and lay down. She wept and she thought, thought back to a time when she had spun cotton-yarn with Pao-erh sitting at her side eating peas flavored with aniseed. With his small black eyes he had stared at her for some time and then had said: "Mom! Dad sold won ton. When I grow up, I'll sell them too, sell lots and lots and lots—give all the money to you." At that time even the cotton-yarn she spun, each and every inch of it, seemed possessed of meaning, of life. And now? Sister Shan-ssu really hadn't given any thought to now.—I said, a long time back, that she was a simple woman. What thoughts *would* she have been capable of? She only felt that her room was somehow too quiet, too big, and too empty.[58]

Here Lu Hsün's subjectivity leads him to a rare breach of artistic and tonal consistency when he needlessly intrudes in the first person.

The dominant tone of Lu Hsün's literary voice is that of a dispassionate news correspondent filing dispatches from Chinese villages and occasionally from the cities. This tone is deceptive. The choice of these seemingly objective news items is highly selective, and their content is always emotionally freighted with the correspondent's point of view. The man behind the voice is lightly touched with melancholy, and his quick, analytic intelligence is held taut by strong emotions which at times drive him to biting sarcasm and satire or loft him to flights of lyric beauty. Ever conscious of the personality of the writer behind the prose, we are likely to imagine such a man as Hsü Shou-shang's description, previously quoted, puts before us: "there was hardly a single

58. *LHCC*, I, 41; *SWLH*, I, 47.

"Dad sold won ton. When I grow up, I'll sell them too."

movement, word, or expression about him that did not reveal a combination of compassion and toughness—the two characteristic qualities that filled his life, pervaded his works, and made him a great writer and brave fighter, the very soul of the Chinese people."[59]

One wonders about the tension that must have existed between the roles of "great writer" and "brave fighter" in the turbulent China in which Lu Hsün lived. Given the high degree of formal artistry exhibited in his stories, how widespread an effect could they have had? Who were his readers? Only a small fraction of

59. *YHC*, p. 16.

China's population was literate to begin with, and it is likely that only a small fraction of that fraction had sufficient literary interest to turn to works of this quality. And yet one must remember that many of the young political leaders of China in the 1920s and 1930s came from the literary class and were quite capable of appreciating Lu Hsün's stories. Hence one cannot entirely discount their practical political impact. The breadth of Lu Hsün's influence is further attested by the biographical and critical literature in Chinese (running to hundreds of books and articles) that has grown up around him. A reissue of his complete works was brought out in the People's Republic the year before last (1973).[60] Finally, however, we ought to remember that his strongest and most heartfelt aspiration (ever since his student days in Japan when he wrote "The Power of Mara Poetry") was not primarily to be an artist, but rather to change China.

60. This is an amended reprint of *LHCC-20*.

12

CONCLUDING REMARKS ON AN IN-BETWEEN INTELLECTUAL

Lu Hsün, like many others of his generation, lacked a function. He had been trained as a traditional intellectual before the abolition of the examination system, and though he rebelled against it, this training left a lifelong imprint. It was an education that was humanist in emphasis, an education that was designed to cultivate a boy morally so that he could, as an adult, become an official and participate in the highest task to which a man might aspire—the governing of society. As a teen-ager, Lu Hsün was wrenched off track and sent off in a new direction; he attended new-style schools that taught such things as mining, naval science, and medicine, but it is likely that none of this was as influential on his development as was his early, more traditional, education.

By virtue of social position and sentiment, again like many others of his generation, he was convinced that the burden of responsibility for the state of Chinese society lay squarely on his own shoulders. Intellectually, his mixed Chinese-foreign training made him into a being quite different from the traditional scholar-officials; in terms of spirit, however, he had much in common with them. Like them, he was convinced that one's aim in life was self-cultivation (*nei-sheng*) carried on for the purpose of improving the human lot (*wai-wang*). In the view of C. T. Hsia, modern Chinese literature differs from that of both the traditional and the post-1949 periods by virtue of "its burden of moral contemplation: its obsessive concern with China as a nation afflicted with a spiritual disease and therefore unable to strengthen itself or change its set ways of inhumanity. All the major writers of the period— novelists, playwrights, poets, essayists—are enkindled with this patriotic passion."[1] Most readers of modern Chinese fiction will probably agree with this assessment. Professor Hsia also notes a tendency among authors of modern Chinese fiction to identify their subjective sufferings with the fate of China as a whole,[2] and one can easily find corroboration of this in the life and works of Lu Hsün.

It is, of course, quite natural that writers like Lu Hsün should see their own experience not as individual, or idiosyncratic, but rather as a microcosm of the macrocosm of Chinese society, history, and culture. The sharp division that sometimes exists in the pluralistic societies of the West between individual and society was (and still is) relatively unknown in China. The traditional scholar-official upon his arrival as the new magistrate of a district often presented himself to the local gods and spirits, announcing that he, and he alone, would now be responsible for the moral well-being of the area, and that he alone ought to be punished in case of any transgression. There are strong elements of continuity between this attitude and that of many modern writers. The modern intellectual did not proclaim his responsibility for the fate of China before the gods of the mountains and rivers, but he did announce that responsibility—perhaps not without a touch of pride—to his reading public in proclaiming the importance of the cultural and political themes on which he chose to write.

Lu Hsün's identification of his private experiences (ssu) with the fate of Chinese society as a whole (kung) was not (given the interim age in which he lived) farfetched. China was in rebellion against its collective past, searching for a new mode of being as a nation; Lu Hsün was also in search of a new mode of being in which men might come to know honesty (ch'eng) and love (ai), the two qualities which (he had decided) Chinese personality most lacked. Since he did not want to be assimilated into the society around him, it followed as a corollary that he should idealize youth. For Lu Hsün, "growing up" was necessarily bad. It meant assimilation into a social structure which he saw as evil: maturing was equivalent to being corrupted.

This idealization of youth is presented most poignantly in "Home Town," in the person of the innocent Jun-t'u whom maturation eventually twisted and thwarted, and in "Village Opera," in the personalities of the children who accompany the

---

1. "Perspective on Chinese Literature: Obsession with China," in *China in Perspective* (Wellesley Hills, Mass., 1967), pp. 101-2.

narrator to the festival play. Earliest of all, it occurs in "Remembrances of the Past" when the narrator recalls those idyllic chats out under the tung tree with Old Wang and Amah Li, when only the children and servants remained uncorrupted against the background of an adult world represented by the unattractive Yao-tsung and Master Baldy. And yet, Lu Hsün admitted in his first colloquial story, "Diary of a Madman," that even children are capable of evil because they have already beeen corrupted by their parents. Apart from the young, however, he saw no hope of salvation—hence the closing line of that story, "Save the children!" In an essay on what fathers ought to be, written in 1919, Lu Hsün said: "Let the awakened man burden himself with the weight of tradition and shoulder up the gate of darkness. Let him give unimpeded passage to the children so that they may rush to the bright, wide-open spaces and lead happy lives henceforward as rational human beings."[3] It was a sentiment that was no doubt shared by a number of intellectuals in the dusk-dawn period of the May Fourth movement. We find, for instance, Hu Shih, an intellectual who saw things quite differently and had his differences with Lu Hsün, telling an American friend in the 1920s:

> Ours is an intermediate generation which must be sacrificed to both our parents and to our children. Unless we would lose all influence, we must marry as our parents wish, girls selected by them for us, whom we may not see before our wedding day—and we must make society happier and healthier for our children to live in. Let that be our reward and consolation.[4]

Perhaps Lu Hsün would have publicly disagreed with what Hu said about arranged marriages (though in private life he submitted to his mother's wishes in this regard); the fact remains, however, that both of these dissimilar May Fourth intellectuals saw the freeing of children for a better life as one of their primary obligations—again a sense of burden, a sense of moral responsibility for China.

2. Ibid., pp. 108-9.
3. Tsi-an Hsia, *The Gate of Darkness* (Seattle: University of Washington Press, 1968), pp. 147-48; *LHCC,* I, 246.
4. In Lewis Gannett, "Hu Shih: Young Prophet of Young China," *New York Times Magazine,* March 27, 1927, p. 10, as quoted in Jerome B. Grieder *Hu Shih and the Chinese Renaissance* (Cambridge, Mass., 1970), p. 12.

Lu Hsün saw the function of his short stories in very serious terms. Even in a purely formal sense, he did not view them exactly as stories. His preface to *Call to Arms* refers to them as "pieces that are something like fiction."[5] And Feng Hsüeh-feng, writing in 1937, remembered Lu Hsün's once having told him: "Even my fiction consists of dissertations; the only difference is that I adapted the short story form to express them."[6] Lu Hsün was a commentator on the classical ideas (if not the classics) of Chinese culture, albeit a very critical and even revolutionary one. No longer able to express himself in commentaries and subcommentaries, living in a transitional period, he used poetry, essays, and the short story to accomplish his ends. He was not just a story teller; he was a philosopher of culture who expressed himself, in part, in stories. And yet, above and beyond the wealth of content in his stories, there is in the best of them a compelling formal and esthetic appeal that arises from the careful planning that went into the structuring of the work, the choice and arrangement of words, and the Spartan (and therefore doubly effective) simplicity in the use of ornamentation and dialogue.

In his student days in Japan, Lu Hsün had written an essay ("The Lopsided Development of Culture") in which he expressed the opinion that both China's weaknesses as well as her strengths were a function of her isolation. It was a belief that he continued to hold, the most noteworthy practical manifestation of it being the prodigious amount of time and effort that he devoted to translating foreign literature into Chinese. Translation provided him with an intimate working knowledge of the structural techniques of authors beyond the walls of his own culture. With great critical acumen, he applied this knowledge to the design of his own works. Thus the form of his stories cannot be explained as a mere continuation of the native short story.

The traditional classical-language tale (the *ch'uan-ch'i* type) was often written to record an interesting anecdote, to record a chunk of history in fictional form, to provide fantasy fulfillment for the reader, or occasionally to show off the literary accomplishments of the writer. With regard to content, far from challenging the

5. *LHCC*, I, 7.
6. Feng Hsüeh-feng, *Kuo-lai-te shih-tai* [The age that has passed] (Shanghai, 1948), p. 22; hereafter cited as *KLTST*.

norms of society, the author of the classical-language tale tended
to take them for granted; with regard to form, he felt free to roam
over thousands of miles and scores of years without the slightest
esthetic compunction, a task that modern literature deems more
suitable to the novelist. In terms of both content and form, Lu
Hsün was unlike the authors of the *ch'uan-ch'i*. Lu Hsün's stories
are also unlike traditional colloquial-language tales in that he did
not present them in stock phrases and devices borrowed from the
tradition of popular storytellers except, of course, in "The True
Story of Ah Q." The traditional storyteller was a popular enter-
tainer who learned his craft through an apprenticeship of imitation; his worth was to be measured not by what he said (with few
exceptions, that was fairly predictable) but by his performance.

In passing, one might suggest that, with the exception of a few
creative geniuses (a Chu Hsi or a Wang Yang-ming), performance
was also the criterion against which the traditional theologian of
culture (the scholar-official) was to be judged. The *shu erh pu-tso*
(transmit-but-not-create)[7] ethic of the big tradition of scholar-
officials permeated Chinese society. Lu Hsün, however, lived in a
period in which the calm righteousness and sense of well-being
that the scholar-officials once enjoyed as a matter of course was no
longer possible. Theology, even the theology of the Confucian
tradition (which was really no theology at all since its bible was
said to have come from men and not God or gods), died in 1905
with the abolition of the examination system. Lu Hsün, as an
in-between intellectual, lived in a transitional period. He himself
was uncertain of the nature of the times:

Alas, alas, if it be dusk, the black night will inexorably come and
engulf me, or otherwise I shall be dispersed by the light of day, should it
be dawn.[8]

Given his historical background, intelligence, and sensitivity, he
could no longer be a cleric in a theological state (he was no longer
a Confucian believer). Therefore he rejected in toto the big
tradition of the scholar-officials who had borne that culture. Even
so, in turning to the little tradition of the oppressed, the ruled, the
common people, and their storytellers he faced a similar problem:

7. Confucius once said that he transmitted the learning of the past, but did not
create anything new.
8. *LHCC*, II, 160-61; *SWLH*, I, 316. From a prose-poem in *Wild Grass*.

the little tradition, though different in detail from the big one, did not essentially deviate from it in spirit. In this regard, Lu Hsün's remark that he was dissatisfied with traditional culture's disdainful treatment of fiction as a frivolous pastime is not to be misread. Traditional fiction, by and large, really was a frivolous pastime. Still it was true that, as Liang Ch'i-ch'ao had pointed out, fiction had a tremendous influence and power in society, and this fact made a deep impression on young Lu Hsün as a student in Japan. Therefore, when he took up fiction as his mode of expression, he was by no means joining the ranks of the traditional storytellers' guilds, nor was he espousing the world view of the little tradition as a replacement for that of the big one. He was, as an intellectual, appropriating from the storytellers a means of expression that was to be more effective in bringing about the reformation of society than traditional commentaries on the classics. Lu Hsün's life-ideal, however, had not radically changed from the ideal of traditional times expressed in the four character expression *nei-sheng wai-wang* ("a sage on the inside, a king on the inside"). The ideal remained that one should be a person who attains wisdom through self-cultivation so as to participate in the task of bringing good order to society at large.

In China there were few models for the intellectual as novelist. Novelists and storytellers had never enjoyed any great prestige, measured against the scholar-officials and their commentarial traditions of scholarship. On the other hand, there were many models available from abroad—hence Lu Hsün's great admiration for the Mara poets and all the writers of oppressed peoples who gave voice to the sufferings of silent masses. In that dusk-dawn period of the 1910s and 1920s, Lu Hsün, in the manner of those foreign novelists whom he admired, used fiction to express his individual viewpoint with regard to the culture in which he lived.[9]

From an abstract point of view, Lu Hsün was writing about the problem of role and self. We all have social roles, parts to play in the society in which we live. But what determines the role? What is the self? "Role" involves society and its norms; "self" involves the individual in relation to society and in isolation from it. In

9. An extensive analysis of the influence of foreign authors on Lu Hsün may be found in Patrick Hanan's article, "The Technique of Lu Hsün's Fiction," *Harvard Journal of Asiatic Studies*, XXXIV (1974), 53-96.

traditional China, Confucianism wrote the script and handed out the roles; Taoism and Buddhism served as critics, critics who asked the ultimate questions of life, death, and meaning. An undercurrent of wonder about such questions lurks beneath the surface meanings of many of Lu Hsün's stories. He expressed this wonder most openly in the prose-poems of *Wild Grass*, but it is to be found in the short stories too and lends them profound meaning.

When Lu Hsün gave up writing short stories after *Wandering*, it might be supposed that the sources of his talent had gone dry, but it is rather more likely that his form of expression changed because his life-style underwent a change. As we have seen, his increasing romantic involvement with Hsü Kuang-p'ing, the young woman who from being one of his students went on to become his wife, coincided with the heightened political involvement that caused him to flee Peking in 1926. Moreover, one ought to remember that during that same period China underwent gigantic changes. The White Terror launched by the Kuomintang against the Communists in 1927 moved vast numbers of intellectuals (especially writers) from the critical periphery of society to its activist center. Then too, it is probable that Kuang-p'ing brought new things into his life which had been noticeably lacking before: love and increasing social involvement. It would seem likely that she enabled him to conquer the sense of loneliness that we see mirrored in "The Isolate" by providing him with the personal warmth of a marriage based on love and by making him a father. During these last years he expressed himself, not in fiction, but in short essays contributed to newspapers and magazines (*tsa-kan*), feeling perhaps that they had a more immediate and a more political impact than fiction.

Lu Hsün never sought to become famous, to be China's Chekhov, Andreyev, or what have you. In addressing alumni of Peking Normal University's Middle School on January 17, 1924 (after the publication of *Call to Arms* but before that of *Wandering*), he spoke out against what he saw as the foolish demand of some that China immediately cough up a literary genius or two:

Then take the "worship of original work." Looked at superficially, this seems quite in keeping with the demand for genius; but such is not the case. It smacks strongly of chauvinism in the realm of ideas, and thus will also cut China off from the current of world opinion. Although many people are already tired of the names of Tolstoy, Turgeniev and Dostoevsky, how many of their books have been translated into Chinese? Those who look no further than our own borders dislike the names Peter and John, and will read only about Third Chang and Fourth Li; thus come the original writers. Actually, the best of them have simply borrowed some technical devices or expressions from foreign authors. However polished their style, their content usually falls far short of translations, and they may even slip in some old ideas to suit the traditional Chinese temperament. Their readers fall into this trap, their views becoming more and more confined until they almost slip back between the old traces. When such a vicious circle exists between writers and readers for the abolition of all that is different and the glorification of the national culture, how can genius be produced? Even if one were to appear, he could not survive.[10]

He wanted to pull China out of its cultural isolation, just as he sought to break down the walls of his own emotional loneliness. Addressing the Chinese Literature Society of Yenching University on May 22, 1929, he said, "It is no easier to translate than to turn out sloppy writing, but it makes a greater contribution to the development of our new literature, and is more useful to our people."[11] Later, when Feng Hsüeh-feng chided him for not writing a novel (he had planned one or two, but never started on them), he replied:

I can't do everything by myself. Great novels are, of course, very important from the viewpoint of cultural significance. But there are other people still left around to do that. I'll just go on *tsa-kan*-ing my way along.[12]

He turned away from creative writing because both he and China had changed. His lifelong aim was to change China; everything else was secondary to that.

Some who read Lu Hsün in English translation object that his stories seem too autobiographical. Perhaps this judgment arises from the fact that he often chose to narrate them in an ostensibly personal manner. Moreover, every writer must, after all, cull experiences from his own life if his stories are to have any claim to versimilitude. And Lu Hsün's stories, however else one may

10. *SWLH*, II, 79; *LHCC*, I, 276-77.
11. *SWLH*, III, 49; *LHCC*, IV, 110.
12. *KLTST*, p. 24.

cricitize them, do have that. François Mauriac has observed that the heroes of fiction are "born of marriage that the novelist contracts with reality."[13] The fictional progeny of Lu Hsün's alliance with reality was a series of diverse characters—male or female, lettered or unlettered, exalted or base—that stalk the pages of his short stories with a disturbing aura of versimilitude. One cannot dismiss them as sheer creatures of imagination. A rare concatenation of individual talent and historical circumstances enabled Lu Hsün to contract a peculiar marriage with reality out of which those characters were born.

He seems to have had an accurate perception of his place in history in an interim generation. His working life was dedicated to a critique of the traditional establishment. (One is reminded of early thinkers of the "School of Han Learning" in the transitional period that covered the end of the Ming and the beginning of the Ch'ing dynasties—thinkers who had enjoyed a somewhat similar interim holiday from orthodoxy during which they were free to view the collective past from a new perspective.) Since 1949, writers have been expected to be, not critics of the state, but propagandists for its new orthodoxy. Whatever one may think of the philosophy of Marx and Lenin as interpreted and expanded by chairman Mao, it is clear that another of those brief dusk-dawn intervals in the history of China where intellectual pluralism thrives is over. Ideology and state are once again united.

Lu Hsün, without retreating into certainties of the past or escaping into fantasies of the future, accepted his place in time. This acceptance of the "nowness" of that period lent spiritual weight to his writings and thought. Lending his voice to the silent suffering of the Chinese people, he took his place in the long line of Mara poets that he had come to admire as a young man in Japan.

It was Lu Hsün's fate to face that from which others averted their gaze and to speak those things which others avoided mentioning. He did not do this lightly; his vision of reality was not won without pain and loss. He viewed Chinese society with a mixture of indignation and compassion; he condemned it so bitterly because he loved it so well. As Maxim Gorky said of Chekhov's relation to the Russian people, one might say of Lu Hsün's relation to the Chinese:

13. *Le Romancier et ses personnages* (Paris, 1933), pp. 95-96.

In front of that dreary, gray crowd of helpless people there passed a great, wise, and observant man; he looked at all these dreary inhabitants of his country, and with a sad smile, with a tone of gentle but deep reproach, with anguish in his face and in his heart, in a beautiful and sincere voice, he said to them: "You live badly, my friends. It is shameful to live like that."[14]

14. David Magarshack, trans. *Reminiscences of Tolstoy, Chekhov, and Andreyev* (New York, 1959), pp. 84-85.

APPENDIX

REMEMBRANCES OF THE PAST
(*Huai-chiu*)

Outside the gate at our house there stood a tung tree which was about thirty feet tall. Once a year fruit would cover it like stars spread out on an evening sky and the children would try to knock them down with small stones—stones that often continued in flight until they came through the open window of the family study and occasionally landed on my desk. Whenever that happened, my teacher, Master Baldy, would run outside and scold the children. The leaves of that tree were almost a full foot in diameter and used to close up like fists in the heat of the summer sun; but when the night air settled in, they would revive again, looking like so many hands opening up and stretching out.

The family gatekeeper, Old Wang, would draw water from the well and damp down the ground in order to dissipate the residual heat of a summer's day. Sometimes he would grab up his pipe and a dilapidated old stool to go off and swap stories with old Amah Li. They would still be trading tales when the moon had set and the only light to be seen was provided by the embers in old Wang's pipe.

Once while Old Wang and Amah Li were thus enjoying the first cool of the evening, Master Baldy was just in the midst of having me do an exercise in poetic composition. He chose a two-word expression for which I was expected to provide an antithetical response. He picked the words "red blossom" and I came back with "green tung." He waved my response aside, saying that I had violated the rules of poetic tonality, and ordered me to go back to my seat and do it over again. At the time I was only nine and had not the vaguest notion of what was meant by "poetic tonality" nor had he ever explained it to me. But for the time being I went back to my seat and wracked my brains at length without managing to come up with anything. Slowly I stretched my hand out, fingers wide, and brought it down hard against my thigh, making a loud slap as though I had just swatted a mosquito. I hoped thus to attract Master Baldy's attention to the trouble I was having in coming up with an answer, but he still didn't pay me the least bit of attention. After a long time he finally called out in those drawn-out pedantic tones of his: "C-o-m-e h-e-r-e." I moved forward smartly and he wrote out the two words "green grass" for me.

" 'Red' and 'flower' are both even tones," he said, "and ought to be balanced by 'green,' which is an entering tone, and 'grass,' which is a low tone. All right. That will do for today." Not waiting to be told twice, I started bounding out of the room. Master Baldy raised his voice again: "No jumping about." I continued on out, though refraining from anything resembling a jump.

I went outside, but no longer dared to play under the tung tree. Previously I used to go there quite often and tug at Old Wang's knees to get him to tell me stories about the mountain people, but Baldy would invariably follow, screw up his face and say: "What a lad! You ought not to waste so much time fooling around. If you've had your supper, why not go back and do your home-work!" If I didn't obey him instantly, he would whack me on the head with a pointer the next day and demand: "Why are you so mischievous at your play and so stupid at your studies?" Since it was obvious that my Master Baldy saw his classroom as a place for evening-up old scores, I gradually came to dread going to school. Since tomorrow wasn't a holiday, what did I have to look forward to? If only early in the morning I were to be taken ill and then get well again in the afternoon, then I could have a good half day's vacation. Better yet, let Baldy be taken ill; or still better, just let him die! If neither illness nor death overtook him, however, then there would be nothing for it but to go to school the next day and study the *Analects* of Confucius.

Sure enough, Baldy was there the very next morning, testing me on the *Analects* and wagging his head back and forth as he explained the meaning of the characters. Baldy was so nearsighted that his lips almost touched the book, as though he were about to gnaw a few pieces out of it. People often accused me of being mischievous and were fond of saying that before I had finished half a chapter of a book, the pages were sure to be in a state of terrible disrepair. If they had only known that all that huffing and puffing from Master Baldy's flaring nostrils did more damage to my book than I ever could have done! After all the working-over that he gave a text with his snorting, how could one expect the pages to be anything but raggedy? Of course the characters had become indecipherable; they had been "breathed" into indecipherability by old Baldy! No matter how mischievous I may have been, I would never have been able to mess up my book the way that he did.

Master Baldy said: "Confucius said, 'When I was sixty my *erh* was in tune.' That's the *erh* in *erh-tuo* of our spoken language, meaning 'ear.' Confucius said that when he was seventy he could freely follow the desires of his heart without exceeding the proper bounds of, uh, uh—morality." I didn't follow his explanations of the text because most of the words were so obscured by the shadow of his nose that I couldn't even see them. The only thing that I was conscious of was that the title *Analects* was capped by the Master's bald head—so glittering and bright that I could see my face in it, albeit somewhat indistinctly, not nearly as clearly as in the old pond out in the backyard.

When he had been explaining for a long time, Baldy would wobble his knees in rhythm with the cadences of the text and nod his head in great sweeps, apparently enjoying himself immensely. I, on the other hand, was getting very bored. To be sure, the light given off by his head was, in itself, interesting enough to hold one's attention, but if you looked at it long enough, you got tired of that too. How could I take it much longer? Fortunately, at this very juncture, from outside the door there came a strange voice: "Master Yang-sheng! Master Yang-sheng!" It sounded as though it came from a man who had just witnessed a disaster and was calling for help.

"Yao-tsung, my honored friend, is it you? Come in!" The Master stopped lecturing on the *Analects*, raised his head, and went out to open the gate and bow in salutation.

At first I was at a loss to understand why the Master should treat Yao-tsung with such deference. Yao-tsung came from the

Chin clan, our very wealthy neighbors to the east. Yet he wore very seedy clothes and broken-down old shoes. Since he lived on a meatless diet to save money, his face was as yellow and swollen as an autumn eggplant. Even Old Wang did not go out of his way to be courteous, and once said of him: "That fellow's only talent is hoarding money. But since he never parts with a penny of it, why should we treat him with deference?" Old Wang treated *me* very well, but was unusually disdainful of Yao-tsung; and yet Yao-tsung never really seemed to notice it.

Actually, in intelligence he was no match for Old Wang. For whenever Yao-tsung listened to people telling stories, for the most part he was unable to follow them, but would not his head anyway and say: "I see, I see." Moreover, Amah Li once told me that, from infancy to manhood, Yao-tsung had been tied so close to his parents that you would have thought he was their prisoner. He never got out of the house to meet people, and hence was a very clumsy conversationalist. If the talk turned to rice, then he would say something about rice, but he didn't know the difference between ordinary rice and the glutinous kind; if the talk turned to fish, then he would manage to say something about fish too, but he didn't know the difference between a bream and a carp. Sometimes when he didn't understand, you would have to give him several pages of the kind of commentary that the scholars do on the classics. Even then there would probably be much in the commentary that didn't get through to him, and you have to provide him with a sub-commentary. But even in the sub-commentary there would, no doubt, still be words that would prove too difficult for him and in the end you would have to drop the whole subject without his having gotten any of it. Since that's the kind of fellow he was, none of us really liked to talk with him.

And yet, much to the amazement of Old Wang and the others, Master Baldy was very partial to him. In the privacy of my own mind, I too sought out the logic for this odd affection. I remembered that in the past Yao-tsung, having reached the ripe old age of twenty-one without having sired a son, had taken three pretty concubines into his household. Baldy had also started mouthing the saying "There are three things that are unfilial and to lack posterity is the greatest of these" as if to justify Yao-tsung's conduct. The latter was so moved by this that he gave Baldy twenty-one pieces of gold so that he too could buy a secondary wife. Thus I concluded that Baldy's reason for treating Yao-tsung with such unusual courtesy was that the latter had shown himself to be thoroughly filial. Although Old Wang was wise in his own way, he was not, after all, so learned as Master Baldy. No wonder that he hadn't been able to fathom the depths of my teacher's wisdom. Even I had to wrack my brains for a good many days before coming up with an explanation for Baldy's strange partiality.

"Master Yang-sheng, have you heard the news today?"

"News? No, not yet. What news?"

"The Long Hairs are coming!"

"Long Hairs? Ha-ha, you must be joking."

What Yao-tsung meant by the Long Hairs was what Baldy called the "Hairy Rebels." Old Wang called them that too. They were the rebels who came around away back during the Taiping Rebellion. Old Wang told me that he was just thirty at the time, and since he was past seventy now, that must have been over forty years ago. Even a lad of nine like myself knew through simple arithmetic that there couldn't be Long Hairs around anymore.

"But I got the news from His Third Excellency over at Ho market. He said that they would be here any day now."

"His Third Excellency? Then you got the news from the government prefect! In that case it won't do not to be on our guard!" Old Baldy held His Third Excellency in even higher esteem than the sages of antiquity; therefore, upon hearing this, his face suddenly changed color and he began to pace round the desk.

"He said that there were some eight hundred of them. I've already sent one of my servants over to Ho market to see what's going on and to try to find out when the rebels will actually arrive."

"Eight hundred Long Hairs? How could that possibly be? Oh, maybe he means the bandits of Mount Tai or the Red Turbans hereabouts."

Master Baldy's brain was in control again and even he realized that they couldn't be Long Hairs. But what he didn't realize was that when Yao-tsung spoke, he lumped mountain bandits, ocean pirates, White Hats, and Red Turbans all together as "Long Hairs," just as he lumped carp and bream together as "fish." Hence when Master Baldy began making distinctions between Red Turbans and Long Hairs, it all went right over Yao-tsung's head.

"We ought to have food prepared against their arrival. The reception hall in my home is only large enough to accomodate half of them, so I have made arrangements to use the Chang Sui-yang temple to feast the other half. Once they've had a good meal, they may be in a mood to issue the usual rebel proclamation stating that they intend the populace no harm." Yao-tsung was pretty thick about most things, but at least his family had managed to inculcate in him the time-honored technique of feasting invading armies. Old Wang too had once said that when his father encountered the Long Hairs, he kowtowed to them and begged for his life. In order to thoroughly convince them of his submission he had kept knocking his head on the ground until he had raised a big, ugly lump on it. But at least the Long Hairs had not killed him. Elaborating on the technique of feeding invading armies, old Wang's father had even gone a step farther and opened a kitchen to provide them with food. As a result the Long Hairs had become especially fond of him and he, in turn, had made a great deal of money. When they were finally defeated, he managed to get away from them, became wealthy in his own right, and finally settled down in Wu town. Thus, in a sense, Yao-tsung's plan of protecting the populace with a single feast was not nearly so farsighted as the strategem that Old Wang's father had employed.

"The fate of such enemies is always short. Read through all of our history and how many times do you find instances of such rebels succeeding in the end? Only a very few isolated examples. There's nothing wrong with feasting them, but Yao-tsung, my esteemed elder brother, see to it that you don't get your name linked up with theirs. Let the village headman arrange the matter of the feast."

"I'll do just as you say. By the way, Master Yang-sheng, could you write the two characters 'Obedient Subject' on a poster that I can tack up on my gate?"

"Don't do anything like that right now. There's no point in being too hasty about such things. If, after all, the rebels actually do arrive, there'll still be plenty of time for writing 'Obedient Subject' posters to welcome them. Elder Brother Yao-tsung, there is still something else that you ought to bear in mind. While it is true that one can't risk incurring the anger of these rebels, it is also true that it doesn't do to be too close to them. Way back when the Long Hair rebels came, occasionally even 'Obedient Subject' posters didn't save the homes of the people who posted them. And then when the government armies came back into the area, such families were really in trouble. We had better wait until the rebels are on the outskirts of Wu town before taking up this business of posters. The only thing that you ought to worry about now is seeing to it that your family finds a safe hiding place as quickly as possible, but don't pick a place too far away."

"You're perfectly right. Well, I'm off now to the Chang Sui-yang temple to tell monk Chang of my plans." Seeming to half-understand what Master Baldy had told him, Yao-tsung took his leave in a flurry of expressions of appreciation for Master Baldy's advice.

People used to say that my teacher, Master Baldy, was the wisest man in all Wu town. They really had something there, for he could have lived in any age of chaos and come through it without the slightest scratch. From the time when P'an Ku created the universe on down through generation after generation of fighting and killing, through alternations of peace and war, through the waxing and waning of dynasties, Master Baldy's forbears had never laid down their lives to preserve a government, nor had they lost their lives by joining rebel causes. Their line had survived down to this very day and now one of them, Master Baldy, was an honored teacher who expounded to mischievous students like myself on the wisdom of Confucius—a man who had been able at the age of seventy to follow all of his heart's desires without exceeding the proper bounds of morality. If one were to explain Baldy's talent for survival on the basis of the modern theory of evolution, then one might attribute his talent to racial heredity. But in retrospect, as I see it today, his peculiar talent must have been gained entirely from books. Otherwise how could you have explained the fact that neither Old Wang, Amah Li, nor myself had inherited this kind of talent? None of us could have even distantly approximated the thoroughness of thought that he had exhibited in his advice to Yao-tsung.

After Yao-tsung left, Baldy did not resume his explanation of the *Analects*. Looking rather distressed, he said that he was going home and dismissed me from class. In very high spirits, I bounded out to the tung tree. Although the summer sun scorched my head as I ran about, I didn't mind in the least. For now the territory around the old tung tree was completely mine and was—for this precious time at least—safe from the incursions of Baldy! Before long I saw my teacher hurrying away with a big bundle of clothes under his arm. Normally he would only go home on the occasion of a special holiday or at New Year's; at such times he would invariably take several volumes of a text on how to write those deadly eight-part essays that one had to compose when taking the civil service examinations. But this time the entire set of the text stood sternly on his desk. He had taken with him only the shoes and clothing that he kept stored in that broken-down trunk of his.

I noticed that there were more people on the road than ants on an ant hill. They all seemed frightened and were wandering about as if they couldn't decide which way to go. Most were carrying things, though a few were empty-handed. Old Wang told me that they were probably preparing to flee the impending difficulties. I noticed that among them were quite a few people from Ho market who were apparently fleeing to Wu town; the residents of Wu town, on the other hand, were obviously fleeing in the direction of Ho market! Old Wang told me that he had been through this kind of thing before and there was no reason to get excited prematurely.

Amah Li had gone over to the Chin family compound to see what news she could get. Now she came back to report that the servants had not yet left to go back to their own families, but there was a swarm of concubines in the midst of gathering up cosmetics, perfumes, silk fans, and sheer silk gowns, all of which they stuffed into their bamboo traveling-cases. These, of course, were the women of the wealthy; it seemed that they took being refugees with all the seriousness of going on a spring outing. On a spring outing, of course, one simply couldn't go without lipstick and eyebrow pencil!

I didn't have time to waste on listening to Amah Li and Old Wang prattle on about the business of the Long Hairs; instead, I went off by myself and caught flies with which I baited ants out from their nests and then trampled them with my foot. then I ladled out a bowl of water and flooded them in order to get those ants who had survived my first onslaught by remaining securely at the bottom of the nest. Before long I saw the sun suddenly drop behind the branches of the trees and heard Amah Li call me to dinner. I couldn't understand why the day had been so short. Ordinarily at this time of day I would have been wracking my brains for an antithetical response to a pair of characters selected by Master Baldy and would have to watch him making a tired face while he waited for my answer.

When the meal was over, Amah Li took me out into the yard. Old Wang had also come out to cool off. All of this was very commonplace; the only unusual thing was that there was a group of local people gathered about him with their mouths hanging wide open as though they had just been frightened by some sort of monster. The beautiful moonlight fell on the multitudinous teeth of the crowd, highlighting their irregularity and discoloration: one rather imagined a display of colored jade. Old Wang smoked and spoke in a very slow and relaxed manner.

"At that time the gatekeeper here was Fifth Uncle Chao. That guy was really thick. When the master of the house heard that the Long Hairs were on the way, he ordered everyone to flee for his life. And what do you think Chao said? 'But if the master leaves, then there won't be anyone here to look after things. I'll have to stay so that those ruffians don't take over the house.' "

"Wow, what a stupid lout!" Amah Li suddenly cried out, hardly able to believer her ears, and glad of the opportunity to castigate roundly the shortcomings of a "former sage" like Fifth Uncle Chao.

"And old lady Wu, the cook, didn't leave either. She must have been seventy-some at the time. She holed up in the kitchen and wouldn't come out for dear life. For several days she heard only the sound of people walking by and dogs barking in the distance, sounds that were unbearably sad and fearful. Then even those sounds stopped, and the atmosphere in the kitchen became so spooky that she thought that she was already in the world of the dead. One day she heard the sound of marching men in the far distance; then she heard the sound of the same men as they marched past outside the wall of the family compound.

"Before long, dozens of Long Hairs suddenly burst into the kitchen. Knives in hand, they dragged old lady Wu outside. Their speech was so guttural that she could barely make it out. They seemed to be saying: 'Old woman! Where's your master? Hurry and bring us whatever money there is.' Old lady Wu bowed and said: 'Great king, our master has run away. The old woman standing before you has herself gone hungry for many days and now beseeches the great king to give her a bit to eat.' One of the Long Hairs laughed and said, 'If you really want something to eat, then we ought to feed you!' With a sudden movement he threw something round into old lady Wu's bosom. It was so matted with blood that one could barely make out what it was—Fifth Uncle Chao's head!"

"Aiya! Old lady Wu must have been almost dead of fright!" Once again Amah Li interrupted his narration with a frightened cry. The listeners standing around him also popped their eyes out a bit farther, and their mouths opened even wider.

"It probably happened something like this. Fifth Uncle Chao steadfastly refused to open up, and instead reviled the intruders, saying: 'You only want to get in to loot the place anyway.' Then the Long Hairs—"

"Is there any news yet?" someone asked, having noticed that Baldy had just returned. I thought that I was in for it, but when I examined Baldy's expression, I noticed that it was not nearly as stern as usual; hence I did not follow my first inclination to skulk away. I was thinking that if only the Long Hairs would come again and toss Baldy's head into the arms of Amah Li, then I could spend every day in flooding ant nests and would not have to study the *Analects* anymore!

"No, it's too early for news yet," Old Wang observed and then continued with his narration. "Then the Long Hairs smashed down the door. When Fifth Uncle Chao came out to see what the rebels looked like, he was frightened out of his wits. Then the Long Hairs—"

"Master Yang-sheng! My servant has returned!" Yao-tsung shouted at the top of his voice as he entered our family compound.

"Well, how do things stand?" Baldy asked the question as he went forward to greet his friend; his nearsighted eyes were popped wide open so that they looked much larger than I had ever seen them before. Along with the others, I hurried toward Yao-tsung for the news.

"His Third Excellency said that the business about the Long Hairs turned out to be nothing more than a rumor. Actually it was only a large group of refugees fleeing through Ho market. By 'refugees' His Excellency probably meant the kind of people who often come round to our homes begging for food." Yao-tsung, fearful lest the crowd not understand the word "refugee," used all the knowledge at his command to define it for them. And all that knowledge was just barely enough to fill a single sentence.

"Ha-ha! So it's only refugees! Ah . . ." Baldy laughed as though he were making fun of his own previous stupidity in having gotten so excited. He began to laugh at the idea of "refugees," for that was not frightening at all. The crowd of local people that had gathered began to laugh too; it wasn't that they had understood what was going on, but rather that, having seen an important person like Baldy laugh, they felt that it was their place to join in.

After having obtained accurate news from His Third Excellency, the crowd dispersed in a lighthearted atmostphere. Yao-tsung went back home too. Suddenly the atmosphere under the tung tree was rather lonely. Only Old Wang and a few others were left. Old Baldy paced around for a long time and then announced that he was going home with the news in order to reassure his own family. Saying that he would be back in the morning, he gathered up his volumes on how to write the eight-part essay and headed for the gate. Just before leaving, he looked at me and said: "Since you haven't studied the livelong day, how do you expect to have the text memorized well enough to recite for me in the morning? Hurry up and get back to your books and stop being so mischievous." Feeling more and more depressed, I fixed my eyes on the glow in Old Wang's pipe in order to avoid having to answer him. Old Wang continued smoking. The flickering light in his pipe reminded me of an autumn firefly fallen into a pile of grass; then I remembered how the summer before I had fallen into a pond of reeds while trying to catch one. Thinking about these things, I managed to put Baldy completely out of mind.

"Eh, how many times have I heard people say, 'The Long Hairs are coming'? When the Long Hairs really did come, it was terrifying. But what did it amount to, after all?" Old Wang stopped smoking and sat there slowly nodding his head in reminiscence.

"Old man, did you ever really see the Long Hairs? What were they like?" There was a sense of urgency in Amah Li's voice.

"Were you ever a Long Hair yourself?" I asked hopefully. I thought that if the Long Hairs came, then surely Baldy would have to go. In that case, the Long Hairs must be good people. Since Old Wang was so good to me, I reasoned, he must have been a Long Hair once himself.

"Ha-ha. No, I wasn't. By the way, Amah Li, how old were you at the time? I must have been twenty-some myself."

"I was only eleven. When it happened my mother took me and fled to P'ing T'ien so that I never had a chance to see what the Long Hairs really looked like."

"I ran away to Mount Huang, myself. When the Long Hairs got

to my village I happened to be away. A neighbor of mine, Fourth
Niu, and two of my cousins didn't get out in time and were taken
prisoner by some of the Long Hairs. They dragged them out onto
the T'ai P'ing Bridge and cut their throats; they were still alive
when the Long Hairs pushed them into the water. That Fourth Niu
was really something; he could carry almost three hundred pounds
of rice for a whole half-mile! They don't make men like that any
more. By the time I got to Mount Huang it was almost evening.
The sun was not yet touching the tops of the tall trees on top of the
mountain, but the rice fields at the foot of the mountain were
already enveloped in the dusk and were a much richer green than
they are during the day. When I got to the foot of the mountain, I
stopped to look back. Fortunately nobody had followed me, and I
felt somewhat safer. But looking ahead and not seeing a soul in
sight, I felt both lonely and sad at the same time. After a bit I
managed to calm down. The night was closing in around me and I
felt even more isolated. I couldn't hear the sound of human voices
anywhere, but I did hear *jer-jer wang-wang-wang!*"

"*Wang-wang?*" I was confused and the question escaped my lips
unconsciously. Amah Li gripped my hand to signal me to be quiet,
as though what I had in the back of my mind would bring calamity
down upon her if I spoke it out.

"It was only a frog. I also heard the hooting of owls and that
was really a weird sound . . . Say, Amah, Li, do you know that a
lone tree in the darkness looks very much like a man? Ha-ha, but
when you take a closer look, there's really nobody there. We were
terrified of the Long Hairs when they first came, yet when they fell
back in retreat and we villagers pursued them with spades and
hoes, then a hundred of them wouldn't dare to stand and fight ten
of us. Later on people went fishing for treasures every day. Isn't
that the way that His Third excellency from Ho market got so
rich?"

"What's 'fishing for treasures'?" I was confused again.

"Oh, 'fishing for treasures'? Well, you see, whenever we villagers were right on the heels of a group of Long Hairs, they would
throw down whatever gold, silver, and precious stones they had in
order to slow down our pursuit. They knew that we'd all scramble
for such things. I myself once got a very bright pearl. It must have
been as big as a good-sized bean, but I scarcely had a chance to
express my surprise and delight when that Second Niu clobbered

me with a stick and made off with it! Otherwise, though I'd never have gotten as wealthy as His Third Excellency, at least I would have been comfortably off.

"Ho Kou-pao, His Third Excellency's father, got back to Ho market at just about that time. When he got home he spotted a Long Hair who had tied up his hair into a large pigtail and was lying in wait in one of the closets that had been broken into. Then he—"

"Oh, oh, it's raining. We'd better go in and go to bed." Amah Li, seeing the rain, had decided to go in.

"No, no! Let's stay here!" I didn't feel at all like going in. I felt much as I did when I reached the end of a chapter in a novel. Just when the hero was in the most precarious situation, the novelist would close the chapter with the words: "If you want to find out what happened after this, then turn to the next chapter." I would usually not only turn to the next chapter, but would read straight through the whole volume. Amah Li was apparently not like me in this respect.

"Come on now, let's go in and that's an end to it! If you get up late tomorrow, you'll get a good taste of Master Baldy's pointer."

As I put my head down on the pillow I heard the rain come down harder and beat against the giant leaves of the banana palm in front of my window. I remember thinking how much it sounded like crabs crawling across the sand.

"Don't hit me, Master Baldy, I promise that I'll prepare my lesson next time . . ."

"Hey, what's going on here? Are you dreaming? With all that shouting of yours you scared me right out of my own nightmare. What are you dreaming about?" Amah Li came to my bed and patted me on the back.

"Oh, it was just a dream. It didn't really happen. Amah Li, what were you dreaming about?"

"I was dreaming about the Long Hairs. I'll tell you about it tomorrow. It's almost midnight. Go to sleep now, go to sleep."

A Note on the Translation

The preceding translation is based on a copy of the original in the *Short Story Magazine* (Vol. IV, no. 1, 1913), obtained through the Photoduplication Service of the Library of Congress. The story was published under the pen name Chou Ch'o. On the whole I have done an interpretive translation, trying to bring out for the English reader those elements which a reader of the original would have filled in for himself. The story has been translated into English once before, by Feng Yu-sing, as "Looking Back to the Past" (*T'ien Hsia Monthly*, VI, no. 2, [February 1938], 148-59). I feel that the present translation is more successful in bringing out the tone and feel of the prose; also it is complete (Feng makes some deletions, the most important one consisting of the narrator's aside on the theory of evolution).

SOME RABBITS AND A CAT
(T'u ho mao)

During the summer, San T'ai-t'ai [Third Brother's Wife],[1] who lives in the rear courtyard, bought a pair of white bunnies for her children. Apparently they had not been long separated from their mother, for a man, although belonging to a different species, could plainly see that they were still extremely naive and trustingly open. And yet when they erected their long pink ears and twitched their nostrils, the expression in their eyes was still rather timid. After all, this new environment was no doubt somewhat strange to them and they felt less secure than they had back home.

If one were to wait until there was a temple fair and then go out and bargain for a pair of small animals like that oneself, they would have only cost two strings of cash apiece at the most, but San T'ai-t'ai had sent a servant to a regular store to buy them for her and hence they had cost a dollar each.

The children, of course, were delighted and chattered excitedly as they gathered round in a circle to watch them; the adults all stood around to observe them too. Even a little dog called "S" came running up and barged in to take a few sniffs which immediately made him sneeze and back off. San T'ai-t'ai scolded him: "S, you listen. You are *not* allowed to bite those bunnies!" She slapped him on top of the head. "S" ran off and never bothered the rabbits again.

She kept them shut up in the little yard out behind the back window most of the time—from what I heard this was because they had shown themselves overly fond of scratching at the wallpaper and gnawing on the legs of the furniture when she kept them inside.

There was a wild mulberry growing in the little yard and when the berries fell off the bunnies would gorge themselves, refusing to

1. This undoubtedly reflects the Japanese wife of Chou Chien-jen, third of the Chou brothers; she was Habuto Nobuko's younger sister.

so much as touch the spinach that had been bought for them. When crows or magpies would try to come down for their share of the berries, the bunnies would arch their backs, suddenly extend their powerful hind legs and, sinews cracking, leap straight up like a spiral of snow taking off into the sky. The crows and magpies would immediately be scared off and after a few doses of that they didn't even dare to come close anymore. San T'ai-t'ai said that she wasn't all that worried about the crows and magpies in the first place. The worst they could do would be to steal a bit of the bunnies' food. What she'd really have to guard against was that obnoxious big black cat who often perched on top of the low courtyard wall, casting savage glances at the bunnies. Fortunately "S" was the cat's natural enemy; perhaps he would serve as a check on the cat so that nothing would go amiss after all.

The children often grabbed them up to play with, and the bunnies on their part were quite friendly. Ears up and noses twitching, they'd tamely remain in encircling hands, but if those hands relaxed long enough to provide an escape route, they'd slip through and scamper away. Their bed at night was a pad of straw in a small wooden crate under the eaves outside the back window.

After things had gone on like this for several months, the now-grown pair of rabbits suddenly began digging their own burrow. They did it with amazing speed, clawing their way in with their front paws and kicking the dirt out with their back ones so that before the day was even half out they had finished a deep burrow. Everybody wondered what it was all about until later, upon closer inspection, it was noticed that one rabbit's belly was considerably larger than the other's. The next day they spent most of their time busily carrying straw and leaves into the burrow.

Everyone was very happy and said that soon we'd have more bunnies to enjoy; San T'ai-t'ai now issued a stern injunction to the children forbidding them to pick up the rabbits. My mother was also very pleased at their fecundity and even said that after the new litter was weaned, she planned on asking for one or two to raise outside her own window.

From then on they kept to the confines of the burrow they had fashioned for themselves, occasionally venturing forth to get a little something to eat. Then they disappeared entirely and we couldn't figure out whether it was because they had stored so much down there that they didn't need to come out, or whether they had simply stopped eating. After another ten days or so, San

T'ai-t'ai told me that the pair had come out again. She assumed that the litter had been born and all died, for though there were many teats visible on the female, there was no evidence that she ever went into the burrow to nurse any young. San T'ai-t'ai seemed rather put out about it as she spoke, but of course there was nothing that she could do.

One balmy day when there was no breeze and not a leaf stirred on any of the trees, I suddenly heard some people laughing over at San T'ai-t'ai's place. When I got to where the sound was coming from I found several people leaning out her back window watching something outside. It turned out to be a bunny bounding about in the courtyard, a bunny that was much smaller than his parents had been when San T'ai-t'ai had first bought them. And yet by firing his hind legs out behind him, he was already able to leap up in the air. The children all competed to be first to tell me that they had seen another little bunny come to the opening of the burrow and poke his head out to look around, but then he had immediately shrunk back into the burrow; he must have been the younger brother of the one in the courtyard.

The latter began gathering bits of grass, but it seemed that his elders would not allow it; they kept pulling it out of his mouth, without however eating it themselves. The children laughed so loudly at this that they startled the young bunny; he bounded over to the hole and started to burrow in. The adult pair followed him and one of them, placing his forepaws on the youngster's spine, helped push him on through. Once they were all inside one of the parents loosened some of the clay around the hole and used it to close up the entrance to the burrow.

After this the little courtyard was more lively than ever and people were often to be seen at San T'ai-t'ai's back window peeking out at the rabbits. And then, old and young alike, the rabbits all disappeared again. San T'ai-t'ai began worrying again that that big black cat had done them in. We were having a cloudy spell at the time and I maintained that it had nothing to do with the big black cat, but it was simply because it was chilly; they were quite naturally all holed up down there to keep warm and when the sun came out again so would they.

When the sun did come out again, however, they were nowhere to be seen. At this point everyone forgot about them. San T'ai-t'ai continued to think of them, however, because she was the one who always went to the burrow to feed them their spinach. One day when she went into the small courtyard outside her back window she suddenly discovered a new hole at the base of the courtyard wall. When she inspected the entrance of the burrow itself, she detected faint paw prints, prints that looked far too large to have been made by one of the adult rabbits. Her mind turned uneasily to the big black cat who so often sat on top of the low wall. At this point she had no choice but to screw up her courage and resolve to excavate the burrow. At last she got a hoe and dug straight down into it. Although she had her doubts, she still hoped against hope that she would be surprised and find live rabbits down there; when she reached the bottom, however, all she saw was a pile of rotten straw with some bunny fur matted in it. The straw had probably been spread there when the female was about to give birth to her litter. Apart from those faint reminders, however, the burrow was utterly desolate. There was not the slightest trace of that snow-white bunny who had, not long previously, frolicked in the courtyard or of his younger brother who had once looked outside but had never ventured forth from the nest.

A combination of anger, disappointment, and a feeling of emptiness so worked upon San T'ai-t'ai that she had no choice but the excavate the new hole at the foot of the wall too. She had no sooner started to dig than the two large white rabbits wriggled out of the hole. San T'ai-t'ai, thinking that they had simply moved house, was very happy. She continued digging and when she reached the bottom, she found a fresh mattress of grass and fur spread out there; sleeping on top of it were seven tiny baby bunnies, bodies all flesh pink! Taking a closer look she discovered that their eyes were still closed.

Now she began to understand all that had happened and realized that it was just as she had feared. In order to guard against future danger she took all seven baby bunnies, placed them in a wooden crate which she then moved into her own room. She even put the parents into the box and forced the mother to nurse the babies.

From then on San T'ai-t'ai not only detsted the black cat but was also more than a little put out with the parent rabbits. As she saw it there must have been more bunnies in that first litter than just those two who had been done in by the cat because a rabbit litter could not possibly consist of only two. Since the mother didn't nurse evenly, those in the first litter who had not been aggressive enough to get a teat had probably died long before the cat got the two that we had all seen. She probably had something there because two of the seven in this new litter were very skinny and weak. That was the reason that San T'ai-t'ai now made it a point to grab up the mother rabbit whenever she had a bit of spare time and then put the seven bunnies to her teats one after the other, not allowing any one to get more than another.

My mother told me that she had never in her whole life even heard of, much less seen, such a fussy way of feeding rabbits; she even thought that it might be worth putting into a book of records.

The family of white rabbits continued to thrive and everyone was happy again. And yet after that I was somehow or other beset by a depression that I couldn't shake. At midnight I sat by the light of my lamp and mused over how those two tiny lives had long since been lost at some unknown time without anyone's even knowing about it, with no evidence of the fact that they once had lived. "S" hadn't even so much as barked.

That started me remembering things out of the past, of how I had once gotten up early when I was living at the hostel and had seen a chaotic pile of pigeon feathers under the big locust tree— obviously the leftovers from a hawk's feast. Later the same morning, the janitor came and swept it all up without leaving a trace; no one would have ever guessed that a life had been cut down there under that very tree. Then I recalled too how once when I had been going past the West Fourth Gate, a little dog caught my eye that had been run over by a horse cart and was just breathing its last. Later that day when I was coming back by the same route, there was nothing; the carcass had no doubt been cleared away and the pedestrians passing by merely hurried along their way. Who would have ever guessed that a life had recently been cut off there by the gate. I recalled how on a summer's night I often heard the long drawn-out buzz of a fly outside my window, trapped no doubt in a spider's web, crying out as the spider bit into it. And yet I was never really all that bothered by the sound and other people weren't even conscious of it to begin with.

If one can call the Creator to accounts, then I think he ought to be blamed for being too prodigal in the creation of life and too prodigal in its destruction.

Yeow . . . A pair of cats fighting again outside my window.

"Hsün-er, is that you beating up on a cat again?"

"No, they're laying into each other. Why in the world would I hit them?"

My mother had long been put out with me for the way I treated cats. She had probably gotten out of bed to ask because she suspected that I was avenging those two bunnies in some particularly vicious way. Furthermore, I had the reputation in the family of being a real enemy of the feline world. I had been known to do them real violence in the past and even ordinarily I would strike them when I had a chance—especially when they were mating. But the reason that I struck them was not at all because they were copulating, but rather because they made so much noise about it that I couldn't get to sleep. As I see it, copulation is no justification for setting up such a hullabaloo.

Moreover since the black cat had killed the bunnies, I was morally obliged to avenge them. I felt that my mother was really far too kind and forgiving and that's why I answered in such an ambiguous—almost contentious—fashion.

"The Creator is really too reckless and I shall simply have to oppose him, although perhaps I shall really be helping him—that black cat is not going to strut and swagger on top of that wall for very long," I thought to myself decisively. Almost unconsciously my glance fell on a bottle of potassium cyanide stored in the bookcase.

October 1922

ABBREVIATIONS

AQHPC Wang Hsi-yen 王西彥. *Lun Ah Q ho t'a-te pei-chu* 論阿 Q 和他的悲劇 (On Ah Q and his tragedy). Shanghai: Hsin-wen-yi ch'u-pan-she, 1957.

CCT Hsü Chung-yü 徐中玉. *Kuan-yü Lu Hsün te hsiao-shuo tsa-wen chi ch'i-t'a* 關於魯迅的小說雜文及其他 (On Lu Hsün's stories, miscellaneous reactions, and other things). Shanghai: Hsin-wen-yi ch'u-pan-she, 1957.

CHWH *Chung-kuo li-tai che-hsüeh wen-hsüan: Ch'ing-tai chin-tai pien* 中國歷代哲學文選:清代近代編 (A selection of Chinese philosophical documents throughout the ages: Ch'ing and modern periods). Peking: Chung-hua shu-chü, 1962.

CNST Chou Ch'i-ming (Chou Tso-jen) 周啓明. *Lu Hsün te ch'ing-nien shih-tai* 魯迅的青年時代 (The period of Lu Hsün's youth). Peking: Chung-kuo ch'ing-nien ch'u-pan-she, 1957.

CSCC Chang Hsiang-t'ien 張向天. *Lu Hsün chiu-shih chien-chu* 魯迅舊詩箋注 (Comments on Lu Hsün's old-style poetry). Canton: Kuang-tung jen-min ch'u-pan-she, 1962.

CTCS *Chuang-tzu, chi-shih* 莊子集釋 (The Chuang-tzu collected commentaries). Taipei: Shih-chieh shu-chü, 1955.

CWHS *Hsü Ch'in-wen hsiao-shuo hsüan-chi* 許欽文小說選集 (A selection of Hsü Ch'in-wen's stories). Peking: Tso-chia ch'u-pan-she, 1956.

ESS Sun Fu-yüan 孫伏園. *Lu Hsün hsien-sheng erh-san shih* 魯迅先生二三事 (A few things concerning Lu Hsün). Shanghai: Tso-chia shu-wu, 1949.

HC Feng Tzu-k'ai 豐子愷. *Feng Tzu-k'ai hua-chi* 豐子愷畫集 (A collection of Feng Tzu-k'ai's pictures). Shanghai: Jen-min mei-shu ch'u-pan-she, 1963.

HHHS Feng Tzu-k'ai. *Hui-hua Lu Hsün hsiao-shuo* 繪畫魯迅小說

(Illustrating Lu Hsün's stories). Hong Kong: Wan-yeh shu-tien, 1954.

HHL   *Chih-t'ang hui-hsiang lu* 知堂回想錄 (Reminiscences of Chou Tso-jen). 2 vols. Hong Kong: San-yü t'u-shu wen-chü kung-ssu, 1971.

HHLH   Hsü Ch'in-wen 許欽文. *Hsüeh-hsi Lu Hsün hsien-sheng* 學習魯迅先生 (Learning from Lu Hsün). Shanghai: Wen-yi ch'u-pan-she, 1959.

HMTP   *Hsin Min Ts'ung Pao* 新民叢報 (New People's Review). 17 vols., reprinted. Taipei: Wen-yi yin-shu-kuan, 1956.

HSJW   Chou Hsia-shou (Chou Tso-jen) 周遐壽. *Lu Hsün hsiao-shuo-li te jen-wu* 魯迅小說裡的人物 (The characters in Lu Hsün's stories). Shanghai: Shanghai ch'u-pan kung-ssu, 1954.

HWHTH   *Chung-kuo hsin wen-hsüeh ta-hsi* 中國新文學大系 (Encyclopedia of the new Chinese literature). 10 vols., 1935. Reprint. Hong Kong: Wen-hsüeh yen-chiu-she.

HYL   Hsü Kuang-p'ing 許廣平. *Lu Hsün hui-yi-lu* 魯迅回憶錄 (Remembrances of Lu Hsün). Peking: Tso-chia ch'u-pan-she, 1962.

HYLH   Shen Yin-mo 沈尹默 and others. *Hui-yi wei-ta te Lu Hsün* 回憶偉大的魯迅 (Reminiscences of the magnificent Lu Hsün). Shanghai: Hsin-wen-yi ch'u-pan-she, 1958.

HYLHHS   Hsiao Hung 蕭紅 (Chang Nai-ying), ed. *Hui-yi Lu Hsün hsien-sheng* 回憶魯迅先生 (Reminiscences of Lu Hsün). Shanghai: Sheng-huo shu-tien, 1948.

JP   Chou Tso-jen. "Jih-pen chin san-shih-nien hsiao-shuo chih fa-ta" 日本近三十年小說之發達 (The development of Japanese fiction in the last thirty years). *Chung-kuo hsin wen-hsüeh ta-hsi*, vol. VI.

KLTST   (Feng) Hsüeh-feng (馮) 雪峰. *Kuo-lai-te shih-tai* 過來的時代 (The age that has passed). Shanghai: Hsin-chih shu-tien, 1948.

KMCLH   Wang Yeh-ch'iu 王冶秋. *Hsin-hai ke-ming-ch'ien te Lu Hsün hsien-sheng* 辛亥革命前的魯迅先生 (Lu Hsün before the Republican Revolution). Shanghai: Hsin-wen-yi ch'u-pan-she, 1956.

KYLH   Chih T'ang 知堂 (Chou Tso-jen). "Kuan-yü Lu Hsün" 關於魯迅 (On Lu Hsün). *Yü Chou Feng* 宇宙風, vol. XXIX (November 16, 1936).

KYLH-2   ———. "Kuan-yü Lu Hsün chih-erh" 關於魯迅之二

(On Lu Hsün pt., 2). *Yü Chou Feng*, Vol. XXX (December 1, 1936).

KYLHCT T'ai Ching-nung 臺靜農, ed. *Kuan-yü Lu Hsün chi ch'i chu-tso* 關於魯迅及其著作 (On Lu Hsün and his works). Peking: Wei-ming she, 1926.

LAQ Chang T'ien-yi 張天翼 and others. *Lun Ah Q* 論阿 Q (Discussing Ah Q). Shanghai: Ts'ao-yüan shu-tien, 1947.

LHC Wang Shih-ching 王士菁. *Lu Hsün chuan* 魯迅傳 (A biography of Lu Hsün). Peking: Chung-kuo ch'ing-nien ch'u-pan-she, 1962.

LHC-1 ———. *Lu Hsün chuan*. Shanghai and Hong Kong: Hsin-chih shu-tien, 1948.

LHCC *Lu Hsün ch'üan-chi* 魯迅全集 (Complete works of Lu Hsün). 10 vols. Peking: Jen-min wen-hsüeh ch'u-pan-she, 1957–58.

LHCC-20 *Lu Hsün ch'üan-chi* (Complete works of Lu Hsün). 20 vols. Shanghai: Lu Hsün ch'üan-chi ch'u-pan-she, 1938.

LHCL Chu Cheng 朱正. *Lu Hsün chuan-lüeh* 魯迅傳略 (A general biography of Lu Hsün). Peking: Tso-chia ch'u-pan-she, 1956.

LHCT Chu T'ung 朱彤. *Lu Hsün ch'uang-tso te yi-shu chi-ch'iao* 魯迅創作的藝術技巧 (The artistry of Lu Hsün's creative writing). Shanghai: Hsin-wen-yi ch'u-pan-she, 1958.

LHHS Pa Jen (Wang Jen-shu) 巴人. *Lu Hsün te hsiao-shuo* 魯迅的小說 (Lu Hsün's stories). Shanghai: Hsin-wen-yi ch'u-pan-she, 1957.

LHHY Ching You-lin 荊有麟. *Lu Hsün hui-yi* 魯迅回憶 (Remembering Lu Hsün). Shanghai: Shanghai tsa-chih kung-ssu, 1947.

LHJC *Lu Hsün jih-chi* 魯迅日記 (Lu Hsün's diary). 2 vols. Shanghai: Shanghai ch'u-pan kung-ssu, 1951.

LHKC Chou Hsia-shou (Chou Tso-jen). *Lu Hsün te ku-chia* 魯迅的故家 (Lu Hsün's old home). Hong Kong: Ta-t'ung shu-chü, 1962.

LHNP Ts'ao Chü-jen 曹聚仁. *Lu Hsün nien-p'u* 魯迅年譜 (A chronology of Lu Hsün). Hong Kong: San-yü t'u-shu wen-chü kung-ssu, 1967.

LHPC ———. *Lu Hsün p'ing-chuan* 魯迅評傳 (A critical biography of Lu Hsün). Hong Kong: Hsin wen-hua ch'u-pan-she, 1957.

LHPP Li Ch'ang-chih 李長之. *Lu Hsün p'i-p'an* 魯迅批判 (A

critique of Lu Hsün). Shanghai: Pei-hsin shu-chü, 1936.

LHS   Shu Hsin-ch'eng 舒新城. *Chin-tai Chung-kuo liu-hsüeh-shih* 近代中國留學史 (A history of Chinese students studying abroad in recent times). Shanghai: Chung-hua shu-chü, 1927.

LHSC   Ch'iao Feng 喬峰 (Chou Chien-jen). *Lüeh chiang kuan-yü Lu Hsün te shih-ch'ing* 略講關於魯迅的事情 (General remarks on the affairs of Lu Hsün). Peking: Jen-min wen-hsüeh ch'u-pan-she, 1955.

LHTC   *Lu Hsün tzu-chuan chi ch'i tso-p'in* 魯迅自傳及其作品 (Autobiography of Lu Hsün together with some of his works). Compiled and translated by Meng Chin 孟津. Bilingual edition (Chinese and English). Hong Kong: Kuang-ming shu-tien, 1959.

LHTPTH   *Lu Hsün tso-p'in t'an-hua* 魯迅作品談話 (Chats about Lu Hsün's works). Peking: Chung-kuo ch'ing-nien ch'u-pan-she, 1955.

LHTS   Ou-yang Fan-hai 歐陽凡海. *Lu Hsün te shu* 魯迅的書 (The writings of Lu Hsün). Canton: Hua-Mei t'u-shu kung-ssu, 1949.

LHYS   Ts'ai Yüan-p'ei 蔡元培. "Chi Lu Hsün hsien-sheng yi-shih" 記魯迅先生軼事 (Notes on some odds-and-ends of Lu Hsün's life). *Yü Chou Feng*, vol. XXIX (November 16, 1936).

LHYW   *Lu Hsün yi-wen-chi* 魯迅譯文集 (Collected translations of Lu Hsün). 10 vols. Peking: Jen-min wen-hsüeh ch'u-pan-she, 1959.

LNPC   Lao She 老舍 (Shu Ch'ing-ch'un). *Lao niu p'o ch'e* 老牛破車 (An old ox and rickety cart). Hong Kong: Yü-chou shu-tien, 1961.

LTC   Liu Ta-chieh 劉大杰. "Lu Hsün yü hsieh-shih chu-yi" 魯迅與寫實主義 (Lu Hsün and realism). *Yü Chou Feng*, vol. XXX (December 1, 1936).

NHCSP   Chou Shu-jen (Lu Hsün). *Na-han: chu-shih pen* 吶喊注釋本 (Call to Arms; annotated edition). Hong Kong: San-lien shu-tien, 1958.

NHFH   Hsü Ch'ih-wen 許欽文. *Na-han fen-hsi* 吶喊分析 (An analysis of the stories in *Call to Arms*). Peking: Chung-kuo ch'ing-nien ch'u-pan-she, 1956.

PCTF   Sun Shih-k'ai 孫世愷. *Lu Hsün tsai Pei-ching suo chu-kuo te ti-fang* 魯迅在北京所住過的地方 (The places where

Lu Hsün lived in Peking). Peking: Pei-ching ch'u-pan-she, 1957.

PHFH   Hsü Ch'in-wen 許欽文. *P'ang-huang fen-hsi* 彷徨分析 (An analysis of the stories in *Wandering*). Peking: Chung-kuo ch'ing-nien ch'u-pan-she, 1958.

PYHP   *Lu Hsün ch'üan-chi pu-yi hsü-pien* 魯迅全集補遺續編 (Pieces left out of the complete works of Lu Hsün, continued). Edited by T'ang T'ao 唐弢. Shanghai: Shanghai ch'u-pan kung-ssu, 1952.

RJ   Takeuchi Yoshimi 竹內好. *Rojin* 魯迅 (Lu Hsün). Tokyo: Sekai Hyōronsha, 1948.

RJ&DT   Imamura Yoshio 今村与志雄. *Rojin to Dentō* 魯迅と傳統 (Lu Hsün and tradition). Tokyo: Keisō Shokyoku, 1967.

RJD   Yamada Norio 山田野理夫. *Rojin den* 魯迅傳 (A biography of Lu Hsün). Tokyo: Chōbunsha, 1968.

RJNP   Nakagawa Shun 中川俊. *Rojin nempu* 魯迅年譜 (A chronology of Lu Hsün). Tokyo: Daian, 1966.

SB   Dazai Osamu 太宰治. *Sekibetsu* 惜別 (Regrets at parting). Vol. 7 of *Dazai Osamu Zenshu* (Complete works of Dazai Osamu). Tokyo: Chikuma Shobō, 1962.

SC   *Lu Hsün shu-chien* 魯迅書簡 (Lu Hsün's letters). 2 vols. Hong Kong: Pai-hsin t'u-shu wen-chü kung-ssu, 1960.

SCC   Liang Jung-jo 梁容若. *Wen-hsüeh shih-chia chuan* 文學十家傳 (Various biographies of ten writers). Taipei: Shang-wu yin-shu-kuan, 1966.

SCK   Lin Ch'en 林辰. *Lu Hsün shih-chi k'ao* 魯迅事蹟攷 (Tracing down some of the facts of Lu Hsün's life). Shanghai: Ḥsin-wen-yi ch'u-pan-she 1957.

SCK-1   1948 edition of the above. Shanghai: K'ai-ming shu-tien.

SHC   Chiang T'ien 江天. *Lu Hsün shih hsin-chieh* 魯迅詩新解 (New interpretations of Lu Hsün's poetry). Hong Kong: Wen-yü ch'u-pan-she, n.d.

SHSC   Jen Wei-yin 任微音. *Shaohsing san-chi* 紹興散記 (Random impressions of Shao-hsing). Shanghai: Wen-hua ch'ü-pan-she, 1956.

SWLH   *See* Chou Shu-jen in Section B of this bibliography.

TCLH   Hsü Shou-shang 許壽裳 and others. *Tso-chia t'an Lu Hsün* 作家談魯迅 (Writers talk about Lu Hsün). Hong Kong: Wen-hsüeh yen-chiu she, 1966.

TJHKP   Ch'eng Chung-en 成仲恩. "Chou Tso-jen yü Hsü Kuang-p'ing chih-chien te en-yüan" 周作人與許廣平之間的恩怨 (The feelings between Chou Tso-jen and Hsü Kuang-p'ing). *Ming-pao Monthly*, May 1967.

TPCH   Hsü Ch'in-wen 許欽文. *Yü-wen-k'o chung Lu Hsün tso-p'in te chiao-hsüeh* 語文課中魯迅作品的教學 (The teaching of Lu Hsün's works in classes on language and literature). Shanghai: Shang-hai chiao-yü ch'u-pan-she, 1961.

TPFH   Chu T'ung 朱彤. *Lu Hsün tso-p'in te fen-shi* 魯迅作品的分析 (An analysis of the works of Lu Hsün). 2 vols. Shanghai: Tung-fang shu-tien, 1953–54.

TPYC   Chiang-su wen-lien 江蘇文聯 (Kiangsu Provincial Literary League). *Lu Hsün tso-p'in yen-chiu* 魯迅作品研究 (Studies of Lu Hsün's works). Nanking: Chiang-su jen-min ch'u-pan-she, 1957.

WHYL   Chou Tso-jen. *Chung-kuo hsin-wen-hsüeh te yüan-liu* 中國新文學的源流 (The course of new Chinese literature). Peking: Jen-wen shu-tien, 1923.

WLLH   Su Hsüeh-lin 蘇雪林. *Wo lun Lu Hsün* 我論魯迅 (I have my say on Lu Hsün). Taipei: Wen-hsing shu-tien, 1967.

WPC   Chou Tso-jen "Wu-p'eng ch'uan" 烏篷船 (Black-canopied boats). In *Hsien-tai Chung-kuo hsiao-p'in san-wen hsüan* 現代中國小品散文選 (A selection of contemporary Chinese informal essays and prose). Shanghai: Chung-kuo wen-hua fu-wu-she, 1926.

WTLH   Hsü Shou-shang. *Wo so jen-shih te Lu Hsün* 我所認識的魯迅 (The Lu Hsün I knew). Peking: Jen-min wen-hsüeh ch'u-pan-she, 1952.

WTTT   Chao Ts'ung 趙聰. *Wu-ssu wen-t'an tien-ti* 五四文壇點滴 (Fragments concerning the literary world of the May Fourth period). Hong Kong: Yu-lien ch'u-pan-she, 1964.

YCTL   Shen P'eng-nien 沈鵬年. *Lu Hsün yen-chiu tzu-liao pien-mu* 魯迅研究資料編目 (A bibliography of materials for the study of Lu Hsün). Shanghai: Shanghai wen-yi ch'u-pan-she, 1958.

YFHC   *Yin Fu hsüan-chi* 殷夫選集 (Selected writings of Yin Fu). Peking: K'ai-ming shu-tien, 1951.

YHC   Hsü Shou-shang. *Wang-yu Lu Hsün yin-hsiang-chi* 亡友魯迅印象記 (Impressions of my departed friend Lu Hsün). Peking: Jen-min wen-hsüeh ch'u-pan-she, 1953.

YLH   Mao Tun 茅盾 (Shen Yen-ping) and others. *Yi Lu Hsün*
       憶魯迅 (Remembering Lu Hsün). Peking: Jen-min wen-
       hsüeh ch'u-pan-she. 1956.

YPSCC *Yin-ping-shih ch'üan-chi* 飲冰室全集 (Complete works
       of the ice-drinkers studio). Shanghai: Chung-hua shu-
       chü, 1917.

YYWP   Chou Tso-jen. *Chih-t'ang yi-yu wen-pien* 知堂乙酉文編
       (1945 essays of Chou Tso-jen). Hong Kong: San-yü
       t'u-shu wen-chü kung-ssu, 1962.

BIBLIOGRAPHY

A. SELECTED LIST OF ENGLISH TRANSLATIONS OF THE STORIES
(SEE LIST OF SOURCE TITLES AT END OF THIS SECTION)

Story	Date completed	Translation source
Remembrances of the Past (Huai-chiu)	Winter 1911	*THM*, VI, no. 2 (February 1938), 148-59, Appendix to this book

Na-han (*Call to Arms*)—1923

	Story	Date completed	Translation source
1)	Diary of a Madman (K'uang-jen jih-chi)	April 1918	*Straw Sandals*, pp. 1-12; *Ah Q*, pp. 205-29; *SW*, pp. 8-21; *Silent China*, pp. 3-13
2)	K'ung Yi-chi (K'ung Yi-chi)	March 1919	*Straw Sandals*, pp. 25-32; *Living China*, pp. 44-50; *SW*, pp. 22-28; *Modern Stories*, pp. 14-19
3)	Medicine (Yao)	April 1919	*Straw Sandals*, pp. 13-24; *Living China*, pp. 29-40; *SW*, pp. 29-39
4)	Tomorrow (Ming-t'ien)	June 1920	*SW*, pp. 40-48
5)	A Trifling Incident (Yi-chien hsiao-shih)	July 1920	*Living China*, pp. 41-43; *SW*, pp. 49-51
6)	The Story of Hair (T'ou-fa te ku-shih)	October 1920	*Ah Q*, pp. 59-64
7)	Storm in a Teacup (Feng-po)	October 1920	*Straw Sandals*, pp. 33-44; *Ah Q*, pp. 65-76; *SW*, pp. 52-62
8)	Home Town (Ku-hsiang)	January 1921	*Ah Q*, pp. 3-15; *SW*, pp. 63-75; *Modern Stories*, pp. 20-29

Story	Date completed	Translation source
9) The True Story of Ah Q (Ah Q cheng-chuan)	December 1921	*Ah Q*, pp. 77-129; *SW*, pp. 76-135; *Silent China*, pp. 14-58
10) Dragon Boat Festival (Tuan-wu chieh)	June 1922	*Comtemporary Stories*, pp. 180-189
11) The White Light (Pai-kuang)	June 1922	*Silent China*, pp. 59-64
12) Some Rabbits and a Cat (T'u ho mao)	October 1922	Appendix
13) A Comedy of Ducks (Ya te hsi-chü)	October 1922	*JOL*, 1 (July 1947), 7-10
14) Village Opera (She-hsi)	October 1922	*SW*, pp. 136-149

P'ang-huang (Wandering)—1926

Story	Date completed	Translation source
1) The New Year's Sacrifice (Chu-fu)	February 7, 1924	*Living China*, pp. 51-74; *Ah Q*, pp. 184-204; *SW*, pp. 150-173; *Modern Stories*, pp. 29-45
2) Upstairs in a Wineshop (Tsai chiu-lou shang)	February 16, 1924	*Ah Q*, pp. 45-58; *SW*, pp. 174-187
3) A Happy Family (Hsing-fu te chia-t'ing)	February 18, 1924	*SW*, pp. 188-97
4) Soap (Fei-tsao)	March 22, 1924	*Ah Q*, pp. 16-30; *SW*, pp. 198-211
5) The Eternal Lamp (Ch'ang-ming teng)	March 1, 1925	*Ch L*, 1963, no. 11, pp. 54-63
6) A Warning to the People (Shih-chung)	March 18, 1925	*Contemporary Stories*, pp. 190-195
7) Schoolmaster Kao (Kao lao-fu-tzu)	May 1, 1925	*China Journal*, 33, no. 1 (July 1940), 11-17
8) The Isolate (Ku-tu-che)	October 17, 1925	*Ah Q*, pp. 130-157; *SW*, pp. 212-37
9) Remorse (Shang-shih)	October 21, 1925	*Straw Sandals*, pp. 107-128; *Ah Q*, pp. 158-83; *SW*, pp. 238-61
10) Brothers (Ti-hsiung)	November 3, 1925	*Renditions*, no. 1 (Autumn 1973) pp. 66-75
11) Divorce (Li-hun)	November 6, 1925	*Ah Q*, pp. 31-44; *Living China*, pp. 85-96; *SW*, pp. 262-73

Sources

Ah Q	Wang Chi-chen, trans. *Ah Q and Others: Selected Stories of Lusin*. New York: Columbia University Press, 1941.
China Journal	*The China Journal*. Vols. 1-35. Shanghai, 1923-41.
Ch L	*Chinese Literature*. No. 1—Peking: Foreign Languages Press, 1951—.
Contemporary Stories	Wang Chi-chen, trans. *Contemporary Chinese Stories*. New York: Columbia University Press, 1944.
JOL	*Journal of Oriental Literature*. Vols. 1-6. Honolulu: Oriental Literature Society of the University of Hawaii, 1947-55.
Living China	Snow, Edgar, ed. *Living China: Modern Chinese Short Stories*. Westport, Conn.: Hyperion Press, 1973. (Reprint of the 1937 edition published by John Day, in association with Reynal & Hitchcock, New York.)
Modern Stories	Jenner, W. J. F., ed. *Modern Chinese Stories*. London: Oxford University Press, 1970.
Renditions	*Renditions: A Chinese-English Translation Magazine*. No. 1—. Centre for Translation Projects, The Chinese University of Hong Kong, 1973—.
SW	Vol. 1 of the *Selected Works*; see Chou Shu-jen in section B of this bibliography.
Silent China	*Silent China: Selected Writings of Lu Xun*. Yang, Gradys, ed. and trans. London: Oxford University Press, 1973.
Straw Sandals	Isaacs, Harold R., ed. *Straw Sandals: Chinese Short Stories, 1918-1933*. Cambridge, Mass.: MIT Press, 1974.
THM	*T'ien Hsia Monthly*. Vols. 1-12. Shanghai: Kelly and Walsh, Ltd., 1935-41.

Note: *Selected Stories of Lu Hsün* (Peking: Foreign Languages Press, 1972) and *Chosen Pages from Lu Hsün: The Literary Mentor of the Chinese Revolution* (New York: Cameron Associates, 1959) duplicate most of the contents of vol. 1 of the *Selected Works*. I have given the pagination of English works cited in the foregoing list because translators often use different titles for the same story.

B. WORKS IN WESTERN LANGUAGES

Alber, Charles J. "Soviet Criticism of Lu Hsun, 1881-1936." Ph.D. dissertation, Indiana University, 1971.

Andreyev, Leonid. *The Little Angel and Other Stories*. New York: Alfred A. Knopf, 1924.

Bishop, John L. "Some Limitations in Chinese Fiction." In *Studies in Chinese Literature*, edited by John L. Bishop. Harvard-Yenching Institute Studies, vol. XXI. Cambridge, Mass.: Harvard University Press, 1965.

Boorman, Howard L. ed. *Biographical Dictionary of Republican China.* 4 vols. New York and London: Columbia University Press, 1967-70.

Booth, Wayne C. *The Rhetoric of Fiction*. Chicago: University of Chicago Press, 1961.

Brière, O. "Un écrivain populaire: Lou Sin." *Bulletin de l'Université l'Aurore*, III, book 7, no. 1 (1946), 51-78.

Britton, Roswell Sessoms. *The Chinese Periodical Press, 1800-1912.* Shanghai: Kelly & Walsh, 1933.

Chang Hao. *Liang Ch'i-ch'ao and Intellectual Transition in China, 1890-1907*. Cambridge, Mass.: Harvard University Press, 1971.

Chen, Pearl Hsia. "The Social Thought of Lusin, 1881-1936." Ph.D. dissertation, University of Chicago, 1953.

Chiang Monlin. *Tides from the West*. New Haven: Yale University Press, 1947.

Chou Shu-jen (Lu Hsün), *Selected Works of Lu Hsün*. Translated by Yang Hsien-yi and Gladys Yang. 4 vols. Peking: Foreign Languages Press, 1956-60. [Abbreviated in footnotes as *SWLH*].

Chow Tse-tsung. *The May Fourth Movement: Intellectual Revolution in Modern China*. Cambridge, Mass.: Harvard University Press, 1960.

————. *Research Guide to the May Fourth Movement: Intellectual Revolution in Modern China 1915-1924*. Cambridge, Mass.: Harvard University Press, 1963.

Creel, H. G. *Chinese Thought from Confucius to Mao Tse-tung*. Chicago: University of Chicago Press, 1953.

Deutsch, Babette. *Poetry in Our Time*. Garden City, N.Y.: Doubleday, 1963.

Fairbank, John King, and Liu Kwang-ching. *Modern China: A Bibliographical Guide to Chinese Works, 1898-1937*. Cambridge, Mass.: Harvard University Press, 1961.

Folsom, Kenneth E. *Friends, Guests, and Colleagues: The Mu-fu System in the Late Ch'ing*. Berkeley and Los Angeles: University of California Press, 1968.

Garshin, Vsevolod Mikhailovich. *The Scarlet Flower*. Translated by Bernard Isaacs. Moscow: Foreign Languages Publishing House, 1959.

Gasster, Michael. *China's Struggle to Modernize.* New York: Knopf, 1972.

_____. *Chinese Intellectuals and the Revolution of 1911.* Seattle: University of Washington Press, 1969.

Gibbs, Donald A., and Li Yun-chen. *A Bibliography of Studies and Translations of Modern Chinese Literature, 1918-1942.* Cambridge, Mass.: Harvard University Press, 1975.

Goldman, Merle. *Literary Dissent in Communist China.* Cambridge, Mass.: Harvard University Press, 1967.

Gorky, Maxim. *Reminiscences of Tolstoy, Chekhov, and Andreyev.* New York: Viking Press, 1959.

Grieder, Jerome B. *Hu Shih and the Chinese Renaissance: Liberalism in the Chinese Revolution, 1917-1937.* Cambridge, Mass.: Harvard University Press, 1970.

Grosier, Jean Baptiste Gabriel Alexandre. *De la Chine, ou description générale de cet empire.* 3d ed., rev. 7 vols. Paris, 1818-20.

Hackett, Roger R. "Chinese Students in Japan. 1900-1910." Papers on China, vol. III. Mimeographed. Cambridge, Mass.: Harvard University, Committee on International and Regional Studies, 1949.

Hanan, Patrick. "The Technique of Lu Hsün's Fiction." *Harvard Journal of Asiatic Studies,* XXXIV (1974), 53-96.

Hsia, C. T. "Obsession with China: The Moral Burden of Modern Chinese Literature." In *China in Perspective.* Wellesley Hills, Mass.: Wellesley College, 1967.

_____. *History of Modern Chinese Fiction, 1917-1957.* Appendix on Taiwan by Tsi-an Hsia. New Haven: Yale University Press, 1961.

_____. *The Classic Chinese Novel: A Critical Introduction.* New York and London: Columbia University Press, 1968.

Hsia Tsi-an. *The Gate of Darkness.* Seattle: University of Washington Press, 1968.

Huang Sung-k'ang. *Lu Hsün and the New Cultural Movement of Modern China.* Amsterdam: Djambatan, 1957.

Hummel, Arthur W., ed. *Eminent Chinese of the Ch'ing Period (1644-1912).* 2 vols. Washington, D.C.: Government Printing Office, 1943-44.

Jansen, Marius B. *The Japanese and Sun Yat-sen.* Cambridge, Mass.: Harvard University Press, 1954.

Keene, Donald. *Modern Japanese Literature.* New York: Grove, 1960.

Krebsová, Berta. "Lu Hsün and His Collection Old Tales Retold." *Archiv Orientální,* XXVIII (1960), 640-56, and XXIX (1961), 268-310.

_____. *Lu Sün: sa vie et son oeuvre.* Prague: Éditions de l'Académie Tchécoslovaque des Sciences, 1953.

Lang, Olga. *Pa Chin and His Writings: Chinese Youth between the Two Revolutions.* Cambridge, Mass.: Harvard University Press, 1967.

Lee Ou-fan. *Lin Shu and His Translations: Western Fiction in Chinese Perspective*. Papers on China, vol. XIX. Cambridge, Mass.: Harvard East Asian Research Center, 1965.

Levenson, Joseph R. *Liang Ch'i-ch'ao and the Mind of Modern China*. Cambridge, Mass.: Harvard University Press, 1953.

Leyda, Jay. *Dianying: Electric Shadows—An Account of Films and the Film Audience in China*. Cambridge, Mass., and London: MIT Press, 1972.

Li Tien-yi. *Chinese Fiction: A Bibliography of Books and Articles in Chinese and English*. New Haven: Far Eastern Publications, 1968.

Lu Hsün. *See* Chou Shu-jen.

Lyell, William A. "The Short Story Theatre of Lu Hsün." Ph.D. dissertation, University of Chicago, 1971.

McClellan, Edwin. *Two Japanese Novelists: Sōseki and Tōson*. Chicago: University of Chicago Press, 1969.

Magarschack, David, trans. *Anton Chekhov: Lady with Lapdog and Other Stories*. Baltimore: Penguin Books, 1964.

Mauriac, François. *Le romancier et ses personnages*. Paris: Editions R.-A. Corrêa, 1933.

Mills, Harriet C. "Lu Hsün and the Communist Party." *China Quarterly*, October-December 1960, pp. 17-27.

_____. "Lu Hsün: 1927-1936—The Years on the Left." Ph.D. dissertation, Columbia University, 1963.

Miyoshi, Masao. *Accomplices of Silence: The Modern Japanese Novel*. Berkeley and Los Angeles: University of California Press, 1974.

Monsterleet, Jean. *Sommets de la littérature chinoise contemporaine*. Paris: André Tournon, 1953.

Nakamura, Mitsuo. *Modern Japanese Fiction*. Tokyo: Japan Cultural Society, 1968.

O'Faolain, Sean. *The Short Story*. London: Collins, 1948.

Parker, E. H. "A Journey in Chekiang." *Journal of the China Branch of the Royal Asiatic Society*, vol. XIX, part I (1884).

Plopper, Clifford H. *Chinese Religion Seen through the Proverb*. Shanghai: China Press, 1926.

Pollard, David E. *A Chinese Look at Literature: The Literary Values of Chou Tso-jen in Relation to the Tradition*. London: C. Hurst, 1973.

_____. "Chou Tso-jen and Cultivating One's Garden." *Asia Major*, n. s., XI, pt. II (1965), 180-98.

Průšek, Jaroslav. "A Confrontation of Traditional Oriental Literature with Modern European Literature in the Context of the Chinese Literary Revolution." *Archiv Orientální*, XXXII (1964), 365-75.

_____. "The Realistic and Lyric Elements in the Chinese Mediaeval Story." *Archiv Orientální*, XXXII (1964), 4-15.

_____. "Reality and Art in Chinese Literature." *Archiv Orientálni*, XXXII (1964), 605-18.

_____. "Quelques remarques sur la nouvelle littérature chinoise." In *Mélanges de Sinologie offerts à Monsieur Paul Demiéville*. Paris: Presses Universitaires de France, 1966, pp. 209-23.

_____. "Lu Hsün's 'Huai Chiu': A Precursor of Modern Chinese Literature." *Harvard Journal of Asiatic Studies*, XXIX (1969), 169-76.

Roy, David Tod. *Kuo Mo-jo: The Early Years*. Cambridge, Mass.: Harvard University Press, 1971.

Scalapino, Robert A. "Prelude to Marxism: The Chinese Student Movement in Japan, 1900-1910." In *Approaches to Modern Chinese History*, edited by Albert Feuerwerker. Berkeley and Los Angeles: University of California Press, 1967.

Schell, Orville, and Esherick, Joseph. *Modern China: The Making of a New Society from 1839 to the Present*. New York: Random House, 1972.

Schiffrin, Harold Z. *Sun Yat-sen and the Origins of the Chinese Revolution*. Berkeley and Los Angeles: University of California Press, 1970.

Schultz, William Rudolph. "Lu Hsün: The Creative Years." Ph.D. dissertation, University of Washington, 1955.

Schwartz, Benjamin. *In Search of Wealth and Power*. Cambridge, Mass.: Harvard University Press, 1964.

Semanov, V. I. "Lu Hsün and his Predecessors." Translated by Charles J. Alber. Unpublished.

Slupski, Zbigniew. *The Evolution of a Modern Chinese Writer: An Analysis of Lao She's Fiction with Biographical and Bibliographical Appendices*. Prague: Oriental Institute in Academia, 1966.

Sun, Shirley Hsiao-ling. "Lu Hsün and the Chinese Woodcut Movement: 1929-36." Ph.D. dissertation, Stanford University, 1974.

Tang Tao. "On Lu Hsün's Two Stories [Pai-kuang and Ch'ang-ming teng]." *Chinese Literature*, XI (1963), 73-77.

Tun Li-ch'en. *Annual Customs and Festivals in Peking*. Translated and annotated by Derk Bodde. Peking: Henry Vetch, 1936.

Walshe, W. Gilbert. "The Ancient City of Shaohsing." *Journal of the China Branch of the Royal Asiatic Society*, vol. XXXIII (1900-1901).

Wolff, Ernst. "Chou Tso-jen, Modern China's Pioneer of the Essay." Ph.D. dissertation, University of Washington, 1966.

_____. *Chou Tso-jen*. New York: Twayne, 1971.

Zi (Siu), Le P. Etienne, S. J. *Pratique des examens littéraires en Chine*. Variétés sinologiques, no. 5. Shanghai: Imprimerie de la Mission Catholique, 1894.

INDEX